WOMEN AT WORK IN PREINDUSTRIAL FRANCE

Women at Work in Preindustrial France

DARYL M. HAFTER

THE PENNSYLVANIA STATE UNIVERSITY PRESS
UNIVERSITY PARK, PENNSYLVANIA

LIBRARY OF CONGRESS CATALOGING-IN-PUBLICATION DATA

Hafter, Daryl M., 1935–
Women at work in preindustrial France / Daryl M. Hafter.
  p. cm.
The research focuses on Lyon, Paris, and Rouen.
Includes bibliographical references and index.
  ISBN-13: 978-0-271-05868-9 (pbk : alk. paper)
  ISBN-10: 0-271-05868-4 (pbk : alk. paper)
1. Women—Employment—France—History—18th century.
2. Women in guilds—France—History—18th century.
3. Working class women—France—History—18th century.
4. Sex discrimination against women—France—History—18th century.
5. Discrimination in employment—France—History—18th century.
    I. Title.

HD6145.H26 2007
331.40944´09033—dc22
         2006034214

Copyright © 2007
The Pennsylvania State University
All rights reserved
Printed in the United States of America
Published by The Pennsylvania State University Press,
University Park, PA 16802-1003

The Pennsylvania State University Press
is a member of the Association of
American University Presses.

It is the policy of The Pennsylvania State University Press
to use acid-free paper. This book is printed on stock
that meets the minimum
requirements of American National Standard for Information Sciences—
Permanence of Paper for Printed Library Material, ANSI Z39.48–1992.

Frontispiece: Processing silk thread from cocoons.
The *dévideuse* starts the thread to unwind cocoons in
boiling water and passes it up to a reeling frame.
"Vermis sericus," engraving by Jean Stradanus (1523–1605).
Photo courtesy of the Folger Shakespeare Library.

CONTENTS

Acknowledgments / vii
Introduction / 1

1
The Political Economy of Guilds / 19

2
The Uses of Gender in Economic Life / 51

3
Guildwomen and *Ouvrières* / 89

4
Turgot's Reforms and Their Aftermath / 145

5
Paths to the Revolution / 207

Conclusion / 291
Bibliography / 295
Index / 309

For the memory of
MY MOTHER AND FATHER
AND
FOR MONROE

ACKNOWLEDGMENTS

This book has been many years in the writing, and I have incurred numerous debts of gratitude to the people who helped me. My research in France benefited from the archivists and friends who made me welcome through the years. In Rouen's Archives Départementales de la Seine Maritime, archivist Mademoiselle Vivienne Miguet extended friendship as well as scholarly expertise. The entire staff of the ADSM deserves hearty thanks for their kind and efficient help. Archive friends who made the days more pleasant were Judith Miller, Gayle Brunelle, Claude Mazauric, Jean-Pierre Bardet, and many passing scholars. For their hospitality and encouragement, I thank Andrée and Michel Callais, Véronique and Jean-Pierre Fruit, Paul and Françoise Toumyre, and the Roland Gerbi family, who made Passover a Sephardic holiday for me.

In Lyon, the chief archivist of the Archives Municipales de Lyon, Monsieur Henri Hours, and the librarian in the reading room took special pains to assist me. I found a real home in Lyon's Musée Historique des Tissus, where I received the help of the museum's heads, Monsieur Jean-Michel Tuchscherer and Monsieur Pierre Arizzoli-Clémental, and the entire staff. Monsieur Gabriel Vial, the extraordinarily knowledgeable and generous expert in textile technology, granted me a veritable apprenticeship, and we enjoyed many luncheons at the nearby restaurant, Tartuffo. It is impossible to express how much I owe to the encouragement of this dedicated scholar. So many staff members of the museum and of CIETA (Centre internationale d'étude des textiles anciens), the organization devoted to making concordances of handloom textile technology, have become friends. I am grateful for the companionship of Mademoiselle Marie-Dominique Frieh, Madame Monique Cogny-Jay, and Mademoiselle Agnès Colas. For their expertise and assistance, the librarians and curators of the Musée Historique des Tissus also deserve my thanks, as well as the staff of the Bibliothèque Municipale of Lyon and the Archives Départemental du Rhône. To Maurice Garden I offer my gratitude for his guidance and help.

Paris houses the Archives Nationales and the Bibliothèque Nationale, and the staff of archivists and assistants there were indispensable to my work. I appreciate the encouragement and guidance of Professors Daniel Roche, Jean-Claude Perrot, Michelle Perrot, and Louis Bergeron.

To the archive companions who have become personal friends, I owe thanks for their scholarly guidance and their cordial hospitality: my work would not have been completed without the encouragement and valuable critiques of Jacques Bottin, Pierre Caspard, Serge Chassagne, Sophie Desrosiers, Dominique Godineau, Liliane Hilaire-Pérez, Christopher Johnson, Judith Miller, Lesley Miller, Philipe Minard, and Nicole Pellegrin. The hospitality of Anne and Odette Lavaud made Paris much more friendly.

At home, the long-standing reading group, French Historians of the Third Coast, including Dena Goodman, Pamela Graves, Christopher Johnson, David Klinck, Anne Meyering, Leslie Moch, Barry Shapiro, and Judith Stone, has been a source of stimulation and encouragement. For help with chapter 5, I am especially indebted to Barry Shapiro. Ellen Schwartz and Joanna Scott provided insights from their own fields along with helpful advice and friendship. Sherri Klassen painstakingly composed graphs. Gabriel Weinreich helped with statistical material early in this project and Gerane Weinreich, with orientation to Paris. Jeffrey Horn has offered references, advice, and encouragement with many parts of this manuscript. Above all, I must single out Leonard Rosenband's steadfast interest in my work. His many discussions about themes in French history informed the entire project, and I am grateful for his inspiration and help. I would also like to thank the Penn State Press readers for their very helpful suggestions and copyeditor Eliza Childs for patience and assistance.

Early research at the Eleutherian Mills-Hagley Library was supported by the American Philosophical Society. Major grants from the National Science Foundation enabled me to spend two years studying the relation of preindustrial technology and women's work. A year's fellowship at the Dibner Institute for the History of Science and Technology contributed handsomely to the project. Eastern Michigan University's sabbaticals and many faculty research fellowships were crucial to every part of my research and writing. The Society for the History of Technology, the Western Society for French History, the Society for French Historical Studies, and the Textile Society of America provided opportunities to present my research and receive informed responses. I also thank the Special Collections Library of the University of Michigan and the Library of Eastern Michigan University.

My parents, Harry and Theresa Maslow, deserve my deep appreciation for giving me a good education and sustaining my historical work with their interest and devotion. My children, Matthew and Naomi, provided welcome distraction, forbearance, and encouragement. My husband, Monroe, merits the lion's share of thanks for carefully reading every chapter, keeping the domestic ship afloat, and for his constant loving support.

INTRODUCTION

The guild system in prerevolutionary France provided a unique opportunity for women fortunate enough to become sworn masters of a trade. Within a world of discrimination and hardship, these women received technical training and legal privilege, enabling them to participate directly in the market economy. Although the law considered women minors, forbidden to do many tasks on their own behalf, the law could also make exceptions and confer on designated women the right to exercise male privileges. Women were dependent on husbands or fathers to make contracts or go to court, but if they became guild masters, they were able to carve out a sphere of legal equality with men. In guilds they went through the traditional steps in training, starting as apprentices and rising to the status of masters in charge of their own workshops and staff of artisans. In this role they negotiated with the royal and municipal government over taxes, they petitioned ministers and royal councils for regulation changes, and they took commercial rivals to court with—in some cities—success. Paradoxically, it was by means of privilege that French society introduced flexibility into its system, enabling some businesswomen to break through the web of restrictions. The structures of privilege actually became a vehicle for gaining economic and personal advantage.

The means these women used to get ahead were embedded in the system of privilege that structured Old Regime France. We might even say that the same restrictive code that hindered their free activity as full-fledged adults carried within itself pockets of opportunity that they used to make their way. France before the Revolution was a society of hierarchical orders, further subdivided into privileged groups, with each given specific rights denied to the general population. Just as nobles were endowed with exemptions from certain taxes, provincial treasurers could borrow money and lend it to the king, and guilds, in turn, could exert monopolies over certain techniques and products. These privileges were liberties given by a monarch, absolute in theory, in return for some benefit or service the group might render him. They stemmed from the early days of the kingdom, mingling public and private functions characteristic of early modern Europe, and habituating people to respond to privilege rather than the natural status of individuals.[1] In this way, women could become business proxies for their husbands and merchants acting with the legal rights of men, but only for a limited time. As guild masters, women could step out of their role as legal minors and behave as adults in the law for their entire lives. In effect, special circumstances made them "surrogate men."[2]

Awarding equal rights in one aspect of life did not mean that the French patriarchy was surrendering its power. On the contrary, as Joan Kelly asserted in her path-breaking essay, "Did Women Have a Renaissance?" exceptional rights that women received in patriarchal society served to maintain and perpetuate the status quo. Taking her example from medieval chivalry, Kelly reasoned that courtly love "reinforced, as its necessary premise, the practice of political marriage," and it provided a loophole to counterbalance the tensions incurred in the system of cementing political alliances with arranged marriages.[3] By the same token in the eighteenth century, permitting women in business to act with the freedom of men benefited the husband, the family, and society. Guildwomen's rights were protected by the system of privilege to such a degree that they could argue in conflicts with other guilds as if they were male. Thus we see the paradox of women gaining a measure of equal rights *by means of* privilege.

---

1. The classic definition of the society of orders was made by Roland Mousnier, *The Institutions of France Under the Absolute Monarchy, 1598–1789: Society and State*, trans. Brian Pearce (Chicago: Chicago University Press, 1979). William Beik challenges Mousnier's approach in *Absolutism and Society in Seventeenth-Century France: State Power and Provincial Aristocracy in Languedoc* (Cambridge: Cambridge University Press, 1985), esp. 3–33. See also Gail Bossenga, *The Politics of Privilege: Old Regime and Revolution in Lille* (Cambridge: Cambridge University Press, 1991).

2. Cynthia Cockburn uses this term in *In the Way of Women* (Ithaca: ILR Press, 1991), 21, cautioning that women's gain of equal rights does not mean that society has been reformulated to do away with patriarchy. See her discussion in chapter 1, "Equal Opportunities: 'Rights' and Wrongs."

3. Joan Kelly suggests that giving women equal sexual rights with men is done only when "1) it can threaten no major institution of the patriarchal society from which it emerges, and 2) men, the rulers within the ruling order, must benefit by it." See "Did Women Have a Renaissance?" in *Women, History and Theory: The Essays of Joan Kelly* (Chicago: University of Chicago Press, 1984), 28. The same reasoning can be taken to apply to other privileges.

While guildwomen received their privileged freedom to act in the context of the artisanal economy, their business reflected how intensely the French economy was responding to the emerging brisk, competitive, capitalist world market. Like the subcontracting in Parisian guilds reported by Michael Sonenscher, Rouen's guildwomen illegally farmed tasks out to rural artisans.[4] They also inspected and purchased goods legally from the stream of knitted items brought to town by country people, and they fought in courts to maintain control of the lucrative wholesale linen goods trade in the city, a benefit awarded in their original guild statutes. Thus they used customs and regulations originating in the Middle Ages to put themselves into the position of modern merchants aiming to keep in charge of the linen industry from yarn to cloth, and to ensure their monopoly of its manufacture and sale.

The lived experience of guildwomen put the lie to theorists dubbing women as unsuited to the public world of the economy. Guildwomen demonstrated aptitude for advancing their business agenda from their ambition to use their assets, to policymaking in guild meetings, to their ability to press their claims for technical and product monopolies in court. Indeed, women were such an integral part of economic production in industry and agriculture that the question of female work loomed large in the preindustrial age. Where and under what terms women could be set to work was a major issue. Whether dealing with the relatively small number of privileged guildwomen or hiring and training the massive numbers of female industrial laborers, the French economy found women to be crucial players.[5]

Moreover, the general view that females were incapable of managing technology had not yet taken hold.[6] In view of society's prejudice against

---

4. Michael Sonenscher, *Work and Wages: Natural Law, Politics, and the Eighteenth-Century French Trades* (Cambridge: Cambridge University Press 1989), 29–41, and passim. Subcontracting, called *marchandage*, was also discussed by Cissie Fairchilds, "The Production and Marketing of Populuxe Goods in Eighteenth-Century Paris," in *Consumption and the World of Goods*, ed. John Brewer and Roy Porter (London: Routledge, 1993), 228–48.

5. Until their suppression in 1791, the Inspectors of Manufacture surveyed French economic resources systematically tallying the number of women workers and their level of skill in their reports. See Philip Minard, *La Fortune du Colbertisme: État et industrie dans la France des lumières* (Paris: Fayard, 1998). See Sonenscher, *Work and Wages*, 55, and Leonard N. Rosenband, *Papermaking in Eighteenth-Century France: Management, Labor, and Revolution at the Montgolfier Mill, 1761–1805* (Baltimore: Johns Hopkins University Press, 2000) for women workers' family ties.

6. The historical implications of ideology separating women from technology have been widely discussed. For a few of the most important works, see Joan Rothschild, ed., *Machina*

women, this statement needs explanation. Historians have argued that labeling women's work "unskilled" simply because it was performed by women obscured the real training and performance that tradeswomen had. It was a political means of curtailing women's wages by investing male training and tasks with prestige rather than an accurate assessment of female capacity.[7] To be sure, people believed that menstruating women spoiled metal casting and that gathering *vertdegris* from copper strips might make men impotent;[8] but these ideas did not keep male and female workers from performing many of the same tasks.[9]

With rare exceptions, until the last quarter of the eighteenth century, Rouen's guilds did not use incompatibility with technology on the basis of sex as an argument.[10] It was assumed that women in guilds were capable of using technology productively. Despite our modern view of historic times as rigidly gender-bound, men and women did a variety of tasks depending on circumstance and need. Only when a deep cleft between male and female *natures* became a general ideology were women branded as technologically incompetent. For the first time social theorists

---

Ex Dea: Feminist Perspectives on Technology (New York: Pergamon Press, 1983); Judy Wajcman, *Feminism Confronts Technology* (University Park: The Pennsylvania State University Press, 1991), Francesca Bray, *Technology and Gender: Fabrics of Power in Late Imperial China* (Berkeley and Los Angeles: University of California Press, 1997); and Ruth Oldenziel, *Making Technology Masculine: Men, Women and Modern Machines in America, 1870–1945* (Amsterdam: Amsterdam University Press, 1999).

7. Within the large body of work discussing the definition of skill in the context of women's work, important discussions are found in John Rule, "The Property of Skill in the Period of Manufacture"; Michael Sonenscher, "Mythical Work: Workshop Production and the *Compagnonnages* of Eighteenth-Century France"; and Maxine Berg, "Women's Work, Mechanisation and the Early Phases of Industrialisation in England," all in *The Historical Meanings of Work*, ed. Patrick Joyce (Cambridge: Cambridge University Press, 1987).

8. For the dangers of women polluting metal in workshops, see Natalie Zemon Davis, "Women in the Crafts in Sixteenth-Century Lyon," in *Women and Work in Preindustrial Europe*, ed. Barbara A. Hanawalt, (Bloomington: Indiana University Press, 1986), 174; for the *verdegris* industry, see Reed Benamou, "Women and the Verdigris Industry in Montpellier," in *European Women and Preindustrial Craft*, ed. Daryl M. Hafter (Bloomington: Indiana University Press, 1995), 7–8.

9. For an example of men doing "traditional" women's tasks, see Gay L. Gullickson, "The Sexual Division of Labor in Cottage Industry and Agriculture in the Pays de Caux: Auffay, 1750–1850," *French Historical Studies* 12, no. 2 (fall 1981): 177–99.

10. An important exception is cited by the Paris seamstresses in their struggle to escape domination by the male tailors. See Clare Haru Crowston, *Fabricating Women: The Seamstresses of Old Regime France, 1675–1781* (Durham: Duke University Press, 2001). The tailors retaliated by declaring the women incapable of making corsets, a more profitable branch of the industry.

suggested that women's nature was not compatible with wage earning and that their role in society ought to be invested in the social capital of nurturing the family. This new idea arose at the same time that the French state was pressing its administrators to analyze the economy in increasingly numerical and abstract terms.

From 1775 to the end of the century, an era of transition brought old assumptions into conflict with modernizing efforts. Unable to abolish the guilds, administrative reformers tried to improve their efficiency by restructuring them along "rational" lines. This way of thinking viewed workers as abstract productive units. Bureaucrats were accustomed to dealing with men in these terms, but could females be considered in the same terms as males in work associations? Taking into account the presence of females as workers, they opened the guilds to men and women irrespectively. The male guilds, however, seized on the new ideology of women as technologically incompetent, and some used it as a bar to deter women from entering their associations.

When the Revolution abolished legal privilege, guildwomen lost the protection that accorded them a more equal playing field in the economy. By suppressing guilds in 1791, revolutionary legislation in France stripped guildwomen of the chance to gain legal exceptionality and threw them into competition with other male and female workers. In the revolutionary critique, nature supplanted tradition as the touchstone of rational social structure. It was not the assignment of man-made categories that should form the basis of the state, but rather that human beings should be assigned to the roles that their natures dictated. While this ideal brought the civil benefits of divorce, equal inheritance, and the chance to speak in court to *all* women, it negated the possibility of *some* women to gain the freedom of "honorary men."[11]

The increasing popularity of Jean-Jacques Rousseau's analysis added to the notion that the natures of men and women were different and complementary, and that in the well-ordered society men conducted activities in the public sector, while women performed the nurturing role of wife and mother in the home. Because citizens were defined by their essential natures, the postrevolutionary conception left an indelible stamp on

11. Elizabeth G. Sledziewski takes the opposite view that revolutionary ideals, experience, and accomplishments provided the direct basis for subsequent feminism. "The French Revolution as the Starting Point," in *A History of Women*, ed. George Duby and Michelle Perrot (Cambridge: Harvard University Press, 1995), 32–47.

the roles assumed by individuals. Women could not escape their role as private, wifely beings, unsuited to public life in business or politics.¹² Following this logic, social rhetoric cast females as lacking in technological aptitude. There was no longer an exception to the belief that women's work was unskilled work as there had been during the earlier period when guilds ordered social roles.

Without orders or privilege, the categories that had composed the Old Regime, French society turned to the grand remaining differences: wealth and sex. Instead of the horizontal separation of society into clergy, nobles, and Third Estate, the modern state arranged itself into a division between males and females. This vertical separation was more deep-seated than earlier ways of organization because it rested on the supposedly indelible nature of men and women and it imposed social norms on every aspect of human life. The separation intensified discrimination against women by defining them as naturally unsuited to public life whether in business, politics, or the use of complex technology.¹³ During their last years, women's guilds turned the tables by claiming a monopoly on gender-specific tasks, such as hairdressing and sewing, to exclude the men who flocked to those trades.¹⁴

To understand how drastic the new order of feminine restriction was, we need to contrast it with the experience of women guild masters under the Old Regime. In this book I will tell the story through case studies of women workers in two major centers of the manufacture of textiles in preindustrial France. I will compare the guildwomen in the city of Rouen with female workers in the silk industry of Lyon in order to analyze how these two groups of productive workers carved out a space for their economic activity and attempted to exert control over their lives. Both sets

---

12. A voluminous literature exists on Rousseau's influence on women's role in the state. For a first orientation, see Susan Moller Okin, *Women in Western Political Thought* (Princeton: Princeton University Press, 1979), 99–194; Gita May, "Rousseau's 'Antifeminism' Reconsidered," in *French Women and the Age of Enlightenment*, ed. Samia I. Spencer (Bloomington: Indiana University Press, 1984), 309–17; and Elizabeth Rose Wingrove, *Rousseau's Republican Romance* (Princeton: Princeton University Press, 2000).

13. The German example was even more clear-cut. See Karin Hausen, "The Family and Role Division: The Polarization of Sexual Stereotypes in the Nineteenth Century," in *The German Family: Essays on the Social History of the Family in Nineteenth-and Twentieth-Century Germany*, ed. Richard Evans and W. R. Lee (London: Croom Helm, 1981), and Merry Wiesner, *Working Women in Renaissance Germany* (New Brunswick: Rutgers University Press, 1986).

14. See Judith G. Coffin, *The Politics of Women's Work: The Paris Garment Trades, 1750–1915* (Princeton: Princeton University Press, 1996), esp. 35–38, for several examples.

of women were occupied with the production of textiles, the most numerous goods produced and sold in the preindustrial world. Both catered to the luxury trade, but their different opportunities depended on their location, what crafts they undertook, and their legal status. By becoming masters in Rouen, then a city of 90,000, the guildwomen gained the chance to trade legally in wholesale as well as retail markets, and to sell primary materials as well as manufactured goods.

The majority of women workers of Rouen were day laborers who toiled for their employers by weaving linen, carding wool, and carrying coal and wood to furnaces; like most female workers, these employees received minimal wages and were laid off in business downturns. At the opposite end of the workforce, Rouen was unique in having many female guild masters ruling over their workshops, deciding collective policy, and going to court to preserve their technical monopolies. With their members numbering more than one hundred, the linen-drapers of new cloth (*lingères en neuf*) were the predominant guildwomen in the city. Much smaller, but highly vocal, the all-female linen-drapers of old cloth (*lingères en vieux*) sold used clothing and continued to operate as a distinct women's commerce throughout much of the eighteenth century. The female knitters (*bonnetières*) excluded men until late-century reforms. Other women's guilds of feather merchants (*plumassières*), hairdressers (*coiffeuses*), seamstresses (*couturières*) and pin makers (*épinglières*) were gradually absorbed into larger guilds with various specialties. Although it seems logical that the all-female guilds had women officers, it comes as a surprise that guilds with male and female masters, like the spinners (*filassières*) and the ribbonmakers (*rubanières*), elected predominantly women officers. All told, the female masters amounted to some 7,000 persons, 10 percent of the city's guild population. They worked as seamstresses; cotton, linen, and silk spinners; hat makers; linen weavers; pin makers; ribbon and fringe makers; shoe decorators; purveyors of feathers and linen; and even grain merchants.[15]

By contrast, Lyon's work force was largely devoted to the silk industry, which outdistanced its production of other goods—wool, iron, and

---

15. The most complete demographic study of Rouen is by Jean-Pierre Bardet, *Rouen au XVIIe et XVIIIe siècles* (Paris: SEDES, 1983). Information about Rouen's guilds is found in Archives départementales de la Seine Maritime, Series 5 E and Series C. For guild statutes, see Charles Ouen-Lacroix, *Histoire des anciennes corporations d'arts et métiers et des confréries religieuses de la capital de la Normandie* (Rouen: Lecointe frères, 1850).

sundries. In this city of 150,000 inhabitants, some 40,000 artisans turned out the luxurious silks for which France became famous. Even its function as a financial center and a hub for transshipment did not outshine the silk business that spread through the flat peninsula and up the steep slopes of Lyon's cliffs. Composed of one large guild that encompassed all the silk techniques, the *grande fabrique*, as it was called, employed at least 20,000 women and children as day laborers. Only one of the trades, the *passementiers* making decorative braid, allowed women to become masters; the rest relied on the work of male apprentices and journeymen, wives and daughters and sons of guild masters, and hired female craft workers. The women and girls active in silk manufacture were divided into two categories: relatives of master silk weavers or wage earners legally excluded from becoming masters. To be sure, like most other French cities, Lyon had its associations of female guilds that included seamstresses, hairdressers, and river barge women, but these trades had neither the prestige nor the economic power of silk making.[16]

The female silk workers of Lyon made their way by assisting their husbands in the family trade or by becoming so skilled that they became indispensable to their patrons. Whether related to a silk master or hired from the ever-renewing pool of wageworkers, the many women gained more social capital than their circumstances might suggest. Where business was king, the practices of the silk guild bent to the realities of demanding customers and the need for technical skill. Wives and daughters of silk master weavers hired themselves out to more prosperous masters with large orders. Wageworkers in the auxiliary trades performed such specialized tasks that their guild masters feared their desertion to other employers and made it illegal. At the top of this group the readers (*liseuses*), who were highly paid and highly sought after, did the painstaking work of making programs that enabled brocade weavers to transform the designer's pattern into cloth. Even the drawgirls, whose tasks required mostly muscular strength, pulling down cordage attached to weights in order to advance the brocading program, were valued enough that that guilds required masters to give them lodging and a yearly contract.[17]

---

16. The most authoritative study of Lyon is Maurice Garden, *Lyon et les lyonnaises au XVIIIe siècle* (Paris: Société d'éditions "Les Belles Lettres," 1986).

17. See Daryl M. Hafter, "The 'Programmed' Drawloom and the Decline of the Drawgirl," in *Dynamos and Virgins Revisited: Women and Technological Change in History*, ed. Martha Moore Trescott (Metuchen, N.J.: Scarecrow Press, 1979): 49–66.

Moreover, the women themselves set up clandestine networks of commerce, stealing raw materials, running workshops to process them, and colluding with merchants who specialized in selling their wares. The underground economy to which these women contributed was not a sideline; it was an essential part of business in the risky silk commerce. Master weavers had to make outlays for an expensive raw material without the assurance that pattern styles would last and that they would be reimbursed for their time and that of their workers. Throughout the industry, masters relied on discounted merchandise and pilfered raw materials to weather the economic uncertainties.[18]

These examples do not change the fact that the majority of women and men labored for subsistence wages in disagreeable and dangerous conditions. It is important, however, to notice that entrepreneurs acknowledged the importance of female employees whether or not they gave the women pay commensurate with their skills. Recognition that the women's work was crucial to the structure of the industry sometimes came in the form of prohibitions against leaving before a contract was finished or strictures against working for rival masters or guilds. These lifelong female wageworkers were excluded from becoming apprentices and eventual master in the guild. Nevertheless, they were the motor force of one of the largest manufactures in the preindustrial era. Contrary to our expectations, even the dispersed nonguild industry of prerevolutionary France employed far more women than men, relying on their cheap labor to transport wood, break coal, tear rags, weave, bleach woolen cloth, and perform any number of other unskilled and semi-skilled tasks.

Research on women's work in eighteenth-century France shows that we have left behind the idea posited by Ivy Pinchbeck and others that women's work outside the home began with the Industrial Revolution.[19] As Robert Lopez, the eminent medievalist has said, the preindustrial world was an era of scarcity, as production relied on wind, water, and animal and human labor for energy. So few surpluses arose from the primitive tools and limited motor power that every person had to work to provide subsistence. As more sophisticated economic structures emerged, merchants at the top of the scale did well, but ordinary people still had to

---

18. For a fuller examination, see Daryl M. Hafter, "Women in the Underground Business of Eighteenth-Century Lyon," *Enterprise and Society* 2 (March 2001): 11–40.

19. See Ivy Pinchbeck, *Women Workers and the Industrial Revolution, 1750–1850* (New York: Routledge, 1930; rpt. A. Kelley, 1969).

worry about their next day's support. Women and children worked at productive tasks as well as men, and even when the trades were conducted in the home workshop, caring for the home itself took low priority. Enhancing the family shelter became important only when industrialization created enough of a surplus to enable a middle class, with wife and children not employed outside the home, to clean and fuss with the family shelter. As Louise Tilly and Joan Walloch Scott wrote, early modern society *expected* women to earn money to help keep the family economy afloat.[20] Mothers had the primary responsibility to provide for their children. Folktales warned young men that wives with no aptitude for work would bring disaster to the home. Whether women assisted their husbands and trained their children in the trade or left the family workshop to earn fees outside the home, women have always worked cleaning, selling, transporting bundles, preparing raw materials for manufacture, and crafting goods.

But there was a paradox here: society expected women to be effective economic participants, but the legal system—embodying the general discriminatory view of women—set strict limits to their independent actions. Marriage coverture was the structure devised to enforce this uneasy and unbalanced relationship. As the British jurist William Blackstone put it, "By marriage, the husband and wife are one person in law: that is, the very being or legal existence of the woman is suspended during the marriage, or at least is incorporated and consolidated into that of the husband: under whose wing, protection, and cover she performs every thing."[21] Women in France, too, under the Old Regime were generally considered minors in the law; they could not make binding contracts, sue, or be sued on their own behalf. Husbands, fathers, or another close male relative had to speak for them in legal disputes, unless—usually with father deceased—they were considered to be in charge of their own affairs as adult unmarried women (*filles majeures*) or widows.[22]

20. See Louise A. Tilly and Joan W. Scott, *Women, Work, and Family* (New York: Holt, Rinehart and Winston, 1978), a classic in the field of women's social history.
21. William Blackstone, *Commentaries on the Laws of England*, 11th ed. (London 1791). Cited in Susan Groag Bell and Karen M. Offen, *Women, the Family, and Freedom: The Debate in Documents* (Stanford: Stanford University Press, 1983), 1:33.
22. *Filles majeures* were unmarried women who had reached their majority and assumed control of their business dealings and finances because their father was deceased or had granted his permission. See the discussion by Sarah Hanley, "Family and State in Early Modern France: The Marriage Pact," in *Connecting Spheres: Women in the Western World, 1500 to the Present*, ed. Marilyn J. Boxer and Jean H. Quataert (Oxford: Oxford University Press, 1987), 53–63.

Women in Rouen had the additional burden of discrimination from the *Coûtumier de Normandie,* Normandy's legal code, which was in operation until the Revolution. These laws required wives to be supervised constantly by their husbands and restricted their inheritance to a smaller percentage of the assets than widows received under other legal codes.[23] Because each generality had its own traditional set of customary law, the rights of women were not the same throughout France. Lyon, which was under the Paris *parlement*'s jurisdiction, posed different obstacles for women. Although the Paris legal system was not as restrictive as that of Normandy, the majority of Lyon's working women labored in the silk industry under master weavers, with no possibility of becoming head of their own business. Contrary to first impressions, however, working women in both cities managed to rise above their restrictive situations, wives in Rouen becoming guild masters and industrial laborers in Lyon taking advantage of an underground economy to compete with legitimate silk masters.

Two important legal instruments helped women to participate in economic life. The first was the designation of *marchande publique,* merchant in the public domain, which gave a married woman the right to conduct business on her own behalf. She could perform all the functions necessary in business just like a man—buying, selling, making contracts, suing, being sued, and investing. Her business and her funds were separate from those of her husband, and his creditors could not accost her if his business failed. Female guild masters automatically became *marchandes publiques.*[24] A second legal instrument was the device of *séparation de biens* that severed a couple's finances, allowing the wife to take charge of her own business and monies. This expedient helped a woman whose husband was wasting the resources of her dowry or was on the brink of bankrupting the family.[25]

---

23. See the discussion of legal obstacles and devices to overcome them in Daryl M. Hafter, "Gender Formation from a Working Class Viewpoint: Guildwomen in Eighteenth-Century Rouen," *Proceedings Western Society for French History* 16 (1989): 415–22.

24. For the eighteenth-century definition, see Rogue, *Jurisprudence consulaire et instruction des négociants* (Angers, 1773), 1:227. The English equivalent was *feme sole,* a wife acting independently. Brigit Hill discusses the legal implications of *feme sole* and *feme covert* (a wife under the protection of her husband) in *Women, Work and Sexual Politics in Eighteenth-Century England* (Montreal: McGill–Queen's University Press, 1994), 196–204.

25. For a discussion of these two legal devices, see Julie Hardwick, *The Practice of Patriarchy: Gender and the Politics of Household Authority in Early Modern France* (University Park: The Pennsylvania State University Press, 1998), 111–20, and her "Seeking Separations:

These exceptions to the rule of masculine domination were hardly attempts at women's liberation; instead they were devices to maintain real estate or goods in the woman's birth family or to promote the welfare of the husband and family. According to French law, the letters of *séparation de biens* and the autonomy invested in the role of *marchande publique* were permissions the husband gave his wife to benefit himself.[26] Nevertheless, the *marchande publique* acted as an honorary man, participating in business with the same instruments a man would use. The practice of awarding rights by means of royal decree or legal title accustomed the French to accept the constructed status of privileged individuals. Thus, despite the general prejudice against women that assumed their lack of intelligence, manipulative nature, and excessive sexuality, women with privilege were accepted in terms of their legal status. As William Sewell put it, privilege trumped gender discrimination to enable women in guilds to behave as guild masters rather than minors under the law.[27]

This resulted in episodes of remarkable behavior in Old Regime France. Women became masters in guilds that were exclusively female and also in guilds of mixed sex. In some places women became officers for female guilds and also for mixed associations. In Rouen, the guilds to which these women belonged had the same structure, habits, and legal rights that male guilds employed. They competed with male guilds on the basis of legal equality, asserting their control over the use of materials and technical and commercial monopolies in opposition to male guilds that challenged them.

With such evidence, this book helps to overturn the traditional view of guilds as bastions of exclusively male privilege. In Chapter 1, "The Political Economy of Guilds," I define the qualities that guilds shared. All guilds, both male and female, had in common the principle that they were sworn trades conferring privileges upon their members. Guilds modeled themselves on the traditional structure of masters, apprentices, and journey workers, training and licensing the producers of medieval and

---

Gender, Marriages and Household Economics in Seventeenth-Century France," *French Historical Studies* 21 (winter 1998).

26. See Hafter, "Gender Formation," esp. p. 417, which cites comments by the eighteenth-century jurist David Houard to the effect that by permitting his wife to become a *marchande publique* the husband gives her freedom in order to enrich himself.

27. See the remarks of William Sewell commenting on Daryl M. Hafter, "The Female Masters in the Ribbonmaking Guild of Eighteenth-Century Rouen," *French Historical Studies* 20, no. 1 (winter 1997): 443–48.

early modern products. These professional associations held monopolies on the goods they created and the technology they used, prosecuting unlicensed interlopers whenever they were found making or selling similar objects. In keeping with their corporate function, guilds each pledged devotion to a patron saint and formed confederations that paid for masses and held ceremonial meals. Despite these common traits, what characterized the range of guilds was how individual and idiosyncratic they were.

Moreover, not every group of sworn tradesmen formed a group with all the institutions of the traditional guild. Some workers took only the first step of guild creation by being sworn as apprentices. Others became legal peddlers, counted among a limited number of itinerant venders of food or secondhand items. Such groups of female peddlers, or *revendresses*, which could not accept a new member until an old one had died, had letters that licensed them to trade only particular goods and forbade them to enter other professions. Since they had no guild structure, they were on the fringe of the corporate system; still their license gave them a monopoly of sales and the right to ply their wares on the streets outside of the market boundaries.

In Chapter 1, I also show that even in guilds with a more traditional formation, the particular products, tools, and specifications for manufacture and sale varied according to the region. It followed that different entrance fees, statutes, initiation practices, and size characterized guilds in various parts of France. Guilds with the same name often had dissimilar technical practices in different cities. The makers of decorative braid (*passementiers*), for instance, were counted as ribbonmakers in Rouen, knitters in Paris, and silk weavers in Lyon, and each guild had particular rights not shared by their counterparts in other cities. This variety worked to the women guild masters' advantage, since the Old Regime abounded in particular privileges that marked out legal boundaries.

In Chapter 2, "The Uses of Gender in Economic Life," I make the case that within the contentious arena of guild politics, gender was a minor element, largely overlooked and of far less significance than it is for us today. This point is illustrated by the contretemps between the female linen-drapers of Le Havre—who sought to expand their business to include selling cotton cloth, material of mixed composition, and linen thread—and the male guild of merchant mercers, which owned the rights to this wholesale commerce. When merchant mercers refused to relinquish their monopoly over these items, the women proposed to

Figure 1. Passementerie, putting brass tips on flax laces used to tighten women's bodices. The brass wire is cut into lengths, pounded, and shaped to make it flexible. Brass decorations were also an economical substitute for gold and silver braid. From Diderot's *Encyclopédie*, courtesy Special Collections Library, University of Michigan.

amalgamate their guild with the mercers and thereby gain the commercial rights. Rightly assessing this proposal as a hostile takeover, the merchant mercers mounted a propaganda campaign that reveals how guild masters regarded gender. Their first arguments rested on the traditional pillars of past practice and incompatibility of goods.[28] Only later did the merchant mercers point out that a male guild and a female guild were two separate entities that should not be joined. The reasons they adduced were not based on the women's lack of skill, but rather on their own, since the *lingères* required an apprenticeship and masterpiece, whereas the merchant mercers did not. Not a word was written suggesting that men and women had different technical capabilities; what they contended, significantly, was simply that since the women were already trained, they would have the advantage over the merchants.

Nevertheless, gender norms did play a role in accustoming society to associate women's work with a domestic setting and justifying women's debased wages. Thus the social construction of gender regulated women's

---

28. Sonenscher, *Work and Wages*, 91–98.

work and their wages throughout the economy, save for places like Rouen where the guilds created an exception. Still, even the Rouennaise guildwomen, with all their privileged protection, earned less than comparable male guild masters. At times, the government emphasized their feminine nature and created guilds expressly for women, like the *couturières* guild in seventeenth-century Paris. And women were not above playing the feminine card themselves when they might gain some advantage. As historians have noted, women played a shifting role that depended on their economic bracket, their particular function, their location, and their personal situation.

In Chapter 3, "Guildwomen and *Ouvrières*," I contrast the daily experience of these two groups of women. We see how Rouen's linen-drapers of new cloth (*lingères en neuf*) used legal instruments to fend off attempts by other guilds to gain access to their technology and commercial markets. Behaving like any other guild, the *lingères* opposed the powerful male merchant mercers' bid to make and sell linen garments, cloth, and knitted objects. They lobbied the authorities in Paris to gain the right to sell colored thread. When woven shawls started to be used as headscarves, they opposed the female knitters' claim to hold a monopoly on headgear. In all these contests, the linen-drapers of new cloth won court decisions and were able to protect their commercial and manufacturing spheres. They countered hostile actions by male and female guilds alike and used the identical legal instruments available to male guilds. They behaved in these arguments exactly like their male counterparts. Considerations of gender fell away before the legal assertion of privileged rights and the equality created by loopholes in the misogynistic law.

Another aspect of government preoccupation with the composition of the workers and their shop-floor discipline can be seen in Lyon. While the guildwomen of Rouen were exercising their privileges and asserting equality between male and female masters, the silk workers of Lyon were using covert means to mitigate the disadvantages of gender-based work. One major issue in the silk guild was the struggle between the small master weavers, who tried to retain their place as merchants as well as producers, and the wealthy master merchants, intent on monopolizing sales and using the master weavers as hired hands. Women's work was a crucial prize in this struggle as the small master weavers tried to exclude nonguildwomen from weaving while maintaining their own wives and daughters at the loom.

In Chapter 4, "Turgot's Reforms and Their Aftermath," I examine changes in the guild structure in the aftermath of reforms made in 1776 by Controller General Jacques Turgot. In an attempt to modernize the economy, Turgot abolished guilds, but this decree, although enforced only in the Parisian region, aroused such hostility that it was soon rescinded. Nevertheless, the strategy appealed to the administration that turned it into a money-raising scheme, abolishing guilds and then forcing them to reconstruct themselves and pay for new patents. To avoid the traditional bickering over monopolies, guilds performing the same technology or making similar products were merged. And men and women were formally permitted to enter any trade in which they were competent.

From the perspective of this book, the crucial changes occurred when men were permitted into women's guilds and also with the banning of female masters from participation in the governing of mixed-sex guilds. Until then, Rouen's female guild masters had been members of the ruling assemblies and officers of the mixed-sex spinners and ribbonmakers. Under the new rules, the spinners, ribbonmakers, knitters, and linendrapers of old cloth were merged with male guilds, and the women masters in these sworn trades were immediately silenced. This step prefigured the consignment of women to the category of "passive citizens" during the Revolution. It focused attention on the difficult problem of considering women as full-fledged economic participants while rejecting them as active citizens. Like other measures designed to curtail their actions, however, archival research shows that women found ways to exert influence as long as the guild structure was in place.

The revolutionary era offered opportunities and disadvantages to businesswomen that no one had dreamed of, a topic I explore in the final chapter, "Paths to the Revolution." Like so many others, ordinary wage earners were caught up in the ferment of ideology that erupted in 1789. In a more fortunate bracket, guildwomen expressed their complaints, demanding education, professional training, and the exclusion of men from traditional women's trades. Discrimination against women's inequitable wages and limited range of jobs was also a theme brought into the marketplace of ideas. But these reforms took second place to the major changes enacted by the National Assembly. Once the abolition of privilege became a cardinal principle, the institutions of France were changed to reflect egalitarian ideals. Legislators reformed taxes, suppressed venal positions, applied civil law equally, and, most significant for our inquiry, they abolished the guilds and opened trades to everyone.

Although some revolutionary legislation bettered the lot of women—permitting divorce, mandating equal inheritance, and offering the prospect of public education—the suppression of guilds in 1791 brought a sea change to women's economic standing. Female masters had enjoyed the legal protection of institutional privilege during the regime of guilds. It was by no means a "golden age" for women economically active, but within the terms of guild membership, female masters could take on the competition of their male counterparts, in some cases and in some cities, as equals. They could protect themselves from competition from nonguild rivals and negotiate with administrators for lower taxes and greater craft freedom. The fall of guilds cast them into the economic marketplace just when trade barriers, expensive raw materials, drastic style changes, and revolutionary wars disrupted commerce. Women's comparative lack of capital and the small size of their businesses also put them at a disadvantage when government contracts were being offered. Nevertheless, in Lyon, more than a thousand women took advantage of the new freedom to start businesses of their own, according to a survey of silk fabric manufacturers.

Commercial obstacles and warfare devastated Lyon's silk industry as hostilities prevented foreign customers from gaining access to Lyon's goods. Citizens living through the unhappy days of the 1793 "revolt" of Lyon and its bitter suppression were in the worst condition. Within the city, the call to arms thinned the ranks of male weavers leaving female wage earners to take up men's tasks. But tragedies do not last forever, and by 1810, with Napoleon's encouragement, silk was once more being produced in Lyon's shops. The changing laws and economic circumstances brought new realities to the industry. As the process of weaving became feminized, salaries for work at the loom declined just as the male guild masters had warned earlier. Paradoxically, however, it was through the support of these underpaid women weavers that the remaining male weavers were able to preserve their intricate hand weaving and their artisanal way of life. The women helped to keep silk masters in Lyon while the Jacquard device, enabling weavers to create figured patterns by themselves, spread ordinary brocade manufacture to the countryside around Lyon in the first decades of the nineteenth century.

In Rouen, the system of privilege became a means of personal and family benefits for those women lucky enough to become guild masters. Separated from the legal and social discrimination that most women in the Old Regime endured, the female guild masters used all the instruments that male guild masters employed to gain economic advantages. Like their male counterparts, they responded to market pressure by subcontracting and hiring workers without credentials. They also aimed at controlling all aspects of manufacture, from preparation to wholesale commerce, in order to extract the maximum profit. Moreover, their position as "honorary men" brought them face to face with royal officials, and they pursued a lobbying effort through legal briefs and contacts with Paris officials. Instead of preparing them to take their place as responsible voting citizens, however, their intervention in government policy fell victim to the Revolution's definition of women as passive citizens whose civic beliefs were expressed through their husbands.[29]

Lyon's women workers, if they were related to a silk master during the eighteenth century, also benefited from guilds, but without such a family tie they fell into the large pool of wageworkers competing for employment. Their skill did not bring commensurate salaries from the masters or journeymen who employed them even though they were indispensable to the silk industry. Some profited by participating in the underground economy of cut-rate work, some married silk masters, while others ended their days in the Hôtel de la Charité among the poor and disabled.

The Revolution disrupted this system of guild and artisanal craft, throwing women and men into direct competition. As the vertical divisions of the three estates and multiprivileged associations were cast away, gender differences became the overriding division in society. No longer could women shelter themselves, even those few women who might earlier have become guild masters in a privileged institution. All were now at the mercy of the market, which continued to extend opportunities to the lucky few and to impose poverty and hardship on the others.

---

29. The problem of women as political actors has received considerable attention. For examples, see Joan B. Landes, *Women and the Public Sphere in the Age of the French Revolution* (Ithaca: Cornell University Press, 1988); Candice E. Proctor, *Women, Equality, and the French Revolution* (New York: Greenwood Press, 1990); and Karen Offen, *European Feminisms, 1700–1950* (Stanford: Stanford University Press, 2000), esp. 50–76.

THE POLITICAL ECONOMY OF GUILDS

When eighteenth-century critics of the guild system looked for ways to discredit the institution, they could dip into any police register and find evidence to support their views. Guilds had monopolies over the techniques, products, and workers in their crafts. They could manipulate their regulations to serve their vested interests or ignore them, when that seemed expedient. The frustration arising from such high-handed behavior deprived many a worker of employment and provided fodder for writers decrying the privileged status of skilled crafts. The court case against Marie Barb Le Gendre brought by the guild of embroiderers and makers of church vestments is typical of the many imbroglios that ensnared workers when they defied guild regulations.

> Marie Barb Le Gendre, wife of David de Claire, was found working with her daughter, Catherine Baron, at a loom, and the officers of the embroiderers–clerical vestment makers' guild said that neither was a member. The guild officer condemned them but de Claire, the husband, lodged an appeal. In response, the sergeant royal, de L'Étang, promised them a new audience, after which he confiscated the women's looms and work, and imposed a fine with interest, all of which would be read out loud, published, and posted.
>
> David de Claire said, "His wife Marie Barbe Le Gendre paid 80 livres for her master's license, twice the fee charged to others."
> Her lawyer said, "The *gardes* did not warn her not to apply. Hence she was received as mistress on the eve of her marriage to the said de Claire. The *gardes* knew perfectly well about her marriage since she was then working for a former guild officer named Sieur de Lamark, under whom she received her training."

Marie Barbe Le Gendre said, "De Lamark himself prompted her to become mistress of this trade and her husband made the outlay of money. The *gardes* were well acquainted with her because for eight consecutive years she had kept a boutique open and worked for most of the guild masters who even brought her the work to do at her own home.

"It was only when her husband returned home crippled with war wounds, asking to be received master of the craft so he could work with her, that they demoted her to the rank of a simple worker. Without her status of master, she could not bring her husband into the trade."

The *gardes* said, "It is expressly written that women who have their mastership by right of *'fille de maître'* [daughter of a master] will lose it if they marry someone who is not in the guild. Since her husband was a journeyman carpenter, she could not employ him in her workshop and in addition she lost her own license to work at home."[1]

Besides showing how the guild officers functioned in arguing a case and the way individuals fought to regain their status as legitimate workers, this court transcript tells us something about the flexibility, one might say slippery flexibility that guilds were capable of in defending their economic goals. The quantity of records like these casts doubt on the definition of guilds on which many accounts of preindustrial manufacture and social dynamics rely. In creating a foil to show its divergence from artisanal work, analysts of the Industrial Revolution have tended to consider the characteristics of guilds as frozen in time. From this perspective, changes in guild practice in response to different market conditions are taken as demonstrating that the guild system was destroying itself, that by changing their practices to deal with new realities the guilds were betraying their ideals. But were the alterations to classic formation signs that guilds were outmoded, or were they examples of healthy adaptation to new economic conditions?

---

1. Minutes of the case of the *brodeurs-chassubliers*' guild against Marie Barb Le Gendre, 29 January 1715; second appeal of the case, 20 February 1715, Archives départementales de la Seine Maritime 5 E 200, Communauté des Brodeurs-Chasubliers.
   The translation here and all subsequent translations are mine unless otherwise noted.

Despite the variety found among guilds, certain common elements stand out and are taken to be the essence of the guild system. In this chapter I will begin with a sketch of the "typical guild," defining the components that were central to these institutions as they developed. Through their response to changes in the political economy, we will then see how guilds freed themselves from restrictive bylaws without giving up their traditional privileges and how they became a source of taxes and control for the king. We will explore the way the different work structure in two contrasting cities, Rouen and Lyon, spanned a variety of organization and offered different possibilities to the workers in their industries. Finally, we will review the evidence of women in guilds to see how closely their experience duplicated that of their male colleagues.

Guild regulations designated the stages of technical training as apprenticeship, practice as day workers or journeymen, and, finally, mastership. In return for swearing that their goods would be made honestly, according to written specifications, and would not cause harm to the public, guild members received exclusive rights to their technology and products. The officers of these associations wrote rules governing license fees, technical processes, and the qualifications of their employees. They tested aspirants by requiring a masterpiece, and they continued surveillance of the guild ateliers with four annual inspections. This, more or less, is the image of the guild that has survived in histories and in the thinking of most students of past economic life—a tidy formulation of workers and their bosses, guided by principles of medieval egalitarianism, charging a just price, producing goods of quality, and rewarding with mastership skilled young people who paid their dues.

But from their very beginnings, guilds were responding to economic pressures that skewed the neat formulation of qualified artisans automatically rising through the ranks, manufacturing each product from start to finish in one workshop, and hewing to the guild regulations. The policing and court procedure that developed to accompany guild activity testifies to the motto that where there are rules, there will be infractions. Or rather, where there are irregularities, rules are imposed. The testimony preserved in Marie Barbe Le Gendre's case shows how guild officials manipulated their regulations in order to secure a skilled labor force at bargain wages.

The officers of the guild of embroiderers and church vestment makers explained to the court that "the regulation says that in a case like this, the artisan can work at the home of the various members of the craft

Figure 2. Wax making. Wax is heated in a cauldron, then cooled by a female worker who passes it back and forth between two sticks. It is then weighed, shaped into four to six equal sections, and heated again. From Diderot's *Encyclopédie*, courtesy Special Collections Library, University of Michigan.

as a day worker (*ouvrière*), but the decision will not be reversed . . . since from the moment when she lost her license by contracting marriage with the said de Claire she could not keep a boutique open and work publicly as a mistress."[2] As for David de Claire, entering the guild even by offering 80 livres for his own license was out of the question. The *gardes* declared adamantly that while they had accepted another worker who had trained elsewhere, they could not think of receiving de Claire because "all the masters agree; he does not know the first elements of the trade." In the meantime, de Claire demanded the return of the 80 livres he had spent to secure his wife's mastership.[3]

The guild masters were more than willing to use Marie Barbe as a perpetual drudge, benefiting from the skill she had learned at their hands,

---

2. Ibid.
3. Ibid. The *brodeurs-chasubliers* reaped the result of their exclusionary policy later in the century when they dwindled in 1770 to a paltry five members, one man, three widows, and one unmarried woman.

but they stuck at the idea of allowing her husband into the craft. Clearly, they were using the guild as a vehicle for themselves, to have different parts of their work finished by specialized wageworkers and even allowing the goods to be finished at their homes, thus extending the capacity of their workshops. But when it came to sharing the benefits of the association with someone they considered an outsider, they relied on the full legal formality to exclude that person and to enhance their own profits. While women's guilds were generally more open to giving their students the mastership than men's associations—perhaps because the monetary rewards were smaller—the female artisans also wanted to save money by exploiting their employees. The basis for guild formation was to protect artisans' livelihoods as well as to serve as a vehicle for training and industrial control.

Guilds in France were already working institutions when the earliest ones received official status in the twelfth and thirteenth centuries by receiving the king's license or *lettres patentes*.[4] These craft associations had special importance for the economic, political, and social institutions of France. Called *jurandes*, because the members swore (*jurer*) to uphold the guilds' regulations, and *corporations*, because they had the privileged legal status to be able to borrow and lend money, the guilds called themselves *communautés*, for their communal nature. Having grouped together as a means of protecting their trade from competition in a medieval economic resurgence, the guilds formed cooperative associations that acquired prestige and power in their municipalities. As the locus of skilled work, guilds imparted training and commercial monopolies to their members. They drew trades into units that offered prestige, fiscal benefits, and social organization, bringing potential trade rivals into bonds of local community and national resource. From the viewpoint of its members, a guild provided a way of life, opportunities in self-government, officials to regulate technology and protect them from unauthorized competition, a guaranteed place in town processions, and, finally, a burial society.

One of the constant elements in guild history is the variety in their structure, membership, products, and technology. Some historians have found their precedents in the trade associations of classical Rome and the Byzantine Empire, but the guilds of the early modern period have a

---

4. Étienne Martin Saint-Léon, *Histoire des corporations des métiers depuis leurs origins jusqu'à leur suppression en 1791* (Paris, 1922), 208–9 (rpt. New York: Arno Press, 1975). He found guild statutes also dating to the twelfth century.

more direct link to the twelfth-century upsurge in trade and manufacture than to the capitalistic factories of ancient Europe. Medieval guilds began as spontaneous trade unions of skilled artisans, who were seeking collective help in fending off the competition stimulated by the new economic dynamism. Born in the ateliers of the Middle Ages, they conformed to the requirements of the craft in their particular economic environment. They emerged throughout feudal Europe, tied to individual cities by family links and political influence.

Guilds developed naturally from the domestic production of urban families. Their earliest records, from the eleventh and twelfth centuries, show them to be as much a part of the urban evolution as city charters and annual fairs. The development of crafts and the honing of particular skills depended on population centers large enough to accommodate specialization. Their techniques expanded only as quickly as workers could master the available natural resources. Skills grew out of earlier experimentation with tools in rural areas and housing clusters, based on the medieval need to make the most of the small supply of labor. A nearby river that could accommodate mills or a source of copper that could be extracted, for instance, lent particular advantages to a locale and shaped its development. Traditional practices of working with particular materials might point artisans in special directions, for example, the gold and silver workers of Florence or the woolen workers of Flanders. Guilds grew out of the resources and the product needs of cities.

It is easy to see why these associations emerged as family businesses, since tools and materials took over the living space in workers' homes and dominated their days. Every family member was drawn into the process, from the young children running to get wood to the wife finishing the process or weaving on an auxiliary loom. The master's entire family participated in each guild workshop for their collective support. This cooperative activity began literally with the mother's milk; society assumed, for this reason, that the guild master's children already had so much training that they were exempted from the obligations of formal apprenticeship and masterpiece when ready to enter the trade. The apprentices and many day workers lived under the master's roof and shared the family table, performing industrial or domestic tasks to support the productive unit. Under the circumstances, the master acted as chief of the workshop as well as head of the family, and since most guild masters were men, the patriarchal nature of society gave a masculine cast to the guilds.

Everywhere craft production was intimately connected with the family. In an era when few secular institutions existed, the family atelier was located within the home and associated with it. The guilds that arose out of this setting gave family members status in the craft and fostered a strong connection between kinship ties and skilled learning. The guild expected relatives to be associated in business with the master. (In early fourteenth century the Florentine guild of food purveyors [*oliandoli*] applied the most liberal entrance rules to masters' sons, nephews, grandsons, brothers, orphaned daughters, and widows.)[5] In guilds without female masters, the daughter of a master could convey the mastership to her husband if he entered the trade. A master's widow could keep the business open for various periods of time, depending on the regulations, unless she remarried out of the guild. There was something besides practicality at work in these special exceptions. The master's family had learned the craft at his side, but more than that, society believed that the family had been steeped in the mystery of the craft, which constituted its inner secrets.

Sharing the craft secrets was at the heart of the masters' union within the guild, a union cemented by the sworn oath to employ this knowledge for the public good. The spiritual bond linking guild masters to each other, virtually as family members, surpassed the closeness of those who were merely workmates.

Masters also benefited from the participation of family members, who undertook all but the most highly skilled process. As a rule, those who worked in the atelier did a variety of tasks. In the classic guild model, each product was made from start to finish in one workshop. The masters not only supervised the work and added the most exacting touches themselves, but they also sold their products under contract, in their boutiques or at a communal trading hall. Thus the masters were industrialists and merchants at once, and their products were guaranteed by the protection of guild regulation over every aspect of this exchange.

Each workshop was headed by a master experienced in the technology of his or her craft. Under the master's tutelage, young persons were apprenticed to learn the craft for a term of four to twelve years. The apprentice's parents or guardians paid for this instruction, and the master

---

5. See Steven A. Epstein's discussion of the changing statutes in *Wage Labor and Guilds in Medieval Europe* (Chapel Hill: University of North Carolina Press, 1991), 208–12.

agreed to provide housing, clothing, and moral care for the youth. In rare cases the apprentice received a small salary. The trainees swore to be faithful and obedient for the period of apprenticeship, after which the initiates could pass into the ranks of journeymen and journeywomen, working for a daily wage until skilled enough to succeed in making a masterpiece.[6] In ideal terms, the aspirants then paid the fee to become masters, provided celebratory festivities, and joined the ranks of masters with ateliers of their own. Not only did the masters provide technical expertise, they were also the heads of the business, negotiating contracts, acquiring raw materials, and taking responsibility for the finished product.

But guilds were far more than simply mediums of production. The guilds were professional associations that linked members of the same craft to provide training, discipline, help, and solidarity. Emile Coornaert called them "an economic association of quasi-public (or semi-public) law, submitting its members to collective discipline for the exercise of their profession."[7] Guilds performed a typical police function in the early modern period that so often split off elements of public authority and placed them into the hands of private citizens. They were empowered by their municipalities to administer training, manufacture, and quality control for their own products.

Guild officers enforced their statutes by periodic inspection tours of the workshops in their organizations; they confiscated goods that did not conform to the craft rules and fined masters who hired unqualified workers or extended the workday longer than standards allowed. The officers' authority expanded into the streets, marketplaces, and courts where they brought suit against unauthorized venders or out-of-town craft workers. In terms of national discipline, we might say that the king delegated the responsibility of determining the standards of their industry to guilds, and then endowed their officers, the *gardes, jurés,* and *syndics,* with the power to enforce the laws through the agency of the town government and the royal courts.

The masters' role had a political dimension as well. They joined in the guild's general assembly to elect officers and discuss what measures the officers should take regarding a wide measure of problems—from

---

6. Ibid., xx. In some trades the masterpiece was made at the end of the apprenticeship. The masterpiece became generalized only at the beginning of the sixteenth century. See Émile Coornaert, *Les Corporations en France avant 1789* (Paris: Gallimard, [1968]), 29.

7. Coornaert, *Les Corporation,* 32.

changes in statutes to apportioning taxes. Large guilds elected an executive council for routine issues, and the entire group of masters met together to debate important policy decisions. Standards for behavior were set out in bylaws to regulate technology and personnel. These rules governed the actions of guild members and their employees; they also specified the monopolies of products and tools, which others were forbidden to acquire. Through elected *gardes* and *syndics*, the guilds policed their own members, bringing to justice those who kept their shops open after dark or used unqualified workers or illicit techniques. They employed the public judicial system to enforce their regulations on illegal workers or venders. By offering their own rules to serve as public regulations and by gaining the help of municipal and royal officers to enforce them, these associations thrived on the Old Regime's mixing of private and public authority. Having begun as free, spontaneous institutions, membership in the guilds soon became obligatory for any who wanted to make or sell products under their purview.[8]

Guild ties were further enhanced by the religious cast of their rituals. The oath of mastership, taken before guild and municipal officers, brought God's sanction to their work and their guild loyalty. Bylaws permitted membership only to Roman Catholics. (This stricture was expressed most often after the Counter-Reformation.) Each guild usually formed a religious confraternity that met in a church or abbey, collected funds for charity, was responsible for paying for the guild masters' funerals and a mass celebrated on the day of the guild's patron saint. Indeed, some historians have suggested that the religious association came first and later gave rise to the guilds.[9] The guild associated itself even more in the public mind with its saint's protection by using that holiday to inaugurate new masters, elect officers, and count out the annual contents of the money box. The saint's day began with a holy procession and ended with a new master's banquets and raucous merrymaking that underscored how intimately the sacred and the profane were meshed.

The medieval themes of a Christian ethic animated the guild's ideals. The oath to make goods according to the highest standards was behind

---

8. Edouard Dolléans and Gérard Dehove, *Histoire du travail en France, mouvement ouvrier et legislation sociale des origins à 1919* (Paris: A. Colin, 1936; rpt. Paris: Domat-Montchrestien, 1953), 29.

9. But the early religious confraternities included members from many different trades. See Edwin S. Hunt and James M. Murray, *A History of Business in Medieval Europe, 1200–1550* (Cambridge: Cambridge University Press, 1999), 34.

manufacturing regulations; the promise to sell honestly justified the guild masters' wish to sell their goods themselves, since they were best informed about the product's quality. Setting work hours, rules against suborning another's apprentice or journeyman, injunctions to have *"boutique ouverte"*—that is, to be actively engaged in the trade—all aimed at allaying unfair competition. Requiring goods to be sold in the public hall to prevent private deals was a means of enforcing a just price. Repetition of these injunctions through the centuries, however, indicates how frequently guild masters opted for personal profit rather than benign fellowship. Even as early as the thirteenth century, guild masters held Christian values as ideals rather than guides for everyday behavior.

For all their corporate and religious ideology, guilds were economic institutions keenly interested in business survival. They originated in cities because there, as islands in the midst of feudal society, could be found an environment compatible with commercial enterprise. To be sure, the early guilds took the role that the market played in more economically sophisticated centuries. As Jean-Yves Grenier remarked, the guild flourished in an era when lack of economic information prevailed and therefore the manipulation of capital was not the primary aim. Guild manufacture existed "in societies without markets, where it [information about techniques of production] is at the same time more ritualized and less necessary because goods sold and circumstances of transactions are so little varied and so well codified."[10] In such periods, lack of technical information in society enhanced the profits of those who were industrially proficient, and for this reason, the "mysteries" of artisan skill proved crucial along with monopolies of technique.

But guilds were a bridge between the feudal era of scarcity and the modern world of production increase. At the same time that they used trade secrets to turn out expensive, finely crafted goods, they were experiencing local and international competition. In fact, as we are told, guilds originated *explicitly* to combat the pressure of competition from nearby amateurs and long-distance traders.[11] They were never oblivious of market considerations; and when historians define guilds as entities outside

---

10. Jean-Yves Grenier, *L'Économie d'Ancien Régime: Un monde de l'échange et de l'incertitude* (Paris: Albin Michel, 1996), 418.

11. As Hunt and Murray suggest, although guilds "arose out of the need for tradesmen to band together to meet the pressure of increasing local and import competition . . . [they] sought to regulate competition rather than to abolish it." *History of Business,* 35.

the orbit of competition or profitability, they portray the guilds inaccurately. In the very century when guilds began writing formal statutes describing trade associations that gave young people training and professional status, masters began using hired labor that had no hope of advancing to the mastership. The *cursus honoris* of apprentice, journeyman, master itself restricted legal competition. To set standards for their collective work, guilds used the medieval terms in their catalogue of metaphors, but the harsh action of business stretched the institutional norms they composed. Collegiality among masters, their freedom to participate in guild governance, their insistence on equalizing opportunities among the workshops and on preserving a just price were medieval elements to balance the rivalry and profit that emerging market pressures exerted.

Competition was always a preoccupation for guild masters. Goods made by artisans outside the guilds always limited guild sales whether the products were made by servants in private bourgeois houses for private use or by rural artisans alternating craftwork with agriculture. Moreover, guilds did not spread into the countryside, or even into every town, and the "free crafts," practiced in peasant homes and in towns without guilds, were constant competitors. In the early Middle Ages, craft products from cottage industry and from village artisans were sold only at local markets, but through the centuries, these nonguild goods became objects of long-distance trade. Nonguild production outdistanced that of the urban guilds. As Henri Hauser wrote, "In the France of the sixteenth century, it is 'free work' that is the rule; work organized into *jurandes* is the exception."[12] Hauser's assessment continued to be true through the seventeenth and eighteenth centuries as well, with the continuing development of proto-industry and merchant capitalism that carried products from dispersed rural manufacturers to national and international trade. As increasing outlets for goods developed, international merchants gained importance; some arose along with nonguild rural production, others emerged as guilds split between master merchants and master workers, each with their separate interests.

In the past, the fact that some industries moved out of cities to take advantage of the flexible labor and work rules has suggested that guilds imposed rigid industrial regulations and turned a hostile eye to new

12. Henri Hauser, *Ouvriers du temps passé, XVe–XVIe siècles* (Paris: F. Alcan, 1899), xxix.

industry and technology. Current historical writing, however, views guild action as far more flexible and profit oriented. Despite prohibitions against work outside the master's atelier, outsourcing, subcontracting, and dealing with clandestine production were widely used. Some of the flexibility was legally authorized and written into guild statutes.

Whereas masters were limited in the number of apprentices they might accept to one or perhaps two, there was no limit to the number of journeymen and journeywomen they could hire as low paid labor. By the twelfth century, guild masters were hiring additional hands from the general labor force in busy seasons or to expedite large or immediate orders. From early times, these varlets or chamberlains joined the ranks of poor journeymen who lacked the funds to pay mastership expenses and spent their lives as wage labor.[13]

In the guild of the Florentine food suppliers, "some enterprising masters had branched out and had more than one 'family workshop'" run by employees.[14] Paris guilds frequently subcontracted portions of fine products for specialists to insert. In Lille, cloth guilds dominated rural manufacture, selling the products under their own name. In Rouen, the linen-drapers of new cloth took charge of the knitted gloves, caps, stockings, socks, and purses brought from country homes and workshops, and resold them to local and national consumers. Lyon's silk master weavers bought their looms from local carpenters and silk thread from the crowd of nonguild female spinners within the city and suburbs. In these cases of legal outsourcing, guilds simply made use of regional labor without apologizing for the fact that the workers had neither been trained in formal apprenticeships nor were eligible to become masters.[15]

Illegal outsourcing and clandestine production was also widespread within guild business. The numerous suits by guild officers testify to the extent of manufacturing both in guild cities and the nearby countryside by workers without guild qualifications. Guild masters had no compunctions against setting up workshops for parts of their products in rural

---

13. Bronislaw Geremek, *Le Salariat dans l'artisanat Parisien aux XIIIe-XVe siècles*, trans. Anna Posner and Christiane Klapish-Zuber (Paris: Mouton,1968).

14. Epstein, *Wage Labor and Guilds*, 212.

15. For Paris, see Michael Sonenscher's pioneering *Work and Wages: Natural Law, Politics, and the Eighteenth-Century French Trades* (Cambridge: Cambridge University Press, 1989) and Steven L. Kaplan, *La Fin des corporations* (Paris: Fayard, 2001. Conditions in Lille are analyzed by Jean-Pierre Hirsch, *Les Deux rêves de commerce: Entreprise et institution dans la region lilloise, 1780–1860* (Paris: Éditions de l'École des hautes Études en Sciences Socials, 1991).

locations, and they also took the risk of organizing craftwork in urban sheds and back rooms. Frequently masters had special arrangements with nonguild individuals around the city, who hired their own workers and channeled unfinished cloth, garments, or dyed goods at lower cost to the guild workshop. The upper stories of workers' tenements housed male and female piece workers (called chamberlains because they worked in their own chambers) whose imperfect work enabled masters and merchants to save on the cost of production.

The frequent use of these illegal workers and the constant inveighing against them in the guild statutes has created a puzzle for historians. What behavior should we consider the norm for guilds? Was the essence of guild work the tradition of finishing an entire product in one workshop? Could the presence of suits against scofflaws be a sign that the guild system was being stretched to its limits by increasing capitalist competition? Were they outgrowing their medieval origins if they found the guild system unequal to the need for cut-rate workers? As we study the evolution of guild production, we need to understand the guild as a more flexible institution than its strict bylaws would suggest. Perhaps guilds were as elastic in their actions as contemporary corporations that give lip service to the free economy and see no contradiction in demanding government subsidies and tariffs.

Guilds as a Fiscal Resource

Despite their limited production, guilds had special importance in the economic, political, and social structure of France. As the accepted mediator of skilled work, guilds imparted training and commercial exclusivity to their members. They organized members of trades into units that offered prestige, fiscal benefits, and the legal right to maintain monopolies over particular craft processes and artifacts. Through these sworn trades, a way of life was formed that drew potential rivals into bonds of local community.

Whereas the guilds had emerged spontaneously in the Middle Ages as professional fraternities, by the sixteenth century they had come under the king's bureaucratizing policy. Edicts of 1581 and 1597 ruled that all crafts be made into sworn associations that could take their place within municipal administration. The legislation also prohibited abuses on the part of *jurés* who demanded too complex a masterpiece or required excessively lavish initiatory banquets; the king was asserting his right to regulate behavior in the trades. In their early days, guilds took the initiative in proposing regulations for industry. Under the mercantilist policy of Henri II and Henri IV, guilds became part of a national plan to encourage the production of exports.

These trade associations, however, never simply accepted royal policy without question. Having become more numerous and more conscious of their common interests, the guilds exerted an influence on the course of history, supporting the Catholic forces during the Wars of Religion and mobilizing against foreign invaders in the Thirty Years' War. The close of these conflicts saw further efforts to encourage industrial development by importing new techniques from abroad and setting up royal industries.[16]

Jean-Baptiste Colbert, controller general (1662–83), continued earlier efforts to bring artisans into the guild system and extend its standards to as many manufactured goods as possible. Although the advantages to be drawn from guild membership did not seem worth the trouble to many craft workers, and the edict of 1673 succeeded in spreading guilds into only a few towns and not through the countryside, Colbert's efforts had a major impact on guilds and industries. Stringent rules for guild governance now supplanted the haphazard practices that were usual—contents of the money strong box had to be reviewed annually and masterpieces could not be overly complex. The controller general took important steps to promote industry for women workers. Among his successful initiatives can be counted the establishing of the *couturières* and flower sellers' guild for women in Paris and creating a guild for *couturières* in Rouen. He also established schools where women could learn to make lace and implanted other crafts for women's work. Colbert's major contribution took place in 1664–69 when he convinced the large textile guilds to cooperate with the government in drawing up regulations for the export industries of woolens, silk, linen, and other textiles and for paper products. His aim was to raise French cloth manufacture to competitive international standards and to import techniques used by foreign competitors.

In the 1690s, the relation of the state to guilds took a new turn. Using the precedent that guilds had raised money for the king in the sixteenth

---

16. Saint-Léon, *Histoire*, 373–81.

century, officials turned to them again. Seeking funds for Louis XIV's war, in 1691 Controller General Pontchartrain issued the first guild edict with a purely fiscal objective. The 1691 law took the pretext that the guilds' elected officers were enmeshed in abuses, such as extortionate entrance fees, expensive masterpieces, and election irregularities, and that the king, therefore, had withdrawn the guilds' right to choose their own officers and was ready to impose men of his own choice. Pontchartrain correctly assumed that the offices the king created would be bought up and suppressed by the guilds. The substantial sums raised by this forced taxation convinced subsequent ministers to turn frequently to the guilds for stop-gap assistance. It also biased eighteenth-century reformers against the guilds because of their role in enabling the king to escape the constraints of responsible taxation.

Even before they rose to fiscal importance, the guilds' place in export trade had given them the king's ear. During the 1614 meeting of the Estates General, guilds complained about the establishment of privileged industries with new foreign techniques and asserted that artisans should direct their own crafts without royal interference. In 1664, the Six Corps—a merchant association in Paris that included woolens makers, grocers-apothecaries, mercers, fur dealers, hosiers, and goldsmiths—had demonstrated its influence by helping to convince Colbert to establish a moderate tariff on raw materials and manufactures, along with twelve entrepôts to facilitate exports. This policy was doubtless a concession to the powerful guilds for cooperating over the industrial regulations. The Six Corps became an arm of royal economic policy, policing the cloth guilds of Paris and intervening in the assessment of taxes, the maintenance of technical monopolies, law suits concerning merchants, requests of individuals for guild entrance, and the right to vote in municipal elections, as well as import and export tariffs.[17]

Once guilds had shown their fiscal capacity, they embarked on a new relationship with the king, who used them frequently to help underwrite military adventures. The same process continued through the eighteenth century. In 1723, the Paris Six Corps found almost a half million livres for the king. In 1722 and 1725, new letters of mastership were bought up and suppressed by the guilds. In 1730, offices reestablishing inspectors of the covered markets and open-air markets were disposed of in the

[17]. Ibid., 374–76, 391–92, 403–9.

same way. Offices were created in 1745 to supervise guild officers and in 1752 to increase the masters' ranks; both sets were bought up and suppressed. The pattern of taxing guilds indirectly became an important, if erratic, resource for the monarchy. And the guilds had the capacity to be taxed since, as privileged corporations, they were entitled to behave like individuals, borrowing and spending money.

But the royal policy was capricious, and it undermined the efforts of government bureaus to promote other economic results. Using guilds for fiscal purposes disrupted their effect on improving technology and reducing the cost of goods. Even the sixteenth-century edicts ordering all the kingdom's trades to form into guilds did not stand without contradiction as some ministers expressed a fear of fomenting labor unrest by giving workers, brought together to vote, an excuse to congregate. Three times in the eighteenth century, the government tried unsuccessfully to transform masterships into venal offices, which would restrict access to technology while simultaneously encouraging inspectors of manufacture to improve looms and spinning devices among workers in towns and rural areas.[18]

Guilds could pay the irregular taxes only by borrowing money, and naturally they raised prices on their goods to repay the loans. But higher prices on manufactures went against the efforts of the Chamber of Commerce and the Bureau of Inspectors of Manufacture to keep French products competitive in the international market. Despite his frequent demands for money, the king forbad guilds in 1763 from borrowing money without express permission, in order to limit their influence. While goods from rural workshops were finally given legal entry to foreign trade in 1759, in 1767 the crown proposed once again to make crafts that were still free into guilds. Ministers in the economic bureaucracy tried to provide more elbowroom for manufacture by curtailing guild prerogatives, but their efforts were undercut by officials in the tax department pressed by the urgent need for funds. As Émile Coornaert wrote, "Evidently royal politics has nothing mechanical about it: it is a force that is alive, changeable."[19]

The trade guilds also had a complexity that was "alive and changeable." They balanced between, on one hand, efforts to withstand the pressures

---

18. Coornaert, *Les Corporations*, 149–50.
19. Ibid., 150–52, citation from p. 150.

of competition from goods made less expensively in the countryside and, on the other, the tradition of furnishing luxury goods made to exacting standards. Emboldened by access to the Spanish colonies and the Atlantic trade, weavers increased their repertory of goods by mixing fabrics, copying foreign cloth, and counterfeiting foreign trademarks of origin. Within the guilds, political struggles took place between the interests of merchants and master workers. In Lyon and other centers of overseas trade, merchants tried to suppress the industrial regulations so they could respond quickly to style changes, while the master weavers held out to retain the complicated work rules. But even this polarization was not universal. In Lille, the wholesale merchants, not the master weavers, requested detailed industrial rules for woolens and mixed-fabric textiles, and merchants there insisted on maintaining these guidelines so foreign customers had confidence in their goods.[20] Promoting high standards for export wares, of course, was also the motive behind Colbert's constitution of industrial regulations.

The royal bureaucracy was also divided in its views for and against a regulatory regime in the second half of the eighteenth century. Reform ideology had convinced some policy makers to reduce the controls extended over industry and trade. In 1759 the prohibition against importing cotton calico prints (*toiles peintes*) was cancelled, and in 1762 rural manufactures were allowed to circulate freely. The guilds protested against these new freedoms but did not prevail because the relaxed laws promoted the government's hope of stimulating trade. Even the decision to ally with Great Britain's rebellious colonies in 1776 carried the hope of fostering trade across the Atlantic.

As for the debate over whether or not to maintain industrial regulations, the survey that inspectors of manufacture undertook on this subject in 1780 showed the spilt in opinion among manufacturers, merchants, and guilds. Each group sought to weigh the advantages of regulation and freedom within its particular circumstances, just as they had applied their shrewdest estimates over what goods to manufacture and to market. In the last resort, guilds had to deal with their individual situations, those physical and moral elements that had formed them and continued to set the parameters of their opportunity.

20. See Gail Bossenga, *The Politics of Privilege: Old Regime and Revolution in Lille* (Cambridge: Cambridge University Press, 1991), 147–52, and Hirsch, *Les Deux rêves*, passim.

Women in Guilds

From the twelfth century when guild women appeared in urban registers along with their male counterparts, to the end of the eighteenth century when the guilds were suppressed, female masters formed part of the privileged workforce. Economic stress and legislation shrank their numbers in the sixteenth and seventeenth centuries, but there were still viable women's guilds and mixed-sex guilds until 1791.

Most women did not have the financial means to take advantage of society's legal devices to shelter women's business. Unskilled heavy drudgery was their lot, whether at agricultural labor, cottage industry, dispersed rural manufacture, or urban crafts. The struggle to stay alive led them to take whatever jobs they could find, and they resorted to charity, theft, and prostitution in bad times. Olwen Hufton's characterization of "an economy of makeshifts" applied especially to women who had the responsibility of supporting their children.[21]

The situation became even worse when bad times kept their husbands unemployed, when their husbands migrated to find jobs, or if they were deserted. Over time the majority of women struggled to eke out a living. But amid records of women working at every conceivable craft—from excavating underground watercourses to architectural labor, from barge polling to spinning—a small percentage of women attained skilled, privileged industrial work. These fortunate individuals entered guilds as apprentices, advanced to practice their trade as journeywomen, and eventually became full-fledged masters in their guilds.

An apparent anomaly in this patriarchal society, guild women were the exception to prove the rule that privilege could overcome all disability, including that of sex. But until recently their activity did not attract the attention of later generations of historians. For many reasons, the historical record of guild women's existence has been obscured and challenged. Twentieth-century historians reasoned that guilds were too patriarchal to admit women on an equal footing. Eighteenth-century Enlightenment critics of the guild system labeled guilds an overwhelming obstacle to women's employment, and they used this argument to help discredit them. Liberal historians in our own day have taken the philosophes' word

---

21. Olwen Hufton develops this idea in her well-researched book *The Poor of Eighteenth-Century France, 1750–1789* (Oxford: Oxford University Press, 1974), see esp. chaps. 3 and 4.

for the malevolent effects of guilds on female employment. Our task is to recover the record of these workers and to ascertain how they managed their lives and businesses.

Women's names appear on the lists of masters in the earliest guild records of the twelfth century. In order to make even a provisional picture, we need to combine fragments of information from far-flung areas, bearing in mind that the particular mores of each place may cast a special light on its workers. Women's involvement in many trades was a continuum from low-skilled wage earners to workers with some formal link to certain guilds. Of course, membership as a master in a guild made all the difference; female wage earners received the lowest salaries in the workforce and their employment had little standing, whereas masters' prestige was acknowledged in legal and monetary terms.

The problem of women's work role in the medieval centuries has been the object of serious recent investigation and reevaluation. Early scholarship painted a favorable picture of female work as involved in many trades, needed, and relatively well paid. These characteristics were found by Eileen Power, E. Dixon, Marian Dale, Alice Clark, Henri Hauser, and others who were among the first to trace the existence of women workers in the past. To some extent, this recovery of women's work served as a platform to show how female wage opportunities have declined in the modern era. Alice Clark led the way by demonstrating the greater equality between women and men when work took place in the family home, an equality that disappeared with the rise of capitalism. This optimistic view has come under criticism by Olwen Hufton, Judith Bennett, and Maryanne Kowaleski who objected to an idyllic picture of the "good old days," when women's work had respect and prestige that it lost in the Industrial Revolution.

In their article "Crafts, Gilds, and Women in the Middle Ages: Fifty Years After Marian K. Dale," Kowaleski and Bennett underscored the fact that English female silk workers, whom Dale had studied, were not organized into a guild.[22] Their survey of medieval women's work concluded that virtually none of the women, no matter how skilled, were permitted to gain mastership and participate as guild members in their own right. The few women who were apprenticed rarely reached the level of guild

---

22. Maryanne Kowaleski and Judith M. Bennett, "Crafts, Guids, and Women in the Middle Ages: Fifty Years After Marian K. Dale," *Signs* 14, no.2 (1989): 474–88.

masters; they did not even become independent journey workers but stayed with one master until they married.[23] Their practice in the guild was most often determined by their relationship to the male guild master. As wives of masters, they helped in the shop and with management; as daughters, they were sometimes able to work, but more often, their marriage to an apprentice or journeyman served to make him a guild master with lightened guild dues. Most guilds, like those in Denmark, permitted masters' wives, daughters, and widows to participate in manufacture and social activities without gaining status in their own right.[24] In time of economic downturn, some guilds forbade the hiring of any women except those related to masters. In those few guilds composed of women, men undertook the chief officers' roles. Paris silk workers exemplified this practice.

We are well cautioned to avoid "the tempting specter of a 'golden age,'" as Bennett wrote, and to be aware that recent scholarship paints a picture "of European women excluded, since at least the twelfth century, from full participation in their communities."[25] But Kowaleski and Bennett are more inclusive in their statement that "the women's gilds of Rouen, Paris, and Cologne are exceptional instances of skilled women who organized and regulated their crafts."[26] With the perspective of knowing that several hundred women in these cities reached the high status of control over their trades, skilled training, and business independence, we might view women's work as activity that spanned the spectrum from a mass of ill-paid women to a small but important cohort who became guild masters. That is not to minimize the gulf separating nonguild from guild workers, but rather to link the actual practice of a craft to women's work, whether privileged or not. To be sure, the small number of women masters is an example of their general denigration within society, but it also documents their experience with male workers and their importance in the manufacturing process. With that in mind, let us see how widespread guild women were in Europe.

---

23. Ibid., 477.

24. Grethe Jacobsen, "Women's Work and Women's Role: Ideology and Reality in Danish Urban Society, 1300–1550," *Scandinavian Economic History Review* 30, no. 1 (1983): 3–20, and "Economic Progress and the Sexual Division of Labor: The Role of Guilds in the Late-Medieval Danish City," in *Altag und Fortschritt im Mittelalter* (Vienna, 1986).

25. Judith M. Bennett, "'History That Stands Still': Women's Work in the European Past," *Feminist Studies* 14, no. 2 (summer 1988): 269, 271.

26. Kowaleski and Bennett, "Crafts," 483.

Much documentation of women's work exists only because statutes signaled restrictions to be imposed on them. Alice Clark cited a statute of 1271 indicating that there were male and female weavers in Flanders. But by 1511, women were forbidden to weave under the excuse that they were not strong enough "to work the wide and heavy looms in use."[27] David Herlihy explained that female workers were crucial to much manufacture in the early Middle Ages, especially in the skilled role of dyeing, but by the late Middle Ages, male guilds had taken over the skilled jobs leaving tasks like spinning and cleaning for women workers. He suggested that women's value in the family fell in consequence.[28]

Evidence of female apprentices must also be taken with hesitation. Although their status had official recognition and might have involved payments to the master in return for training, in many cases these girls were never expected to become masters. Where this was the case, the females could not bring training for a lucrative trade to their families unless they married men who became masters in it.[29] The Paris wigmakers' papers mentioned female, not male apprentices, causing us to wonder if only masters' sons were eligible to become masters. Daughters of master silk ribbon weavers (*tissutiers-rubaniers*) could work as apprentices, but they had to stop if they married out of the trade.[30] Paris tanners' daughters were the only females allowed to become apprentices in the guild, but they could not have apprentices themselves if they married out of the trade.[31] Sixteenth-century Geneva allowed girls to be apprenticed in dressmaking, pin making, silk carding, and taffeta making, without their expectation of becoming masters. In watch making and passementerie, girl apprentices had been permitted in the seventeenth century, but they were gradually excluded in the next hundred years, as widows' rights also declined.[32] In the Parisian guild of fruit and butter merchants, which had

27. Clark, *Working Life*, 102.
28. David Herlihy, *Medieval Households* (Cambridge, Mass.: Harvard University Press, 1985), 84n86. But Herlihy also conceded that "the relation of women to the work force in the late medieval towns remains very obscure."
29. Epstein, *Wage Labor and Guilds*, 123.
30. Gustave Fagniez, *La Femme et la société française dans la première moitié du XVIIe siècle* (Paris: J. Gamber, 1929), 110–11. Because the statutes referred only to *apprentisses*, not male apprentices, Faigniez reasoned that the men making up half the guild were only figureheads. It is more likely that the female apprentices were a permanent proletariat.
31. Epstein, *Wage Labor and Guilds*, 115.
32. E. William Monter, "Women in Calvinist Geneva, 1500–1800," *Journal of Women in Culture and Society* 6, no. 2 (1980): 200, 203.

a majority of female masters, the dispute over whether to have female officers was settled by the lieutenant civil who ruled that the officers should be half and half. But this decision was rescinded when the *parlement* of Paris declared in 1589 that only men would be *jurés*. The linen-drapers of Paris who had acquired some women officers were also restricted afterwards to male *jurés*.[33]

In Germanic guilds we find a similar story of enabling women to participate through the mid-fifteenth century as masters in some trades and curtailing their membership afterwards. The Basle furriers had women as full members in 1226 and this practice was followed in Cologne, Frankfurt am Main, Regensberg, Lubeck, and Quedlinburg. In the fourteenth and fifteenth centuries, women entered many textile, clothing, and light metal guilds. The early fourteenth century brought women felt hat makers' guild rights in two cities. In the Strasbourg woolen weaver and cloth makers' guild, the mid-fifteenth century saw unmarried women and widows as full members, alongside females in the gardeners' guild. Weaving guilds with male and female members in Frankfurt am Main, Munich, and Stuttgart produced wool, veils, and linen. Cologne was unusual in the number of guilds open to women: these included the linen-weaving and fustian-and-blanket-weaving guilds, Cologne linen yarn makers in mid-fourteenth century, silk makers, the mixed-sex guild of heraldic silk embroidery, and the Cologne and Leipzig butchers. In fifteenth-century German cities, women running guild businesses often made up from 10 to 15 percent of guild membership in "weaving, needle making, yarn spinning, hat making, and tailoring," and widows sometimes maintained their husbands' metal works for years. In Nuremberg, a female guild to spin gold thread was founded in 1597.[34]

German workingwomen's tenure in guilds, however, did not survive the political and economic changes of the fifteenth and sixteenth centuries. Like those in other cities of Germany and the Lowlands, Cologne's guilds were evolving "from an association of family shops into a political organization made up of individual male artisans."[35] It was considered

---

33. Fagniez, *La Femme*, 93–103.
34. Erika Uitz, *The Legend of Good Women: The Liberation of Women in Medieval Cities*, trans. Sheila Marnie (Wakefield, R.I.: Moyer Bell, 1994), orig. published as *Die Frau in der mittelalterlichen Stadt* (Leipzig: Edition Leipzig, 1988), 54–58.
35. Martha C. Howell, *Women, Production, and Patriarchy in Late Medieval Cities* (Chicago: Chicago University Press, 1986), 133.

inappropriate for women to have access to political involvement, so as guilds achieved urban power, they excluded women from the mastership. Whereas guilds earlier had simply done without laws against women and had included the occasional female master and the work of masters' wives and daughters, mid-fifteenth- and early sixteenth-century German guilds officially prohibited women. Only trades practiced outside the home were considered honorable, and women were excluded from them. Public rhetoric in German cities warned men against having women as coworkers because their presence would taint the male workers, both journeymen and masters.[36] Economic pressure to keep the jobs for men led to restrictions on the masters' female relatives within the guilds and to wide-ranging prohibitions against women's doing many industrial tasks inside or outside of guilds. This curtailed work not only for women in guilds but also for independent female workers.

Gradually stocking knitting, hat making, weaving, and dyeing either came to have restrictive guild regulations or were changed from free trades at which all could work into guild crafts that admitted only sworn members. Only dressmaking and sewing, especially of old and cheap garments, remained open to all women. The exceptions were Cologne's female guilds—the silk workers, gold spinners, and yarn makers—which persisted because their structure provided benefits for their families' commerce.[37] By mid-seventeenth century, most German workingwomen could find only the crudest and lowest paid work, which did not even offer a subsistence wage.[38]

Lyndal Roper has shown the wide divergence between religious rhetoric that expected husband and wife to work harmoniously for their living and the actual expectation that women should care for house and family and pick up "odd bits" of work to add to the family economy. "Beneath the façade of the gender-neutral conception of work as 'sustenance,' there were in reality careful divisions of task and skill within workshops which served to underline women's adjunctive role within production."[39]

Official acts removing women from public life and curtailing women's freedom to participate in guilds also typified the movement in France

36. See Jean Quataert, "The Shaping of Women's Work in Manufacturing: Guilds, Households, and the State in Central Europe, 1648–1870," *American Historical Review* 90 (December 1985): 1122–48.
37. Howell, *Women, Production, and Patriarchy*, 124–33.
38. Weisner, *Working Women*, 151, 167–68, 172, 176, 184–85.
39. Lyndal Roper, *The Holy Household* (Oxford: Oxford University Press, 1989), 45.

in the sixteenth and seventeenth centuries toward a stronger patriarchal state. In addition to restricting widow's choice of new husbands, raising their age of majority to thirty, and hindering their use of property, royal edicts put pressure on married women to make contracts only with their husbands' consent. Political pressure intensified by economic urgency caused many guilds to restrict women's work. Thus in 1561, Lyon silk weavers were limited to two male apprentices and female apprentices were forbidden. Journeywomen could be engaged, but only to work inside a master's atelier, not independently.[40]

But workplace culture in Germany, the Lowlands, and England was distinct from that of France; the presence of the French court as consumer of luxury goods made in Paris and Rouen, the historic use of guilds as sources of royal revenue, and the entrenched nature of privilege combined to maintain the guilds and extend tolerance to guildwomen. The fact that France had a viable national existence, unlike Germany and the Lowlands, also helped women to survive in guilds. Although French guilds developed considerable power within cities, the cities themselves were not politically independent and the incongruity of women voting on national policy did not occur. In addition, as royal power intruded into municipal governance, it sometimes used women's guilds to curtail powerful associations like the mercers and to increase competition in manufacture and commerce. Therefore even under the obstacles of economic downturns and increasing restrictions, women persisted in some French guilds.

In Paris, the tradition of female guildmasters can be documented from the thirteenth century. Étienne Boileau's *Livre des métiers* counted one hundred trades, of which five belonged to women: silk spinning with a small spindle and with a large one, makers of fastenings, ribbon making, and silk handkerchief weavers. Pin makers, flax dressers, and hat makers were mixed-sex guilds.[41] Female linen spinners and weavers worked in Paris guilds, as did female silk workers whose officers consisted of three men and three women.[42] Embroiderers, makers of fancy purses,

---

40. Natalie Zemon Davis, "Women in the Crafts in Sixteenth-Century Lyon," *Feminist Studies* 8, no. 1 (spring 1982): 68.

41. See E. Dixon, "Craftswomen in the 'Livre des métiers,'" *Economic Journal* 5 (1895): 209–28.

42. Andrée Lehmann, *Le Rôle de la femme dans l'histoire de France au moyen âge* (Paris, 1952), 440–45.

and headdress makers were other female guilds noted from the thirteenth century. The tax roles of the 1291 and 1300 *taille* listed some seventy-seven trades with female members.[43] Gustave Fagniez believed that the Paris linen trades continued their fifteenth-century practice of accepting daughters of bourgeois families as apprentices for the next two hundred years.

Within the Paris women's guilds only the linen-draper's trade had a female officer; but surprisingly a number of guilds of mixed sex did have female officers. The Rouen woolen weavers, ribbonmakers, and spinners had mixed membership and some women officers. The Paris grain merchants, embroiderers, and linen and canvas weavers were staffed and headed by women and men. In Reims, the knitters were guilds with women as *gardes* and *jurées*.[44]

There is no lack of evidence showing that throughout Europe, barriers to women's guild participation increased after 1550. We do not have to posit a golden era in order to demonstrate that women's behavior was gradually restricted as the early modern era emerged. Women had never been included as masters in every guild; they were more likely to work as wives, daughters, and widows of masters rather than as skilled workers in their own right. Nevertheless, the structure and function of the guild was so entrenched that some women's and mixed membership guilds persisted into the eighteenth century and some even received new life. Although seamstresses had lost their independence in many cities, being incorporated into male guilds, the Paris *couturières* received an existence separate from that of the tailors during Louis XIV's reign as Clare Crowston has shown.[45]

Women's role in manufacture was crucial whether as day labor hired to perform the range of unskilled tasks that preindustrial industry required,

---

43. Gustave Fagniez, *Études sur l'histoire de la classe industrielle à Paris au XIIIe et au XIVe siècles* (Paris, 1877), 7–19.

44. Ernst Levasseur, *Histoire des classes ouvrières et de l'industrie en France avant 1789*, 2nd ed. (Paris: Arthur Rousseau, 1901), 2:221. The names of these guilds reflected their mixed membership: in Rouen, woolen weavers (*drapiers-drapières*), grain merchants (*marchands et marchandes de grain*), ribbonmakers (*rubaniers et rubanières*), and spinners (*filassiers et filassières*). In Paris, grain merchants (*grainiers-grainières*), embroiderers (*brodeurs-brodeuses*), linen and canvas weavers (*tisserands-tisserandes en toile et canevas*). In Reims, the knitters were called (*bonnetiers-bonnetières*).

45. For the fullest account of Paris seamstresses (*couturières*), see Clare Haru Crowston, *Fabricating Women: The Seamstresses of Old Regime France, 1675–1791* (Durham: Duke University Press, 2001).

to add the force of their arms and feet to heavy work, or to accomplish the skilled techniques done by the guilds. But what different experiences did the two categories of women workers have? Was it far more advantageous to have a formal apprenticeship and a place in a sworn trade? Or did the prejudice against women, which was responsible for their low salaries as day workers, also harm their economic place in guilds? Was the effect of guild work in a city like Rouen different from that of the unprivileged female workers in a large, market-oriented industry like the silk *fabrique* of Lyon? Which experience was closer to the pattern of early industrialization in the nineteenth century?

Guilds in Lyon

With a population of more than 150,000, Lyon was France's premiere industrial city in the eighteenth century. Its history—very different from that of Rouen—shaped the city's large-scale industry and international trade. Lyon was a frontier area in the Holy Roman Empire until its incorporation into France in the fifteenth century. Its proximity to Italy, the German states, and France had for years drawn merchants and bankers to its fairs. With a bank established in 1543 and a commercial tribunal of exchange in 1549, Lyon acquired the tools to become a powerful center of commercial capitalism. A long tradition of free craft made the city especially inviting for entrepreneurs; even in the eighteenth century, its lack of restrictions and commercial vigor encouraged large-scale industry.

Lyon's municipal government reflected its business outlook. From early times, the mayor and aldermen came from wealthy commercial families, and they maintained the city's right to oversee the urban crafts without royal interference. This unusual policy made Lyon more like Italian or German city-states, which allowed the heads of guilds and prominent crafts to direct the trends of urban life for their own advantage and for whom foreign economic policy was within their purview. The entrepreneurs who made up the city council needed two things from the local economy: flexible industrial practices to accommodate the fashion-conscious international market and workers available to be hired for unorthodox work schedules. For both criteria, a city full of guilds separating the crafts into self-contained units would have been detrimental.

With these preoccupations, the consulate—as Lyon's city government was called—leaned on the side of preserving the city's tradition of free work. This pattern was not spoiled even when Louis XI helped to found the silk industry in 1466. While the silk-making specialties were arranged in six separate crafts, the loose structure of business institutions allowed them to work together as one industry. To be sure, royal initiatives did encourage some small guilds to emerge; seventy-two were listed in the Royal Almanachs of the seventeenth century. But these guilds did not exercise a monopoly of their trades, and in principle workers were allowed access to every trade without having to join them.[46]

Moreover, the small trades were dwarfed politically and economically by the overwhelming power of the silk *grande fabrique*. The consulate jealously kept its own jurisdiction over the crafts in order to maintain conditions advantageous for silk production. The mayor and aldermen preserved their control by appointing two members of each guild to choose six new aldermen each year.[47] The freedom to shape cloth trade at will and to make policy without deference to other authorities was too important to lose. When workers in various trades agitated to set themselves up as separate guilds by which to curb competition and gain privileges, they reached a sympathetic audience in the *parlement* of Paris, which was accustomed to the regime of guild production. But the royal Conseil d'État, "convinced by the appeal of Lyon's prévôt of merchants," intervened several times "in its turn and maintained the municipality of Lyon in possession of its privileges." Thus Lyon's consulate kept the ultimate jurisdiction over the personnel and technique of its industries.[48]

Guilds in Rouen

A city of 80,000 or so inhabitants, eighteenth-century Rouen, by contrast with Lyon, was a typical *ville jurée*, a city whose medieval guild tradition went back at least to the eleventh century and continued until guilds were suppressed in 1791. Some commentators even ventured that guilds

---

46. Saint-Léon, *Histoire*, 323.
47. Ibid. Saint-Léon commented succinctly, "La haute bourgeoisie était ainsi absolue maîtresse du pouvoir, puisque investie, originairement des fonctions municipales, elle désignait elle-même des électeurs à sa convenance."
48. Levasseur, *Histoire*, 2:483.

had a continuous presence there since Roman times.⁴⁹ Despite their early appearance, guilds did not play much of a role in the formation of its municipal government. The city had never been an independent enclave. Rouen had a long history of political domination from the tenth century by the dukes of Normandy, and after its conquest by King Philip Augustus in 1204, by the kings of France. Rouen took her place as a major administrative and economic provincial city securely within the kingdom. A way station for grain bound for Paris, the emporium had come within secure royal control. However, as the site of the *parlement* of Normandy, Rouen had an institution to express its differences with royal policy. Some of the tension between royal and municipal control manifested itself in a tug-of-war over economic governance.

Rouen was ruled by a coalition of wealth, and the city's municipal structure was, like Lyon's, an oligarchy. The richest bourgeoisie and merchants chose an electoral group of one hundred peers that named the mayor, the twelve aldermen, the twelve councilors, and a general council.⁵⁰ Although this group periodically challenged the king's policies, the royal will usually won the contest. Like other guild cities, Rouen received the right to govern its own trades, but that privilege slipped back into the hands of the royal lieutenant general of police several times. Even though the king ceded supervision of the fairs and most trades in 1710 and formally reduced jurisdiction of royal police to the reception of guild officers, the examination of the masterpiece, and swearing in new masters in 1747, royal representatives still played a major role in disciplining the guilds.⁵¹

They acted in cooperation with elected officers of the trades, because guilds ruled the streets and shops of this Norman city. Rouen had ninety-two recognized guilds in 1750. Although they produced a range of goods from arquebuses to lace, their strength lay primarily in textiles and the luxury needle trades. Like the other successful manufacturing cities, Rouen had a long tradition of textile production. Legend has it that the sale of fine woolen cloth (*draps*) made from English and Spanish wool paid for one tower of the cathedral (and that donations to gain exceptions for consuming butter and eggs during Lent paid for the other—appropriately called the Tour de Buerre). The manufacture of woolen and linen

49. Saint-Léon, *Histoire*, 73–74.
50. Ibid., 338.
51. Levasseur, *Histoire*, 2:482–83.

cloth found markets throughout Europe during the Renaissance. The non-guild woolen manufactures that opened in Elbeuf, Louvois, Darnetal, and other nearby locations and light woolen *sayettes* from the Lowlands came into competition with Rouen's products. But in late seventeenth century, Rouen's textile trade received a boost from the invention of two new textiles: the *rouenneries,* cloth made entirely of cotton, and *siamoise,* made from a silk warp and cotton weft, later a mixture of linen and cotton. Both of these textiles, colored in stripes and checks, became hugely successful in the domestic market. They also went to clothe slaves in the Spanish Empire and to the French colonies. Their export signaled the enlarged scope of Atlantic trade that provided markets in the eighteenth century.[52]

Rouen was also an important administrative, legal, and ecclesiastical center, with lawyers, parliamentarians, royal officials, municipal clerks, church dignitaries, and wealthy merchants from France or abroad living within its walls. This fashionable local clientele supported the luxury industries. And the skilled crafts were not limited to local sales; Rouen, and indeed all of Normandy, was within the network of the Parisian market. Silk, linen, and cotton fabric were woven and made into garments on the rue Gros Horloge and the rue aux Carmes. The eastern and western edges of the city hummed with industry; from the impoverished rue Martainville came thread and from the western workers' quarter on outlying rue Cauchoise, woolens. In the city center, below the cathedral, lived the craft workers who made mirrors, harnesses, ribbons, shirts, barrels, and shoes. To the north of the cathedral, close to the Église St. Ouin one might find hosiers, embroiderers, and makers of church vestments. Slightly to the west, the rue Eau de Rebec flowed alongside the apartments, providing a site for dyers who hung cloth from poles sticking out of their attics. It hardly seems possible that tenements like those on the crowded rue Malpalu (or the ironically named red light district's rue des Hauts Mariages) could house the workshops for the delicate lace or fancy reticules they produced.

Another important source of commerce was the cottage industry spread throughout Normandy, which produced spun linen, knitted articles, some metalwork, and of course the cider, butter, and beef that upheld the local cuisine. By the eighteenth century, it included a brisk

---

52. Ibid., 2:524.

new source of prosperity—the spinning of cotton thread. While this production competed with that of the urban guilds, attempts were made to derive some advantage from it by bringing it under the control of Rouen's trades and merchants. Thus the rural workers and factors were obliged to bring their linen and cotton thread, cloth, knitted hats, stockings, socks, and mittens into the Halle aux Toiles, which was built in the sixteenth century as a central clearing house for regional textiles. There the goods would be inspected and bought by the appropriate guilds or by merchants and set out for sale in local shops or bundled up for transport to domestic and foreign markets. But the urban guilds went further than this; they responded to expanding rural industry by forming their own links with cottage craft. They wanted to reach beyond the confines of the urban workforce at the same time that they used guild regulations to protect their economic privileges in town.

In Rouen many levels of commerce were going on at the same time: fine finished luxury goods made by urban guilds; products like thread, which was bought by guild weavers or shipped away in wholesale trade; finished or semi-finished cloth destined directly for overseas commerce. The large picture reveals competition between city guilds and nonguild country producers. The smaller picture shows rivalry among the guilds themselves, scrambling for advantages in technology or products. A further layer of antagonism can be seen between the guilds producing goods and clinging to their right to sell them, and the merchant mercers eager to take over the privilege of sale to become the sole commercial agents.

Rouen's long-standing tolerance for female guild masters made possible the existence of tradeswomen in mixed-gender guilds and in guilds with only female members. Embedded in the bustle of commerce, these businesswomen competed successfully with their guild colleagues and their nonguild competitors. In the next chapter we will explore the implications that commerce in this city of guilds had for its female workers.

Conclusion

Guild manufacture, which had begun with the twelfth century revival of medieval commerce, carried on as an important part of the economy until its suppression during the French Revolution. Concerned at first

Figure 3. Needle making. A female worker pounds a length of wire and another makes a point with pincers. Next, a male worker pierces the metal to make an eye, hitting the needle on a press with his mallet. The needle is then burnished and whitened. Contrary to our assumptions, women workers were often employed in making metal objects and tools. From Diderot's *Encyclopédie*, courtesy Special Collections Library, University of Michigan.

with local markets and limited to craft within the guild master's family, guilds produced items that were made entirely within the family atelier. While the guild master had formal training and the license to produce and sell the work, members of his family, his apprentices, and journeymen and women took part in the manufacture, perhaps interchangeably. As the era of merchant capitalism brought increased competition to the guilds, they began to use strategies to reduce the cost of manufacture. Adapting their family workshop to more sophisticated manufacture, they subcontracted parts of the work, brought in varlets or servants to help, and used the services of unqualified workers, called chamberlains, living in nearby tenements.

The guilds were privileged bodies within the state, whose masters had sworn to uphold standards of manufacture and sale. Because of their privileged status, they were called corporations, created by the king's license to behave as privileged individuals. This gave them the right to borrow and lend money, to police themselves and their manufacture, and to take part in the rituals and rights that were an important part of

French institutions. Although we customarily think of guild masters as fathers of the family, as privileged institutions guilds were also open to women who became full-fledged mistresses in their own right. This book compares the role of guild women in the northern city of Rouen with the nonguild female workers in Lyon's silk industry to see how the conditions of work and life were similar and different in surprising ways.

THE USES OF GENDER IN ECONOMIC LIFE

On 29 January 1750, the guild of female linen-drapers (*lingères*) of Le Havre learned that their formal request to join the guild of merchant mercers had been turned down by the *parlement* in Rouen. The *lingères*, a group of sixty-nine women, had brought suit to link the two guilds. By this means they would gain the legal right, now exclusively in the hands of the mercers, to sell cotton cloth, goods of mixed composition, and linen thread. Unable to get the rights to sell the popular cottons by a simple change of law, the linen-drapers proposed that their all-female guild should be amalgamated with the all-male guild of eighty-eight merchant mercers and woolen cloth manufacturers.[1]

Their bylaws had limited the linen-drapers to sales of pure linen goods, either clothes they manufactured and decorated, or cloth from the loom. They must have looked with longing at the mercers' shops and stalls, filled with the popular cotton-woolen blend of goods called *siamoise*, various cotton novelties, and kerchiefs made of a cotton and silk blend. The mercers had several advantages in trade over the linen-drapers. Not only could the mercers sell a wide variety of textiles, their guild had earlier incorporated with the jewelers, hardware merchants, and woolen manufacturers to become an association of multiproduct merchants. In addition, the mercers had been awarded the prerogative of wholesale trade, which was the most lucrative commerce. With this license they could sell goods in large lots or those tied up in packets of a dozen items. Emphasizing their wide-ranging license, the guild was officially called the "association of amalgamated merchant mercers, wholesalers, jewelers, hardware purveyors, and woolen manufacturers of the city and suburbs of Le Havre."

---

1. Archives départementales de la Seine Maritime (hereafter cited as ADSM) 5 E 89, "Mémoire pour les maîtres et gardes du corps des marchands merciers-grossiers-joaillers-clincaillers et drapiers unis de la ville & faubourgs du Havre, servant de réponse à la requête présentée au conseil par les gardes en charge & maîtresses de la communauté des lingers et lingères de la même ville, au fins d'obtenir leur union au corps des merciers."

The linen-drapers' campaign to effect another amalgamation, linking their guild to that of the mercers, rested on traditional rhetoric. First they offered arguments of similarity.[2] Both guilds sold textiles and clothing; in fact, the mercers sold pure linen articles, as long as they were tied up in packages of a dozen. Uniting the guilds would do away with the squabbles and lawsuits that arose when two like trades were artificially separated. It would also stimulate foreign trade, the women asserted, as many husbands of *lingères* were sea-faring traders who became discouraged when their wives could not sell the goods they imported.

The merchant mercers mounted a battery of arguments to refute this line of reasoning and to defend their separateness. They accused the women of hypocrisy in pressing for an amalgamation of the guilds, since their projected scheme would maintain the separate governance and finances of the two crafts. It seemed clear to them that the women were trying to take over the mercers' commerce, to sell a wider variety of goods, and to enter wholesale trade. Indeed, the *lingères* admitted that their retail limitation discouraged them from buying goods in large lots because they feared they would be unable to resell them.

Then the mercers used arguments from past practice to underscore the differences between the functions of the two guilds. For over a century, the *lingères* had jealously guarded their exclusive right to handle linen goods, and they had been particularly chary of the mercers' incursions into their trade. Turning their own words against them, the mercers asserted that the *lingères* "have taken the precautions that they thought appropriate to entrust the manufacture and commerce in lingerie, which is their province, only to experts who have been licensed [*gens experte et qui ont fait leurs preuves*]. It is thus a contradiction to claim that they can associate with the mercer ignorant of a craft which is incompatible with his bailiwick."[3] The *lingères* had been keeping the mercers at bay by taunting them as unskilled at dealing with linen goods, but now the mercers picked up that argument to use on their own behalf. A telling refutation now made use of the *lingères'* higher qualifications as reasons against a merger. The mercers objected that the linen-drapers could easily enter their trade of commerce, since it had no masterpiece, but the mercers

---

2. Michael Sonenscher shows the ways in which arguments from similarity and past practice formed the basis of guilds' legal protest. See *Work and Wages: Natural Law, Politics and the Eighteenth-Century French Trades* (Cambridge: Cambridge University Press, 1989), esp. 91–98.

3. Ibid., 6.

would be at a disadvantage in reciprocal arrangements, since the *lingères'* business involved the ability to actually manufacture something and thus required a period of apprenticeship and a masterpiece. They were defending their separate status by asserting that the women were more skilled and had more rigorous standards. The women would gain more by the merger, especially access to the wholesale trade, while the men would unfairly be kept from adopting the *lingères'* activities by the lax standards of their own craft.

The third category of argument brought in the element of gender and this area is the most telling for our narrative. "The difference of the two sexes alone [should] suffice to disqualify the sort of amalgamation proposed by the *lingères*," wrote the mercers. One guild consisted solely of men, the other of women. Thus a male guild effectively fought off the aggression of a female association, calling on the principle of separation of sexes in society.

What they did not say was even more significant. No qualitative comment was made about the nature of the genders involved. Men and women were not directed to work in separate spheres. In fact, the mercers specifically pointed out that a union of mercers and *lingères* might be practical for the neighboring city, Caen, because there the linen-drapers' guild included both men and women. In Le Havre, urban tradition separated the sexes, and because of that, they should remain apart.

Nor were males and females told to develop separate technologies. There was no mention that males could not learn the practices of the *lingères,* just that as merchants they had not required these skills and therefore they had not developed them. Nor did the mercers contend that the linen-drapers were incapable of functioning as wholesale traders because they were women. Although the workers' sex was mentioned, the mercers did not treat it as an important argument, in itself, to determine their separateness. Instead the rhetoric of past practice and specific guild requirements served to protect the male mercers, while the female *lingères* used the argument of similarity of products and the history of frequent interguild litigation as justification for amalgamating the guilds. These were the classic forms of argumentation that French guilds used to assert domination over their rivals and to defend their status against the pressures of competitors. In Normandy, male and female guild members rarely used sexist rhetoric to fight hostile takeovers, preferring to base their legal defense on the traditional modes of expression.

Gender in Legal Distinction

How was gender understood in eighteenth-century France? It was, of course, an indicator of sex, based on different generative roles. But more than that, the scholarship of the past two decades has provided new insights that show how gender works as a social category to preserve patriarchal advantage. No longer considering women's restrictions as natural or universal, social theorists have been engaged in mapping the ways that ascriptions of maleness or femaleness inheres in activities that have little to do with sex differences. As Joan Walloch Scott has written, gender is "a primary way of signifying relationships of power."[4] Always a constructed relationship that defines and expedites the dynamics of power, gender divisions assign particular characteristics of the male or the female to spheres unconnected with sex. In eighteenth-century Europe, for instance, male students expected to study "tough-minded" subjects like Latin, mathematics, and geography, while females (if they had any schooling) found as their curriculum "decorative" topics like freehand, sketching, music, and embroidery. So pervasive was gender ideology that even purely sexual characteristics were fitted into the social pattern, with women assigned the passive role of nurturing the egg and sperm, both of which came supposedly from the active male.[5]

Work also showed the effects of gender separation. Women generally had less access to resources than men, and they were seldom able to compete in industries that required fixed capital outlay. Because they were rarely given formal training, they usually did not have access to high-paying jobs. Circular reasoning determined that since most women's work was low skilled and poorly paid, any work done by women became, by definition, low skilled. The skill was found in the worker, not in the difficulty of the task, and since males were thought to be more intelligent, they were considered naturally to have more skill. "Women's work" could be counted on to draw lower wages, one-half to one-third that of men's work. This took into account not only differences of skill and strength but the prescribed marital structure. Olwen Hufton suggests

---

4. Joan Wallach Scott, "Gender: A Useful Category of Historical Analysis," in *Gender and the Politics of History* (New York: Columbia University Press, 1988), 42.

5. Thomas Laquer, *Making Sex: Body and Gender from the Greeks to Freud* (Cambridge, Mass.: Harvard University Press, 1990).

that one factor in keeping wages for wives low was the general expectation that their husbands supplied their shelter.[6]

The eighteenth century inherited generations of assumptions about gender that colored and reinforced its use in creating social division. The practice of considering gender in binary opposites began in classical times. Aristotelian definition of women as cool and wet, men as hot and dry provided a basis for women to be thought inconstant and nonintellectual while men derived power and intellectual ability from their fiery nature. Christian tracts from earliest times warned that every woman was a potential Eve, untrustworthy, likely to sin unless led and corrected by a male. The evolution of ideology about women and men thus reflects the principles of patriarchal society by giving men commanding roles. Women in Old Regime France were defined by their inferiority, their lack of independence, and their subordination to men. But if this were true, how would it be possible for women to exist in guilds, which were powerful, legally sanctioned institutions? Is it not a contradiction in terms to imagine women—who were not even adults in the law—undertaking roles of privilege and independence? Let us return to our first premise that gender is socially constructed. It responds not only to major power divisions of society, but to the variety of ways that power is manifested.

Each nation, each region, each valley may have a different manner of building and presenting gender. That is why history must look at the particular, the situational. And cutting through these specificities, class brings its own markers. As Joan Scott reasons, "Gender, then, provides a way to decode meaning and to understand the complex connections among various forms of human interaction. When historians look for the ways in which the concept of gender legitimizes and constructs social relationships, they develop insight into the reciprocal nature of gender and society and into the particular and contextually specific ways in which politics constructs gender and gender constructs politics."[7]

As long as historians of Western culture have been analyzing patriarchies, the expression of gender shows women at a disadvantage. Joy Parr argues that we should not "lose sight of 'the multiple determinants' that constitute any individual's social position and access to power and also of the ways in which social identities are simultaneously formed

---

6. Olwen H. Hufton, *The Prospect Before Her: A History of Women in Western Europe, 1500–1800* (New York: Alfred A. Knopf, 1996), 158.

7. Scott, "Gender," 45–46.

from a multiplicity of elements."⁸ As we try to understand how the expression of gender benefits patriarchy, we may encounter complex situations in which *some* women gain lifelong advantages and others acquire benefits *some* of the time. This warning bears on women's entrance into guilds; it demonstrates the means by which guildwomen conveyed gains and flexibility to their families. In a seeming paradox, it shows how the presence of some privileged women reconfirms the patriarchal pattern of male dominance in French society. For it is important to learn how exceptions to the denigration of females help to maintain the social structure, and it is also worthwhile to see how women and men respond to these windows of opportunity. In what follows, I will discuss how a variety of forces—class, religion, national culture, particular historical era, and privileged institutions—shaped the expression of gender that made possible French women's participation in guilds.

If we select class as our first influence on gender, we will see that different groups spelled out the behavior of men and women in very different terms. Aristocratic men, in addition to being brave and loyal, were expected to display knowledge about refinements of action and speech that showed their awareness of social status. It was the male prerogative to make decisions, to act as head of household, to care for and correct his dependents—that is, his wife, children, and servants. Female aristocrats were to be elegant, devoted to their families, discreet, and to show delicacy. Male and female standards for working people were different. Both were supposed to labor as hard as possible, for each had to contribute to the family economy. The ideal husband was a steady worker who did not spend too much money on wine at the neighborhood cafe; the employer's ideal of the working man was that he be hardworking and docile, satisfied with his pay, and honest enough to refrain from stealing material or tools. As for the wife, the modesty she needed was to refrain from making a cuckold of her husband. Delicacy and social modesty would have been considered ludicrous. "Hard work, however, was essential; and thrift, for she looked after the household."⁹ Even if tasks were not the same, the urgency to bring in enough to support oneself and one's children, was the overriding preoccupation for the woman as for the man.

---

8. Joy Parr, *The Gender of Breadwinners* (Toronto: University of Toronto Press, 1990), 9.
9. David Garrioch, *Neighborhood and Community in Paris, 1740–1790* (Cambridge: Cambridge University Press, 1986), 75.

A contemporary observer of French eighteenth-century society, Louis-Sébastien Mercier, contrasted the differences between the usual appearance of working women and those in the upper class.

> It gives me pain to see the unfortunate women, who, with their baskets weighing on their shoulders, their faces red, their eyes almost bloodshot, preceding the dawn on muddy streets or on a road on which the ice screeches under the first footsteps that fall upon it. . . . You don't see the work of their muscles as you do with men, it is more hidden, but you can guess at it from their bloated necks, their hard breathing, and sympathy strikes you to the heart when you hear their tired step, as they utter an oath in a strange, yelping tone. . . . What a contrast [to the society ladies]! The first are covered with sweat under a double burden of pumpkins and gourds, calling out. . . . "Give way, make room for me!" The other group, in a jaunty carriage which flies down the street sweeping away the large, over-stuffed basket, [the ladies] under their makeup, fan in hand, expiring from idleness. Are these two groups of women the same sex? Yes![10]

Such a variety of norms identified different classes. It was usual for wealthy or noble women to look, talk, and act in a way distinct from the manner of working women. Their code of behavior elicited an expected response. Peasant women and urban wives, for instance, who led bread marches depended on administrators' reluctance to deal harshly with mothers and pregnant women. It was understood by both groups that the women were responsible for feeding their children, and that this imperative caused police to tolerate, for the moment, the illegal act of making public protest. Olwen Hufton has written that to insist upon the peaceful and moral nature of their protest, the women of the October 1789 Bread March, for example, threw out of their group the men who had helped them to storm the Hôtel de Ville.[11]

The Reformation brought new standards for women, differentiating female norms in Protestant and Catholic communities. In Germany and the Lowlands, the Protestant ideal was personified in the wife and mother

---

10. Louis-Sébastien Mercier, *Le Tableau de Paris* (Paris, 1781–88), 4:33–35.
11. Olwen H. Hufton, *Women and the Limits of Citizenship in the French Revolution* (Toronto: University of Toronto Press, 1992), 7–18.

who stayed within the home, occupying herself with domestic duties, and left the paid jobs to the men. This was a new stance for women; it coincided with the sixteenth- and seventeenth-century movement to close the guilds to them.[12] The new mentality did not mean that clerics advised early modern Protestant women to be idle. Misogynistic writers called on Protestants as well as Catholics to cure women's alleged inconstancy, weak intellect, and hysteria with work, religion, the law, and husbandly discipline. The prescriptive literature for every wife recommended "honest work that busied her hands,"[13] but as we shall see, whether they wrote that it was to be done within the home or not had for a long time been part of deep-rooted prejudice, the undoing of which had far-reaching implications.

Women in German cities, for example, were gradually excluded from guilds.[14] As honorable work came to be defined as work done by men outside the home, journeymen shied away from participating in workshops with women. It was just a step away for women to be considered ineligible to learn the "secrets of any craft" and so to be distanced even further from learning about or producing goods that required skill.[15] The gender ideal for the German female worker was to create homemade items in her own house, where her skill and her products were considered amateurish. This primitive manufacture was, by definition and by circumstance, outside the capitalist market. The German workingwoman, stripped of privilege, was expected to do merely incidental business that would not bring her into economic or legal competition with men.

The French situation provides a contrast. While the post-Tridentine sixteenth- and seventeenth-century Catholic Church inveighed against

---

12. Merry E. Wiesner, *Working Women in Renaissance Germany* (New Brunswick, N.J.: Rutgers University Press, 1986), see chap. 5, "Guilds, Crafts, and Market Production," passim; Lyndal Roper, *The Holy Household* (Oxford: Oxford University Press, 1989); and Hufton, *Prospect*, 493. Hufton writes, "In the context of the sixteenth century, religious reform provided the rhetoric to insist that the proper place for a woman was in the home under patriarchal control. The rhetoric endorsed, in effect, an ordering of society coincident with male claims to jobs."

13. Natalie Zemon Davis, "Women on Top," in *Society and Culture in Early Modern France* (Stanford: Stanford University Press, 1965), 126.

14. Merry E. Wiesner, "'Wandervogels' and Women: Journeymen's Concepts of Masculinity in Early Renaissance Germany," *Journal of Social History* 24 (1991): 767–82.

15. Merry E. Wiesner, "Guilds, Male Bonding and Women's Work in Early Modern Germany," *Gender and History* 1, no. 2 (summer 1989): 130–31.

women's sinful, concupiscent nature and enclosed religious orders, this rhetoric did not impose upon laywomen the obligation to avoid work outside the home. Women's role in guilds did diminish, but they remained masters in some guilds and in others took up auxiliary wage work alongside men. Olwen Hufton's description of the post-Reformation wife and mother did not apply to them. As Louise Tilly and Joan Scott have shown, for ordinary people, work was the order of the day and employment went to support the family economy.[16] The ideal of the "family wage" paid to the husband in support of his dependents was absent in the preindustrial era. All individuals—wife, husband, children—had the obligation to support themselves by contributing to the family budget.

Thus the work environment was different for French and Germanic women, and we would see other differences as well if we included Spain, England, and Scandinavia. Even with these few examples, it is evident that societies fully invested as patriarchies could prescribe the role of women differently. That of upper-class women differed from workingwomen; German female workers lived with strictures from which their French counterparts were free. Differing norms did not appear at random; each expectation of male and female behaviors grew out of a particular situation, each region, each local economy with its own dynamic needs. This was also true of customs that, while apparently running counter to the patriarchal establishment, gave benefits that ranged from cultural capital to financial perquisites.

In her reevaluation of medieval institutions, Joan Kelly has suggested that courtly love could be viewed as a loophole enabling nobles to tolerate the irritations of arranged political marriages. Troubadour poetry and the conventions of noble women choosing partners in adultery became widespread among late medieval aristocrats. "But this could happen only if such ideas supported the male-dominated order rather than subverted it."[17] Under the conventions of courtly love, the noblewoman had the freedom to accept a lover and to express her preference for him over her husband. "And while passionate love led to adultery, by that very fact it reinforced, as its necessary premise, the practice of political marriage."[18]

---

16. Louise A. Tilly and Joan W. Scott, *Women, Work and Family* (New York: Holt, Rinehart and Winston, 1978).

17. Joan Kelly, "Did Women Have a Renaissance?" in *Women, History and Theory* (Chicago: University of Chicago Press, 1984), 26.

18. Ibid., 26–27.

In another example, the cultural inversions of sex that Natalie Zemon Davis shows in "Women on Top" may confirm rather than overturn the sexual order of the society.[19] Neither Kelly nor Davis, however, discounts women's own experience in these activities and the new personal power that they might have achieved from their participation. But we know that participants in a patriarchal society benefited unequally from its resources. Perhaps the award of liberties to some women provided a counterweight to gross sex inequalities in the social structure as a whole. Would these fortunate women behave as allies to the patriarchy, supporting the status quo? Before we can consider this question, we need to know more about the institutions that seemed to override patterns of gender control and how they managed to emerge within the society.

Guildwomen are a quintessential example of privileged women in a man's world. Cynthia Truant, Judith Coffin, and Clare Crowston have shown how privilege overrides gender in Parisian women's guilds.[20] Women in guilds behaved like adults, as men did, using economic and legal advantages to advance their business interests. The adoption of adult freedom for a lifetime's work, rather than just during the temporary period of a festival, must seem like an extravagant inversion of women's role. But like manifestations of women on top, women in guilds did not act to overturn the patriarchal reality. Rather, they exposed the complex institutional structure by which the norms are reinforced. They introduced flexibility by using women as conduits of opportunity. Most significantly, they underscored how factors other than dialectical expression of male and female can become vehicles of social confirmation. As Mary Povey reasons, gendered differences rely on the polarity of the sexes for definition and march together in paired opposites: male/female, rational/irrational, leaders/subordinates. But "the epistemological term *woman* [will] guarantee men's identity only if difference [could be] . . . fixed—only if,

---

19. Davis, "Women on Top," 130–31.
20. See Cynthia Truant, "La maîtrise d'une identité? Corporations féminines à Paris aux XVIIe et XVIIIe siècles," *Clio, Histoire, Femmes et Sociétés* 3 (1996), and "Parisian Guildswomen and the (Sexual) Politics of Privilege: Defending their Patrimonies in Print," in *Going Public: Women and Publishing in Early Modern France*, ed. Dena Goodman and Elizabeth C. Goldsmith (Ithaca: Cornell University Press, 1995); Judith Coffin, "Gender and the Guild Order: The Garment Trades in Eighteenth-Century Paris," *Journal of Economic History* 54 (December 1994): 768–93; and Clare Haru Crowston, "Engendering the Guilds: Seamstresses, Tailors, and the Clash of Corporate Identities in Old Regime France," *French Historical Studies* 23, no. 2 (spring 2000): 339–71.

that is, the binary opposition between the sexes [becomes] more important than any other kinds of difference."[21]

Gender was but one kind of difference in the Old Regime, a social system constructed on myriad categories. Based on the principle of hierarchical authority that was at the heart of the medieval state, centuries of special privileges had accrued in France. Beginning in the early medieval period, the king had alienated portions of his sovereignty by awarding particular nobles the responsibility of carrying on public functions like tax collecting, providing an army, and judging legal disputes. By the Renaissance, these governmental functions had become linked to offices that were sold to raise revenue for the king. In the seventeenth century, Louis XIV was able to extort funds by threatening to create dozens more offices that would debase the value of those already purchased.

These offices contained the rights to perform governmental tasks, first as life-long privileges and later as inherited prerogatives. The various attempts to reintegrate these functions into royal hands had, in fact, confirmed their alienation from the sovereign power. Kings seldom had the funds to buy up the offices to remove them. It was not only the high nobility that protested vigorously when their patents of office were threatened. Guild members also guarded their monopoly to train, manufacture, and sell those goods that the privilege of their license allowed. The notion of simply suppressing them would have been deeply shocking to the king as well as his subjects, for all shared the belief that society was constructed of these units of privilege.

In a hierarchical society like the French, privilege governed permission to do any number of activities. Whether one was allowed to walk in a holiday procession or whether one could wear a hat in a workshop were as important to working people as whether one might sit in the presence of the king was to courtiers. These gestures confirmed the importance of the individuals permitted to make them. They were worth money and power. Not only did they sometimes confer direct pensions and grants, just as importantly they gave their performers the standing of creditworthiness, enabling them to borrow money, to delay paying it back, and to attract the confidence of investors. In the Old Regime, people might complain that they had been unfairly robbed of one or another privilege, but until the Enlightenment, the system itself was unchallenged.

21. Mary Povey, *Uneven Developments: The Ideological Work of Gender in Mid-Victorian England* (Chicago: University of Chicago Press, 1988), 80.

In terms of political science, this sort of a hierarchical structure is called a society of orders. William Beik has called attention to the disagreement of French historians who presented the past in terms of an absolute monarch working through the estates, or orders, to gain control of the kingdom. Beik's primary complaint is that writers who envision the state in terms of orders discount the effect of economics to change the political weight expressed in the "ordered" institutions. My approach does not deny the importance of economic factors; rather it shows how different forms of patriarchy can exist within the accepted framework of society and use economic tools to express them.[22]

The permission of each separate group to behave in certain ways, to enjoy certain rights, rested on the deeply rooted acceptance of the king's right to fragment his authority and to alienate parts of his sovereignty. Each of these groups had gained the right to enjoy political and economic privileges in exchange for the obligation to perform bureaucratic functions. The external gestures were important in part because they signified legal rights to transgress another person's potential liberties. The structure of society was a honeycomb of exceptions. Ordinary human beings, unexceptional in their native origin, were endowed with special rights by virtue of the king.

Moreover, the habit of getting permission to perform exceptional acts, thus gaining monopolies over functions in the public realm, legitimized privilege as an overriding imperative. As the philosophes complained, the award of special functions to individuals who paid for the right to have them or who gained them by inheritance was irrational. It had the function, however, of desensitizing people to incongruities between the function and the nature of individuals in privileged roles. M. le Curé had the right to receive the living, even if his assistant had to perform the Mass and the parish duties. M. le Parlementaire had the nominal right to occupy his inherited place at a young age, while his legal assistants told him what to say and when to nod. In the Middle Ages this gap between title and performance had permitted some women to act for their noble husbands defending the estate or to cast a vote in lieu of their husbands on a city council.[23] French society defined itself by the infinite possibility of

---

22. See William Beik, *Absolutism and Society in Seventeenth-Century France: State Power and Provincial Aristocracy in Languedoc* (Cambridge: Cambridge University Press, 1985), esp. chap. 1, "Absolutism and Class."

23. Joan Kelly asserted that women's power to inherit and administer feudal property

privileged distinctions. Of course, the division between male and female was important, but so was the separation between noble and commoner, between provinces with a legislative body (*pays d'états*) and provinces without such protection, between city dweller and rural peasant. From the right to wear rich clothing that would cause others to defer to them on the public road, to the chance to speculate in public finances, this society was attentive to separate categories that mandated special behavior. Because "male" and "female" constituted one normative category in an array, other classifications could subordinate it.

This social flexibility underlay women's guilds in France. We can see how the very rigidity that enabled the society of orders to function provided a system of immunity from discrimination for guildwomen. To test this theory, let us return to the story with which this chapter began, the Le Havre merchant mercers who were defending their guild from amalgamation by the female *lingères* of the town.

A closer look at the mercers' argument from the point of view of gender, laying out the reasons why the two guilds should not be unified, is instructive here. The mercers used the argument from gender to prevent the "hostile takeover" that they feared for purely economic reasons. They asserted that the provisions of statutes regarding daughters would enable the females to infiltrate the mercers' ranks. "Advantage [*lingères*], because their daughters would come into full rights of both guild sections, while the mercers' daughters could not, according to the mercer's statute, become masters in their fathers' guild. That is, unless the right were accorded them in a total revamping of the mercers' statutes."

In order for the mercers to regain balance, they would need their daughters to be admitted into the linen drapers' trade. This, however, would constitute another "Advantage—*lingères*." Currently the *lingères*' daughters were excused from long apprenticeships and from masterpieces altogether because they had already learned the trade at their mothers' knee. The mercers' daughters would have to undergo the training and to make the masterpiece. This in itself seemed an inequity, but if the mercers' daughters were excluded, it would also be unfair.

---

helped them to stand in for absent husbands. "The lady presided over the court at such times, administered the estates, took charge of the vassal service due the lord. She *was* the lord—albeit in his name rather than her own—unless widowed or without male children." "Renaissance," 27.

Nowhere in this document did the mercers make a global comment suggesting that women were inferior workers. They did not argue that the guildwomen were incapable of learning and performing the trade of mercer. Quite the contrary, they claimed to worry about their own lack of knowledge in the lingerie trade. Because the trade of linen-draper required manual skills, the mercers would have to undergo an apprenticeship and show a masterpiece to gain access to the women's activities. The linen-drapers, however, would only have to make room on their shelves to sell the mercers' goods. Even the comment that "the trade of the linen-draper is little suited to men" was belied by the mercers' acknowledgment that men in Caen could become master *lingers*. The mercers' defense did not deal with qualitative differences of gender; it was not ideological, but legalistic. And the legal strictures fit into a society in which power was awarded on the basis of particular categories in possession of special privileges. This is one of the meanings of gender to working people in prerevolutionary France.

Handmaidens of God in Society: Gender as Economic Restraint

Earlier in this chapter, I argued that gender in the Old Regime was submerged within many categories of difference and that it did not have the polarizing effect that we see in today's society. But the problem of gender is highly complex. At the same time that it diminished in comparison with other indications of difference, gender loomed large in the society, pervading all human activities. As Joan Wallach Scott wrote of political interaction: "We can write the history of that process only if we recognize that 'man' and 'woman' are at once empty and overflowing categories. Empty because they have no ultimate, transcendent meaning. Overflowing because even when they appear to be fixed, they still contain within them alternative, denied, or suppressed definitions."[24]

Of these hidden definitions, associating women with religion has long been a powerful belief. In medieval society, the figures of Mary and the female saints served both to indicate the religious sensibility of women and to prescribe women's role as essentially spiritual. As the female figures representing the Virtues on the cathedral at Chartres showed,

---

24. Scott, "Gender," 49.

humankind may act righteously in practical life by working. The injunction *"laborare est orare"*—working is a form of prayer—came to be applied particularly to women.[25]

The theological precedent for showing Mary and other female figures at work in textile manufacture comes from a story of her early life. In writings of the Apocrypha, five virgins were selected to make a curtain for the Temple; the spinning of purple and scarlet wool fell to Mary, signaling her royal lineage. According to the second-century Protoevangelium of James, Mary had been placed under the guardianship of Joseph in her twelfth year. She took wool for the sacred task to his home to spin, performing her function of a servant there. Thus Mary is a virgin of royal blood humbling herself by working at servants' tasks. In early representations, it is while she is spinning that the archangel Gabriel announces she will bear Jesus.[26]

Mary's work in preparing material for the Temple curtain is holy service. Its worth is beyond price because it is a sacred product, representing service to God. By analogy, as Mary came to be the model of the Christian woman, the interpretation of women's work as service became generalized. Standing beyond the mundane arena of commerce, women's work became ideologically dissociated with market price. Late medieval representations of Mary knitting blended the secular and profane uses of activity. The knitted garment (shown after knitting was adopted in the thirteenth century from the East) was a perfect, seamless covering for the perfect Child. The weaving of veils represented in cathedral statuary showed nuns performing manual labor for a religious purpose. Paintings and tapestries displayed wealthy women busy embroidering, weaving on belt looms, spinning, and weaving at broadlooms in imitation of sacred figures.[27] The injunction that to labor is a means of extolling God applied to men and women alike. But as men became increasingly tied to the secular network of the market economy, women's work remained linked in a special way to religious significance. From this perspective, female employment became conflated with service to family. As Mary

---

25. Lynn White Jr., "Dynamo and Virgin Reconsidered," *American Scholar* 27, no. 2 (spring 1958): 183–94.

26. B. Harris Cowper, *The Aprochyphal Gospels* (London: Williams & Norgate, 1867), 12.

27. For discussion on the representations of Mary's textile work as holy activity, see Rosalie Green and Iso Rogusa, *Meditations on the Life of Christ* (Princeton: Princeton University Press, 1961), 12, 27–28, 42, 74–76, 140–41.

labored for the holy family, so the female worker in the preindustrial era performed essential services for hers. The paintings of Mary as spinner, knitter, weaver, cutter of clothing were the normative icons of the working woman of historic times.

Investing women's work with religious significance gave two advantages to patriarchal society. Such investment maintained a sentimental segregation for women. It put them on a pedestal in idealized form and thus assured society that its force and brutality would be balanced by a pure goodness before which evil bows. Secondly, it removed women from the economic arena in ideological terms. In this way society justified underpaying women's work and defining their contribution to the economy as nonessential.

In the preindustrial era, the institutional framework lent itself to this formulation. Women's work was seen in a family context since workshops or farmhouses also served as family homes. The law underscored this apparent separation of women from the economy by not having women participate in public functions. Her work might consist of unpaid tasks performed directly for the benefit of the household like cooking, childcare, or tending a kitchen garden. Or she might do craft work at home or earn wages from a neighboring farmer or artisan outside the home. In either case, her labor was considered to benefit the family, headed by the husband. Hence its immediate definition was that of service rather than productivity.

In the guild system of work, such a definition found a natural concordance. Bylaws of Lyon's silk guild, for instance, permitted journeymen in the seventeenth century to set up one loom for their own work and one for that of their wives. In the eighteenth century, when conflict between weavers and merchants wracked the guild, it was commonly understood that wives of masters produced one-quarter of the workshop's output under the license of the male head of household.[28] In Lyon, the silk guild permitted masters' wives, daughters, and sons to weave as journeymen in workshops outside their family. For the daughters' work, a special ledger requesting individual permissions from the guild officers cast the young women's work as a form of charity toward their parents. The guild register recorded each request in the following form: "Jacques

---

28. See the discussion in Daryl M. Hafter, "Women Who Wove in the Eighteenth Century Silk Industry of Lyon," in *European Women and Preindustrial Craft* (Bloomington: Indiana University Press, 1995), 42–64.

Potel and his wife Angelique Normand, aged parents of so and so, [the daughter's name] request permission for their daughter to work in the atelier of . . . ." The guild withdrew this privilege in 1744 when the merchants gained control of the industry, but it was quickly reinstated in response to weavers' demands. In the tailors' guild in Lyon we find the theme again. A master's daughter, apprehended after the guild had canceled daughters' rights, insisted that she still had authority to work at the trade because she was helping her old infirm father, a master tailor no longer able to work. The argument that wives and daughters may earn wages outside the home in order to sustain their families remained a strong theme in the moral economy.[29]

From a societal point of view, defining women's work as service had several advantages. Women's wages were pegged at subsistence level because they were a form of "just price." To ask for more would be to take advantage of hardship, in the same way that adding interest to loans was considered usury. This scheme provided society with a form of flexibility, a sort of economic insurance policy that kept a group of workers in reserve who were not linked to the market economy. Without professional credentials, they could take up any number of minimally skilled tasks in succession and enter or leave the workforce depending on their families' needs. They could adjust to one husband's trade yet accept new instruction if a second mate were in a different guild or business. Either by taking jobs in advanced technology outside the home or by accepting the low wages that came from remaining in outmoded technology, they enabled the male masters to persist as skilled craftsmen rather than joining the ranks of industrial workers. In the nineteenth century, as Tessie Liu has demonstrated, the Cholet woolen weavers' female relatives became day workers outside the home to enable their fathers and husbands to continue as handloom weavers, even when handweaving was economically unfeasible.[30]

Ascribing religious connotations to women applied to their role as accepting charity as well as giving it. Every society has provided a means

29. Permission for masters' daughters to work outside the home was sought for each job. These records are found in the silk guild's papers under "Registre, Permissions Accordés," Archives Municipales, Lyon, HH 586. Justin Godart discusses their favorable salaries in *L'Ouvrier en soie* (Lyon: Bernoux et Cumin, 1899), 169–72.

30. Tessie Liu, *The Weaver's Knot: The Contradictions of Class Struggle and Family Solidarity in Western France, 1750–1914* (Ithaca: Cornell University Press, 1994), and "The Commercialization of Trousseaux Work: Female Homeworkers in the French Lingerie Trade," in *European Women and Preindustrial Craft*, 179–97.

for impoverished women at the fringe of the social structure to earn a subsistence living. It was a form of charity that kept the women from having to resort to prostitution. In classical Greece, women were not permitted to own property, but poor tradeswomen might have the equivalent of three days' worth of goods to peddle. The Old Testament example of Ruth and Naomi gleaning the fields after harvest enjoined farmers to leave some grain for the poor. Medieval guild statutes made exceptions for individuals to sew and spin for their own use and small sale. Fourteenth-century London guilds were ordered by the king to permit craftwomen without guild affiliation to take up needlework for a minimal sum, even if the skill belonged to the trade associations. In eighteenth-century France, reforming minister Jacques Turgot justified his edict suppressing guilds on the basis that opening needlework and other female trades to all women would enable them to live "honorably."

Society confirmed women's segregation from the market economy by defining their needs, as well as their salary, as minimal. It was therefore inappropriate for women to make a profit from their work. Guilds were aware that there was a possibility of this happening. Some of their bylaws kept women workers from taking advantage of the market. Guild statutes also set limits on male masters, but it was assumed that the man was head of a household—in Lyon's silk guild for instance—and the male weaving master could have at least four machines to support his dependents. By contrast, the female masters who produced fancy decorative braid in Lyon graduated from their apprenticeship with the right to set up only one loom.

Widows' rights in their husbands' guilds were another expression of charity to benefit the guild master's children until they could become masters themselves. Where a widow received the privilege of carrying on the family business, it was heavily restricted. She might retain only the apprentices in service at the time of her husband's death. Or she might be permitted to take on one assistant but no more. Usually she forfeited the privilege if she remarried outside the trade. Thus by casting working women as separate from economic gain, as servants to the family imitating Christian motherhood, society acted to undercut their competition with men. Women's work was defined as service to the family on behalf of the husbands' interest.[31] But this separation from men, this insistence

---

31. For a discussion of this idea as it relates to later history, see Joan Kelly, "The Doubled Vision of Feminist Theory," in *Women, History, and Theory*, 58.

on women's otherness, provided the basis by which to treat women's resources differently from those of men. Although the law constantly acted to enhance the power and wealth of men, it reacted to women's separateness by providing a legal segregation of their funds and status. A series of legal provisions based on women's partition in society became important devices for families as they navigated the unstable preindustrial economy.

Dividing the Indivisible: Marriage in Customary Law

Patriarchal society considered women in terms of their family relationships, in particular, as wives. The legal definition of the wife, however, posed a difficult conundrum for jurists in the eighteenth century. At issue was the balance between the husband's supremacy in the marriage and the wife's physical and moral independence in fact. Legal commentators have tried to dissociate the construction of the French marriage from that of the early English union, asserting that in France the wife had greater theoretical separation from her husband. For the English jurist Blackstone, the "wife is submerged in the husband."[32] Commenting on the traditional law, Renée Génestal, a twentieth-century legal scholar, thought that in Normandy "the reality is not so simple." The wife "is not an [legally] incompetent creature [*une incapable*], a being without judicial personality, as one would say in England. She has a personality and a capability; but the authority of the husband requires, even if his interest is not at stake, that nothing should be done without him and apart from him."[33]

The role of the wife in legal documents highlighted the importance of the family in supporting male privilege. Social and kinship benefits were organized to flow to husbands and fathers. Each nuclear family comprised a knot of subordinates grouped around a male head of household. Each extended family formed links that could become political spheres of influence.[34] In economic terms, most women participated in the husband's

---

32. William Blackstone, *Commentaries on the Laws of England*, 11th ed. (London, 1791), L3, chap. 7.

33. René Genestal, "La Femme mariée dans l'ancien droit normand," *Revue historique de droit français et étranger* (1930): 477, 487.

34. Sarah Hanley, "Family and State in Early Modern France," in *Connecting Spheres: Women in the Western World, 1500 to the Present*, ed. Marilyn J. Boxer and Jean H. Quataert

trade, helping to produce goods, manage the workshop, feed the journeymen and apprentices, and take up the slack in any way they were needed. If families had been set up as clusters of adult males or of an equal husband and wife, they would lack the surplus value that women as nonadults added to the family economy.

In the area of customary law (*loi coutumière*) under which Rouen and Lyon were governed, the law codes would not appear to contain any clauses enabling women to act with independence.[35] Areas ruled by written law (*loi écrite*) allowed the wife's independence from her husband on the books but then curtailed it by exceptions.[36] For the most part, women were not considered adults in the law. Only if they survived parents or were designated by a father as *fille majeure*, an unmarried woman with adult status, or as widow standing in for her husband, were women freed from being minors. The role of wife, which was an economic and moral necessity according to Christian theorists, placed most women in a subordinate and mute position. "From the instant the marriage has been celebrated, the wife is deprived—among us—of the right of acting without the authorization of her husband; but that does not mean that he can dispose of all her rightful gains [*droits*] without informing her."[37] With these words the eighteenth-century legal scholar David Houard expressed the basic tension within the definition of marriage in the Old Regime: the wife and the husband are one person in the law and the wife is under the husband's coverture. The married couple was a corporate unit with only one head. This equation was constructed to benefit the family; because the husband was its representative in the law, he controlled its economic affairs. Or perhaps the sequence of cause and effect should be reversed. One might say that since the society was a patriarchy that gave men control over the family's economic rights, they were its legal representatives. It is important to note that Houard's *Dictionnaire analytique* was a compendium of customary law in Normandy, but that Paris and

---

(New York: Oxford University Press, 1987); and "Engendering the State: Family Formation and State Building in Early Modern France," *French Historical Studies* 16, no.1 (spring 1989): 4–17.

35. Lyon used a combination of customary, royal, and commercial law made by the special law court called the *Conservation*, see J. Vaesen, *La Juridiction commerciale à Lyon sous l'ancien régime* (Lyon, 1879); and Francois-Xavier Emmanuelli, *État et pouvoirs dans la France des XVIe–XVIIIe siècles* (Paris, 1992), 128–29

36. David Houard, *Dictionnaire analytique, historique, étymologique, critique et interprétatif de la coûtume de Normandie* (Rouen, 1780) 2:259.

37. Ibid., 1:264–65.

Lyon conformed to the customary law of Paris. Although there were many rules that appeared in both jurisdictions, the customary law of Normandy was especially harsh on women.

Provision had been made in some provincial law codes for wives to have a bit more control over resources and activity. Acquisitions made by the wife, especially from her commerce or industry, could not be sold or traded away in the southwest of France.[38] *Bourgage*, real estate acquired during the marriage, under Normandy's code was inherited equally.[39] But despite this clause, in Normandy the husband was the master. Even when it came to giving testimony in court, the wife retained only a grudging margin for her conscience. As Houard put it: "In this province . . . the husband may not cease for an instant to guide the will of his wife, to enlighten her on the actions she must take. [To be sure] it is possible for her not to follow his advice nor to testify as he wishes; she may retract what she already consented to, such is her liberty. But she may not give witness against the wishes of the husband, nor consequently be, for an instant, without his special permission. Such is her dependence. In a word, it does not suffice that the husband consents; it is necessary that he *permits* and *authorizes*" (emphasis mine).[40] It is hard to imagine a more forceful expression of the power of the male head of household.

The husband exerted his power over the wife by virtue of his "quality of superiority and as head of the conjugal association." The twentieth-century legal scholar Jean Portemer concludes that the husband's power in the Old Regime "makes of the married woman, not a perpetual minor, as common understanding has it, but in reality a person much more effaced on the juridical scene than a minor."[41] While the wife might not obligate her husband or deal with his goods without his approval, the husband, needing only to consult his own wishes, could dispose of all their married resources. Thus, when it came to the fruits of his wife's

---

38. Jean Portemer, "Le Statut de la femme en France depuis la réformation des coûtumes jusqu'à la rédaction du code civil," *Recueils de la Société Jean Bodin* 12 (1962): pt. 2, 454–55.

39. However, Julie Hardwicke suggested that non-noble women gained more access to property under customary law prevalent in northern France in *The Practice of Patriarchy* (University Park: The Pennsylvania State University Press, 1998), 54–55. See also Barbara Diefendorf, *Paris City Councillors in the Sixteenth Century: The Politics of Patrimony* (Princeton: Princeton University Press, 1983), 225n26.

40. Houard, *Dictionnaire*, 1:264–65.

41. Portemer, "Le Statut de la femme," 454–55.

inheritance or work, he had the right to make any disposition with the exception of selling real estate that she brought into the marriage.[42]

These trenchant provisions converted into law the patriarchal ideology that had become even more intense with the Catholic Counter-Reformation as clerical and lay reformers tried to impose new standards of moral discipline on society. Just as the king sought to bring his realm ever more surely under his command, the husband needed to exert authority to guide and control the natural waywardness and inconstancy of the wife. The legal personification of marriage was a microcosm reflecting society's organization. As the absolute monarch ruled his kingdom by means of constant attention and control, the paterfamilias was obliged to govern every action of his wife. As the resources of the state were the king's to dispose according to his will, the husband received the same freedom to handle the joint belongings of the marital community that were set forth in the marriage contract.[43]

The means to greater flexibility reflected the mechanism we have already seen, by which the Old Regime used privilege to pacify potential rivals or to license various functions within the state. The absolute monarch delegated some of his sovereignty to aristocrats and functionaries in order to expedite bureaucratic responsibilities. To get the tax collected, courts staffed, and the army captained, he sold offices and gave participants special privileges. In parallel fashion, just as the king treated certain problems by conceding to each a separate category of privilege, the law was able to treat women as a special group and award them particular activities. While society officially endorsed a strong position for husbands within marriage, other pressures called for more flexible management of the couple's resources. Faced with a marital union headed by an all-powerful husband, the legal code "fenced off" certain capacities and resources pertaining to wives. In these cases women received the same

---

42. René Genestal modifies this view by saying of the wife, "She is not an incapable entity, a being without juridical personality as they say in England; she has a personality and a capability. But the authority of her husband requires, even when his interest is not at stake, that nothing be done without him and outside of his purview." "La Femme mariée dans l'Ancien droit Normand," *Revue historique de droit francais et étranger* 29 (1930): 498.

43. James R. Farr, *Authority and Sexuality in Early Modern Burgundy, 1550–1730* (New York: Oxford University Press, 1995). Of course laws had to be authorized by various traditional bodies to come into effect.

sort of license or monopoly enjoyed by other privileged groups within the state.

As we consider how a woman's relative freedom or power contributed to the functioning of this society, what sort of exceptions did the families need women to convey? Three economic problems stood out to be solved in the marital equations of old France: first, the issue of the resources invested in the new union—the dowry and the real estate that would both revert to the wife's father (or his heirs) after the husband's death; second, the possible need to shelter the woman's resources from her husband or his creditors; and third, the practicality of permitting the wife to participate in business on her own behalf.

Each of these goals held tensions generated by conflicting ideals of the society. Efforts by the patriarchy to keep power in male hands were so intense that they produced the negative effect of setting sons against fathers or fathers-in-law. Men heading the new families were beholden to fathers in the generation before them for money and land. Women completed the new families and provided the next generation, but they still had obligations and ties to their families of origin. We see this clearly in their usual signatures, written with both the name of the birth family and that of the husband—for instance, "Marie Angelique Normand, Femme Houard." Besides that, reality did not always live up to the ideal of husbands who succeeded in business and did not squander their wives' dowries. Even though the patriarchal family assumed that husbands were naturally superior to their wives, families benefited from the efforts of women with more skill, daring, health, determination, or luck in business than their mates. The construction of a marital corporation, one of whose partners was to find expression *only* through the agency of the other, had an inherently artificial and awkward quality. Ironically, the legal system of the Old Regime itself provided the means to make an advantage out of women's separated state.

In concrete terms, each legal provision had its difficulties and complications, as it assigned resources to the new family while keeping the tie of the family of origin. The dowry and real estate were major concerns of the marriage contract. The dowry might consist of household goods, clothing, jewelry, annuities, mortgages, promises of inheritance, cash, the title to debts, and promises of benefits in kind—like living rent free with the bride's family. Such provisions can be seen in the marriage contract of Jean Raphael Dubos, journalier, and Marie Malmaison. The contract gave

Dubos 100 livres, the right to dine, "*souper*," at his mother-in-law's house, and the gift of two chickens a year.[44] The wife's father had a competitive claim on parts of their belongings; thus another man's family wanted assurance that the real estate and the dowry given to the new spouses would pass back to the wife or her relatives undiminished. To protect that succession, the law forbad the wife to consent to having her dowry alienated or mortgaged. But in the interest of the Royal Patriarch, the goals of subject patriarchs could be suborned. In 1664, Louis XIV permitted wives in regions around Lyon to obligate themselves for their husbands and to alienate their dowries whether liquid assets or real estate in order to stimulate business and pay taxes.[45] In general, however, exceptions permitted to the wife by law, like allowing her to transmit certain feudal rights, were constructed to benefit her family.[46]

The *douaire*, or marriage portion, was the second instrument to assign resources expressed in the marriage contract. It listed the proceeds that would fall to the widow on her husband's death—one-third of the husband's goods in Normandy, one-half in Paris and Lyon. These assets came from the husband's property and they would revert to the children or the husband's heirs after the widow's death. Only in special cases did the wife come into full ownership of these assets; ordinarily they were simply to support the widow during her lifetime. The marriage portion was not a repayment of the dowry, for that fell to the wife's father. Rather it was a benefit made by the husband to the wife. In this way "she should be ensured of profiting from the wealth of her husband; to recompense her for the cares and troubles that she takes for his household, raising his children, and for the increase and preservation of the communal property."[47] The marriage portion was the sole support a widow could expect.

Legists devised formulas to mitigate these conflicting claims. Despite the overwhelming right of the husband to their complete use, the resources that made up the dowry were protected during the marriage. Special rules

---

44. ADSM 5 E 89, marriage contract, 15 July 1760. Both principals made the sign of an X.
45. Claude-Joseph Ferrière, *Dictionnaire de droit et de pratique contenant l'explication des termes de droit, d'ordonnances, de coûtumes et de pratique*, 2nd ed. (Paris, 1740), 1:702.
46. Jean Portemer, "La Femme dans la législation royale des deux derniers siècles de l'ancien régime," *Études d'histoire du droit privé offertes à Pierre Pétot* (Paris: Le Boucher, 1959), 445–46.
47. Citation from Ferrière, *Dictionnaire*, 1:707. See 1:707–16 for information about the *douaire*. The clause permitting a remarried woman to keep her funds originated in cannon law.

applied to protect this wealth from private creditors, and even from the state. Citing precedent, the eighteenth-century jurist Claude-Joseph Ferrière explained, "By Roman law, the wife has only a tacit mortgage over the belongings of her husband for the claim for recovering her dowry, but this same mortgage carries a preference over all the other mortgage creditors that contracted with the husband before his marriage." The *parlement* of Toulouse even maintained that debts to the state made after the marriage might not be assessed against the wife's property.[48]

As for real estate that the wife brought, the husband had its usufruct, but he was forbidden to alienate it. Legal scholars have suggested that husbands were encouraged not to act as despoilers of this resource, though of course there were no sanctions against it. At least the husband was not to keep business affairs concerning that property hidden from his wife. Moreover, unless she gave him power of proxy, he was not allowed to intervene in lawsuits dealing with this resource.[49] Urban property acquired after the marriage was in a special category called *bourgage* and was inherited by both spouses.[50]

The very marriage contract by which the family was constituted into an indissoluble economic unit could also be used to introduce exceptions to the husband's control. For the most part these were economic protocols, but permission to behave in an "insubordinate" manner could also occur. The wife, for instance, might acquire in the marriage contract the right to testify without her husband's permission. "Stipulations have [also] been invented to exclude the wife's liquid assets from falling into the community and to produce the same effect as real estate, in order to conserve in some sort the equality between conjoints, and not to leave all the advantage on the side of the husband."[51] By contrast, one might stipulate that real estate may enter the community thus coming into the husband's ownership.[52] Or the marriage contract might substitute for the dowry, a gift of liquid assets (*don mobile*) that the husband could take possession of immediately. An exception even more radically opposed to the definition of legal norms might direct that the dowry remain in the husband's

---

48. Ferrière, *Dictionnaire*, 1:703. Public debts made before the marriage, however, or debts that the wife incurred before the marriage may be assessed on her funds.
49. Houard, *Dictionnaire*, 3:214, 259.
50. Charles Lefebvre, *L'Ancien droit matrimonial en Normandie* (Rouen: Impt. de L. Gy, 1912), 20–22.
51. Ferrière, *Dictionnaire*, 1:706. The legal term for this was *stipulations de propres*.
52. Ibid., 1:703, 702.

hands after his wife's death. If the widower had nothing else to live on, he was not obliged to return the dowry.[53] The list of exceptions following these rulings suggests why lawyers were important in this society.

It is instructive to learn how thoroughly the stipulations could undo virtually any general provision of family finance. They provided wedges to introduce the claims of the brides' and grooms' families into the inflexible unit of the newly married couple. By this means the marriage contract became a more malleable financial device than it would otherwise have been. And this flexibility was achieved in the time-honored manner of Old Regime law: building personal exemptions and privileges into the construction of patriarchal absolutism, which constituted, in this case, traditional marriage.

We now come to the second problem that Old Regime marriage was not constructed to solve: the occasional need to shelter the wife's finances from the husband. The all-encompassing nature of the legal tie provoked an equally forceful remedy to disengage the husband's control over the wife's goods and person when circumstances called for it. Two major types of marital separation provided remedies for financial problems or incompatibility and abuse. They were civil separation of property (*séparation de biens*) and civil separation from bed and hearth (*séparation de biens et de corps*). To be in force, legal separation had to be authorized by a judge and registered with letters from the chancellery.

While the *séparation de biens* gave the wife control over her own belongings, its first purpose was not to foster women's independence. As Houard wrote, "The civil separation has been established to prevent the dissipation of the wife's property, by the bad management of the husband, for it is agreed that the husband may not, even with the consent of his wife, alienate or mortgage the dowry resources."[54] When the wife noticed that her husband's business dealings were weakening assets awarded by the marriage contract, it was advisable for her to obtain a civil separation to preserve the dowry for its eventual return to her own family.

With the exception of provisions made in the marriage contract, civil separation was the strongest legal device to segregate the wife's possessions. It had repercussions on the relationship of the wife and husband to each other as well. The shifting limits assigned to male and female

---

53. Houard, *Dictionnaire*, 3:231.
54. Ibid., 2:261.

actors under the regime of "separation" reveals how malleable the expression of gender could be. As Ferrière's dictionary put it, "When a wife is not civilly separated, you could say that her actions and the administration of her property are in the husband's hand; but separation puts her outside his guardianship and gives her the right to use her property or just to keep it: in that case, her husband can no longer act for her without becoming her formal proxy nor could he convey her property to someone else or mortgage it."[55]

In theory, the civilly separated wife could act with as much independence as she chose—she could undertake business affairs under the same provisions as a man. Legislation of 1701 and 1747 required her to pay her own income taxes of *capitation* and *taille*.[56] But the law did not completely forget that she was a woman. She was no longer entitled to receive her marriage portion in the usual manner, but a judicial settlement ordinarily gave her the marriage portion or a pension of one-half of the husband's estate at his death. During his lifetime, the husband was still considered head of the family, with the power to make the normal decisions over the children and the household, and to do whatever seemed useful (which kept the "separation from oppressing him"). He "never lost the authority . . . over the conduct and the habits of his wife" and could always sue her for adultery. But because he did not have access to the dowry, his authority and resources were diminished. For this reason, he could not be chosen officer in a guild.[57]

The civil separation blocked the husband's power in other ways too. In one case, Sieur de la Vaunudière, auditor in the Chambre des Comptes in 1723, forbade his wife to accept the inheritance of her brother, Abbé Longuet. In order to enable Madame de la Vaunudière to inherit from her brother, the judge imposed a *séparation de biens* on her by his own authority. Her husband objected saying that his own refusal was only "a reasonable precaution to keep him from blindly becoming responsible for his brother-in-law's debts." His protest against this legal remedy did not sway the judge who may have been more interested in gaining a means of settling the debts that technically would devolve on the wife's

---

55. Ferrière, *Dictionnaire*, 2:232.
56. Portemer, "La Femme," 451 n10. Declarations of 12 March 1701 and 19 March 1747 asserted that she must pay these taxes "as a charge on the gains and revenues whose administration and profit she has."
57. Houard, *Dictionnaire*, 2:231; Ferrière, *Dictionnaire*, 2:862.

funds alone. The civil separation was reinstated, solely to enable the wife to receive her brother's legacy.[58]

Many examples reflect situations in which there was antagonism between wife and husband. Hostility between the wife's parents and the son-in-law who borrowed money and lost it; complaints by a businesswoman that her husband intruded into her trade; anger over the husband's wasteful, careless practices: these situations all provoked *séparations de biens* as a means of withdrawing assets from the husband's incompetence or malfeasance. But the civil separation did not necessarily indicate that the marriage itself was falling apart. On the contrary, it came to be used as a technique to protect the family resources and save the household. Begun as a means of protecting the dowry for the wife's heirs, and an exceptional remedy at that, the *séparation de biens* began to be used, illegally, as a regular business technique.

Bankruptcy records show how families resorted to hasty letters of separation tailor-made to save dowry assets from creditors; of course this example of bad faith was against the law but that did not stop families from trying to use it. In taking this step the wives and husbands acted not as antagonists but in collusion. The creditors responded with irritation and outrage complaining against this use of the wife's special protection to escape from paying debts of the family business. The law may have taken the high road and exempted family debts from the dowry; the husband may have been enjoined not to diminish it; but these were the resources the family lived on. When debts fell due, the creditors came looking for their money. Few families had enough assets to pay off their obligations comfortably. Thus the quick drawing up of letters of separation was cause for creditors' harsh words.[59]

When Jacques Duval and his wife presented their new letters of separation, his creditors balked at the usual procedure of agreeing to accept a percentage of the debt. Instead they imprisoned him. Only when the wife's letters were annulled did they agree to a debt settlement that included his release. A similar situation faced Dame Mouchet whose husband was apprehended trying to ride out of town. In a dramatic series of events during 1768, she rescued her debt-ridden husband from jail by agreeing

---

58. Houard, *Dictionnaire*, 2:261.
59. Creditors were on guard against "*les abus, les surprises, et les fraudes.*" Houard, *Dictionnaire*, 2:294. Ferrière recommended that the creditors find out the extent of the debts and see the papers in order to prevent "*collusion entre le mari et femme.*" *Dictionnaire*, 2:862.

to give up her letter of separation.⁶⁰ Sometimes by gaining separation, sometimes by giving it up, the wife's special category endowed her with leverage to help the family economy.

Because of its important repercussions, the *séparation de biens* written into marriage contracts of merchants and financiers should be a matter of public record, warned jurists, "so that creditors in good faith are not fooled by a separation they didn't know about."⁶¹ After all, many wives handled aspects of the family business and were assumed to be reliably following the husband's instructions when they accepted deliveries or bargained over goods. A great deal of informal proxy activity went on in the normal course of commerce; wives doing business at the family workshop or sales stall were assumed to have their husbands' confidence. But unless one had actually asked about the legal situation, it might be risky to make a contract with the wife. A commentator warned, not in jest, that trumpets, drums, and the town crier should make known every declaration of *séparation de biens*.⁶²

The *séparation de corps et d'habitation* (separation from bed and hearth) was another exception to the marital power, to protect the abused wife whose husband threatened her with death or the husband whose wife tried to kill him, committed adultery, or attacked his honor.⁶³ (The woman, however, had grounds for complaint only if blood was flowing, an eye had burst, or a limb had been broken.) Given the legal acceptance of wife beating, this provision may have been more theoretical than actual. Still, it existed on the books as another remedy, which could be invoked in a court of law. Civil separations provided a means of preserving the dowry, sheltering assets from bankruptcy, and they offered a measure of protection against abusive spouses. There was yet another legal device that ameliorated the strictures governing women's lives, giving them a measure of personal liberty as they enhanced the family's wealth. This was the

60. ADSM 201 BP 604.
61. Josse, *Commentaire*, 137–38. Merchant families' letters of separation should be registered at the Juridiction Consulaire or at the city hall, listed in a table of such categories and set up in a public place. The customary law of Orléans required that their names, addresses, and nicknames should be included and that three days after the separation was made, the couple had to inscribe their names, addresses, and the court that registered it on a poster hung in the chamber of hearings at the Châtelet.
62. Houard, *Dictionnaire*, 2:261. An edict in March 1673 required widows and *femmes séparées* to make known if they had mortgaged property. In the same year, merchants with *séparation de biens* were told to publicize their status. Portemer, "La Femme," 451n10.
63. Houard, *Dictionnaire*, 2:291.

device called the *marchande publique,* a privilege that made possible the existence of women in guilds.

While the home provided a place for many families to work at one business, it was sometimes an advantage for a wife to practice her own trade separately as a *marchande publique.* Even the Romans had made provision for the wife's independent business. The provision existed in Germany by the thirteenth century.[64] In France, this legal device could enable her to belong to a guild or to continue in a business that her family of origin had founded. No matter how restricted the wife was in respect to family assets, society recognized that some women could benefit themselves and their families if they had a public role. "If wisely conducted," one source declared, "the advantages and even the well-being of the husband have made it permissible to wives, having talent and industry for commerce, to undertake a separate trade, and to become *marchandes publiques.*"[65] The women could then maintain the skill and business network developed during an apprenticeship. The husband's acquiescence in each decision would not be required. If the wife conducted a business without separating her resources, then her husband's bankruptcy could devastate her business as well. Declaring a wife to be *marchande publique*—businesswoman in the public sphere—would protect her assets from her husband's creditors.

As Houard concisely put it, the *marchande publique,* a "merchant in the public realm, is one who conducts a business separate from that of her husband, under his witness and knowledge [*à son vû et scû*]." (In England a woman whose husband gave her the independence to conduct her own business was called feme sole.)[66] As with the device of *séparation de biens,*

---

64. Erika Uitz, *The Legend of Good Women: The Liberation of Women in Medieval Cities,* trans. Sheila Marnie (Wakefield, R.I.: Moyer Bell, 1994), orig. published as *Die Frau in der mittelalterlichen Stadt* (Leipzig: Edition Leipzig, 1988), 48. Early evidence of this special status was provided by the Augsburg town law of 1276, which stated: "No woman has the right to give someone else a part of her husband's estate, neither as surety nor in any other form without her husband's consent, unless she has her own business, run from her own shop or cellar or she is involved in trading activity independent of her husband; neither may a woman take any matter to court without her husband's permission . . . unless she goes to the market and buys and sells." A woman with a separate trade could dispose of her own estate and had to pay her own debts. In Russia the wergeld of a "handicraftswoman" equaled that of her male equivalent, not the reduced fee expected for other women. G. Vernadsky, *Medieval Russian Laws.* My thanks to Dr. Walter Moss for this reference.

65. Houard, *Dictionnaire,* 2:292–93.

66. Kay E. Lacey, *Women and Work in Preindustrial England* (London: Croom Helm, 1985),

this legal function was not construed as a benefit for the wife, but for the husband. It was always possible that "the husband could publicly revoke the liberty he has given his wife to become *marchande publique*."⁶⁷ Despite this formal caveat, the woman merchant enjoyed considerable autonomy, and it is clear from the feisty behavior of guild mistresses that the power to revoke the "liberty" was a dead letter. The *marchande publique* could manage her funds and products as she pleased; she could buy, sell, make contracts, lend, borrow, and initiate suits as she thought best. The law formally authorized her testimony as binding in respect to her business dealings, just as it would have credited her complaints if she were wounded, for only she would be in a position to know about both events.⁶⁸

Every woman who entered a guild, automatically became a *marchande publique* because each guild mistress, like every guild master, was legally responsible for actions the guild took. Whether the guild voted to collect a tariff from members, to go to court, or to protest a tax assessment, each member's vote was duly noted in its minutes and stood in the public record. The guild mistresses' pronouncement of satisfaction in apprentices' training legally gave the young people permission to set up their own shop and produce for the public. The female masters' officers had the right to confiscate merchandise and to arrest nonguild artisans for illegal work. Even women in licensed trades that were short of being full guilds, like the *revendresses*, who sold small quantities of goods on the street, had the independent standing of *marchandes publiques*. As an eighteenth-century jurist wrote, casting the pronouncement in the most commonly accepted situations, "Mistresses of some business or craft, like linen-drapers, seamstresses, small-scale retailers, fish merchants [*lingères, couturières, regratières, marchandes de poisson à la Halle, revendeuses*], and other similar commerce are public merchants."⁶⁹

That the benefit was not an abstruse legalism known only to attorneys we can see from police records of guild activities. On 17 October 1750, a linen-draper mistress married to Jacques Couture was accused of

---

esp. 40–45. Unlike the device of *marchande publique*, the *feme sole* did not provide a basis for women to enter guilds in England.

67. Rogue, *Jurisprudence consulaire et instruction des négotiants* (Angers, 1773), 1:227.

68. Isambert, Decrusy, Taillandier, *Recueil général des anciennes lois françaises* (Paris, 1833), 2:546. See Daryl M. Hafter, "Gender Formation from a Working Class Viewpoint: Guildwomen in Eighteenth-Century Rouen," *Proceedings Western Society for French History* 16 (1989): 417.

69. Rogue, *Jurisprudence*, 1:227.

harboring an unknown peddler and allowing him to sell cloth at her house. She and her husband claimed to know nothing about the incident. Using scorn as a defense, they protested: "It would be too childish to impose an arrest! How could anyone ever think that a *marchande de lingère*, who is *marchande publique*, who keeps a workshop, who has workers with her, and who can oblige herself since not under her husband's control, would be ignorant of the regulations of a profession to which she is a party."[70]

One of the key aspects of the *marchande publique* was that she was responsible for her debts, even to the point of being in jeopardy of losing her liberty from court actions. Her "freedom" to go to jail was linked to her permission "to trade in the public realm" (*marchander publiquement*)—both were authorized by her husband who had authority over her actions and her body. The wife of Sieur Fevret learned this to her chagrin. Having accepted a delivery of fruit with a verbal agreement, she and her husband found themselves unable to pay within the accepted six-month term "due to the harshness of the times." The court was unsympathetic; it fined the husband and put the wife into prison.[71] With the possibility that she stood responsible for her business affairs to the point of risking a sentence of imprisonment, she was considered to be trustworthy and good for the money (*bonne et valuable*). As the statute declared, "Although by our custom the wife may not make a business engagement without the authority of her husband, this maxim has an exception when, at the consent of the husband, the wife undertakes a trade separate from that in which he engages." If a court order required her to settle her debts by selling the family real estate, she was obliged to do so without consulting her husband; only if it were a private debt would her husband have to come before a judge to authorize it.[72]

The tension involved in giving the wife independence within a framework of dependence became evident in legislation on debts. It was understood that every husband was obligated for a wife's "agreements and contracts" with a few exceptions; in the case of a *marchande publique*, the husband was obligated whether he was present or not. Since she was legally a minor under his guardianship, actions she took were supposed to be carrying out his wishes. For this reason, her creditors were entitled

70. ADSM 5 E 508.
71. ADSM 201 BP 178, *Plumatif*, January 1760.
72. Rogue, *Jurisprudence*, 1:223–24.

to dun him, take him to court, and even imprison him if he could not discharge debts she had incurred. The debts that she contracted in the course of her business put at risk "her own liberty and also that of her husband." Neither in Germany nor in England were husbands responsible for their wives' obligations; this may have been both a symptom and a cause of the decline of women in guilds in those countries during the early modern period.[73] Having the husband obligated to make good on the contracts his wife undertook was an important resource. The legal dependence it revealed may ironically have fostered women's public activity.

On the other hand, declaring a wife to be *marchande publique* signaled that her business was "distinct and separate from that of her husband," a circumstance that these women used to utmost advantage. To ensure that it was separarte, "the commerce of the wife must be incompatible with that of the husband, or with his status." Nor was the husband permitted to dispose of his wife's merchandise.[74] (Of course the reality saw couples like Marie Catherine La Motte and her husband who put their funds together into a variety of linen goods to stock a store [*conjoinctement avec son mary mis ses fonds en marchandises de diverts toille dans une Boutique* (original spelling)].[75] When a court was involved, it insisted that the husband's financial obligations had a separate status. This legal device was a means of segregating the wife's part of the family resources. Here, then, is another example when allowing women to act independently became a strategy enabling the patriarchal society to function more effectively. It was understood that the wife received this "liberty" by her husband's permission.[76] She acted within the parameters of his agreement, using the resources agreed to. She then "could mortgage by stipulation his liquid assets, his acquisitions, the revenue of his possessions from the dowry, and her liberty." Her personal freedom was an issue; since the wife belonged to her husband, both in goods and body, it would be a form of lèse-majesté to carry her off to debtor's prison without his agreement.

That the husband permitted his wife this freedom in order to enhance his own wealth was at the heart of the privilege. This understanding

73. Wiesner, *Working Women*, 169–70. "Husbands were not required to pay back debts their wives had incurred without her knowledge; the unfortunate and unwise creditor had simply lost his money."
74. Rogue, *Jurisprudence*, 1:226.
75. ADSM 5 E 511.
76. Houard, *Dictionnaire*, 2:291. This is the term used in the original. "*Liberté*" was a privilege awarded to an individual.

provoked much legal dispute "when creditors of wife and husband vied for repayment." Four closely argued pages appear under the entry *"femmes marchandes publiques"* trying to prove that the wife's resources should be open to the husband's creditors because her business is just another means of enriching him. The case at issue treated the merchandise of Dame Vorillon, *marchande lingère,* whose husband went bankrupt. Could her husband's creditor, Sieur le Sauvage, seize her goods to pay his personal debt? A written opinion by Maître Flaust in 1766 argued that maintaining this separation would privilege the wife's creditors in an unseemly way. If anybody's creditors are to be advantaged it should be those of the husband! Would it not reverse the established order to give precedence to creditors of the wife "who can only work and trade for the husband, being where she is under his control [*puissance*], [rather than the wife] who earns for him, who loses for him, who can neither acquire nor lose for herself?" After all, the argument continued, where do the resources of the *marchande publique* come from? According to the lawyer for her husband's creditors, the fact that she is dependent on her husband's resources confirms the idea that even though separate, all the trades of one household form one enterprise. It is obvious that the wife pays the expense of her household from her husband's business and she draws from his funds to sustain hers or to reassure her creditors.[77]

While no one disputed informal sharing of funds, the argument whether the husband obligated his wife in his debts and vice versa continued. The precedents seemed to lead to an uncertain conclusion. In the *loi coûtumier,* the customary law of Beri and other regions, the debts of the *marchande publique* were her own; in the customary law of Normandy, this was arguable. In his influential manual *Le Parfait Négociant,* Jacques Savary asserted that the husband cannot take his wife's merchandise nor does he have anything to do with her business debts. But the judges of Normandy made more of the original circumstances by which the wife became *marchande publique* upon the consent of her husband. "They have thus judged that the commerce of the wife belongs to the husband, that it is for the husband that the wife has made profit, and that the husband is able to take it for his debts." The court finally resolved this case in an *arrêt du parquet* of 10 March 1766 with a compromise that maintained the financial integrity of the *marchande publique.* The wife's creditor,

---

77. Ibid., 2:291. For a discussion of *femmes marchandes publiques,* see 291–95.

Sieur le Sauvage, was to receive his repayment first. Only then would any surplus of the Dame Vorillon's spill over to pay off her husband's debts.

The court called on the requirement to maintain public confidence that expected the obligations of the *marchande publique* to be privileged within her resources. It also acknowledged the need to intervene in the traditional marital contract to redress the balance between resources assigned to wife or husband. If the wall surrounding her debts were not maintained, the wife would "be reduced to the most extreme impotence. If her goods could be seized to pay her husband's debts . . . it would be impossible for her to pay off her own debts, for she would remain exposed to the pain of corporal punishment without any of the resources that her industry and economy would offer her."[78]

It seemed harder to build a protective wall around the husband's resources. Harkening back to the assumption that the husband is guardian of the wife and that she remained under his ultimate control, jurists concluded that he was obligated to pay off her debts. For this reason, they asserted, one could make the claim that a guildwoman's legal status was uniquely favorable. "The wife has an object of consolation that the husband lacks: her possessions are protected [*à couvert*]; the real estate remains hers, it is not mortgaged. Instead all the belongings of the husband are the object and warranty of the wife's creditors. In declaring herself *marchande publique,* the wife thus risks less than the husband."[79] That opinion, however, was reasoned from the point of view of theoretical business risk; as for what she owned, the wife controlled neither liquid assets, goods in the house, purchases, nor goods acquired by both partners, while the husband was alive. Becoming *marchande publique,* as guild mistress, was one of the few means for women without noble ties or fortune to gain freedom of action in Old Regime France.

Above all, women added flexibility to the system by having multiple roles.[80] As helpmates, women contributed wherewithal and money to the family. As the silent part of the marital corporation, women enlarged the husband's capacity for gain. As daughters, they enabled resources to be circulated to new families and returned to the family of origin. Another advantage of keeping female power contingent on their relationships

78. Ibid., 2:293–94.
79. Ibid., 2:294.
80. Natalie Zemon Davis was a pioneer in making this point in "Women in the Crafts in Sixteenth-Century Lyon," *Feminist Studies* 8, no. 1 (spring 1982): 49–53.

was that the society could then reverse that norm and award women particular rights in special circumstances. Thus females could behave in a subservient mode, or with any degree of activity that might be needed. Tender and nurturing at their hearth, women could, in an emergency, pick up weapons and fight, lead bread marches, or conduct assertive business dealings. The female was conditioned to be the flexible sex. On one hand, they bore children and undertook a variety of activities to accommodate changing life conditions, as women; on the other hand, as deputies for their husbands, they could be endowed with the capacity to participate in the external world, as if they were men. In the patriarchal society, women were multivalent.

Conclusion

One of the most important aspects in the development of women's history has been the light it can shed on the working of society and the infinitely flexible and ingenious ways that people have constructed their ideals, including exceptions that proved the rule and loopholes that enabled their ideals to stand in their era. Women have always worked to help support their families, and in the preindustrial era they were responsible for providing food for their children. The kinds of work they did, the salaries they received, and the prestige of their jobs were all conditioned by their place in society. From antiquity, male and female were endowed with different, sometimes opposite, characteristics. Conforming to patriarchal norms in Western European society, women were classed as legal minors, less intelligent, less capable, and more emotional than men. For this reason, women typically were given unskilled work with commensurately low salaries, and their association with such employment came to taint all work done by women. The skill was in the worker, not the work. Moreover, women's association with reproductive function and home inclined society to consider their employment in farming or crafts as service to the family rather than productivity for the market. While a man's industry tied him to the public world, a woman's activity seemed to benefit the family alone and was accounted a gesture of sentiment, an unpaid service of affection.

Christian writers, turning away from pagan ideals, invested all human work with dignity and spiritual quality, since it was ordained by God.

In tracts and images, Mary appeared spinning, knitting, and presiding over the holy family's household. Combined with the ideology pervading Christian society, this example fostered the belief that women's work had religious significance rather than market value. It was a form of charity to allow women to work since that labor would sustain the family, help elderly parents, and not least, keep the women from prostitution. These notions justified paying women low wages or setting their recompense at room and board.

But putting women's work into a separate category emphasized the difference between the sexes and reinforced women's role in society as "other." In societies with a hierarchy of orders, the separateness of women formed another category, which conformed to the accepted nature of things. In Old Regime France, the law had created numerous categories of privilege, each of which stood as a separate unit within the kingdom. In certain ways, women's "otherness" became one of these categories, allowing benefits to adhere to its legal definition. It was understandable that a woman's dowry was preserved as a separate category of the family resources, and that letters of separation could shield a wife's funds from her husband's creditors. Therefore, even though marriage created an indissoluble unit, the law offered certain exceptions in which the weaker party could preserve some assets or act alone.

This was especially important in Normandy, where the customary law governing behavior decreed that the wife could take few actions without her husband's permission. In practice, the overwhelming authority of the husband and the relative incapacity of the wife would make for a society with too much rigidity, one that disempowered the wife's birth family. But women's control over their resources, whether as inalienable dowry real estate or through marriage contracts, could reestablish some balance. Other practices, like that allowing wives to be proxies for their husbands, also introduced flexibility.

The legal device of the *marchande publique* permitted women to run their own businesses as adults in the law, separate from the coverture of marriage. It helped to support the patriarchal system by doubling the productive members of the marital unit and by introducing suppleness to male economies. Guild mistresses were by definition *marchandes publiques,* and their freedom to participate as adults in economic life contributed to the wealth and productivity of family and community. This freedom also demonstrated women's capacity to organize effectively in professional associations and to gain success in the public realms of manufacture and commerce. The framework of the ordered society in which privilege trumped gender allowed the guildwomen to deal with their male counterparts on an equal basis.

It seems curious that Normandy, whose customary law restricted women so much more than that of other provinces, was one of the few places with flourishing women's guilds and mistresses in mixed guilds in the eighteenth century. Perhaps we can attribute the apparent anomaly to the need for multiplying the number of *marchandes publiques,* giving women explicit rights to participate in economic activities whereas in other places a looser legal structure simply assumed women's varied roles. There is no doubt that this northern province, with its orientation to Atlantic trade and its proximity to Paris, had a long tradition of industry and commerce. Its equally long experience of women's productivity—growing flax, knitting hats and gloves, making rope and canvass for merchant vessels, processing silk textiles, weaving woolen cloth—predisposed urban women to join guilds. Once in the professional associations, they used their independence to conduct vigorous, assertive, and successful businesses. Revealing the strength of guilds, the guild mistresses had an entire legal universe of privilege to use. As long as guilds were a vital element in economic life, they provided a framework in which their members, male and female alike, could nurture commerce and industry.

3

GUILDWOMEN AND *OUVRIÈRES*

As we search the documents to discover the range of women's jobs in the era before the Industrial Revolution, two groups call for attention: the privileged women in guilds and those in large industrial complexes. It is difficult not to see these two employment situations through a modern lens. We expect to find guild women enjoying privilege as mistresses, and manufacturing drudges performing menial, unskilled, low-paid jobs in industries. Given that women received less technical training than men, we might imagine that the guild women made frequent use of skilled male operatives and that female industrial workers, the *ouvrières* who were day laborers or piecework artisans, worked only at repetitive, crude tasks. We would be wrong on both scores. In order to ascertain the technical ability of women throughout Old Regime society, it is instructive to compare the elite female craft workers with the least favored ones. What we discover is that guild women were in full charge of their businesses and technologies, while the *ouvrières* brought skill and boldness to gain their own advantages. Using Rouen as a case study of women's guilds and Lyon to demonstrate a huge, capitalist silk industry, this chapter and the following ones will compare the work discipline, business strategies, and technical access of women in these two manufacturing centers. We will see that in the preindustrial world, women's role depended not only on wealth but also on the economic and social environment in which they found themselves.

Rouen, City of Women's Guilds

Guilds were vigilant in policing their rights, and charges against those who pursued trades illegally can be found in records of the day. Frequently as guild officers pushed their way into houses converted into clandestine workshops, they discovered servants hired ostensibly for domestic duties but actually set to work at crafts in competition with the guilds. In the following example, the female officials of the mixed-sex spinners' guild give testimony against a man they accuse of illegally dying thread.

> We [spinners'] guards confronted Sieur Delabos in his house, and we asked . . . if the hired girl Delanos did not keep his house and lodge there. He replied shortly, "Yes." And then he went inside. Despite his lack of cooperation, we made an inventory of the objects in his kitchen: fifty-six strands of silk thread dyed black stretched over the back of one chair, thirty-one other pieces of the same thread and color resting on the back of another chair, in a box three other pieces of the same thread and color, in another box three pieces of red thread and twelve pieces of grey thread. . . . On a table resting in front of crosses a small pair of balances with copper basins in one of which [was] a half-ounce of copper and in the other basin an unfinished ball of silk thread dyed black . . . a small [coue-socket?] of wood called a wheel to put the balls of thread into play, a friction-roller to flatten out the fibers in the wound up balls of thread, and a small piece of cloth called an "*étriquez*" to give luster to the thread . . . [when used] along with [a piece of] lead. In one small box we found 20 pieces of silk thread recently dyed black.[1]

Sieur Delabos could not claim he had no idea that thread was being dyed and processed illegally in his home, or that someone else had put the servant up to it. No hired girl would have supplied the copper basins for coloring and the wooden tools for processing thread on her own. Sieur Delabos had to submit to a trial initiated by the female guild officers in cooperation with the bailiff who accompanied them on their rounds. The court confiscated and sold his thread, and he had to pay a stiff fine to the women's guild. An appeal on his part would certainly have led to a decision against him and the ignominy of having it cried and posted in the town square.

The lure of manufacturing for a black market was a constant temptation for those, like Sieur Delabos, who bargained against the neighbors

---

1. Archives départementales de la Seine Maritime (hereafter ADSM) 5 E 527, "Procés Verbal," n.d.

noticing an unusual bustle at his door. No doubt he hoped to keep his clandestine craftwork unobtrusive so as not to attract the suspicions of the guild officers during their four regular inspection tours of the town. But the narrow streets and half-timbered buildings of Rouen, housing tenements on the central rue Malpalu and the outlying rue Martainville, were not likely to conceal much illegal industry from the sharp-sighted guild officers. Even when they were not making formal inspection tours, guild officers swept up and down the streets, alert to condemn unauthorized manufacture and sale that would cut into their guild's business. Male and female officials were equally assertive in their seizures of goods and tools and their accusations of illegal work as they protected their guilds.

For at the heart of guild life was the privilege that gave the group exclusive rights to a technical or commercial process. It followed that protecting the monopoly from competing guilds or from self-styled interlopers would occupy a high place in guild activities. And Rouen was a guild city par excellence. Far from the freedom which "free crafts" (*libre métiers*) had, or from the easy license to switch from one industry to another in Lyon, Rouen's guilds hewed to a strict line of regulations that supported their proprietary stance over ways to make and sell goods. Tradition justified the continuance of guilds with products as varied as mirrors, stone cutting, and embroidery. Guild discipline produced an abundance of woolen and linen cloth, which had been Rouen's staple for centuries. The eighteenth-century novelty product, cotton, quickly passed into the skilled hands of the city's weavers. As for the luxury textile goods that many of the craft organizations made—fine linenware, fancy headdresses, ribbons, garments—guilds maintained control of this fashion-sensitive production. The habits of the urban population, the role guilds played as municipal and national institutions, the advantages of guild membership for many city workers, the expectations of apprentices' parents in the region, and the excellence of the guild workmanship all collaborated to maintain the central place of guilds in the city.

Although guild membership for women had diminished in many cities, Rouen's female masters persisted throughout the eighteenth century along with their male counterparts as both contributed to the economic life of the region. Located on the crowded streets at the base of a moraine that ended at the Seine, Rouen's busy manufacturers produced for markets in Normandy, Paris, a semi-circle around Lyon, the Spanish and French colonies in South America and the Caribbean, and other Atlantic ports. Although other regions may have diminished guild control of local crafts, Rouen's guilds—following those of Paris—intensified their hold on city life as the centuries wore on. Because of its strong guild presence, Rouen fostered the activity and assertiveness of its guild mistresses. The proliferation of rural spinning and weaving, which gradually developed capitalist opportunities in the countryside, passed into the hands of the guildmasters who reaped added benefits from goods they certified and resold. Since Rouen's guilds had long profited from the cottage industry flourishing in the countryside, the increasing volume of international trade did not make them archaic. Rather, as the guilds acquired rural products and channeled them into foreign commerce, from the fairs of Cádiz, Caen, and Guibray to the Spanish Indies, they benefited directly from the new overseas opportunities.[2] Spanning proto-industry and global markets contributed to the guilds' importance in urban business and municipal policing. This was particularly significant for women's guilds, which flourished in the atmosphere of exclusive law and close surveillance.

A city whose skilled trades were virtually all represented in guilds, Rouen provided an envelope of toleration and encouragement for guild members' rights, and this included the privileges of guildwomen. Rouen's police and court officers were well accustomed to treating guild regulations as laws of the land and guild officials as a branch of civil law enforcement. Under these conditions, it was not surprising to find that guildwomen were taken seriously in eighteenth-century Rouen. Female guild masters who had acquired the mastership in their own right numbered some seven hundred women in 1775, approximately 10 percent of all guildmasters then in Rouen. This figure does not take into account the guildmasters' widows, who numbered another 10 percent within the men's guilds.

Of the city's 112 guilds, women participated as full-fledged masters in 8 that were involved in textile production, 1 in the grain trade, and 1 that made light metal objects. The linen drapers of new clothes (*lingères en neuf*), linen drapers of used clothes (*lingères en vieux*), makers of knitted wear (*bonnetières*), and seamstresses (*couturières*) were all-female guilds.[3]

---

2. ADSM 5E 527, Papers of the *marchhands merciers*, 1704.

3. See Clare Crowston's discussion of Colbert's influence in establishing an independent guild of seamstresses in Rouen in December 1675, *Fabricating Women: The Seamstresses of Old Regime France, 1675–1791* (Durham: Duke University Press, 2001), 193, 107.

Women also earned masterships in the mixed-sex guilds of spinners (*fillassiers*); ribbonmakers-lacemakers-fringers-decorators (*rubanières-dentellières-frangères-dorlotières*); creators of feather ornaments and religious vestments (*faiseurs des plumes-chassubliers*); grain and flour merchants (*marchands de grain*); and pin, button, and chain makers (*épingliers-boutonniers-chainetiers*). The 25 women who acquired licenses to peddle small quantities of food or sewing notions as *revendeuses* were also included in the government's list of sworn trades. Midwives (*sage-femmes*) also formed a loosely organized group that was sometimes considered a guild. In addition, records show that a handful of female workers, like Femme Coulon a mirror maker in 1711 and Marguerite Hebert a furrier in 1770, entered male guilds as daughters of masters. One can find two unmarried women selling books, three married women among the male grocers (*épiciers*), and even two wives in the mercers' guild in 1757, along with four wives in the linen-weaving *toiliers* and six among the woolen weavers. These numbers are not significant in themselves, but they invite us to evaluate male guilds' sex exclusivity in less inflexible terms.[4] In addition, the women's guilds were unusual in that they were open to individuals from outside the guild circle and that their members were married, single, and widows.[5]

The *lingères en neuf* was the most important women's guild in terms of membership and taxation, with an imposition of 1120 livres in 1750. Reputed to have had 300 masters at one time, its membership was 103 masters in 1757 and 217 in 1775.[6] As in all the women's guilds, the linen-drapers' guild structure followed the classic model of masters, journey-workers, and apprentices. The mistress *lingère* had to show that she was actively engaged in the trade, with an open workshop (*boutique ouverte*). To be permitted to establish an open workshop, the mistress must be twenty years old or married. With these conditions met, each mistress was allowed one apprentice, at least twelve years old, who spent three

---

4. ADSM 4 BP L B 1 / 4, Register of Guild Entrance. Marie Catherine Jourdain was sworn to be "capable et suffisante d'êre reçue maîtresse . . . linguière [sic], boutonnière, chaînetière . . . pur par elle jouir et l'exercer à l'avenir aussy que les autres maîtresses dud. Métier." December 1720. Register of Infractions Against Guilds, 21 July 1711. Even though married, Femme Coulon was permitted to keep her status as *fille de maître* and to work in the mirror makers' guild. For anomalies in 1757 and 1765, see ADSM C 344 and C 350, "Rôles de capitation des communautês d'arts et métiers de la ville de Rouen."

5. Steven L. Kaplan found evidence that entrance to guilds by nonrelatives of masters was more prevalent than historians have assumed. See *La Fin de Corporations* (Paris: Fayard, 2001), 215–18.

6. ADSM, *Capitation*, 1757.

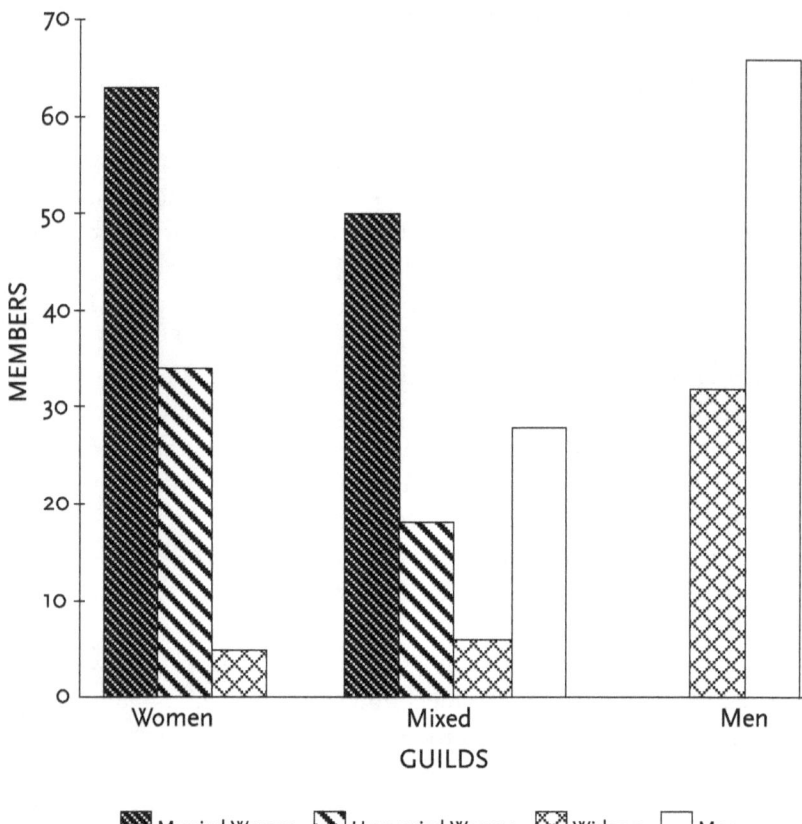

Figure 4. Composition of Rouen's guilds in 1775. All the women in guilds were counted and compared with a composite of male guilds that included apothecaries, butchers, hat makers, woolen cloth makers, *passementiers*, tailors, and dyers. The 1775 capitation tax on guilds is found in Archives départementales de la Seine Maritime, C 360.

years in training and another three as a journeywoman. To become a master, the apprentice would undertake the test of making six different kinds of goods under the eyes of the *gardes en charge:* if they approved of the work, they would swear her into the guild. The new mistress would give each of the four *gardes* 30 sous, each of the six *anciennes gardes,* 20, another 30 livres to the guild, 20 sous for the poor, and 5 sous to the *confrèrie.* In total, the entrant to the guild would pay a total of 43 livres 5 sous for her mastership. Daughters of guild mistresses received the mastership

Figure 5. In this feather merchant's shop, a worker fixes a headdress for a duke or peer and another sews an ensemble of short plumes while listening to a customer. A third worker is making a ceremonial head covering for a horse, and the last worker attaches a border of feathers to a dress. Their expensive materials and elegant clothes show that these businesswomen dealt with titled, wealthy clients. From Diderot's *Encyclopédie*, courtesy Special Collections Library, University of Michigan.

without becoming an apprentice, simply by showing their mother's letter, and paying the reduced fees of 20 sous for each of the *gardes en charge* plus 30 livres for the guild, 20 sous for the poor, and 5 sous for the *confrèrie*.[7]

Rouen's *lingères en neuf* chose officers from among their own ranks. The four *gardes*, elected by a public assembly of all the master *lingères* were charged with the duty of making four tours of inspection to check that all the guild workshops were run according to the statutes. In addition

---

7. Charles Ouin-Lacroix, *Histoire des anciens corporations d'arts et métiers* (Rouen: Lecointe Frères, 1850), 684–88, for the 1700 "Statutes of the Lingères et marchandes de toiles en gros et en détail."

Figure 6. Nail making. After cutting wire into lengths, a worker makes nail heads with one or two blows of his hammer. Using a hammer and press, a female worker then rounds off the nail heads, while another man is busy making a grill with iron or brass wire. Diderot's *Encyclopédie*, courtesy Special Collections Library, University of Michigan.

six elected *anciennes gardes,* helped with governance. Writing a century before French women received the vote, Charles Ouin-Lacroix described the scene of the election that was held every year on the Friday after Christmas as if it were an exotic exhibition. "[With] the number of sworn mistresses rising to more than two hundred, there is no doubt that the spectacle of a public assembly of this kind was quite singular [*très curieux*]. Their election, made only by a plurality of voices, often occasioned lively opposition which usually translated into the sallies and reposts that one could imagine coming from two hundred female tongues overheated by the storms of debate."[8] Despite the touch of misogyny running through these remarks, it is likely that guildswomen stepped outside the bounds of feminine gentility in their activities. The *lingères*' activities centered in the Cloth Hall (Halle aux Toiles), where they bought goods from merchants coming from outside the city, carried on the election of their

8. Ibid., 121–22.

Figure 7. A well-stocked linen-draper's shop showing bolts of cloth on the shelves and busy saleswomen. From *Encyclopédie Méthodique*, courtesy Special Collections Library, University of Michigan.

officers, held their general convocations, and shared and cut the pieces of linen they bought.[9]

These women had the responsibility not only to manage their businesses, but to work in them as well. Before a *lingère* could take up a stall in the Cloth Hall where garments and cloth were sold on Friday and Saturday, she had to have an open workshop (*boutique ouverte*), which showed that she was engaged in manufacturing. Documents show that as early as 1262, the *lingères* also held designed space in the market at the Old Tower (Vieille Tour), a building adjacent to the Cloth Hall.[10] A rental agreement drawn up on 2 September 1706, for 70 livres, reserved a space in the Old Tower to serve as a warehouse and sales center.[11] With such official consideration, the linen-drapers were able to establish themselves as important makers of shirts, bedding, underclothes, handkerchiefs, and other items of lingerie. The mistresses of this guild had the "right to sell and have manufactured all sorts of products made of linen cloth, in every

9. ADSM 5 E 511.
10. ADSM 5 E 506, "Copie de la Chartre du Roy Saint Louis du mois de Novembre 1262."
11. ADSM 5 E 511. The space included "the length of the vault where the traditional race on St. Roman's Day begins, up to the beam of the vault where the door of the Vieille Tour closes on the side of the fish market, but not including the pillars." The leasor pledged to replace "the beams in the sides of the stalls, and the leasees to take care of that the beams on the other side are maintained in good condition and to keep the area as clean as possible."

color, and to decorate the products with all sorts of linen thread, to the exclusion of all other crafts."[12] Throughout the Middle Ages, the linen-drapers continued to expand their range of processes and goods. Their monopoly, from the fifteenth century, over damask linen and cotton for table linen added to their prosperity.[13] When the king reestablished normal commerce after a sixteenth-century plague, he gave *lingères* the new right to dye their cloth themselves and to have it dyed by others. When cotton became popular in the eighteenth century, *lingères* received the right to have the cloth dyed or worked on a machine called the calendar to make a *moiré* or "watered" finish. This put Rouen's drapers of new linen in charge of the confection and coloring of goods that would be the first purchases of families with comfortable or even small incomes.

Besides these manufacturing monopolies, significant commercial privileges benefited the *lingères*. Since commerce, even more than manufacture, was the road to wealth, all guilds sought to retain the right to sell their own products and to expand their repertory of trade. These makers of sheets and fichus understood the advantages of extended commerce. Their earliest existing statutes dating to 1538 show that *lingères* were already involved in the retail and wholesale trade of linen cloth. In this capacity, they frequently clashed with the weavers of linen, the *toiliers*, a male guild that also sold linen as yard goods. The women must have sought justification for their claims by researching their sister guild of "*marchandes, maîtresses toiliers, et lingères*" in Paris, judging from the 1645 copy of the Paris bylaws found among the Rouen *lingères*' papers. In order to avoid problems and legal entanglements, the Rouen authorities tried unsuccessfully to relegate its *lingères* to retail trade and the *toiliers* to wholesale commerce. The *lingères*, however, managed to regain their right to both retail and wholesale trade of linen. Finally, conflicting decisions by both groups led the *parlement* of Normandy to make the unusual ruling in 1664 that each guild had to invite the other to sit in on their deliberations, on pain of a fine of 200 livres. In addition, the *lingères* received a monopoly on the retail and wholesale trade of cotton cloth, in all sizes, whether decorated or plain, dyed or natural, foreign or domestic.

The commercial privileges were added to others that the linen-drapers had received when the Cloth Hall was built in the sixteenth century. Their

---

12. Ouin-Lacroix, *Histoire*, 685
13. Ibid., 122.

officers had the obligation to inspect goods coming from the rural areas to be sold in Rouen. Since the cottage industry in farms and hamlets of Normandy produced a steady stream of textile products that contributed to the prosperity of Rouen and its surroundings, their place as inspectors was important. They acted in concert with the royal administration's inspectors of manufacture and had the power to enforce national standards and to authorize or to exclude goods. Under their eyes passed bleached linen, ticking, fine cloth, linen that was unbleached and tied into bales, and untied bales of cloth. Inspection meant fees, of course, and also an early chance to assess the market and buy the most saleable goods before any of the competition was allowed entrance.

The linen trade brought the *lingères en neuf* into contact with dozens of merchants, intermediaries, and country factors from the valleys around Rouen. The bustle of rural merchants carting bales of goods, some of which were organized into batches of six, others simply bound up in old sacking, added to the possibility of sharp practice. The peasant craftworkers were enjoined to make the packets and bales available for inspection and to avoid harming the public with goods packed to deceive (*fardes empaquetées*). Traders from outside Rouen called *forains* were supposed to bring their goods tied up in bundles to the "large, spacious and very commodious" Cloth Hall;[14] those bringing batiste, Hollande, muslin, Laval, linen, Bretagne, and other fine goods were specifically forbidden to expose it for sale at inns, on the street, or in a private house. Rules were also in place to prevent individuals from buying at the Cloth Hall and reselling the cloth elsewhere, or from intercepting the merchants on the pretext of encouraging them to set higher prices, or from contracting for the cloth before it reached the Hall. All in all, the linen and cotton commerce provided opportunities for gain, by fair or foul means.

The linen-drapers' trade was set aside for women; only master's daughters, not their sons or husbands, could benefit officially from their relationship. This ostensibly put into practice the clause ordering the *marchande publique* to keep her business separate from her husband's. Here the husbands were forbidden to have anything to do with their products, and especially not to become agents for their wives' cloth trade. The bylaws specifically ruled that husbands of mistresses might not buy cloth at the

---

14. ADSM C 154. The 28 June 1594 ordinance establishing covered markets in Rouen required them to have these characteristics.

Cloth Hall or in rural markets. In addition, they treated the *lingères'* widowers as the most exigent guilds behaved towards widows: the husbands were entitled to only three months to end their deceased wives' business affairs and close the shop. By contrast, the widows of linen weavers (*toiliers*) were allowed to maintain two looms provided that they had able workers.

But it is clear that the *lingères* continued to do business with unauthorized merchants and that their husbands were involved in the transactions. An article from the statutes of the Paris *lingères* paints a vivid picture of the forbidden activities.[15] The husbands were not to socialize with the country merchants, nor sit down at a tavern and eat and drink with them. We can visualize the web of sociability and business intrigue that must have arisen from cases that the *lingères'* officers brought to court. In 1664, for instance, the linen-drapers' officers obtained a successful suit against Antoine Bence and Anne de Noyon, his wife, mistress *lingère*, for having bought thirty pieces of linen cloth for resale to out-of-town merchants.[16] When Gabriel Crestien, a merchant from outside Rouen, was apprehended in 1757 for having bought cloth at the Hall and leaving it in the house of Pierre Chefderue, an intermediary trader and a baler of linen cloth who had married a mistress *lingère*, both Chefderue and his wife were fined.

In 1675, the *lingères* made an object lesson of a *toilier* named Bigault and his sister, whose array of goods included squares of linen, cotton, muslin, and ticking, all of which was bleached and unbleached or partially sized and finished. The *lingères'* seizure of these goods was validated by their winning the suit. From this case grew the specific regulation that master *toiliers* should not sell cloth they did not weave; and to prove it, they had to weave their initials into the fabric. The *toiliers* could sell their own linen goods at the Cloth Hall, their shops, or their workshops, but they were specifically forbidden to buy cloth either wholesale or retail for resale.[17]

The statutes and the legal cases that helped to create them portrayed the guilds in their full regalia of medieval craft ideals, with apprentices

15. For information on the legal status of women in Paris, see Janine Marie Lanza, *From Wife to Widow in Early Modern Paris: Gender, Economy, and the Law* (Aldershot, U.K.: Ashgate, 2006).

16. ADSM 5 E 599, "Arrest de la cour de parlement de Rouen, servant de règlement entre les marchandes lingères et tissserans en toile du 17 Novembre 1686," Rouen, 1732, 4–7.

17. Ibid., 8–11.

who became masters, workshops turning out goods that conformed to regulations, and commerce that offered exchange wholesale in its transparency. But one reason guilds were able to survive was that they had incorporated so many of the traits that early capitalism had brought to France. After all, guilds had first originated to serve the needs of an economy of scarcity, building a process that would spread resources and profits in the most equitable way. As the requirements and possibilities of business changed, nonguild workers emerged to produce cheaper products for a larger sphere of consumers. The guilds could not ignore the increasing competition or the enlarged market that was beginning to appreciate cheaper and more plentiful goods. Each guild adapted itself to the capitalism of early modern Europe in one way or another. Each clung to its statutes and national regulations, using the police apparatus to suppress competition. At the same time, guild members were incorporating into their own practice activities that their officers condemned, just as twentieth-first-century corporations praise free enterprise while at the same time they seek government favors and subsidy.

Thus the *lingères* guild presented itself as an advocate of traditional guild values, especially in commercial relations. Strict rules forbade merchants to purchase linen goods at the Cloth Hall for immediate resale. Brokers or agents of merchants were fined if they acquired goods for their own account. The products made outside Rouen had to be inspected and displayed for immediate sale, starting at five o'clock in the morning in summer and seven o'clock in winter. These regulations aimed at avoiding the price increase that would accrue if the merchandise passed through several hands. As a special privilege, Rouennais citizens who were sufficiently well-off to be classed as "bourgeois" were permitted to undertake petty sales of certain clothes (*blancards, fleurots,* and *bouves*) and even to use their own domestics or agents for the transactions, but not to set these assistants up with any "places, stands or stalls" in the Cloth Hall. These areas were for the use of the *forains* to sell their products "freely" on Friday or Saturday, or later at specified fair days, and for the *lingères* to inspect and buy. Since places in the Cloth Hall were not equally good, the *lingères* would get their assignments by lots. It was even ordered that any *lingère* must allow other members of her guild to buy sections of the cloth she bought at the Hall if they had spotted it at the same time and wanted it.[18]

18. Ouin-Lacroix, *Histoire*, 686–88.

These stringent rules to equalize opportunities for the guild mistresses and to avoid a complex mercantile system express only one aspect of guild activity. The statutes may also be read as a catalogue of behavior that was current and that seemed to undercut the original precepts of guild structure. From this viewpoint the *lingères'* caveats are a lexicon of strategies for business success. In clear exasperation, the officers went so far as to forbid any self-styled "assistant" to approach the foreign merchants under pretext of helping them to set more advantageous prices; indeed, no agent, whether male or female was to sell goods in the merchant's absence, to speak during the sale, or to do anything more than point out the houses where merchants should go to collect their money. These exaggerated instructions for a "dumb-show" had little chance of being obeyed, but the *gardes* had written them "inasmuch as it has been discovered in the past that many people meddled in the merchants' coming-and-going, in order to make themselves indispensable."[19] By the same token, other warnings also aimed at preventing current behaviors. The prohibition against "lending" the rights of guild masters signaled that *lingères* were joining others with skill or capital to facilitate new enterprises. They surely elbowed sister *lingères* out of the way in the Cloth Hall to reach for particularly handsome pieces of cloth.

Breaking the rules was not the only way that guild members were able to put new business practices to work. Guild administrations themselves also took steps to gain benefits for their members. The multiple lawsuits that made some guilds objects of derision appeared to concern only petty details; they were actually life-and-death fights for trade survival. The guilds and free craft had to be responsive to a constantly changing economic climate. Atlantic trade offered vast new markets to seventeenth- and eighteenth-century merchants. European colonies to the west and east provided exotic raw materials and the hope of new consumers. As the tempo of commerce increased, the Lowlands and England joined Italy and Germany as trading partners and competitors of France. French ports and major cities benefited financially from the triangle trade, and seventeenth- and eighteenth-century domestic markets increased in size and sophistication. Under Colbert's initiative, regulatory standards had aimed at raising French manufacture to a national level. Amassing capital and increasing business flexibility became more important than in

19. Ibid., 688, Article 27.

the past. Whether by disregarding the rules or by altering them, guilds struggled to maintain their purchase in a changing sea.

Under these new conditions, guild survival depended on four aspects of business expansion. First, the associations needed to defend their monopoly of manufacture while also trying to enlarge it. Second, it was important to keep the right to sell what they had made and to increase the kinds of commerce that they could handle to include retail and wholesale, linen and cotton, finished and unfinished. Third, the sworn trades had somehow to incorporate nonguild workers, or guild workers working outside of guild supervision and materials produced under free circumstances, into their work processes. Fourth, guilds found it expedient to separate manufacture into component parts and to use specialists to complete them.

The first category, defending and expanding the monopoly of manufacture had an official boost in the sixteenth century when the king gave the *lingères* of new cloth the right to dye fabric and have it dyed and to use a calendar to give special finishes to cloth.[20] An *arrêt de la Cour* of 31 January 1665 confirmed the *lingères'* use of woolen goods priced at 30 sous and less for linings of cloaks, hats, jerkins, jackets, and vests (*manteaux, casques et juste au corps*). On the same day they were given permission to make and sell all sorts of clothes as long as the material cost of no more than 30 sous per yard.[21] In 1697, an *arrêt du Conseil d'État* confirmed their right to dye linen and cotton.[22] The other side of the story is that with each new privilege, if it were exclusive, the guild would defend its rights by challenging anyone who seemed to be using the technique without authorization.

The second criterion, keeping the license to sell what they had manufactured and increasing their commercial rights actually ran counter to the tendency of merchant capitalism to dominate manufacturing and keep the makers of products beholden to the merchants. The medieval guild originally made and sold its own products, sacrificing the efficiency of specialization to the integrity of knowledge. This practice also kept commercial expenses to a minimum. And it allowed the original guild to

20. ADSM 5 E 508, Court case, 12 August 1753. "*Marchands merciers drapiers*" appealing a sentence of 3 February 1753.
21. ADSM 5 E 714.
22. Archives Nationales (hereafter AN) F 12 751, *Statuts et Règlements, des marchandes de toutes sorts de toiles, tant Français qu'étangeres, en gros et en détail, et Maîtresses Lingères en la ville, faubourgs, et banlieu de Rouen* (Rouen: Étienne Vincent Machuel, 1772), 10.

benefit from any small price increase the guild attached to its products for the bother of selling them. Maintaining access to the market was crucial to a guild's autonomy; without it, the guild mistresses would be reduced to working drudges, unable to defend themselves by exerting flexibility in their business dealings. Branching out to gain control of goods one did not manufacture oneself or sales in several kinds of markets was always a desired aim. The *lingères* accomplished this goal with extraordinary success when they gained the liberty to sell linen cloth wholesale and retail, in competition with the *toiliers* in 1686.[23] By curtailing the *toiliers'* incursion into the *lingères'* monopoly of selling linen cloth retail and by allowing the *lingères* to continue to sell it wholesale, the courts gave the linen-drapers the legal means to compete against the *toiliers*.

The third criterion, to find a way to incorporate nonguild workers and materials into their work processes, was built into the guild statutes.[24] The *lingères en neuf* had ready access to the linen goods brought into Rouen from the villages and farms in the countryside. They did not need to undertake the chancy role of farming out thread to rural workers and collecting the woven products themselves; instead they occupied the key position of inspectors as rural craft workers themselves carted their products to the Cloth Hall. (They were in a better position than the *passementiers* and *toiliers*, for instance, who worked in the countryside when they could find no work in town.)[25] But the pressure to expand manufacture of clothing did encourage guild members to participate in illegal cooperation with nonguild workers. Statutes prohibiting these activities reveal what else the mistresses were up to. For instance, each was forbidden to associate with anyone outside her guild or to lend her name to any other enterprise. The timeliness of the rule can be seen by the accusations on 19 July and 18 August 1703 against "la femme Lambert, living at the Basse Vieille Tour." She was found with four corselet-bodices with sleeves, some made of used silk, and six other linen garments dyed grey,

---

23. Ibid., 10. The permission was granted by an *arrêt* of the *parlement* of Rouen, serving as a *Règlement*, 17 November 1686.

24. ADSM C 148. Although one man renting a house where he stationed fourteen or fifteen looms was singled out for punishment, the *toiliers* overlooked their official limit of two looms per workshop to a number of others if they were located within the city or its suburbs. Apparently this was also the policy of the central government. In 1750 Machault overruled the punishment of depriving a weaver of his mastership and imposing a fine of 500 livres for having many looms in his atelier.

25. ADSM C 148, letter from Orry to La Bourdonnay, 3 February 1738.

red, and blue, and decorated with buttons. Two male neighbors of hers were also found displaying goods for sale and in their workshops. Officers found linen culottes, yard goods, and garments with copper and thread-covered buttons in their rooms.[26] Clearly la femme Lambert had been involved with two nonguild artisans in turning out illegal garments.[27]

The fourth step, using specialists to complete various parts of their trade, was not legalized, but here again the guild's bylaws give the clue to what was happening in the *lingères* workshops. *Lingères* were forbidden to take into their shops workers who were not part of the guild. The bylaws specifically banned their hiring any mistress *lingère en vieux*, maker of socks, *mercer*, *passementier*, dyer, ribbonmaker or lacemaker. They might not "employ any work in secret, nor buy or sell any used goods" either. It was also against the law for *lingères* to work in the shops of other guilds.[28] Judicial records show that these rules were continually broken as linen-drapers took workers from other crafts into their shops to facilitate cheaper and speedier confection, to supervise carrying out orders, and to expedite delivery.

From guild laws and court records we learn that guild members and merchants had introduced flexibility into business with illegal, but widespread, practices. Merchants were supposed to keep their pieces of unbleached linen at the Cloth Hall until they were sold. But instead they withdrew the linen écru from the stalls if it did not find ready buyers and put it out to be bleached and reexposed for sale. Each merchant and linen-draper was meant to set a distinctive mark on his or her cloth so its provenience was known, but it was common practice for noncity merchants who were well informed to "borrow a mark from a *lingère* or from another person as if the piece of cloth had been sold," thereby permitting it to be removed from the Hall.[29]

The fact that they were infringing their own statutes did not convince any guild member to lower the penalties when members of other guilds broke their rules. For this reason, the history of guilds is traced out in terms of competition and lawsuits. Each group held tightly to its monopolies as protection against outside competitors while its members themselves ignored restrictions on their own and others' trades. Thus crafts

26. ADSM 5 E 714.
27. ADSM 5 E.
28. ADSM 5 E 508, "Nouveaux statuts," *lingères en neuf*, 22 July 1700.
29. ADSM 5 E 508, Case of Sieur Vieillot, merchant in Rouen, 26 April 1760.

whose technology overlapped or whose products became indistinguishable as they responded to fashion changes were destined to be known by hostility to their antagonists as much as by their own characteristics. As we broaden our scope of investigation to include the range of guilds in which women were masters in their own right, certain clusters of trades emerge. The *lingères en neuf* and the *bonnetières en étoffes*, fought against the mercers who wanted to take over their right to sell their goods. The *lingères* and the *bonnetières* opposed each other for control of the right to make women's head coverings. The spinners who were allowed to dye as well as to spin thread clashed with the *lingères en neuf* and the male guild of dyers. There were no more hostile antagonists, though, than the two all-female guilds of linen-drapers, which dealt in such similar goods. The *lingères en neuf*, whom we have already met, concerned themselves with new linen; they bought and sold new yard goods and made new garments and bedclothes. The *lingères en vieux* had to confine themselves to dealing in used goods; like their male equivalent—the *fripiers*—they were forbidden to make or sell new items. Organized like the new linen-drapers under the patronage of Saint Barbara, their religious confraternity met at the Church of Saint Denis.[30] They were a relatively small group whose work did not bring in much revenue, with thirty-five members in 1750 and a tax of only 140 livres on their guild.[31] Despite their small number, this guild had more than its share of feisty, obstinate members who got into altercations not only with the other *lingères*, the male sellers of used clothes, and the tailors, but with the municipal and royal government as well.[32]

The *lingères en vieux* obtained many of their goods from the closets of the deceased; in fact, they had the right to inventory these clothes after a death and before any other tradesman was allowed into the house. (Did the families greet them with irritation or matter-of-factness?) The remainder of their products came from trade in used items, and this activity caught police attention. The search for used clothing took them out of Rouen, with its busy surveillance, and into hamlets and isolated marketplaces in the Normandy countryside. Like used clothing dealers

---

30. ADSM 5 E 498, The *lingères en vieux* also paid for masses on the holidays of St. Gervais and St. Paul.

31. Ouin-Lacroix, *Histoire*, 377, 385.

32. ADSM C 146, "État des maîtres et veuves de la communauté des lingères en vieil [sic]," Inquest of 1762. At their height in 1762, they numbered only forty-eight.

everywhere, they were suspected of stealing and fencing stolen goods.[33] To minimize this possibility and to ensure that they did not encroach on the market of the *lingères en neuf*, the old clothes dealers were restricted to using a special stitch for their repairs. The *lingères en neuf* used an ordinary stitch known as *"pliés"* or folded; the used clothes dealers had to sew with a stitch called *"à la taquette,"* or by angleblocks, in order to distinguish their products from those of the other *lingères*. The technique of the *lingères en vieux* required much more arduous work as the needle had to go back and forth several times in contrast to the simple overcast stitch of the *lingères en neuf*.

But even this expedient was not a foolproof way to keep the *lingères en vieux* from selling new garments, as an important lawsuit from 1751 indicates. The decription of the trial that follows documents the testimony for both sides, the *lingères en vieux* and the *lingères en neuf*. It is an example of the vigorous self-promotion found across the classes whenever economic disputes occurred.[34]

On 20 February 1751 the officers of new linen brought Femme Nicolle, *lingère en vieux*, before the lieutenant of police, claiming that in her stall in the Cloth Hall she had five men's shirts of thick gray new linen with collars and one with linen cuffs, another with flax, and that she also had sold three new women's shirts of gray linen and flax. The officers of the new linen-drapers complained that not even the many judgments they had obtained against these rivals "had made it possible to stop the old clothes dealers from squeezing into the trade of new goods—even with their restriction to sell only used goods, that is, [garments] which are used and gotten rid of, which they had to sew *à la tacquette*. . . . But Femme Nicolle's shirts were not like this, they were new and sewn *'à l'ordinaire.'"* The *lingères en vieux* were using a big subterfuge by claiming that "they had just refreshed or washed and boiled the shirts in question."

Another old clothes seller, Femme Bunel, had used this artifice without success, the new linen-drapers continued, and her merchandise had been confiscated. Femme Nicolle could not excuse herself by pointing to the fact that the shirts were of coarse linen, because she had been caught using the new linen products in the past. It was important to curb "this ruse which will bring the whole guild of new linen-drapers to destruction."

33. ADSM C 146, letter de Crosne to Tolozan, 6 March 1785.
34. ADSM 5 E 508. The entire transcript and papers of the trial are found in this box.

The used clothes dealers reposted that "since they pay their taxes and were permitted by the king to ply their trade, they should be able to carry it on with tranquility." But instead of this, the new linen officers had come into the Old Tower, ferreting out merchandise among the stalls, but found no new goods. So they approached Femme Nicolle, who had eight linen shirts packaged up, with their queues and heads [properly marked], after having been purchased, and challenged her to prove that the shirts had been given to her in a dirty condition.

The *lingères en vieux* said they were not trying to use Bunel's case as precedent: that was a clear contravention of the rules, since her shirts were new and had never been washed and another part of her merchandise was certainly new. No, the action on the part of the new linen guards was nothing but "a pure vexation" caused by envy (*"lanvie"*).

The *lingères en neuf* replied that "the old clothes sellers have a lot of nerve [*il y a de la témerité*] to insist on an inspection of the shirts in question... since everybody who casts an eye on the state of the cloth and the seams would be convinced that they are new. The *lingères en vieux* were trying to argue captiously and with cunning that the shirts were dirty before they were washed."

Femme Nicolle and her husband excused themselves from testifying "saying, it was a scandal to name publicly the persons who had sold their shirts out of necessity." Upon hearing this excuse, their opponents jeered that it must have been quite a coincidence to find a man and a woman in the same financial straits at once. And what about the seams, which were not sewn *à la taquette?* Femme Nicolle replied that the seams were not *taquette* because the shirt was already made up when she bought it. One is not obliged to examine how a shirt is made when buying it used and already washed, she said.

Their ingenious arguments did not convince the judges, however, and the *lingères en vieux* lost the case. Femme Nicolle was assessed a relatively mild fine of 20 livres, with a warning that another contravention would cost more. Dame Montmiery, *ancien garde contable* paid the expenses of the case, 112 livres, 17 sous, 8 deniers, for the *lingères en veux*.[35]

---

35. ADSM 5 E 508. The judges agreed that a verdict against the *lingères en vieux* was one way "to prevent the impunity of those who steal and facilitate the fencing of stolen goods which can certainly be sold with the assurance of the *vielles lingères* without discovery when they make no mention of the name of their supplier."

This case shows something of the way the courts became a platform for sorting out guild precedents. With each clash of interests, a dramatic struggle ensued in which the protagonists had the floor to justify their suit with exaggerated reasonableness, scorn, precedent, puffed up vulnerability, and declarations of innocence. Although the statutes imposed separations between rival guilds, guild members inevitably took the underground route to expand their businesses. The pressure to branch out into another guild's product or process put the effectiveness of the regulations into question. Moreover, the guildwomen who took part in these theatrical displays expanded their range of activity into yet another arena of the public sphere. From their home ateliers to the Cloth Hall where they inspected, bought and sold linen; then for more business to the Old Tower, and even further to the courtrooms, and finally to the impressive high-ceilinged court of last local appeal in the *parlement* of Rouen. As with male guilds, the mistresses' officers turned the city's streets into their "police round" just as they laid claim to particular chapels in parish churches or in the cathedral to house their confraternities. The guild mistresses employed the same arguments the male guild members used to win court cases. They also asserted the claims of priority of time, accuracy of category, and appeals to natural rights, which Michael Sonenscher attributed to male guilds.[36]

All the guilds were ready to use their public testimony in as convincing a way as possible. But the old clothes sellers carried their assertive stance into other questions as well. In 1769 the king imposed on every guild the responsibility to provide and outfit soldiers, the numbers to be based on each guild's size and wealth. This was not an unusual procedure. Early in the eighteenth century, the *lingères en neuf* had received a royal request for twelve soldiers. In 1702 they paid 600 livres for the soldiers and 1,300 livres to outfit them.[37] But in 1769, both sets of *lingères* prepared to resist this tax with unique rhetoric. In discussions of women's guilds earlier in this chapter I have taken pains to show how similar they

---

36. Michael Sonenscher, *Work and Wages: Natural Law, Politics and the Eighteenth Century French Trades* (Cambridge: Cambridge University Press, 1993), esp. 55–61. Sonenscher commented that in guild legislation, "Precedent, difference and appeals to natural rights could all be invoked to demonstrate that rights that appeared to have been sanctioned were, in fact, inappropriate, irrelevant or illegal" (61). See also Daryl M. Hafter, "Female Masters in the Ribbonmaking Guild of Eighteenth-Century Rouen," *French Historical Studies* 20, no. 1 (winter 1997): 8–11.

37. ADSM 5 E 508, Guild accounts, 1702.

were to male guilds. The guildwomen shared their male colleagues' assumptions and benefited from being treated as guild members rather than as women who happened to be workers. They traded on the phraseology that male guilds used. But the guildwomen had another string to their bow that they employed when it seemed appropriate: casting themselves as poor females who deserved different treatment because of their woman's nature.[38]

Accordingly, both sets of linen-drapers demurred from paying the tax for a *"milicien"* because their groups were made up entirely of women, and so, they claimed, this call had nothing to do with them. They argued that the tax was really a substitute for serving in the army. Guilds with males could either offer one of their journeymen or apprentices or pay for a proxy to fill the role. But because women's guilds were by definition ineligible to send one of their number into the ranks, it was senseless to levy a payment on them. By 1771, tax collectors were able to convince the *lingères en neuf* to reverse their strategy; they paid three men to serve in the army for two years and nine months, at the rate of 1 livre per month.[39] The *lingères en vieux*, however, remained obstinate. Perhaps they were encouraged by the intransigence of the spinners who refused to pay 550 livres for one soldier, offering instead to pay 150 livres to show their good will.[40]

When the mayor and aldermen told the linen-drapers of old clothes to join other guilds in taking a census of their masters and journeymen (*garçons, ouvriers, servants*) to ascertain how many soldiers each could support, the *lingères en vieux* replied with a unanimous motion that counting male workers was irrelevant (*"pas dans le cas"*). In a general meeting of the guild held at eight o'clock on a January morning in 1777, Dame de Laplanche[41] suggested that the guild should refuse to pay the

---

38. Crowston shows how arguments from modesty helped justify a separate guild for seamstresses, *Fabricating*, 191.

39. ADSM 5 E 508, Guild accounts. The *lingères en neuf* subsequently agreed to pay him 8 sous a day and 200 livres after six months of service. But they offered only 100 livres to his heirs if he were killed in action (ADSM C 137). By 1766, the *rubanières* pledged to support one *milicien*. The *marchands merciers*, fifteen; the *boursiers-gantiers-platriers-couveurs, charrons, talonniers*, one; the *perreuquiers* and *chaudronniers*, two.

40. ADSM 5 E 499. Minutes of guild meeting.

41. ADSM 5 E 497. Widow de Laplanche, as she was called, was a prominent leader in guild affairs. She was spokesperson for a group of guild voters in their 9 January 1773 general assembly. She was a trusted *garde* named to oversee the opening of the coffer in 1776 and was a guild officer again in 1778. See *"Recette, Lingères en vieux,"* 1778.

royal subscription for the soldier "under some pretext" and that the *gardes* should deliver the transcript of this meeting to the city hall. Two years later, Nicholas Laurent Naval, bailiff to the guild, appeared at their meeting and told them that they must contribute to the fund for a soldier. Once again Madame de Laplanche balked, declaring that she was "of the opinion that this guild should make no contribution except for those who are able to be chosen from a "blind" drawing to satisfy the ordinances of the king." (Qu'elle c'est d'avais que la communauté ne fera aucun abonnement sauf a ceux qui sont dans le cas de tire au sort à satisfaire aux ordonnaces du roy [sic].) Since the all-female guild had no males who could be chosen, it ought to be exempt from the tax. Not only did she appear to question the right of the civic officers to collect the money, she again urged that the guild should authorize its officers to register this decision at the city hall, putting it, so to say, under the noses of the municipal officials.[42]

What made the old clothes sellers oppose the financial levy for a soldier? And why did they hold out against making the payment for so long? Did the exigencies of their profession have something to do with their attitude? Had they learned to be tough as they searched for used clothing outside of Rouen? Or had the authorities' suspicions that they dealt in stolen goods soured them against cooperating? Municipal politics may have played part in this dispute, encouraging the guildwomen to discredit the mayor and aldermen.[43] The social standing of some of the women surely placed them in the higher brackets of non-noble status and may have encouraged them to be obstinate. Documents tell us that a number of their guild officers were married to men of "quality." In 1702, Margureite Brehaine was the wife of Henri Aubin, commissioner of gabelles, and Anne Elisabeth Jean was the wife of Sieur Cauchois, master plasterer and bourgeois. In 1759, Dame Marie Catherine Boisleau was widow of Claude Bernard Le Rat, dean of bailiffs in the court of accounts, indirect taxes, and finances of Normandy, and Dame Marie Genneviève Manger was married to Sieur Jacques Charles Grave, master surgeon in Rouen. In 1764, Dame Marie Anne Jorre was the wife of Master Pierre Francois Geffroy, royal attorney of the *parlement* of Rouen. In 1770, a marriage was celebrated between a mistress *lingères en vieux* and Louis Sabastien

---

42. ADSM 5 E 499. Minutes of guild meeting.
43. ADSM 5 E 499. Minutes of guild meeting, 13 February 1779.

Cousin, regular bailiff of the king. Another *lingère* married Francois Nee, merchant mercer.[44] It is not surprising to find in these circles that the linen-drapers had a relatively high degree of literacy. From five-sixths to two-thirds of the women signed their name at guild meetings where very lively discussions took place. Most of these linen-drapers were married, and perhaps this provided a secure financial basis that encouraged their assertiveness.[45] But there must also have been individuals among the *lingères en vieux* with exceptional self-confidence and feisty personalities that led them to take provocative, independent positions.

The third guild composed entirely of women was the makers of cloth head coverings and knitters, embroiderers, and hat decorators (*bonnetières en étoffes-brodeuses en tavelle-enjoliveuses des chefs-frets*), who made hats from cloth and knitting, embroidered with a mechanical device, and embellished head coverings, as their name suggests. The 1762 guild survey listed them as having 179 female members, the 1775 tax rolls assessed their *capitations* at 500 livres. The guild did not have a separate confraternity but was associated with the one at Notre Dame de Recouvrance, run by the Carmelites.[46]

This all-female guild of knitters had early stepped out of the interminable litigation carried on by the other two guilds involved in knitting, the male guilds of manufacturers of knitware (*bonnetiers fabricants*) and the merchants of knitware (*marchands bonnetiers*).[47] In sorting out particular technologies to differentiate the guilds, the women were assigned knitting by hand, the men, knitting by hand or with mechanical knitting frames.[48] Here we have a classic example of female workers being

---

44. ADSM C 154. Through the entire century a struggle between the mayor and alderman and the royal lieutenant of police plagued Rouen's administration of guilds. In 1707, 1747, and 1781, officials tried to lay it to rest by giving the lieutenant of police the jurisdiction over the induction of guild officers, examination of the masterpiece, and the swearing in of masters in manufacturing guilds alone. The city officials were supposed to judge questions about the actual technique and products, as well as to verify the guilds' account registers. See *arrêt du conseil* of 21 March 1747, edict of February 1778, and letter to Tolozan, 14 April 1781.

45. ADSM 5 E 506.

46. ADSM 5 E 598, Register of Accounts. In 1770, the guild totaled 21 wives, 4 widows, and 9 single women.

47. ADSM 5 E 598, "État de ses Revenus," "État de ses Charges," 1762 survey. Since the guild did not have its own confraternity, it had no banquet.

48. ADSM C 137, letter to Tolozan, 12 May 1774. To settle the litigation, officials assigned particular rules for manufacture and commerce to the two guilds. The *marchands bonnetiers* sold goods made on the machine or by hand, but they could only manufacture goods by hand, although they were permitted to decorate goods. The *fabricants de bas* knitted by machine.

restricted to an older technique while their male counterparts progressed to the advantages of machine work. But their experience afterwards shows how inaccurate it would be to let that fact alone signify their economic decline. The women made up for their technical disadvantage by expanding horizontally to include hat making with cloth, embroidering with a tavelle machine, and decorating women's head coverings. These industrial functions became the bailiwick they defended as their monopolies both in manufacture and sales, fulfilling two of the criteria for guild survival. They had also managed to lay their control on a wide range of costly decorative materials from well before their published bylaws in 1449. More remarkably, they used arguments based on three categories—craft process, body location, and product—to assert their monopolies.

Their widest latitude came from their right to manufacture items that covered the head, ears, and necks of women and girls. On the basis of their products for women's heads, they claimed exclusive rights, even to

Figure 8. Artificial-pearl makers. In this all-female workshop, a young woman harvests fish scales for coloring and dissolves them in a liquid that others suck into pipettes, afterward introducing a drop into the artificial pearl. One worker puts a tiny roll of papier-mâché into the pearl and another cuts off the paper with a knife. Women workers were praised for their ability to accomplish painstaking tasks like these. From Diderot's *Encyclopédie,* courtesy Special Collections Library, University of Michigan.

the exclusion of barbers and wigmakers, to furnish all sorts of additions to the hair. This included buying hair from "all sorts of persons" in the city or outside and reselling hairpieces to others in their guild. Over the furriers' objections the *enjoliveuses* won the right to attach fur pieces to hats. They made a wide variety of hats, in fur as well as silk, gold or silver cloth, velour, wool, and waxed or unwaxed linen. Their experience with fur led them to make and sell purses, game bags, and ladies' tote bags. They catered to women, children, and men, creating toques and mortarboard for judges and special head coverings for clerics. They also made every sort of decoration for hats, from bushy toppings and tufts for casques, to feathered fringes and artificial flowers for women's bonnets. Their involvement with women's garments justified their right to decorate trousseaus. The range of expensive goods they considered exclusively theirs to use included satin, velour, cloth of gold, silk, or wool and decorations of ribbons, lace, pearls, sequins, gold, silver, silk, buttons, and boutonnières.

For this range of decoration, the *bonnetières* used specialized tools. Presses, needles, and devices to attach rivets were crucial for embellishing the surface of their goods. They made lace with bobbins, on the pillow, and with their fingers. They also had two more complex tools: the *machine à tavelle* for embroidery—an early sewing machine that resembles the device used today to stitch up mesh bags for potatoes and flour—and the high warp loom (*métier à tisser haute lisse*) to apply tapestry technique to decorative bands. To create the extravagant traditional hats worn by the countrywomen of Normandy, they had devices to manipulate and to cover iron wire with cloth and thread.

Not only did this guild exert control over a wide range of lucrative techniques and products, they also managed to make themselves indispensable to other guilds for help in finishing products. Hat makers in Rouen were obliged to employ the embroiderers to decorate any kind of band on their headgear, although the *chapeliers* might decorate the body of the hats themselves. Shoe makers also deferred to the embroiderers who added decoration of silk figures, pearls, or sequins to footwear. To this involvement in working with leather, the women added the right to make elaborate book covers. Thus, while other guilds forbade workers from outside their association to enter their workshops, the *bonnetières en étoffes-brodeuses en tavelle-enjoliveuses des chefs-frets* saw to it that other guilds were forced to hire its members. They enacted the sort of specialized work discipline that Michael Sonenscher and Steven L. Kaplan discovered in

Paris, except that in this case, the products stayed in one workshop and the skilled workers came to them, rather than being farmed out to craft workers in their own ateliers.

By amalgamating the hat makers, embroiders, and specialists in hat decoration in one guild, the *bonnetières* integrated their trade. Their success in enabling their own workers to visit the workshops of shoe makers and hat makers provided another source of income and kept the hat decorators' skills in their own guilds. These were legal provisions that the guilds' officers had established to enhance the position of the knitters' guild, but they also facilitated efficient manufacturing.

Pressure to gain more workers, whether in legal or illegal ways was also present. The statutes limited all masters in the *bonnetières*' guild to only one *"apprentisse"* at a time, who would be *"nourrie, couché, levée, et blanchée"* (fed, housed, reared, and her clothing laundered). But in an unusual provision that Steven L. Kaplan calls entrance by experience or by *"suffisance,"* the knitters' bylaws allowed trained women from outside Rouen to enter the guild either by making a masterpiece or by taking the oath of loyalty, and paying double the usual entrance fees. By 1709, evidence suggests that the officers may have tried to keep these outsiders as permanent day workers. Guild officers were specifically forbidden to use trickery to prevent apprentices from becoming masters. "It is understood," the rules declared, "that if the *gardes* give the apprentices a masterpiece that is too difficult or if they refuse unjustly [to install] her, justice will prevail." The guild masters must have tried to lay their hands on additional workers by every means, for the statutes spell out in exceptional detail what they are forbidden to do. Masters should not take on nonguild workers. Masters were not to suborn one another's apprentices. And if two masters shared a house, they were permitted to have only apprentice between them.[49]

Four all-women's guilds among 112 such associations; some 539 guildwomen governing themselves, using the court system to defend their rights and intrude on the prerogatives of others; 28 women officers charged with making inspections, handling funds, apprehending illegal workers, charting a course that was alert to threats and vigilant in seizing advantages—how significant was this minority in eighteenth-century

---

49. Ouin-Lacroix, *Histoire*, 580–84, "Statuts des brodeuses en tavelle, bonnetières en étoffees, enjoliveuses des chefs-frets et autres ouvrages," 1709, citation p. 583.

Rouen? They occupied the peaks of a large mass of women workers located throughout the industrial sector. Unlike the great majority of women and men, they had the standing to receive the government's respect and compliance. Equals in the law to their male equivalents, guild mistresses in Rouen challenged every trespass they perceived on the same terms as the men did. They accustomed the inhabitants of Rouen to dealing with privileged working women; in this part of France, a women worker could not automatically be classified as a downtrodden drudge or an illegal interloper. In the bustle of business activities, women were everywhere in the city, and some might exact fast retribution if they believed they were mistreated.

More guildwomen were associated with men in the five guilds of mixed-sex membership. These organizations ran the gamut between the spinners, a guild with few men and even fewer male officers, and the seamstresses, once a separate association but later dominated by the tailors. The spinners were some 58 persons, paying 214 livres in the *capitation* of 1775; the 99 *couturières* paid 299 livres. Besides these organizations, women were members of the embroiders of church vestments' guild (*brodeurs-chasubliers*), the pin makers' guild (*épingliers*), the butchers' guild, and the grain merchants' guild. Without the good fortune of their Parisian counterparts, the *couturières* of Rouen were subsumed into the tailors' guild, where they competed with the tailors' wives for employment.

Rouen's most important mixed-sex guild was the ribbonmakers-fringe-makers-lacemakers (*rubanières-frangères-dentellières-dorlotières-lacetières*), who claimed to have established their regulations in 1292. Their subsequent statutes grew out of their struggle against the sixteenth-century attack of the *bonnetières-enjoliveuses* who claimed the exclusive right to furnish women's fancy goods. The ribbonmakers successfully defended themselves and sustained their privilege of selling fringe, ribbons, and lace. In 1750 they numbered some 80 individuals; in 1770, there were 140 with an assessed tax of 949 livres.[50]

The ribbonmakers' statutes gave them the privilege of manufacturing and selling products for women's adornments and also selling materials that figured in their production. But they were not permitted to make thread, except for a small amount for their personal use. Their involvement with thread brought them into conflict with the spinners since they

---

50. Ouin-Lacroix, *Histoire*, 123; for 1770 figures, see ADSM C 355, *Capitation*.

were apparently allowed to have some of the same tools that the spinners used. This ambiguity must have provoked the authorities, as we see in a seventeenth-century example. In 1660, Pierre Regnard and his wife, ribbonmakers, lodged a successful complaint against guild officers who had "maliciously . . . thrown their machines used for adding luster to thread [esquilles] into the street."[51]

Although one-third of the ribbonmakers were male, their officers were women in the eighteenth century. By the same token, if we examine the origin of children of masters and mistresses entering the guild, about one-third of them had fathers who were masters, and two-thirds owed their entrance to their mother's masterships. Privileges for the spouses of masters were also evenhanded, as both widows and widowers were allowed to keep their shops open after the death of their spouse. The value of this opportunity is underscored by the fact that guild members could sell the kinds of materials they used for their own manufactures in wholesale and retail trade.[52] In addition, they could deal in items made by others, as long as the materials used were among those the ribbonmakers themselves employed. These entitlements helped them to manufacture goods necessary for fashionable clothes and interior home furnishings, as well as to commission their manufactures in locations outside of their workshops.

As a mixed-sex guild, the spinners had included male and female masters from their earliest statutes in 1309. The 1736 statutes required male apprentices to be taught by male masters and female apprentices, by mistresses. Of the four officers, two were to be female and two male. If there were not enough male candidates among them, the female spinners were to choose from among themselves, and in this case the men were forbidden to stand among them in an attempt to exert influence.

The entire guild assembled a week before the Thursday of Mardi Gras week and chose two officers by a plurality of votes. Lest we be misled into thinking that this was an orderly process, we learn further from the regulations that a rotating advisory council of sixteen was also chosen on election day, so that the general assembly of all guild masters did not have to be called into session for ordinary guild affairs. When the sixty or so master spinners gathered, there was "tumult and confusion"; indeed, the day they picked for having elections and passing on the money box

51. ADSM 5 E 457.
52. ADSM 5 E 603, "Mémoire pour les maîtres et gardes . . . rubanières," Articles 12, 14.

of the confederation, Jeudy Gras, was notorious for its noise and public celebration.⁵³ Their confederation, dedicated to Saint Anne, met in the cathedral and celebrated mass there on Jeudy Gras. One can easily imagine the festivities erupting into the large square facing the cathedral, one of the few open spaces in the city. To cover the expenses for one year's celebration, the spinners paid 4 livres for posters advertising their Te Deum, 4 livres for the *tapissier*, 3 livres for the *musicians* who played their instruments, and 2 livres, 4 sous for the drummers.⁵⁴

Given that spinning was so widespread, nonguild workers and thread must have appeared in the workshops and boutiques of many guild members. A four-year term of apprenticeship and limitation to one apprentice at a time (except for the last six months of the old apprentice's term when the next one could be started) set in place restrictions to the guild's permanent ranks. But the spinners had considerable leeway to purchase thread either at the Cloth Hall or at markets anywhere in the vicinity, and they were permitted to buy material for their own use or for resale. In addition, they were entitled to hire "all and as many male and female journeyworkers as they needed to accommodate their commerce, as long as they are in the guild."⁵⁵

From the early days their product included spun flax from which ship cordage and sails were made. They also produced cords, rope, and spun linen thread for clothing and table furnishings. The seventeenth century saw this guild spin silk thread for use by weavers, *passementiers*, and button makers; the eighteenth, cotton thread for the newly popular light fabrics. Moreover, on 4 August 1671, the spinners won the right to dye thread, as well as to spin and sell it.⁵⁶ This process brought so large a part of their profits that they began calling themselves the guild of the "*marchands et marchandes filassières teinturières en touttes couleurs*" [sic] (male and female merchants, female spinners and dyers of all colors).⁵⁷ Their statutes limited their dying to thread "used in their commerce only." To

---

53. ADSM 5 E 457, Statutes, 1736, "Sire, La Communauté des maîtresses, marchands et marchandes, Filaciers en couleurs en blanc et demiblanc de toutes façons de la ville, faubourgs et banlieu de Rouen."
54. ADSM 5 E 463, Account Book, "Mise dudit Nicolas Campion suivant ses quittances."
55. ADSM 5 E 457, Statutes, 1736, "Ils pourront prendre tous et autant de compagnons ouvriers et ouvrières dont ils auront besoin pour la facilité de leur commerce pourvue qu'ils soient de la jurande au dit mestre."
56. ADSM 5 E 455, "Arrêt qui accorde aux filassières la qualité de teinturière."
57. ADSM C 144, Account Book, "Compte que rend à la communauté."

prevent them from competing with the guild of dyers, the spinners were forbidden to color thread belonging to other individuals or to offer their dyeing skills to the public.[58] With this careful regulation, officials extended a hand to help the spinners expand their industrial possibilities while trying not to threaten the survival of the dyers' guild.

Maintaining the integrity of the corporate system and at the same time awarding various guilds scope for new enterprise was a challenge for the municipal and royal officials in charge of economic affairs. They had to deal with the guilds' efforts to increase their industrial and commercial reach in the prosperous era after the death of Louis XIV in 1715 while protecting their privileged monopolies. The most destabilizing influence came from the actions of the powerful *marchands merciers* who tried to increase their business throughout France during the 1730s and 1740s. The largest and wealthiest guild in most cities, usually among the prestigious Six Great Corps, the merchant mercers were originally confined to trading in the class of goods known as "findings."[59] These goods consisted of a wide variety of sewing notions and haberdashery that included silver buckles, aprons, thimbles, snuffboxes, and other "indispensables." Selling small items that others had made, however, had limited profitability. The mercers' ambitions and their access to funds encouraged them to expand into manufacturing and additional commerce. Early in the eighteenth century the Rouennais mercers incorporated the drapers into their guild.[60] Although the woolen cloth that the drapers wove no longer dominated the market as it had in the late Middle Ages and the Renaissance, it did swell the guild membership to some four hundred members. In addition, they added the wholesale merchants (*grossiers*) and jewelers to become the "*marchands merciers drapiers grossiers jouilliers de la ville de Rouen.*"[61] From this base of support, the mercers

---

58. ADSM 5 E 457, Statutes, 1736, Article 27.

59. *Almanach Royal*, 1775. In Rouen, the Six Great Guilds that formed the upper tier of guild associations were the *drapiers, apoticaires-épiciers, merciers, pelletiers, bonnetiers, orfèvres*. The *marchands de vins* were sometimes included in this group.

60. To stop the disputes over woolen sales in Paris, an aborted proposal was made in 1680 for the drapers to absorb the merchant mercers. They remained competitors until consolidated in 1776. Carolyn Sargentson, *Merchants and Luxury Markets: The Marchands Merciers of Eighteenth-Century Paris* (London: Victoria and Albert Museum, 1996), 13.

61. ADSM 5 E 603, "Factum, pour les marchands merciers, grossiers, jouailliers ... demandeurs et défendeurs contre Charles-César Leroux se distant batteur d'or à Rouen, défendeur et demandeur, en laquelle instance est encore partie Jacques Laigle aussi marchand mercier à Rouen."

launched a campaign to take over the commerce of many other guilds in Rouen, as they seem to have been doing elsewhere.

It was a struggle that ran into obstacles. The first third of the century saw the mercers successfully maintaining their role as merchants for beaten gold leaf but losing their sally at taking over exclusive sales of glassware, bottles, vials, porcelains, and faience ware;[62] cards; wholesale linen; and goods belonging to the *apoticaires-épiciers* and the *épiciers-ciriers*.[63] They based their claims on Article 14 of their statutes, which declared they could trade in the items specifically spelled out as permitted "and generally all the other sorts and kinds of merchandise."[64] By the 1740s, increasing commerce, especially in the realm of fabrics, encouraged the mercers to make a grandstand play at expanding their trade to include all the products made in Rouen. They circulated tracts arguing that they alone knew how to animate the trade that enabled France to find foreign buyers, keep the artisans employed, and provide access to international markets with their complicated treaties and standards.[65]

A general lobby of smaller guilds opposed the mercers' pretensions with memoirs, petitions, and countersuits. The smaller guilds knew that this was a battle they had to win. If the mercers had been able to take away the guilds' right to sell their own produce, their independence would have ended. In the words of the ribbonmakers, they would fall into the category of "simple wage-earning laborers, product makers, or might we say, drones [*l'état de simples fabricantes*]."[66] We can imagine the deprivations such a state would bring to the manufacturing guilds. Gone would be the guild masters' ownership of the mysteries of the craft; gone the integrity of the family atelier with its hierarchy of age and skill. No longer would the guild benefit from extra privileges, like selling raw materials

---

62. ADSM 5 E 603, *Mémoire sommaire pour les maîtres et gardes merciers de la ville de Rouen, intimés en apel, contre les maîtres et gardes fayanciers* . . . (Rouen: Viret, 1739).

63. ADSM 5 E 603, *Mémoire pour les marchands merciers-drapiers unis* . . . *contre les maîtres apoticaires-épiciers, et les maîtres épiciers,-ciriers* (Rouen: Charles Osmont, [1730]).

64. ADSM 5 E 603, "Factum, pour les marchands merciers." The original reads "et généralemente toutes autres sortes et especes de Marchandise."

65. ADSM 5 E 603, *Observations importantes sure le commerce, une des plus precieuse parties de l'état avec un strait des statuts, arrests, et réglements, qui prouvent que les marchandes merciers-grossiers-jouaillers, sont seuls, capables de l'entretenir dans l'interieur et dehors le Royaume, et d'en procurer au public les grands advantages* . . . (original spelling) (Paris: Mesnier, 1735).

66. ADSM 5 E 603, "Mémoire pour les maitresses et gardes de la communauté des marchandes rubanières-dentellières-frangères-dorlotières-et lacetières . . . contre les maîtres et gardes de la communauté des marchandes merciers-drapiers et corps-unis . . ." (original spelling) [1762].

they used in their goods or buying items made outside the guild for resale. The mercers would be able to act as factors, providing workers with raw materials and tools, setting the standards for goods, and determining their wages. One had only to look at what was happening in Lyon to the silk masters, as the silk merchants began to occupy the workers' only link to the market. There the master weavers were sinking into the role of a proletariat as the master merchants streamlined the business in response to the opportunities of merchant capitalism.

Although written later, the ribbonmakers' condemnation of the mercers graphically expressed their intentions in the 1740s. The marchands merciers, "displeased with the competition useful to the public, repeatedly make new efforts to shut off the commerce of the other guilds.... The right that they have to sell all kinds of merchandise is not at all wide enough for them. Envious to appropriate all the trade for themselves, they wish to reduce the other guilds to the state of simple workers."[67] Both the merchant mercers and their opponents perfectly understood the sort of guild reconfiguration needed to survive in the brisk, commercial world of the midcentury, which pressed merchants to measure profit and loss with new acuity. Those who controlled access to the market could wield more exacting controls over the productive units in the economy, while they profited from their experience as go-betweens to manipulate style, price, and preservation. This is why the *lingères en neuf* went to court to safeguard their right to sell linen fabric in competition with the *toiliers*. This was the motive for the *bonnetières'* expansion over not only the sale of ornaments for women's heads, but also their shoulders and necks. Or the ribbonmakers' privilege of trading in the raw materials they used, as well as every sort of ribbon, band, lace, and shoe lacing that could be imagined. Or the spinners' permission to dye and sell thread in every color and material composition.

Objections to the mercers' pretensions came to a crescendo when the mercers took steps to institute new statutes permitting their increased scope for sales. In an unprecedented political effort, twenty-seven of Rouen's guilds joined in one lawsuit in 1742, to oppose the mercers. (The authorities encouraged them to concentrate their complaints for the sake

67. Ibid., The merchant mercers' guild "en est toujours qui, fâchés d'une concurrence utile au public, font à chaque instant de nouveaux efforts pour anéantir le commerce des autres Communautés. . . . Le droit qu'ils ont de vendre toute espèce de marchandise n'est point pour eux un droit assez étendu. Envieux de s'approprier tout de commerce, ils voudroient réduire à l'état de simples fabricants les autres corps de métier."

of minimizing court costs, saying that "if the mercers replied to each one, there would be as many law cases as guilds in the town.") Trades as varied as tinsmiths, wigmakers-barbers, spinners, embroiderers, linen-drapers, knitters, scale makers, kettle makers, sword cutlers, rope makers, and knifesmiths took part, without any distinctions between guilds with women members or without. The mercers, for their part, bridled at articles in sixteenth- and seventeenth-century statutes with which the separate corporations tried to discredit them. When presented with clauses that allowed the manufacturing guilds to sell everything they made, the mercers sputtered that such a regulation was "ridiculous, since the merchant mercers could then sell nothing! For if each merchant and each artisan took back from the merchant mercers the right to sell in retail market the works belonging to this trade and their manufacture [*de sa dependence ou de sa fabrique*], nothing but the name of the [mercers'] guild would remain. They would have to shut their shops" because wholesale trade alone would give them so little recompense that they would "be forced to become slaves."[68]

Officials in all branches of administration took note of this exceptional shared lawsuit that stood out as a defining episode in guild history. M. Brunel, the king's chief attorney, made the point that a great deal of work had gone into the framing of arguments and claims, not only on the part of the opposing corporations but from the other bodies of crafts and artisans in the city. The royal Conseil d'État itself had worked on it as well as the Bureau of Commerce, preparing materials for the chancellor's judgment on the new *letters patentes* (licensing letters) that the mercers requested from the royal court. Accordingly, the guild masters understood that the new statutes spelling out the relation between the mercers and the manufacturing guilds would determine the fate of Rouen's crafts. Would the rules protect the integrity of the various contemporary associations, allowing them to trade as well as to manufacture goods? Or would the mercers gain the upper hand and become the commercial cartel that called the tune for the craft workers?[69]

In the end, the administration opted for a characteristically balanced regime that protected the craft guilds' access to trade as well as the mercers'

68. ADSM 5 E 607, Manuscript with commentary on Article 9 of their statutes, "Il faut renvoyer à M. Bourdonnaye."
69. Ibid., Comments on Article 13 providing the mercers' goods were to be inspected by *bonnetiers, drapiers-drapans, épiciers, orfebvres, fourbisseurs,* and *cordiers.*

need to be involved in commerce. All guilds were entitled to buy raw materials at first hand without passing them through the mercers' hands. Contrary to the provocative claims of the ribbonmakers for having the right, as an older body, to inspect the mercers' boutiques during normal trade and even at fairs, officials ruled that the mercers were to have control over inspections of their own goods, with a few exceptions. Officials also turned down the conservative request that all guilds should be forbidden "to sell, have sold, or expose for sale any merchandise unless it was made by themselves, their servants, or domestics in this city."[70] The government chose provisions that would foster the greatest competition without destabilizing the welfare of the variety of crafts. Rouen's businesses would be able to maintain their artisanal posture uniting manufacturing and sale under one roof. On the other hand, the officials' relaxed attitude toward goods that were subcontracted, or those made by servants and domestics, shows that they knew the guilds were not making each object, from start to finish, in their own ateliers and that they wanted to encourage that sort of production. As with the guilds, the government wanted to have the advantages of control and innovation at the same time. The administrators' stance allowed Rouen to maintain its guilds and continue to be a *ville jurée* whose business climate was compatible with the presence of women in guilds.[71]

Lyon and the Silk *Fabrique:* The Ways of Big Business

By the eighteenth century, Lyon was the preeminent center of silk production in France and in Europe. With its 40,000 workers, the silk *fabrique* had one of the largest single concentrations of manufacture in preindustrial Europe. It was an industry with markets in England, Germany, Italy, Scandinavia, and Russia, as well as France. Raw materials came from the Near East, Italy, China, and some valleys in southern France. Geography and history encouraged the large-scale trade and flexible sources of money that underlay the silk industry. Lyon became part of France only in the fifteenth century; it had developed as a trading city on the edge of the

---

70. Ibid., Comments on Articles 12 and 13.
71. For the best discussion of the tension between these two goals, see Jean-Pierre Hirsch, *Les Deux rêves du commerce: Enterprise et institution dans la region lilloise, 1780–1860* (Paris: EEHESS, 1991).

Holy Roman Empire, with industrial and banking ties to Germany, Italy, and Central Europe. Long accustomed to managing commerce over the Alps and down the Rhône and the Saône rivers, Lyon tailored its urban institutions to the needs of business. At the head of its government, was the consulate with its commercial court, the aldermen (*échevins*) and the provost of merchants, the ecclesiastical establishment that gave charity to workers, and the traditional Lyonnaise jurisdictions. All were intimately involved in ruling on economic policy and commercial detail.

The city had a long tradition of free trades that, the master weavers boasted, even Louis XIV respected. Funded in 1554 by King Henry II, the silk industry outgrew its hothouse origin to become a viable, market-worthy, autonomous industry. Its official name was the sonorous title, "the guild master merchants and master manufacturing workers in cloth of gold, silver, and silk" (la communauté des maîtres marchands et maîtres ouvriers fabricants en étoffes d'or, d'argent et de soie). The silk *fabrique* became a group of separate recognized guilds only in the 1660s when they adopted industrial regulations, bylaws, and a regular process for the sequence of becoming apprentice, journeyman, and master. A few smaller trades also answered Colbert's demand for formal incorporation by becoming guilds, but most of Lyon's crafts remained as they had always been, free professions in which any artisan could undertake orders commensurate with his skill and reputation. It was well known that in Lyon, "all the trades were unrestricted—grocers, woolen goods merchants, mercers—have free commerce."[72] Although not strictly true, even the guilds did business with nonguild firms without insisting that the letter of their statutes be followed. The flexibility of the auxiliary trades, especially in textile work, helped enterprises to switch from one design to another and to fill orders quickly.

Three other elements influenced the structure of Lyon's economy. First, while the usual trades of hardware, manufacture, linen weaving, and wine merchants could be found, silk production dominated crafts in the city and drew into its subspecialties the bulk of the working population. Maurice Garden estimated that it occupied 25 percent of Lyon's working population in the 1780s. As a memoir of 1784 extravagantly put it, "The *grande fabrique* of Lyon is the nourishing mother of all the other manufactures and professions that this city of commerce encloses in its

---

72. AN F 12 765, "Grande fabrique," [1777].

bosom. It sustains more than 15,000 workers, occupied solely with its products, and it brings to a hundred thousand merchants, manufactures, and artisans of all kinds, its benefits and bounty."[73]

The second factor influencing Lyon was that besides offering employment to thousands, the silk business was an expensive and complex enterprise. Purchasing silk, gold, and silver thread required large amounts of capital. Orders from far-flung markets needed salesmen and designers. Merchants were in charge of seeing that raw silk was spun into thread of good quality, warped, woven, and finished. It took months before the order was completed and paid for, so the owners of firms had to be solvent enough to live on long-term credit and to extend credit to their master weavers.[74]

Third, the scale of the citywide business far surpassed most preindustrial enterprises. With 5,500 masters; 2,000 journeymen and apprentices; some 4,000 women weaving legally, 1,000 weaving illegally; 5,500 children; and many part-time workers, the entire *grande fabrique*, including the auxiliary women and children workers must have contained some 35,000 to 40,000 persons[75] The scale of manufacture can be imagined from the report of just one illegal workshop on the second floor of an apartment house overlooking the Saône. The court officers found one mill with four wheels containing 55 bobbins, a hand mill with 60 bobbins, and another mill with 18 spindles; the weight of the silk discovered came to eleven pounds.[76] Even though the silk weaving and selling was included within one guild, its cost, complexity and size combined to make the silk industry into an early capitalist venture.

The work discipline of the silk industry becomes more understandable in terms of its technology. From thread to finished cloth, silk manufacture included dozens of painstaking steps. To obtain the thread alone required cultivating silk worms until their cocoons could be dipped into boiling water to unwind the filament. Using steam to clean the raw silk,

---

73. AN F 12 765, "Grande fabrique," Projet de letter patente, 5 August 1784, and Maurice Garden, "Ouvriers et artisans au XVIIe siècle: L'exemple lyonnais et les problèmes de classification," *Revue d'histoire èconomique et social* 48 (1970): 29–32, 53–54.

74. Lesley Ellis Miller, "Paris-Lyon-Paris: Dialogue in the Design and Distribution of Patterned Silks in the Eighteenth Century," in *Luxury Trades and Consumerism in Ancien Régime Paris*, ed. Robert Fox and Anthony Turner (Aldershot, U.K.: Ashgate, 1998), 147.

75. Garden, "Ouvriers et artisans," 53–54.

76. Archives Municipales Lyon (hereafter AML) HH 85, "Les Mouliniers de Soye," 14 February 1744.

Figure 9. Unwinding cocoons. The seated *dévideuse* dips her hand into a cauldron to loosen the cocoon's strands of silk. (The bowl at her feet holds water into which she dips her hand to cool it from the boiling water.) She then slips the strands from several cocoons into a wooden grill to ply them, while another worker winds them onto a large swift. From Diderot's *Encyclopédie*, courtesy Special Collections Library, University of Michigan.

the female unwinders (*dévideuses*) classified each strand as white, gray, or yellowish and then took it home to spin or to give it out to other spinners. The spinning itself had its complications as strands were twisted right into an S or left into a Z formation. They might afterwards be combined with other threads and respun for greater strength. (The first spinning process was called *filage* and *premier apprêt*, the second twist was then *tors* and *deuxième apprêt*.)[77]

The second application went under the general name of "throwing" (*moulinage*) and used tall circular "mills" to ply several strands together.

---

77. These techniques are described in Georges Gilonne, *Soiries de Lyon*, 2 vols. (Lyon: Éditions du Fleuve, 1948). For spinning and milling, see 1:140, 150.

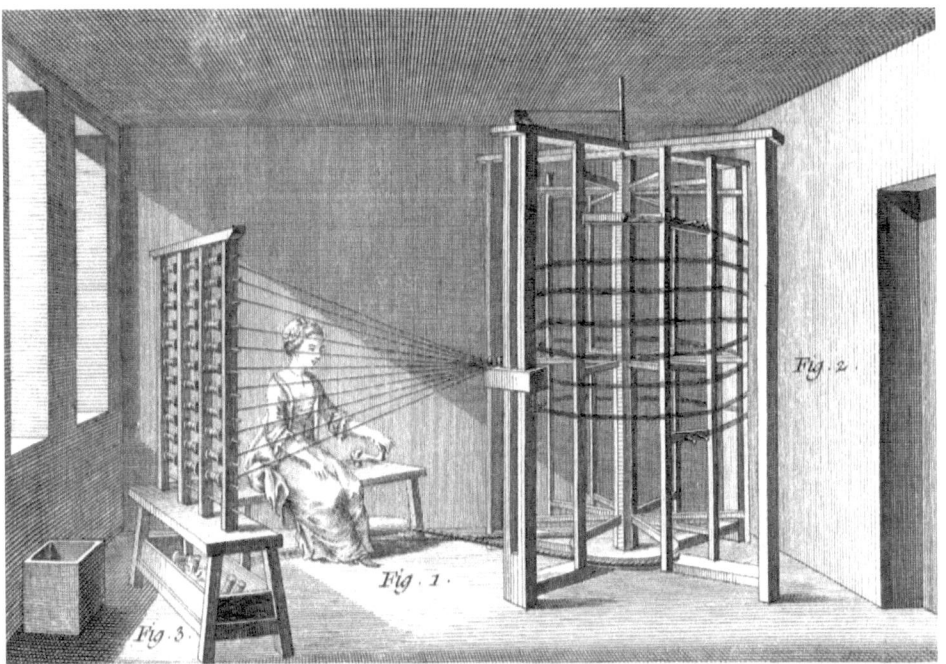

Figure 10. Milling thread. One of the many devices invented to facilitate the process of warping a loom. Here an *ourdisseuse* cranks a cage in which warp threads, fed from bobbins, are gathered into a small bundle. The thread is then detached from the cage and stretched onto a loom. Having the operator seated and using a crank were considered important innovations. From Diderot's *Encyclopédie*, courtesy Special Collections Library, University of Michigan.

Throwing, doubling, and texturizing changed the threads' characteristics, giving them greater shine and elasticity, and because it also increased their girth, it shrank the length. In this process the strand was finished with wax or resin to maintain twist and flexibility. Fusing yarn with resin-bonded substances also improved the appearance of the fabric by filing in any holes that might be left after weaving. These steps prepared yarn to be used in different ways, whether for warp (the length of the fabric) or weft (the width), and for a variety of kinds of cloth, whether crêpe, taffeta, twill, satin, or plain weave. The next process was dyeing the threads according to the needs of the various master weavers. If the filaments were destined to become gold or silver thread, they were laminated with extremely thin sheets of metal and wound onto bobbins. Winding the various kinds

Figure 11. Beating sheets of gold was an important industry until the Revolution. First a worker would heat the gold to make it malleable and another would beat it with a mallet. Next, the gold would be weighed. Finally a woman worker would incise a design with a stylus. From Diderot's *Encyclopédie*, courtesy Special Collections Library, University of Michigan.

of thread onto separate bobbins (*canetage*) was the next task before the bobbins were inserted into the shuttle.[78]

Other steps were taken for yarn intended as the warp. This yarn had already sustained a kind of spinning and throwing to make it particularly strong and durable. If two different sorts of material were to be used, the tougher one becomes the warp. Combinations of linen and cotton, for instance, usually had linen warps. Warp yarns were also placed closer together than the weft, or filler yarns, to sustain the length of the piece and make sure there were no empty spaces in the weave. This was an important consideration in the next process, preparing the warp for the loom (*ourdissage*). In warping, all the threads needed for the length of a cloth were stretched into a parallel bundle before it was fastened onto the loom.

Warping included three occupations. The first was attaching alternate threads to an apparatus that enabled weavers to make the shed through

---

78. Ibid., 150–51. Complicating the technique further, each category of weave had numerous variations.

which the weft or crosswise thread could be passed. The second was winding the yarn around a warping frame or reel, and the third, called *pliage*, saw the strands rolled around a free standing drum or horizontal board that was slowly and carefully unwound with a back and forth motion. Strips of carton or cords tied and placed at intervals kept the threads from tangling.[79] At this point, two persons were needed to attach the warp to the loom. One fitted the end loops of the warp bundle through a set of teeth on the loom, and the other slowly wound it onto the warp beam keeping an even tension. The warp then underwent a painstaking process of threading through the eyes of the heddles in order to determine the construction of the fabric.

Finally, the loom was ready for weaving. Seated on a bench, the weaver depressed the pedals in turn, raising half the warp threads to allow an open area, or shed, to be formed. He then passed the shuttle, with its bobbin, across the warp threads advancing the weft. Another push down on the pedal, alternate warp threads rise; another pass, or pick of the shuttle, the next line of weft is made. Brocade was the most complex kind of fabric, requiring a patterning device called the *semple* to be attached to the loom. On a signal from the weaver, a drawgirl standing alongside the loom lifted and then pulled down on the *semple*, enabling the surface pattern to be woven. For brocade, numerous bobbins with different colors had to be passed through the shed before the next thread forming the background of the weft could be advanced.

For each kind of cloth, whether taffeta, serge, satin, gauze, velvet, or an even more unusual weave, there were prescribed formulas for threading the heddles to ensure the desired crossing of warp and weft threads. Nevertheless, the technicians had to rethink each fabric pattern in order to produce cloth accurately representing the designer's scheme. Both the background of the textile and the figures, if they existed, posed special challenges. Silk can be made as light as crepe or as heavy as satin, with a surface as textured as twill or as smooth as plain fabric; it can be turned into filmy gauze or sturdy upholstery covering. These variations all depend on the quality of the thread and the manner of threading the heddles. Given the intrinsic cost of silk, it is the product most likely to have a complicated structure, and its labor force necessarily must be skilled and experienced to get a successful result.

79. Ibid., 156–57.

The complexity of the industrial process, the large amount of capital involved, and the importance of its far-flung markets combined to make the *grande fabrique* into an unusual sort of guild. Its labor structure evolved into an institution serving merchant capitalism. The silk-weaving guild split according to economic interests in the late seventeenth century, as the wealthy became master merchants (*maître marchands*), and those less well off took on the name and function of master workers or master weavers (*maître ouvriers*). Master merchants received contracts and assigned them to master weavers to make the cloth in their own family ateliers. Forbidden to work on their own behalf or to solicit orders by statutes of 1731, the master weavers were becoming a proletariat that had more in common with their own journeymen *compagnons* than with the master merchants. By 1737, the master weavers were working for wages as if they were journeymen. They made a great effort at this time to regain the capacity to sell their wares and succeeded in changing the bylaws to benefit themselves. But the explosive reaction of the master merchants overturned the statutes in 1744, taking control of their commerce and of the guild to themselves. By the new rules, the master weaver would have had to pay 800 livres to become one of the 150 or so major merchants, or 300 livres to join the ranks of the 700 small merchants.[80]

The gap in their fortunes and opportunities was searingly apparent to the master workers. To the royal government's dismay, officials found that "although the two branches [of the guild] had a common interest, they were nevertheless diametrically opposed to each other." The master workers claimed the right to meet in a separate caucus, to have their own officers within the guild, to pay lower entrance fees, and most significant of all, to negotiate their wage rates *en bloque*. In a trenchant understanding of class consciousness they realized that "work [is] their entire wealth and their sole resource."[81] They continually demonstrated with their companions to demand that the city government raise the tariff, the negotiated wage rate that applied to all workers in their category, and improve working conditions. This was a guild whose male workers—both master weavers and journeymen—behaved like members of a modern labor union.

80. See Garden, *Lyon*, 572–82 for an analysis of the antagonism between the groups.
81. AN F 12 766, Statutes . . . Grand Frabrique [after 1786], Title 9, Article 2, "Police de la fabrique." The original sentence was an argument against making it expensive to become a journeyman. "Le travil étant toute leur richesse et leur unique recourse, le suspender sans nécessité, c'est, pour ainsi dire, attendrir à leur vie."

The overwhelming majority of workers, however, were women. As wives and daughters of master weavers, they had the right to weave in their family ateliers or in the workshops of other masters in the guild. If they were unrelated to guild members, they were hired as daily wage labor or as technicians paid by the job. Historians have treated these women as unskilled labor, with neither the privileges nor the status of guild members. But a close examination of their relation to the work discipline of silk manufacture shows that the guild regarded them as crucial to the industry. The provisions of their work treated them as separate individuals, bound to obey the regulation of the *grande fabrique*. "Whether they be drawgirls of cords or buttons, and spinners who are married or widows, employed by the day, masters, sons of masters, daughters or widows of masters, all those [who] have the right to work as *compagnons*, when they are employed at the home of other masters are equally bound to conform to all the regulations . . . under the stated punishments."[82]

As individual workers, these women were stripped of their coverture protection. The *grande fabrique* statutes of 1744 specifically required those paid as piece workers (*ouvriers à façon*) to put themselves at the disposition of their employers, and if they refused, "they could be constrained by imprisonment of their person." Without this provision, the married women would have been able to insist that they could not be taken into prison without the permission of their husbands. While this argument might not have kept them out of jail, the fact that the statutes of the *grande fabrique* set the protections of coverture aside adds to the picture of the silk industry as motivated by economic considerations rather than guild customs or marital legalities. The same conclusion may be drawn from the list of trades whose less fortunate masters would be working as piece workers: "All master workers employed as piece workers—dyers, silk throwers, crushers and spinners of gold and silver, warpers of silk, spinners, and all persons to whom the master merchants will have given merchandise to finish, to warp, to condition, to dye, and spin . . . must present themselves or take the consequences of prison."[83]

An unorthodox guild tradition and a dominating industry that was, moreover, only possible for those with access to some capital: these were

---

82. AN F 12 766, "Statuts et Règlements pour la communauté des maîtres marchandes et maîtres ouvriers à façon en étoffes d'or, d'argent, et de soie . . . de Lyon; et pour la fabrique desdites étoffes," Title 9, Police de la fabrique, Article 42, 19 June 1744.

83. AN F 12 "Statuts," June 1744, Title 9 Article 5.

Figure 12. Artificial-flower making. In this workshop, men, women, and children process the popular artificial flowers. Judging from the scene, plenty of gossip enlivened the long hours of work. From Diderot's *Encyclopédie*, courtesy Special Collections Library, University of Michigan.

the elements that stood against the development of vital women's guilds in Lyon. To be sure, Lyon had a few women's guilds—laundresses (*blanchisseuses*), artificial flower makers (*fleuristes*), and seamstresses (*modistes*). As in many other cities, Lyon's *lingères en vieux* was a female group under the control of the tailors. Women also worked in guilds of mixed sex: the barge women encountered by Natalie Zeman Davis had become a guild called *bateliers* by early eighteenth century, and women could also achieve masterships along with men as ribbonmakers (*rubanières*), decorative braid makers (*passementiers*), metal forgers (*fondeurs*), and embroiders (*brodeurs*).[84] But despite the presence of a few female masters, Lyon did not experience the vigorous presence of guildwomen in the same way that Rouen did. One might say that while women were at the top in Rouen, they were at the bottom in Lyon. Rouennaise guildwomen were

---

84. Municipal and royal officials were not entirely sure that the embroiders constituted a guild, which only reinforces for us the lack of emphasis on guilds in Lyon.

living examples of the power of privilege in the Old Regime: in Lyon, women's guilds were numerically and economically insignificant. Women became masters in a handful of guilds, but for the most part they worked as proletariat, excluded from legal entry to the mastership and closed out of any legitimate chance to manage an atelier.

Nevertheless, women's labor was crucial to running the *grande fabrique*, even at the heart of the silk industry where the master workers wove the cloth in family ateliers. The right of wives of master workers to assist their husbands at the loom became an angry point of contention in guild politics, suppressed in the statutes of 1737 and restored in 1744. An estimated one-quarter of the home atelier's output might come from the wife's work. Wives' utility reached beyond the family workshop; they also worked, as did their sons and daughters, as journeymen and women for other masters, bringing in crucial funds for the home industry. As widows, they supported themselves by weaving or doing auxiliary tasks for their neighbors' looms. Women in guild families worked as licensed technicians, who learned the trade through experience in the family.[85] The privilege of allowing a journeyman to skip his years of work if he married a master weaver's daughter was justified by the information the master's daughter could impart to the young man.[86] Despite the competence the silk *fabrique* attributed to women within master's families and the "honor" they derived from the living in the bosom of the silk weavers' guild, they did not have the opportunity of becoming masters or establishing a family atelier in their own cognizance.

The dissonance between skill and status, competence and wage, pervaded work practices in Lyon, starting with the clash between the master merchants and the master weavers of the *grande fabrique*. The largest group to suffer from this gap were the thousands of women who prepared the silk thread ready for weaving and helped to ready the cloth for sale. These auxiliary workers provided the labor without which the industry would have ground to a halt. In one of the earliest women's work stoppages recorded, drawgirls caused the production of brocaded silk to shrink

---

85. See Daryl M. Hafter, "Women Who Wove in the Eighteenth-Century Silk Industry of Lyon," in *European Women and Preindustrial Craft*, ed. Daryl M. Hafter (Bloomington: Indiana University Press, 1995), 42–64.

86. AN F 12764, "Mémoire," no. 2623, to M. de la Michodière, 11 July 1762. "Ces marriages ruissants les talent de ces filles, elevées des leur jeune age dans la profession suploroient aux connoissances que ces compagnons auroient acquiescher" (original spelling).

drastically in the 1770s by leaving Lyon and returning to their homes in Savoy. Silk merchants were obliged to travel to the mountainous areas trying to recruit girls and to train more boys for the backbreaking job. Raising their salaries was never considered as an employment lure.[87]

Despite their low pay, however, the girls and women spinning silk into threads, creating the warps, or crushing metal to make gold and silver thread were adroit and capable. Because the machines that had been devised for each function were not well calibrated or standardized, like all early wooden devices, operators needed considerable skill in regulating and controlling them. This presupposed that they had training and experience. So although the female Lyonnais proletariat may not have owned the tools or the raw materials with which they worked, they had skill and judgment essential to their tasks.[88] While their low salaries betokened low status, they were an element of primary importance in the success of an industry. Recognizing the value of these workers and their dependence on them, masters took pains to offer benefits and restrictions to bind them to the guild.

Virtually all the corporation statutes laid claim to the *compagnons* and *filles* working in their ateliers, warning masters to hire only those who were in "their" own workforce. Although none of these female hired hands would ever rise to the mastership, and they were formally outside the guild, they nevertheless had a de facto standing in the craft. Fines were levied on masters who lured workers away from other masters and on employees who left a master without his permission in the form of a written discharge (*congé*). The drawgirls received a measure of job security from the silk weavers who had to give them annual contracts and board. Masters with throwing machines were also obligated to provide sleeping quarters in their homes for girls they hired by the year. In addition, they housed some day workers to keep them from signing on with others.[89] Other benefits also helped the female workers. The *écacheuses*,

---

87. See Daryl M. Hafter, "The 'Programmed' Brocade Loom and the Decline of the Drawgirl," in *Dynamos and Virgins Revisited: Women and Technological Change in History*, ed. Martha Moore Trescott (Metuchen, N.J.: Scarecrow Press, 1979), 49–66.

88. See John Rule, "The Property of Skill in the Period of Manufacture," in *The Historical Meanings of Work*, ed. Patrick Joyce (Cambridge: Cambridge University Press, 1987), 107, for a discussion of how skill was cast as an exclusively male possession.

89. ALM, HH 85, "Reconnoissance [sic] . . . Granjon Maître," Workers hired by the day often found their own lodging. This was one way of distinguishing the basis of a work force since the guild bylaws required of masters that "chacun doit avoir ses filles chez soy."

"girls" involved in hammering gold and silver into shavings to be made into thread, were to receive time off when they requested it for "necessary" holidays. The statutes do not specify whether the women wanted to pause for menstrual problems, or to attend to personal or family matters in their place of origin.

Another level of advantage saw female workers making their own world of illegal work that paralleled legitimate production of silk. While there were always male and female workers caught up in clandestine workshops funded and supervised by male entrepreneurs, Lyon offered the spectacle of women's initiative. Trusted and experienced in guild workshops, some female workers went out on their own initiative and created networks of illicit manufacture and trade. This took place in guilds that forbade women to become masters as well as those where they could rise to masterships. In midcentury, officers of the button makers complained "that for a long time many female workers, to whom they and the other masters entrusted materials to manufacture buttons outside their workshops, encroached on the hiring sequence and meddled to hire for their service young girls, to teach them this craft and from whom some pulled in considerable sums of money; and what is more, some of these women workers made buttons that they sold for their own profit."[90] Profiting from the work of unqualified workers turning out buttons for the unknowing masters, while making buttons themselves that they sold without permission, the women workers carried on their own business and successfully competed against the guild.

The female button makers were part of a thriving underground Lyonaise tradition. Women workers in the hat-making trade shared their strategy. In 1780, the hat makers complained that women and girls who worked at shearing skins (*coupeuses de poils*) for the hat makers had established a thriving black market some twenty-five years earlier. These women were originally girls hired by the day and wives of hat makers who had learned their trade in their husbands' workshops. Not content to remain dependent workers, they set themselves up as independent artisans with

90. AN F 12 768, "A Monseigneurs les Prévosts des Marchands et Échevins," [1758], "Que depuis long-temps plusiers ouvriers ausquelles ils confident de meme que les autres maîtres des matières pour fabriquer des boutons hors de leurs ouvroirs, s'ingerent d'engager à leur service des jeunes filles pur leur apprendre cette fabrication et dont quelques-unes retirent des sommes considérables; outré ce quelques-unes de ces ouvriers fabriquent des boutons qu'elles vendent pour leur compte ce qui est une contravention formelle aux règlements" (original spelling).

Figure 13. Making button moulds. Two male workers saw off pieces of wood that others pierce to make a variety of button moulds. In the center, a male and a female worker pull a drill-bow back and forth to ream out spaces in a block of wood. From Diderot's *Encyclopédie*, courtesy Special Collections Library, University of Michigan.

their own workers. To pay the debts they incurred, they turned to the illegal practice of encouraging legitimate workers in the hat workshops to steal materials, which were then used in clandestine manufacturing or resold. Master hat makers hurled the worst insult they could think of by accusing the *coupeuses de poils* of buying the stolen materials cheap and selling them dear, making large profits and forcing up the price of pelts.[91]

The women's bold actions received a surprising confirmation when royal administrators responded to their evident economic importance and treated them as legitimate workers. Master hat makers were just about to take some means of punishing the women, when the edict of 1777 formed a corps of these workers and amalgamated them into one guild with the furriers, feather merchants, and their former masters, the hat makers. With this approbation, the self-styled *coupeuses de poils* mistresses expanded their trade, and according to hatters, the women increased the number of fences with whom they dealt. Despite their illegal actions,

91. AN F 12 768, no. 4979, "Les Jurés Gardes des Corps réunis des Chapeliers, Pelletiers, et Plumassiers de la Ville de Lyon." This document was noted as being received in the Bureau de la Liquidation, 15 March 1789. But de Flesselles's response is dated 15 May 1780.

these female craft buccaneers received formal masterships and one guild officer to represent them. Then they took the next step of demanding certification as hat makers on the basis of being fellow guild masters.

The outraged *chapeliers* appealed to officials to check the *coupeuses'* pretensions. The trade of shearing pelts was so lacking in skill that it required neither apprenticeship nor *compagnononage*, the hat makers claimed. "The dullest laborer [*le plus lourd manouvrier*] could learn to do it in three days, as well as the *coupeur de poils* [who spent] thirty years." It was highly inappropriate to let the *coupeuses* have guild status; in fact, they should be retired to their original position as unskilled manual laborers, dependent upon the male hatters for work. In the end, the intendent of Lyon, de Flesselles, recommended that the *coupeurs* and *coupeuses de poil* not be made into a separate trade for fear of bringing unfair competition on the hatters, and that they could not become hatters unless they underwent apprenticeship and became journeymen. They could, however, continue to have their own guild officer. This plan legitimated their work but kept the *coupeuses* as dependent workers.

When the workers were powerless to extract benefits from their status in guilds, they resorted to industrial theft. The fact that separate parts of the weaving process were done in dispersed workshops increased opportunities for stealing and caused the business managers to worry. One police transcript shows how many shops might handle an element legally and illegally before it reached its final loom. In May 1761 police, "seized some silk and a black warp at the shop of master weaver Revel who could not show an invoice for the warp which he had from the Femme Rigot, a tapestry maker, who had it without an invoice from someone named Clerc, master manufacturer, who had it with an invoice from a woman named Bibete, also master manufacturer, who had it with an invoice from Sr. Fahy, former merchant manufacturer."[92] Outwork itself was not against the law in Lyon since the authorities realized that the machines were too large and the number of hired workers too many for the master's own atelier. But a constant preoccupation with *picqueuse d'once*, the phrase commonly used in Lyon to indicate someone who stole precious thread thus lightening the "ounce," accompanied the weavers' statutes and memoirs. (And since so many female workers were involved in it, petty theft seemed to acquire the stamp of the woman worker.) Masters

92. AML, Grande Fabrique, Tome 1. The sequence bears a striking resemblance to the pedigree of syphilis passed down in Voltaire's *Candide*.

levied the most frequent complaints against the spinners. These female workers installed themselves in their own rented rooms or at the workshops of journeymen or master weavers. Typically they received raw silk to spin from merchants, who weighed it before they entrusted it to the spinners. Paid little for their work, they were constantly tempted to skim off a quantity of thread and make up the missing "ounces" by adding water or grease to the bundle they returned. If undetected, they sold the stolen thread to manufacturers of silk goods. Although they were the most frequently cited for theft, the spinners were not the only workers benefiting from under-the-counter activities.

Working in their homes, female *ordisseuses* made up the warps that the master weavers used on their own looms. The warps were ordered by master merchants who furnished the plan and materials, but the warps themselves were carried to the weavers by women called *remettreuses* who made their living fetching materials from one workshop to another. Having brought the warps, they took it upon themselves on their way out to gather up the remnants of the thread left over from earlier jobs and buy them from the master wavers. Always in difficult circumstances, the master weavers must have considered the spare cash coming from a product that they had not themselves paid for to be a windfall. But while they were in the workshops, these women took the opportunity to "seduce the spinners, drawgirls, apprentices, and domestics, inciting them to steal silk and gold thread."[93] The master workers could not be safe from theft even in their own workshops. The very skill that enabled women workers to do their jobs gave them the "facility" of keeping back thread, committing fraud, and altering foreign merchandise as they cleverly worked their machines. Master silk winders accused their female workers, *tourneuses*, of making the items look whole to hide their stealing.[94]

Where did the stolen thread go? The master merchants accused the master weavers of substituting stolen material for the thread the merchants provided them. The master weavers denied the accusation, claiming that their orders required an assortment of thread already prepared and chosen; they had to weave according to a plan that required a particular sequence of silk, colors and gold. The trades that could make use

---

93. AN F 12 764, "A Monseigneur l'Intendant de la Généralité de Lyons. . . . Pour les maîtres-ouvriers à façon . . . servant de Réponse aux Mémoires des Maîtres-Marchands de le même fabrique."

94. AN F 12 773, Statutes of *Tourneurs*, p. 31.

of small lengths of thread, they asserted, were makers of ribbons, stocking knitters, embroiders, glove makers, and makers of decorative braid.

Documents suggest that the master weavers could well have been right to point a finger at the makers of decoration for upholstery and drapes, who also knit silk stockings. The *passementiers'* guild statutes could serve as a negative blueprint of illegal workshops and hiring practices. The picture of illegal workshops staffed by female workers either in or outside the guild takes shape from articles in the bylaws. *Passementiers'* hired girls were forbidden "to associate with other girls in the trade or to live together, except for the daughters of masters who were deceased." It was "prohibited for anyone outside the guild to make or to have manufactured any decorative braids and tassels, nor any work of any sort made on the *petite navette* (the small shuttle), whether of linen thread, wool and cotton mixed with silk, or linen thread wrapped with silk if not made into lace, under pain of confiscation and a 50 livre fine." "No one should give orders for goods made with the *petite navettte* to anyone but masters." Masters, journeymen, women and girls, and all others working on the *petite navette* were forbidden to work for or place orders with people outside the "art." Nor should anyone who had not been an apprentice reel the warp, use the calendar, or other finishing machines, except of course for masters' widows or sons. To avoid clandestine production, no daily worker might accept a more ambitious order than could be finished at her home, under pain of 25 livres fine. This suggests that legitimate artisans habitually angled to get large orders that they could distribute to low-wage, undocumented workers, while they pocketed the difference in pay. Within these bylaws we can see the outline of black market manufacture in which female workers living together made use of the *petite navette,* warping reels, calendars, and other tools. They were ready receivers of thread remnants that had been lifted from legitimate workshops or filched from silk given out to individuals for spinning. Merchants and other factors bought their decorative braid, tassels, and silk stockings at cut-rate prices.[95]

Constant distribution of illegal materials and goods kept the under-the-counter business going. There was no shortage of individuals who simply made it their business to circulate between spinners and decorative braid makers, silk throwers and silk weavers, channeling stolen

---

95. AML HH 167, Statutes of *Passementiers.*

thread to workshops making the next stage of the silk products. Inns, taverns, food stores, and private houses also served as way stations to pass uninspected goods along. Besides the self-styled fences, legitimate venders were also involved in this trade. Merchants' trade in their own goods or those of others amounted to theft as they filtered through stores and houses in "clandestine processions" (*cortèges secrets*). Of the 120 licensed street hawkers in Lyon, both male and female sellers were accused of mixing authorized and unauthorized goods in their wares. These *revendeurs* and *revendeuses* competed with the tapestry makers in selling new furniture coverings, but their most irritating practice—according to the *tapissiers*—was to accept "goods made by simple *garçons en chambre* who had not even passed an apprenticeship." Not only were the products made with prohibited materials, but even more galling, "the brisk trade occupied the unqualified piece workers more lucratively than the [masters] working according to the rules of their trade." This was the natural result of having traders who only buy goods to sell them. They "buy indifferently from all hands without asking, and without inquiring if the goods are stolen or if the materials are meant to be used *en chambre* by simple journeymen [making] a quantity of goods that they sell dirt-cheap because they are made of poor materials."[96] But the street hawkers were not always the ones to initiate illicit commerce. The female *tourneuses* who wound silk used peddlers, *revenedeurs* and *revendeuses*, and mercers to dispose of their stolen thread.[97]

That masters themselves tried to profit from unlawful work, either in their own ateliers or secret workrooms, is also clear. As the *passementiers*' statutes warns: "To avoid several big disadvantages which happen only too often, it shall be very expressly forbidden to all masters to have their dependents, servants, and any others work [in the trade] if they have not done their apprenticeship."[98] With the crush of workers seeking employment, especially the girls who came from poor farms in the surrounding areas, it was inevitable that masters would find hands willing to process silk in irregular situations. We have seen that theft and the use of unqualified workers existed in all the trades from the first steps in silk

---

96. AN F 12 722.
97. AN F 12 773, Statutes of *Tourneurs*, p. 31.
98. AML HH 167, Article 19, "Pour obvier à plusieurs grands inconvéniens qui n'arrivent que trop souvent, sera très expressement défendu à tous maîtres . . . de faire travailler leurs serviteurs et servants ny autres qu'ils n'ayent faut leur apprentissage" (original spelling).

preparation done by the *devideuses*, who started unwinding the cocoons; the spinners who wound the first threads; *mouliners*, who spun together several strands of silk; and warpers who prepared warp for application to the loom. But it was more than a question of falling into temptation because opportunities presented themselves. Using nonguild workers, buying cut-rate materials, and selling at a discount were all means of survival in a very competitive business. Illegal work went hand in glove with legitimate work. The proud manufacture of "cloth of silk, silver and gold" would not have been able to exist without it.

Even the hat makers who excoriated the women pelt shearers for breaking away from the guild to carry on their own business had their own connections with irregular trade. Trying to cover all possible contingencies, their rules forbade "all masters, widows of masters, and associates to buy directly or indirectly from any commissioner, apprentice, journeyman, male or female worker, or all other person without license or status, material and merchandise manufactured or not manufactured, that applied to the trade."[99]

With all their complaints about unfair practices of the other trades, the master silk weavers also indulged in questionable hiring. And the master merchants, winked at the deceit. As the statutes of the *grande fabrique* put it, errors in the execution of silk cloth stem from lack of proper inspection and from merchants who consciously ignored this abuse. "They tolerate the master weavers employing all sorts of persons in the manufacture, provided that they get their wages at the best bargain." (Ils soufflent que les maîtres-ouvriers employent toutes sortes de personnes à la fabrication pourvu qu'ils ayent à meilleur marché le prix des façons.) Once again, the imperfect work from these unqualified weavers gets sold because it is mixed with the cloth manufactured by capable and legal workers (*maîtres habiles*). "The merchants gain something with this contravention, and the manufactures loose a lot for their reputation."[100]

But who are the *"toutes sortes de personnes"* offering to work for the lowest wages? We learn that the statutes prohibit "from occupying with work

---

99. AN F 12 763, "Statuts . . . Chapelliers, Pelletiers, Plumassiers et Coupeurs," Article 13. It is prohibited to "tous maîtres, veuves de maîtres et agrégées d'acheter directement ni indirectement d'aucun commis, apprentis, compagnon, ouvrier et ouvrière ou de toutes autres personnes sans droit et sans qualité aucunes matières et merchandises fabriquées ou non fabriquées relativement au métier sans avertir les Maîtres Gardes."

100. AN F 12 762, Statutes . . . Grande Fabrique.

on the looms any person of one or the other sex who has neither the right nor the qualifications of masterships."[101] The phrase "persons of '*l'un ou l'autre sexe*'" is only used when referring to a group with a majority of female workers. Although masters railed against the illegalities of *garçons* too, the prevalence of *filles* and *femmes* in so many auxiliary jobs where theft or illicit work took place seemed to give women workers something of an affinity with underhand activities. The masters did not complain about the female nature as untrustworthy, only about the problems occurring in the course of daily business. But those problems clustered around ill-paid workers excluded from guild mastership who were, quintessentially in Lyon and elsewhere, the women.

Conclusion

Just as the silk masters depended on the rights of their wives and daughters to earn money weaving in the ateliers of nonfamily masters, the men profited from the technical skill and business acumen of other women's illegal activity. In legal activity as well, women provided the muscle and the competence without which the *grande fabrique* could not function. Within the silk guild, female wageworkers were skilled technicians responsible for virtually every aspect of preparation from unwinding the cocoons to sizing the fabric. They had the training but not the economic and political benefits of guild mastership. The guildwomen of Rouen, in contrast, took full advantage of their privileged status as guild masters. Not only did they use the courts to protect their technical monopolies, they also established vertical industries that encompassed everything from the manufacture and sale of their goods to retail and wholesale commerce of the raw materials they used.

The differences between different groups of women are evident here, and they make us understand that generalizations about women, even

101. AN F 12 762 B, Statutes . . . Grande Fabrique. The statutes of 1744 forbad women who were not guild masters to make or sell cloth, stockings, passementerie and other goods, as well as thread. Title 9, Article 7 reads, "Défenses . . . à toutes personnes de quelque sexe, âge et condition qu'elles soient, d'avoir, d'acheter, vendre, offrir, exposer en vente, ou colporter aucune soie teinte servant aux fabriques et manufactures desdites étoffes . . . dans lesquelles défenses ne sont néanmoins compris les soies teintes servant à coudre, broder, à faire des tapisseries, et autres que ne peuvent être employées aux fabriques et manufactures des étoffes, bas de soie, gallons, rubans, raiseaux, passemans, et autres semblables ouvrages."

when they are in the economic sector, must be handled with care. In both cities, the major differences between those with access to formal training and legal maintenance of a business and those forced to be daily wageworkers (*journalières*) was their relation to a guild. In Rouen, guild mistresses and wives of guild masters had the support of organizations that would protect their interests at court, help moderate their taxes, and extend their rights to increasing technologies. The female linen weavers, spinners, and day workers at the dozens of other trades in Rouen had no such protection. For them a daily wage in good times, public charity, theft, and prostitution in bad times were the facts of their lives. In Lyon as well, the women members of the city's few guilds and the wives and daughters of silk masters had skills that generated support for themselves and their families. The female auxiliary workers, even though their work was crucial to the industry, were often fired in economic declines and left with very slim resources.

As for the difference in scale between Rouen's guilds and Lyon's outsized silk industry, one could say that Rouen's relatively small size with seven hundred guild mistresses was actually a factor that nurtured the independence of these women. In Lyon, the capitalist nature of the silk industry, with its merchants dominating expensive commerce, created a less favorable environment for guild women. Also, the few guilds in which women rose to mastership were far less significant amidst the city's far-flung international trade. Paris, which was the premiere center of varied manufacture in France, drew hundreds of *ouvrières* to its trades and also produced its groups of guild women, like the *couturières* Clare Crowston studied. Although these privileged women rose above the mass of female workers, in comparison with their male counterparts, as we have seen in Rouen, their profits usually were lower. They acquired equality through privilege, and yet it would seem that their society, in the end, could not put aside the fact of their being women.

TURGOT'S REFORMS AND THEIR AFTERMATH

> *Women were not allowed into the* passementiers' *guild. So the guild officers of the decorative braid makers used to give women who wanted to earn their living at fashioning decorations for clothing permission only to do piece work for the masters. The* gardes-jurées *would extort rather large sums of money for this permission. But the women had no other choice—if they started working at the trade without the guild's authorization, the officers took them to court and had them fined.*
>
> —ARCHIVES NATIONALES F 12 770,
> "LIQUIDATION: COMPTE DES COMMUNAUTÉS," MARCH 1780

The last half of the eighteenth century saw a crescendo in the efforts of enlightened administrators to reform the economy of France. Opposition to the guilds was a key element in the enlightened campaign to make French institutions conform to natural law, gaining the prosperity sure to follow. Pamphlets and tracts denounced the guilds, accusing them of impeding technical advance, adding costs to manufactured goods, and keeping able-bodied subjects from getting work. The writers found an especially useful image in the plight of poor women kept from earning an honest living by the guild monopolies. Liberal reformers overlooked the existence of female guilds and corporations with male and female membership as they inveighed against the artificial privilege in French society that curbed the natural right to work. In fact, the conditions of women's work had occupied royal officials for years as part of a larger program of economic modernization.

Influenced by the Physiocrats and other enlightened writers, royal administrators of financial and industrial affairs were trying to encourage new manufactures and stimulate French commerce. The inspectors of manufacture reported on the health of industry in various regions and recommended new initiatives. The Chamber of Commerce offered subsidies for inventors to establish new industry and to teach skilled workers the new techniques. The royal councils heard requests from guilds and artisans to enlarge their scope of work. Controllers general had initiated surveys of guild activity from early in the century.

By midcentury the state's long interest in encouraging economic activity combined with proponents of laissez-faire to make French industry more competitive. Of course, as Philippe Minard tells us, there was a strong contingent among members of the economic administration convinced that greater rigor, rather than relaxation, in industrial regulations was the path to success.[1] While the tension between liberal and conservative ideologies continued, legislation that encouraged a new sense of liberty was put in place. Laws enacted in the 1760s included a royal declaration to increase women's access to work. "It is understood by His Majesty, that *'les personnes de l'autre sexe,'* whether married, widows, or girls, are permitted to take out letters or licenses for all the [mechanical] professions in which their sex can manage to work, and that they can exercise without difficulty."[2]

This effort to put more trades into women's hands did not expressly open male or female guilds to women workers. Administrators had in mind that women would undertake this work in their homes and that they would be protected from harassment by the guilds that "owned" the monopoly to the technology. There would be a special category of "free *métiers*" for women who were not guild members, allowing them to carry on small-scale enterprise, enough to earn their subsistence. This formulation must have satisfied both liberal and conservative officials, since giving women a modest chance to earn their bread honestly had a long history.

The next major official to propose reforms, Controller General Anne-Robert-Jacques Turgot, was a devotee of Physiocratic thought, and he

1. Philippe Minard, *La Fortune du colbertisme: État et industrie dans la France des lumières* (Paris: Fayard, 1998).
2. Bibliothèque Municipale de Lyon, 10198, "Arrêt du Conseil d'État du Roi, portant règlements par les professions d'arts et métiers, et autres intéressants dans le commerce, et qui ne sont pas en Jurande," 12 August 1767, Article 4. "Entend Sa Majesté que les personnes de l'autre sexe, soit mariés [sic], veuves ou filles soient admises à se faire pouvoir desdits lettres ou brevets pour toutes les professions don't leur sexe peut être susceptible, et qu'elles puissant les exercer sans difficulté, après avoir été reçue en la forme préscrite par l'art premier."

planned more drastic change. Supported by Enlightenment ideology that condemned artificial obstacles to economic activity, Turgot in 1776 suppressed the Paris guilds as a first step to eliminating them throughout France. He argued that guilds injured the state by inflating prices and restricting commerce. Guild privilege was an obstacle to technical innovation and kept able workers from finding employment. Guilds also discriminated against women, in particular by denying them access to jobs. "We wish, consequently," his edict pronounced, "to abrogate these arbitrary institutions which do not allow the poor to live from their work, which constrain a sex whose lack of strength has given it more needs and fewer resources, and which seem, in condemning it to an inevitable misery, to add to [its] seduction and debauchery."[3]

Women's access to work was a topic of serious consideration for administrators, church officials, and social thinkers. Without the means to support themselves, women would be unable to feed their children and they would be at risk for prostitution. As one tract discreetly put it, "Misery exposes them to dangers which are only too frequent, even when necessity does not constrain them." Thus women's employment was crucial to social order even as their physical ability to perform heavy tasks was limited. Enlightened reformers like Turgot blamed guilds for shutting needy workers out of honest employment because the latter did not have funds to pay the entrance fees. They castigated the guilds for limiting entrance to master's sons. Helping the poor and females to secure the God-given "right to work" was a rhetorically significant part of institutional reform.[4]

But those who stood to lose money and prestige from Turgot's attack on privilege excoriated his goals and his methods. Steven L. Kaplan has likened to a carnival the resulting confusion and lawlessness caused by journeymen eager to partake of the complete freedom they thought the new law brought. Turgot's edict of February 1776 suppressed the Paris

3. Emile Levasseur, *Histoire des classes ouvrières et de l'industrie en France avant 1789*, 2nd ed. (Paris: Arthur Rousseau, 1901), 2:627. As Judith G. Coffin put it in *The Politics of Women's Work: The Paris Garment Trades, 1750–1915* (Princeton: Princeton University Press, 1996), "Most social critics considered 'corporate' and 'male' privilege synonymous. Systematic discrimination, epitomized by male guilds, had made it difficult for women to get work and deepened women's vulnerability—such was a frequently voiced criticism of the corporate organization of work."

4. Levasseur, *Histoire*, 2:627. Turgot's preamble to the Six Edicts of 1776 evoked the highest authority for the right to work: "God, in giving man needs, in making necessary the resource of work, had made the right to work the property of all men, and this property is the first, the most sacred, and the most imprescriptible of all."

guilds; in August 1776 guilds were reinstated according to new regulations. (Rouen and Lyon were spared the outbursts of labor unrest because the edict suppressing guilds took effect only in Paris.) Public outcry and political influence in court circles precipitated the minister's downfall from power and caused the government to revive the guilds. Although Turgot's edict suppressing the guilds had declared that women had the right to work in guilds, the edict reestablishing guilds in August 1776 only generalized that "hired girls and women will not be excluded." But as the rules for establishing guilds were elaborated to fit particular provinces, details of the criteria for women's entrance were set into place. The edict of January 1777 opening Lyon's guilds to women workers imposed an important limitation. The king declared, "In what concerns the admission of girls and women into the guilds of the mechanical arts and crafts, we reserve the right to authorize it *according to the regulations of each of the said guilds*" (emphasis added).[5]

Economic administrators charged with reinstating the guilds tried to shape a system that reformed the arbitrary entrance fees and requirements, opening the professional associations to standards considered modern. Edicts of 1777 and 1778 aimed to redesign the new guilds on rational and efficient lines. Many trades lost their guild status and were open to all who simply registered with their city officials, making work available to women and the poor. Old guilds with similar technologies were amalgamated in the hope of avoiding a repeat of their past lawsuits over competing monopolies. French cities were classified according to amount of commercial activity each experienced and allotted a specific number of guilds: fifty for Paris, forty-one for large cities like Rouen and Lyon, and twenty-five for smaller ones. The new structure provided for two classes of guild members: masters, who paid to have their license renewed, and associates (*agrégés*), former masters who declined to make

5. Archives Nationales (hereafter AN) F 12 763, January 1777, "Édit du Roi pour les Communautés d'Arts et Métiers de la ville de Lyon." AN F 12 37, letter from de Cotte, intendant of commerce, to Claude Rivereiux de Chambost, *prévôt de marchands*, 10 June 1777. When a Sr. Lafabregue asked Bertin to arrange to get his daughters a license in the *guimpiers*—gauze makers' guild so they could make gauze and handkerchiefs in the workshop he outfitted, the official replied that "he could not comply since Article 8 of the 1777 edict states, 'and in what concerns the admission of girls and women into the guilds of arts and crafts, we are limited to the statutes of each of the guilds.'" De Cotte, who subsequently asked that a special exception be made, by means of a royal *arrêt du conseil*, underlined the quotation. To follow Steven L. Kaplan's discussion of the "carnival" begun by Turgot's edicts, see *La Fin des corporations* (Paris: Fayard, 2001), chaps. 3 and 4.

the outlay of money. The masters governed the guild while the associates took up a subordinate position, for they could neither become officers, nor vote, nor deliberate in the assemblies. Entrance fees, generally lower than the earlier ones, were standardized according to trade and category of city. Half the entrance fees went to the royal treasury to pay off the heavy debts of the old guilds. Correcting one of the most glaring faults of the traditional system, an error that even Turgot's enemies acknowledged, women now gained the possibility of entering all the guilds, although they were banned from taking part in guild assemblies or becoming officers of mixed-sex associations.

Rouen Fights Liberty

The reform era came at a particularly difficult time for Rouen. The demand for Rouen's luxury exports declined in the 1760s as King Charles III of Spain restricted French imports in order to nurture Spanish industries. Commercial obstacles during the Seven Years' War also caused the trade in linen cloth from Normandy and Brittany to shrink, while the new and competing industry of printed cottons expanded. Even the producers of calicoes found their difficulties mounting as the cost of cotton thread rose as the price of cloth fell. With European markets partly blocked, Rouen's traditional crafts of linens and knitted goods had to find new outlets, even as more workers turned to these trades. Once responsible for Rouen's chief product, woolen weavers in the city had largely switched to making linens, cottons, and cloth with a mixture of silk and other materials both in the *passementiers'* and linen-weavers' (*toiliers*) guilds or as unaffiliated manufacturers. The displaced trade swung largely to colonial markets, bringing elegant fabric and clothing accessories for the Creoles and *siamoises* for the slaves.[6] Even with this economic haven, sharp European commercial crises in 1763 and 1770 upset production before a new colonial boom caused cloth prices to rise again.[7]

6. *Siamoise* was a muslin made of silk and cotton spun in the Rouen area from the beginning of the eighteenth century. *Rouenneries*, a yarn-dyed or printed cotton or linen fabric, also formed part of the export trade to clothe slaves in Spanish America. See Phyllis G. Tortora and Robert S. Merkel, eds., *Fairchild's Dictionary of Textiles*, 7th ed. (New York: Fairfield Publications, 1996).

7. Archives départementales de la Seine Maritime (hereafter ADSM) C 360, "Capitation des Communautés de Rouen," 1775.

Prosperous again by 1780, Rouen's textiles reached some 166 percent of their 1740 prices, and they joined other dry goods streaming from industrial centers in the north and west of France to the Antilles and South America, or even Cuba and Mexico. As Hanseatic vessels challenged French domination of the trade with northern Europe, merchants had to shift their reliance on vessels leaving Le Havre to non-French merchants. Although Germany and Switzerland remained strong importers, England's prohibitive tariffs curtailed the linen imports that had formed so large a part of trade from Normandy and Brittany during the reign of Louis XV. Consumer demand was high, but the conditions of commerce required flexible, adroit strategies.[8]

With a colonial trade to supply and many economic uncertainties to overcome, Rouen's guilds scrambled to maintain some measure of corporate unity in the administrative reconfiguration of the sworn trades. The competition of new local industries—like the printed cottons in Rouen's suburb of Saint Sevère and the efficient Norman industrial woolen centers of Elbeuf and Louviers—drove the guilds to reaffirm their privileges, even as they transformed some of their practices to respond to new circumstances. But the guild structure remained central to the understanding of work and trade. In Lyon, the *grande fabrique* resisted the royal command to divide into separate guilds, preferring to remain in one large guild with the freedom of all silk professions to work within it. By contrast, Rouen's masters clung to their individual guilds, opposing the king's order to amalgamate with other trades or to disband and become free crafts.

Rouen's guilds were suppressed and reinstated by the edict of February 1778. If they wished to continue their business on a professional scale, masters of the now defunct guilds needed to enter the new ones formally, with a swearing-in ceremony and entrance fees. Artisans who agreed to work as individuals, selling just their own products in their homes, might simply register with the lieutenant of police with no obligation to join a guild. Of the guild fees, four-fifths went to the king to help defray the cost of guild debt, the rest to guild officers and the poor. To encourage former masters to join the new guilds, the government offered lower entrance fees in a grace period. Finally, women were permitted to enter any guild whose work they were qualified to do.[9]

8. Paul Butel, *L'Économie française au XVIIIe siècle* (Paris: SEDES, 1993), 55, 66, 74, 82–83, 105.
9. Levasseur, *Histoire*, 2:637–70.

As in Lyon, carrying out the edict provided a forum for political tensions in the city. The *parlement* of Rouen, which had to reissue the royal edicts in order to make them legal in its own jurisdiction, took advantage of its position to further an ongoing political struggle with Paris. The influential president of Rouen's *parlement,* Bigot de Sainte Croix, sided with the old masters who balked at paying the new entrance fees.[10] Contrary to the requirement of the king's edict, the *parlement* charged former masters nothing to join the new guilds and dispensed with the new oath of entrance. The *parlement*'s insubordination fed the guild masters' continuing resistance to joining the new guilds. The police judge was faced with a "large number [of masters], who were always tumultuous, and the pretension of some individuals who announced loudly that the *arrêt du conseil* did not have the proper letters and that it had not been registered," so they did not have to obey it.[11]

Individual royal officials also showed unexpected loyalties. The Paris Bureau of Commerce was taken aback when M. Vasse, the royal soliciter of police in Rouen, began rewriting the edict to give local guilds a boost. The bureau's secretary and longtime inspector general of manufactures, Louis-Paul Abeille,[12] immediately chastised Vasse for taking the language of the edict into his own hands: "When I replied that I would be delighted to work with you, Monsieur, on the problems which could crop up in the execution of the edict, I never dreamt, nor could I imagine, that you proposed to reform or even more to change almost completely, a law rendered with a clear understanding of its necessity."[13] Despite his

---

10. See his letter of 21 May 1779 cited in Geneviève Blondel, "Les Communautès rouennaises d'arts et métiers à la veille de la Révolution," Diplôme d'Études Supèrieures d' Histoire, Caen, 1962, 22. ADSM F 82.

11. ADSM C 154, letter from Trugard de Maromme, the lieutenant of police, to M. Barthelon, clerk in the intendant's office, 5 February 1782.

12. Abeille held the post of inspector general from 1765 until the office was closed in 1791. See Minard, *La Fortune du colbertisme,* 500. Minard gives an excellent analysis of the politics that embroiled the king's economic administration—controllers general, bureau of commerce, intendants, intendants of industrial sectors, general inspectors, and circulating inspectors. Regulation and laissez-faire, fiscalism and productivity were the major poles of tension for their policies. See also Liliane Hilaire-Pérez, *L'Invention technique au siècle des lumières* (Paris: Albin Michel, 2000) for governmental policy toward industrial inventions.

13. AN F 12 203, letter to Vasse, 24 April 1779. "Quand je vous ai mandé que je serais charmé de me concerter avec vous, Monsieur, sur les difficultés qui pouvaient naître au sujet de l'exécution de l'édit, je n'ai jamais entendu, ni pû entendre que vous proposerez de reformer ou plutôt de changer presqu'en entire une loi rendue en parfaite connaissance de cause." Vasse's title was *procurator du roi de la police de Rouen.*

liberal leanings, Abeille was putting into effect the view of the new chief finance minister, Director General Jacques Necker, that standardizing the rules regarding guilds and their production was a significant reform in itself. Thus Abeille was clearly irritated by Vasse's greater interest in local politics than in a consistent national policy. Besides rewriting the new legislation, the Rouen official also supported requests for changes on behalf of the guilds lobbying against the royal edict.

In the field, royal officials like Vasse might be caught up in sympathy for the guilds they were supposed to discipline. *Parlement* could side with guild masters, not because they favored the guild members, but because they took issue with Paris. The king's command to replace the sixty-some guilds in Rouen with forty new ones made for conflicting policy as well as strange political bedfellows. The financial officials had made it known that paying off the guild debts was a primary goal of the new corporate restoration. Indeed, critics then and now have condemned the new institutions as fiscal devices to line the kings' pockets. But since political pressure insured that the guilds would be restored, reformist administrators seized the opportunity to suppress egregious faults and to free some urban enterprise from guild control. Unlike the government's push to make the silk processes within the *grande fabrique* into separate guilds, the plan for Normandy was to employ a labor force of nonguild craft workers alongside the guilds. No doubt the administrators thought it would be easy for women without jobs to take up the shirt making, spinning, or hat embroidery that Rouen's guilds kept out of their hands. By contrast, in Lyon workers in the *grande fabrique* presented a collective intransigence that sometimes broke out into strikes. The authorities may have thought that splitting the silk industry into separate guilds would offer a means of making its workers more docile. The new program took into account both unaffiliated and guild workers, analogous to Jacques Necker's intermediate system tolerating free and regulated manufacture at the same time. As a letter from one official to another put it, "I do not want to dissemble, my dear colleague, that the intention of the administration is to disengage commerce as much as possible from the obstacles that stand in the way of individuals who want to enter trades, especially those which do not require any strict rigor."[14]

14. AN F 12 203, Letter to the intendant of Caen [June 1779]. "Cependant, je ne vous dissimulerai point, mon cher confrère, que l'intention de l'administration est de dégager le plus qu'il sera possible, le commerce des entraves qu'éprouvent les Particuliers qui veulent entrer

To remain in force, guilds had to convince officials that their work processes met the criterion of "strict rigor." Hiring lawyers to present their case to the courts and the public, guild members followed the traditional practice of circulating a flurry of tracts and broadsides called *mémoires*. These printed pamphlets emphasized how necessary the guilds were for maintaining standards and protecting the public from fraudulent goods. The linen-drapers of new clothes expressed alarm that the edict of February 1778 seemed to allow persons without qualifications to make all sorts of products and to sell them at home.[15] The guild of linen-drapers of old clothes struggled to keep their guild status. They claimed that they needed the bona fides of guild memberships to avoid suspicion of being thieves when they entered the homes of the deceased to collect used garments. The *couturières* and ribbonmakers were also candidates for guild suppression. Royal administrators wanted to transform the making of candles, cords, brushes, whisks, pins, and containers into free trades, reasoning that these jobs were not highly skilled and that they could be done just as well from the home as from a large industrial workshop. They asserted that coal pickers were casual workers, too poor to muster an effective guild, while scribes and instrument players took their jobs mostly as individuals. Many of the guilds sent tracts insisting on their need to exist in sworn trades. Even the paper makers, though few in number, requested formation into a guild, dismayed by the government's refusal on the grounds that they were too scattered to function as a unit.[16]

For trades in which women predominated, like ribbon making, Jacques Necker expressed the official belief that the profession should be free and open for "women and girls to undertake in their homes," with only the wholesale components installed in a guild.[17] Here was a distinct separation of economic function, the framing of small trades worked by individuals in their homes to earn a subsistence wage. While the notion of the "honorable poor," whose work barely sustained their needs, applied to men as well as women, females were special subjects of reform when

---

dans les communautés surtout dans celles qui n'exigent point une capacité qui soit de rigeur absolue." Guilds were also suppressed if they had just a handful of members or if the trade was so decrepit that few could pay entrance fees.

15. ADSM 5 E 500, "Délibérations," 14 May 1778, "permet atouttes personnes sans calitte de faire touttes sorte douvrage, et de les vendre dans leur chambre" (original spelling). They sent a memoir to Paris with their "remonstrances."

16. AN F 12 204, letter to de Crosne, 3 July 1779.

17. AN F 12 203, letter from the Directeur Général to de Crosne, 7 July 1779.

it came to increasing jobs. Without a way to earn an honest living, women fell into depravity and prostitution; therefore, providing them with work qualified as a moral benefit. Turgot's intention of suppressing women's guilds in order to open suitable work to poor women remained a powerful motive for his successors. All the guilds in which women predominated—dressmaking, linen-draping, lace making, spinning, embroidery, and other needlework—were candidates for suppression in order to open them up to every female worker. These trades were considered the natural preserve of females who "learn it from birth" and needed no special training to turn out a few products daily.[18] Although ribbon making involved complex machines that required careful training, it also came to be considered a craft that could support poor women at home because it fell into the category of women's work.

A hailstorm of tracts greeted the administration's plans for suppression as guilds argued for their own survival. We can see the guild in its political dimension, as its members gathered information from Paris counterparts, consulted with attorneys, sending memoirs, hired advocates, and administered bribes to influence the king's council of state. In terms of political action, I believe the women's guilds (like the others) were far more knowing and canny than many women's rights groups of later centuries. They were already part of the establishment and they understood how to use it for their own benefit. Marshaling copies of their old statutes as certificates of venerability and past practice and fortifying their goals with currently accepted rhetoric, they made the jump from local quarrel to royal court, sure of their right to be heard. They dealt with the suppression of guilds as a political issue with economic implications, well within their long experience.

The degree of shrewd strategy displayed by these guilds revealed that women, as well as men, used a high degree of economic and political reasoning as they sought to maintain their privileges. Within guilds they were well positioned to protect technological and product monopolies from competitors. Their voices commanded the ear of Paris ministers as they lobbied for tax relief or tariff protection. Their solidarity even convinced

18. ADSM C 142, letter from de Crosne to Tolozan, 28 May 1779. See Clare Crowston's cogent analysis of how essentialist thinking both gave entitlement to women for the creation of the Paris *courturière*'s guild, but also helped limit female employment to "women's work" in *Fabricating Women: The Seamstresses of Old Regime France, 1671–1791* (Durham: Duke University Press, 2001), 64–66, 182–84.

some bureaucrats to suspend traditional regulations for completing products within one workshop and turn a blind eye to out-sourcing in urban sweatshops or rural cottages. In fact, they were aware that belonging to a guild enhanced their ability to participate in capitalist ventures, supposedly anathema to the corporate structure. Instead of viewing the chorus of requests to maintain Rouen's guilds as backward looking, the raft of letters and petitions suggest that women, as well as men, were embracing a new culture of capitalism. Rouen's intendant made it a point to insist that subcontracting should be specifically prohibited, another indication of its wide practice.

The most important women's guild, the 217 linen-drapers of new cloth (*lingères en neuf*), showed how to mount an efficient lobbying campaign. Immediately after they assembled to hear the king's edict in May 1778, they decided to "make our remonstrances" in the form of a memoir to Paris and to contact a Paris attorney. They spent 144 livres "for consultation with two lawyers on the occasion of the king's edict concerning the mistresses." In June, one of their officers declared, "We must spend the little money we have in their treasury to expedite the affair of the guild." That effort cost them 342 livres for memoirs.[19] Two years later they sent a spokesman to Paris for 28 days, spending 72 livres for a furnished room, 114 livres for food, and 72 livres for carriages in Paris. The expenses also included 120 livres to a lawyer for a memoir and 18 livres for the copyist.[20] In the meanwhile, they were in contact with the Paris linen-drapers of new clothes, sending money on the advice of their sister *lingères* to an influential person who visited key officials in the capital.[21] The money was well spent: the linen-drapers of new clothes was one of only two women's guilds preserved in Rouen.

The other all-women's guild, the makers and merchants of knitted goods, expanded to include the makers and merchants of fashionable dress, dealers in feathers, and dealers in women's hairdressers. At its height in 1776, the combined guild numbered 198 women, and paid 568 livres in *capitation* taxes.[22] The favored position of these trades in an all

19. ADSM 5 E 500, *Lingères en neuf,* "Délibérations,"14 May and 10 June 1778.
20. ADSM 5 E 502, *Lingères en neuf,* "Comptes Rendu."
21. ADSM 5 E 511. See the rare letter from Paris *lingères* to their colleagues in Rouen, "Mesdames Patri, Hellot, Dupré, et Guibellé, 14 June 1783.
22. ADSM 5 E 611, "Tableau," Communauté des marchandes et métiers de la ville et faubourgs de Rouen, bonnetières, faiseuses et marchandes de modes, plumassières, et coeffeuses. "Capitation."

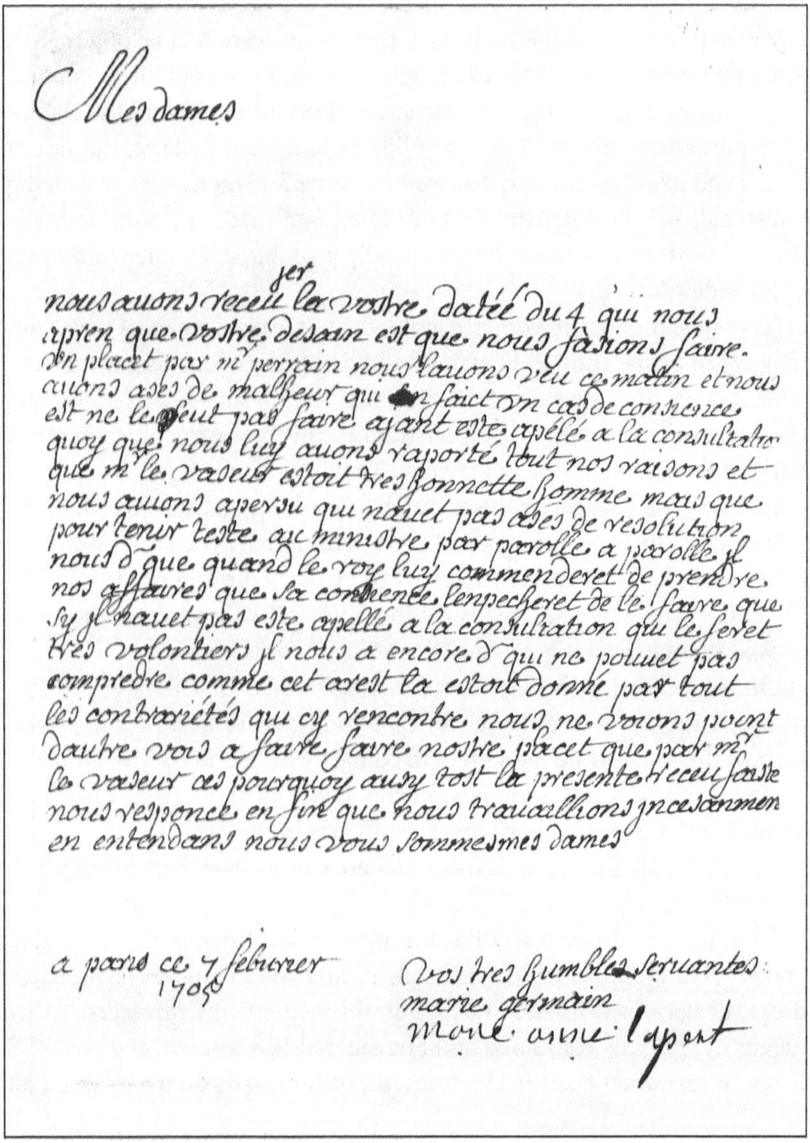

156 WOMEN AT WORK IN PREINDUSTRIAL FRANCE

> Mesdames
>
> nous auons receu la vostre datée du 4er qui nous apren que vostre desain est que nous fasions faire un placet par m. perrain nous l'auons veu ce matin et nous auons ases de malheur qui en faict vn cas de conscience est ne le peut pas faire ayant este apélé a la consultation quoy que nous luy auons raporté tout nos raisons et que m. le vaseur estoit tres honnette homme mais que nous auons aperşu qu'il n'auet pas ases de resolution pour tenir teste au ministre par parolle a parolle il nous d que quand le roy luy commenderet de prendre nos affaires que sa contienće l'enpecheret de le faire que sy il n'auet pas este apellé a la consultation qu'il seret tres volontiers il nous a encore d qui ne pouuet pas compredre comme cet avest la estoit donné par tout les contraretés qu'cy rencontre nous ne voions point d'autre vois a faire faire nostre placet que par m. le vaseur ces pourquoy ausy tost la presente receu faitte nous responce en sure que nous trauaillions jncesanmen en entendans nous vous sommes mes dames
>
> a paris ce 7 febvrier 1705
>
> Vos tres humbles seruantes
> marie germain
> marie anne lapert

Figure 14. This rare letter, dated 4 February 1704, from the linen-drapers of Paris to their compatriots in Rouen, advised the Rouen linen-drapers that an agent they had trusted does not have the "resolution" to confront the minister with their petition. Courtesy Archives départementales de la Seine Maritime, 5 E.

women's guild, separate from male trades, might be attributed to the high social status and networks of these women, 49 percent of whom were married to mercers.

The all-female guild of linen-drapers of old clothes was as assertive as its counterparts in new clothes, but its small size—40 members in 1776—precluded its restoration as an independent guild. (With only 5 members, another guild that allowed female masters, the makers and embroiderers of church vestments, was folded into the tailors' guild.) Despite its size, the feisty group of 40 linen-drapers of old clothes had advantages it could use: it generated numerous memoirs justifying its contribution to the community, and it had a patron in Vasse, the royal solicitor of the *parlement* who had tried to rewrite the king's edict of February 1778. Vasse was energetic in forwarding the linen-drapers' tracts to the Bureau of Commerce, along with his assurance that it was "necessary" to reestablish their guild. In May 1779, the commissioners of the bureau allowed that "there would perhaps be no great inconvenience in restoring this guild."[23] The next month, the commissioners were convinced to retain the old linen-drapers as a guild but suggested linking them to the male guild of secondhand clothes dealers (*fripiers-tailleurs*), with a tariff of one-third the normal entrance fee for current entrants and the whole fee later. This required a letter from the director general to the intendant, authorizing the amalgamation. Sure enough, in July, Necker wrote to Louis Thiroux De Crosne, intendant of Normandy, permitting the linen-drapers to join the old clothes sellers–tapestry makers' guild by paying only one-quarter of the entrance fee, a further reduction for current entrants.[24] As this example shows, a patron's interest could promote financial discounts as well as reincorporation.

But what was done on the level of official directives and high influence was only one side of the story. The linen-drapers of old clothes now had to conduct a four-year campaign to compel the 357 tailors and used clothes dealers to let them in. Guild minutes provide a rare glimpse of this dispute over women's entrance into the heart of male privilege. The

---

23. ADSM C 146, letter from Tolozan to de Crosne, 11 May 1779. In typical bureaucratic style, Tolozan would acquiesce to the reestablishment if the procureur général du Parlement thought it necessary and the intendant furnished information to that effect.

24. AN F 12 203, number 404, letter to Vasse, 1 May 1779; AN F 204, letter to de Crosne, 11 May 1779; letter to De Lessart, 29 June 1779; letter from Directeur Général to de Crosne, 7 July 1779.

account of the tailors' intransigence and the linen-drapers' astute confrontations demonstrate the strategic ingenuity of these experienced businesswomen. In March 1778, the women's officers met with the tailors in an extraordinary session to discuss the merger. (It was an extraordinary session because the new laws forbade women to speak at the assembly meetings of male guilds.) When the tailors' syndic, Jacques Boittout, moved that the amalgamation be presented for ratification, Jean Louis Bonnet, another officer, objected. Bonnet began a campaign against the linen-drapers by declaring that "he cannot understand the reason his Majesty has made this union." What possible rationale could there be for accepting the linen-drapers, "who have already been deposed from guild status, when the new laws forbid them to use either the old journeymen tailors and workers, or the day work seamstresses, the *'filles couturières'*?" He proposed that the guild make a formal remonstrance to protest linkage. Bonnet's views were unanimously repudiated this time, but his efforts to keep the *lingères* out were just beginning.[25]

Two years later, in a meeting in March 1780, Bonnet conceded that the guild's lawyer had advised acquiescing to the king's edict. But this did not stop him from moving formally in an assembly that the lieutenant general of police, the chief municipal officer in charge of commercial disputes, should name two other guild officers (*adjoints*) who could lead a protest with the intent to nullify the royal law.[26]

Tension continued to mount, and in an April 1780 session guild members debated whether to take their lawyer's advice and enroll the linen-drapers in the register. On June 3, the lieutenant of police opened an ad hoc court session to consider the "complaint of the *dames lingères* at not being admitted." Two briefs, one by tailors urging exclusion and one giving the lawyer's advice favoring acceptance, were read. Emphasizing the reasons for opposing entrance, Bonnet declared that admitting the linen-drapers would "be prejudicial to good order and would bring trouble and division into the guild." As a desperate measure, Bonnet interrupted the orderly proceedings, initiating a lawsuit that would bring

---

25. ADSM 5 E 675, "Délibérations." The material for these and subsequent episodes is taken from this source. The *lingères en vieux* enlisted the help of M. Vasse and other administrators with a memoir complaining that the officers of the tailors and old clothes dealers made difficulties preventing their incorporation even though they had paid the entrance fees. AN F 12 204. Letter from Vasse, 10 August 1779.

26. ADSM 5 E 675, "Délibérations."

discussion to a halt by means of the Norman legal device called a "*Haro.*" The lieutenant of police decided the case against Bonnet on the spot and imposed its cost on him.[27]

At this point the guild register records some comic relief amidst the acrimonious debate. An official who tried to verify the documents was thwarted by their sudden disappearance. He discovered that some guild officials had made a "furtive exit through the door carrying the guild register." They were found later drinking at the nearby cabaret of Sieur Revère on the street of the Petit Porche. Thus they added concealing documents and avoidance in a male retreat to the list of devices they used against the *lingères*. Finally the register was placed into the guild strongbox but without the proper formality and witnessing; the tailors' officers were fined and publicly chastised.[28]

At the next guild meeting, two linen-drapers, Dame Thérèse Le Jeune, wife of Grenier and Dame Françoise St. Pierre, widow of Edeline, brought a test case by paying the fees that should legally ensure their entrance to the tailors' guild "in peace and freedom." They met further opposition. The factions stood twelve against, six in favor, with four absent. Once again Bonnet set obstacles in the women's path. He reasoned that since their guild had been suppressed in 1778, its papers, or *lettres patentes,* were no longer binding. This line of argument convinced several members of the assembly. Jacques Pottier the elder moved that the *"dames vielles lingères"* had committed a serious offense and that they must wait until the *lettres patentes* were refurnished. Indeed, he asserted that the tailors' obligation to accept the linen-drapers was legally void because the women could not justify themselves with their papers.

Finally the king's officers took steps to compel the tailors to admit the women by opening a session in the police court of the *baillage.* Two of the linen-drapers' officers, Dames Le Guet and Petit, brought eleven *lettres patentes* that confirmed the legal status of their guild under the *parlement* of Rouen. The first of these dated from the "month of March 1421 before Easter," and their confirmation had been repeated by King Henry IV, Louis XIII, Louis XIV, and Louis XV. In the course of this demonstration in a hostile camp, the two women are quoted as saying, "let it be judged here that only M. Bourdon [the sergeant royal of the *baillage* of

---

27. Ibid.
28. ADSM 5 E 675, "Déliberations," *Marchands tailleurs.*

Rouen] has been for them." Nevertheless, the court session undercut the tailors' last subterfuge, their false claim that the linen-drapers were not a guild. In July 1780 the tailors finally voted to admit the linen-drapers into the guild.[29]

Few guild records allow us to trace in such detail the obstinacy of male guild members in thwarting the royal will, nor the persistence of female guild masters in overcoming their opposition. Legislating their silence did not destroy the women's political acumen. Instead, the artificiality of the new procedure revealed itself in the numerous "special sessions" the tailors had to convene to deal with the linen-drapers. Reaching to the past, the women found support in the tradition of guild privilege, and they used it to counter the modern trend, which was beginning to curtail women's public activity.

Led by its female officers, the mixed guild of ribbonmakers also struggled for its future, leafleting administrators in Rouen and Paris with tracts and letters. With a membership of 160, comprising 112 women (64 percent) and 58 men (36 percent), and a *capitation* tax of 1,037 livres in 1775, this was a guild of significant proportion.[30] The ribbonmakers were already amalgamated with the lacemakers, fringe makers, and decorators, all women's trades, which made administrators think of this as a women's guild.[31] Administrators were reluctant to maintain such trades in a guild setting because they fit so nicely into the notion of female's home work. Reminders by ribbonmakers that the complicated machines turning out brocaded ribbons and other decorations required skills taught in a guild workshop did not persuade officials to reinstate them as they were. At least the director general was willing to consider the girls and women who made these ornamental goods in their home in a category separate from the commercial retailers.[32] As Necker further commented, "In

29. Ibid., "il ne la été que dudit M. Bourdon pour elles."
30. ADSM C 149, "Capitation, 1775."
31. AN F 12 204, de Crosne, n.d. [1779]. The idea that ribbonmakers consisted solely of women was reinforced by their own false assertion, intended to justify their entrance into the *lingères en neuf*, that "their profession has only been exercised by women."
32. AN F 12 1430. Trying to convince the ribbonmakers—who had supposedly lost guild status—to join their guild, the mercers described guild ribbonmakers as needing "to have the faculty to sell their ribbons and to have them dyed, bleached, and completed by the dyers and finishers . . . or to do what many female ribbonmakers have done, to furnish ribbons already dyed and completed, [but] as for the small products [*petits ouvrages*] [made] on the bushel, the small loom, crochet hooks, the bobbin, etc., this part [of the trade] remains free, like the way lace is made and [how] ordinary folk occupy their children."

regard to the sale of ribbons and similar goods from an open craft shop [*boutique ouverte*], this commerce may be done by women as well as men, there is no doubt that they [*"ceux et celles"*] who undertake this enterprise are considered *Rubaniers* [in a guild]."[33] But, since administrators were reluctant to reinstate them as before, what guild could they join?

This situation inspired its own form of political byplay. The ribbonmakers took the initiative to choose a guild to join on the basis of the commercial gains it could offer. They asked to be amalgamated with the male guild of old clothes sellers and tailors, whom they accused of shutting them out of retail stores by allowing them to sell goods but not to buy them. They justified their entrance by the fact that the female linen-drapers of old clothes were already part of the guild, and had been given a discount in their entrance fee. When this union did not materialize, they singled out the linen-drapers of new cloth as guild partners. This time their goal was regaining their ancient right to make fringe on *passementerie* looms, a technique that the new linen-drapers had won from them in an earlier lawsuit. When the new linen-drapers rebuffed them because the ribbonmakers' statutes allowed for males, the ribbonmakers relinquished the chance to recover technical advantages in favor of commercial ones. Unless joined with another corporation, they would have lost guild privileges altogether.

Even at this point the ribbonmakers were selective, rejecting an offer to join the mercers' guild, which was forbidden to manufacture. With this choice the women showed their preference to continue as producers rather than simply as traders. They may also have been leery of becoming overwhelmed by the 600 mercers, whose earlier efforts to absorb craft guilds they surely remembered. Finally they managed to become part of the *passementiers'* guild, which they mobilized in 1786 to challenge the mercers' inspection of ribbons made locally and outside the city. The next year, they opposed the mercers' control over sales of ribbons at fairs. Amalgamating with the *passementiers* placed the ribbonmakers in one of Rouen's three most important guilds—the mercers, linen weavers, and decorative braid makers—which took steps to become one large guild in 1790.

The mixed-sex guild of fifty-eight spinners with its overwhelmingly female membership managed to join forces with the twenty-two male

33. AN F 12 204, letter from Director General to de Crosne, 7 July 1779.

cord makers. The resources in this amalgamated guild helped the spinners launch a successful suit against the ribbonmakers. By the time of the Revolution, the ribbonmakers' trade had declined since they could no longer sell thread in short lengths but had to deal in large rolls of thread, suitable only for industrial workshops.[34] Even without being an official part of its ruling board, the spinners used the guild to their own advantage. It is worth noting, however, that some male guilds, especially in Paris, acquiesced to women entrants and developed a new set of behaviors and outlook.[35]

Other circumstances called forth different strategies and arguments. The female licensed dealers in secondhand clothes were a group of two hundred women who had bought licenses to peddle their goods from house to house. They begged to be linked with the old clothes dealers instead of being made a free trade. At stake, of course, was their sales monopoly since guilds and municipal authorities dealt harshly with unauthorized street vendors. Even though they did not figure as a traditional guild, they inflated their use of two elected *gardes* as justification for claiming guild status. In fact, they reminded the authorities that their members were already sworn in by two officers of the old clothes dealers as well as by their own *gardes*. Moreover, they claimed they deserved compensation from the government's suppression of their licenses, and the administration admitted that they had a case. But the commissioners remarked that unlike the old clothes dealers, they could sell only what had been given to them, and they could well survive as a free trade.[36] The female food peddlers were in a similar situation. Permitted to peddle small quantities of candles, cheese, wood, eggs, fruit, vegetables, grain, milk products, and cooked and salted fish, the monopoly of these women also fell before the king's wish to open small trading to poor women. In the case of this trade, government policy to stimulate food provisioning was also an issue.

The women's trades that survived in guild format, whether alone or consolidated with men, owed their existence to the lingering power of legal privilege. The statutes of their old guilds gave them the authority to

34. ADSM C 149, "Mémoire" requesting union with the *fripiers tailleurs;* ADSM 5 E 501, "Mémoire" asking to be joined to the *lingères en neuf,* 18 December 1779.
35. Kaplan, *La Fin,* 230–32.
36. But they resisted incorporation with the mercers, who were eager to take over the lucrative ribbon trade that included ribbons woven in the countryside and sold in the Halle aux Forains. See AN F 12 1430, letter from Controller General to Intendant, 5 December, 1786.

claim that the public needed the integrity of sworn artisans to make their products, and that commerce required their knowledge and experience. Their old licenses entitled them to enter new guilds with reduced fees, either as masters or associates. Administrators' discussions over amalgamations dealt with the traditional elements of guild discourse—compatibility of technique and product, adding discussions of the financial condition and the size of the group needing incorporation. Except for the *petits métiers* of unaffiliated women and girls, no mention was made of the workers' sex. In the guild debates we have followed, at least in the notes taken by association clerks, the sex of workers does not appear. The *lingères*, ribbonmakers, *couturières*, and spinners used time-tested guild evidence of antiquity, monopoly of technique, and royal confirmation to argue their cases.

The Reform Era Makes Gender Problematic

Because the law caused guilds to change their format, the issue of gender caught the spotlight for both the government and guild members. The order to decrease the number of Rouen's guilds from more than sixty-six to forty forced administrators to link some guilds and suppress others.[37] In the course of changes, the technology, the products, the circumstances, and, inevitably, the sex of the guild masters came under scrutiny. While the Chamber of Commerce and the king's provincial officers remained faithful to the asexual tendency of guild precedent, the world was adopting new standards and assumptions. New social trends following on a long-standing bias against women and stimulated by followers of Rousseau heightened the importance of female and male traits and widened the differences between women and men. This was one motive behind the action taking *petits métiers* out of guilds and transforming them into free work for poor girls and women. Done at the lintel of the house, such work was still in the domestic sphere, unlike the guild *boutique ouvert*, which was an industrial workshop with hired operators and public sales.

37. Amalgamation of ribbonmakers and *passementiers* was decided by a letter of the director general, Necker, 7 July 1779. See also Blondel, "Les Communautés," 46–47. The three guilds—*passementiers, toilliers,* and *merciers*—took the trouble to create a unified list of statutes.

Paradoxically, the administrators' aim to standardize guilds and bring them into modern symmetry worked to set women workers apart from their male counterparts. Lining up female and male workers on their tableau of reform invited comparison. Even if the administrators were trying to create balance between male and female workers, acknowledging that the women in a particular trade could form their own subcouncil in a mixed guild, they still placed the men in the assembly that made guild policy and kept women out of the officials' role. Since one aim of guild reestablishment was to remove old-fashioned medieval anomalies, the prospect that women would act politically in public space—and public space was defined by the presence of men—was clearly an old eccentricity that should come to an end. The sheer fact that the state had now to consider technologies and decide which were compatible brought into focus the issue of technical skill and the question of who had it.

When guilds had competed for technical monopolies and exclusive rights over particular products, it was assumed that women's work was indistinguishable in quality from that of men. Competition in this arena was not gendered in Rouen. Nevertheless, female masters in general earned less than their male counterparts. Whether this was because their guilds made goods that were not as commercially desirable, because the women had less capital to invest in outsourcing activities, or because women's work commanded lower prices, the fact remained that in commercial enterprise, males held the economic power. This unequal balance remained hidden in the legal jousting that dealt in a rhetoric of privilege and precedent, but it came to the fore when administrators grappled with each trade.

Wishing to standardize and increase the workforce, and at the same time to overcome the particularity of guilds, the administration opened guilds to all. It then faced the problem of having to judge anew which trades should be available to female workers. What work could women do? What jobs *should* women do? In typical fashion, the state combined a new outlook with an old one to guide policy. The king declared that women could enter any trade that was appropriate, and that appropriate trades were those whose guild statutes did not exclude women. Since most corporation rules were mute on the sex of their workers, some guilds now began to invent rationales to exclude the women petitioning for entrance. Was it misogyny, fear of competition, or a combination that motivated them?

To complicate matters further, the economic situation of the late 1780s was not an auspicious time for innovations in work discipline. The Anglo-French treaty of 1786 removing French protective tariffs to make French goods attractive to the English and Dutch markets had the immediate result of flooding the French market with cheap English textiles. Even though the cotton prints did not meet French taste and were not as commercially successful as the British had expected, Normandy cloth manufacturers blamed the treaty for their declining prosperity and complained bitterly to Paris. As hundreds of local artisans lost their jobs, city officials collected money from guilds and wealthy individuals to help the destitute. The disastrous harvests of 1788 and 1789 raised the price of bread beyond the reach of ordinary people and left little for them to buy manufactured goods. These severe conditions were reminiscent of earlier economic downturns, which pitted groups of workers against each other and restricted the guild privileges of women. With more social emphasis on the differentiating qualities of sex, the old prejudices against women, which had never disappeared, came to the fore. It grew harder for working women to break the solidarity of male groups, and they may well have felt beleaguered. With that in mind, the behavior of women incorporated within male guilds shows how they persevered in fending for themselves, even when submerged and officially silent in general guild matters.

What was the opinion of female guild workers about joining a male guild, in which they were expected to accept silently the policies determined by the men? At least one group may have disliked the idea so much that its members preferred to be dissolved. The *couturières*' previous experience as part of the tailors' guild had revealed the difficulties of being a subordinate group. They put forth the usual request to be reinstated as a separate guild. If that was impossible, they requested that they be allowed to continue during their lifetimes, or at least for twenty years, "the exercise of their *état* as they had enjoyed it before their suppression." Sewing, however, was another profession administrators wanted "to remain free, and it must be permitted to girls and women who wish to go into the trade, on making a simple declaration to the police."[38]

In opposition to this government policy, the tailors made it a practice to accuse nonaffiliated seamstresses of running *"boutiques ouverts,"* competing illegally with their guild. Showing its determination, the government

38. Ibid.

issued an *arrêt de parlement* on 24 August 1781 prohibiting all tailors and those with exclusive privilege to make linen goods from harassing the unaffiliated seamstresses. In 1785, when tailors tried to gain the right to inspect the work of *couturières* outside the guild, the king again checked their ambition. The government put a high premium on maintaining freedom for individual women and girls to earn their daily bread.[39]

As for women who kept open shops and sold ready-made men's and women's clothes, the government said they should enter the guild of the tailors and old clothes sellers and pay one-quarter of the entrance fee. Those who wished to enter fully into the profession of clothes-construction, like Femme Heuye who engaged ten to twelve workers annually, had to pay the entire entrance fee.[40] The professional *couturières* got only half of the request they made when their guild was suppressed in 1779; they managed to maintain guild status but only as part of the tailors. *Couturières* could not legally open a boutique with workers unless they joined the tailor's guild.

When women workers became amalgamated with a men's guild, they lost their right to participate in professional governance—they could no longer become guild officers, deliberate in the general guild assembly, or vote. These restrictions were consonant with general trends as the government took steps to shrink the power of organized labor, steps that led eventually to the revolutionary government's system of active and passive citizens. After 1779, no guild was allowed to convene its entire membership in deliberations, a sometimes rowdy, disruptive affair. Instead, a prescribed number of deputies was chosen (according to guild size) to discuss the issues and set guild policy. Any male guild master had the potential to be chosen for the elite assembly, but women were permanently excluded because of their sex, just as they would be when the Revolution brought suffrage to France.

We might well ask how the guild women, long accustomed to vigorous participation in the public sphere, reacted to this loss of power. These were women who had charted their own policy, who accosted illegal workers and confiscated their goods, and who had lobbied municipal and royal officials and challenged rival guilds in court. Forbidden to speak

---

39. AN F 12 203, letter to de Crosne, 11 May 1779. The dealers in secondhand clothes (*revendresses à la toilette*) and food peddlers (*regratières*) sometimes willed their numbered licenses to female kin or friends.

40. Blondel, "Les Communautés," 10–13.

in the general guild assembly or to become guild officers, they had to find other means of influence. We have already seen how the linen-drapers of old cloth managed to win an audience in the tailors' guild by petitioning their grievance at not being inducted. Because their exclusion from the tailors' guild also crossed royal policy, the lieutenant of police allowed them to appear at an official meeting and testify for their cause. They continued to find other expedients within the guild framework to defend themselves.

To some extent the equalizing power of guild privilege fortified their status even when the political rules changed. Trades amalgamated into larger units would surrender their monopoly over their specific technique, allowing all masters to hire workers to make and sell the products represented in the new enlarged guild. The specific relation of the entrants to the old guild had to be negotiated, and here there was room for women's trades to insert a sliver of autonomy. Their success depended on using prerogatives from their own guild statutes and on maintaining themselves as a separate unit within the larger association. This was possible because the trades in amalgamated guilds retained some segregation—one guild officer was frequently drawn from the ranks of the newly inducted trade—and they continued to conduct business according to their existing industrial and procedural regulations.

When, for instance, the tailors' officers began to inspect the work of the *couturières* now in their guild, they infringed upon the seamstresses right to make their own inspection. Pressing the issue, Dames Mulat and Vauveurs, who had belonged to the earlier women's guild, refused to pay for the visit of the tailors' officer and won two court proceedings on the issue.[41] Next year, "la fille Binard," *couturière*, also won exemption from tailors' inspection through a court suit. The tailors recognized this as a test case; "the effect of this judgment, if it stood, would cost the guild 600 livres a year." Declaring that "such a considerable loss merits the whole attention of the guild," the officers prepared to take the matter to the king's council, consulting three of its lawyers, and having two syndics themselves lobby in Paris to change the statutes. Mobilizing their own guild statutes, using past practice and priority of time as their defense, even the *couturières*, so often subordinated to tailors' rights, managed to keep some measure of self-determination in a male guild.

41. ADSM C 142, letter from Tolozan to de Crosne, 17 April 1782. *Couturières* outside the guild were restricted to working without assistants and to making only female clothes.

The most powerful example of a women's guild making its own way was the track by which the linen-drapers of old clothes asserted themselves within the tailors' and *frippiers'* guild.⁴² This epic story pitted the forty female linen-drapers against the guild, the local and royal authorities of the Old Regime, and even the chief judiciary officer under the early Revolution. Having won their right to enter the guild after a struggle, the *lingères* immediately declined all responsibility to repair the hall where they sold their goods. Since earlier account books show payments to workers for repairs, their intransigence seemed to be a form of civil disobedience, a concrete way of retaliating for the tailors' earlier obstinacy, or disagreeing about policy, perhaps combined with personal pique. We shall see, however, that the *lingères* knew their rights and how to defend them. The details of this dispute show how women workers contested inequities when they had no vote or voice in a male enclave.

In May of 1783, officers of the tailors' guild took building experts, plasterers, and other workers to the hall occupied by the old clothes dealers and the linen-drapers of old clothes to examine damage that had been done in the course of the past year. They came to an agreement about the repairs and their costs, and they issued a statement charging each of the masters and mistresses who used the hall a yearly sum to help the guild defray the expenses. In addition, all who used the hall should contribute to the annual rent paid to city hall for the space. By September, the guild had paid for the repairs, and it decided to levy a rate of 2 livres a year on the *vieilles lingères* to defray the costs. The motion of M. Bonnemaison to pay 3 livres did not carry.⁴³

The next year, the old clothes dealers were charged at a rate of 3 livres and the linen-drapers, 2, to pay for the roof, the beams, the stalls, and additional plastering needed to preserve the masonry. Given the linen-drapers' difficulty in paying the king's taxes, the guild officers hoped these sums would not be excessive. Discharging this debt seemed a moral obligation to the guild syndics. They declared: "It would be shameful . . . if those women who occupy the hall were not willing to pay, even if they paid less than the 2 livres." The officers continued that they themselves had gone to the hall at different times to have the women honor the

---

42. Blondel, "Les Communautés," 54–55. In 1781 they secured a judgment against one dressmaking workshop.

43. ADSM 5 E 675, "Registre des Délibérations, 1779 à 1787," 187 recto, October 1783. Request for tax relief from Femme Heuye, *couturière*.

payment, but they had to content themselves with *"le mauvais propos."* For that reason they were obliged to go to the police, and their case was placed with the disputed claims court. The guild assembly voted to let them present the case to the lieutenant of police by means of a remonstrance.

In 1785, in order to avoid even greater damage, the linen-drapers' hall quickly needed a large repair to the ceiling, which was completely wrecked. A year later, Dame Le Cas, "or those [*celles*] belonging to the guild," authorized replacing a lock and bolts to the fire wall, which had remained open for a long time. The guild minutes asserted that it would be only fair if the *lingères* compensated the guild for the expenses. In April 1786, the officers were still requesting payment: "these halls were subject to different large repairs which became onerous to the guild." Each linen-draper must pay the 2 livres fee, owing since 1783. A subsequent guild meeting repeated the demand, an officer commenting that "this modest sum is hardly capable of defraying the repairs and the guild has another hall being enlarged, so it has many expenses."[44] This time the syndics voted in favor of opening a suit against the linen-drapers to attach their goods.

There the matter hung for another year, when the officers asked permission to take steps against the *"anciens maitresses lingères en vieux"* for 110 livres they still owed for their *capitation* tax and for the rent of their hall from 1778 to 1781.[45] In 1788, reports on the matter, including a debt for renting the hall since 1783, brought the information that the officers had to enact a new deliberation, demand payment from the linen-drapers, and when the women refused the officers could proceed to appropriate their belongings. They pursued this judgment because, as they said, "it is natural that those who occupy [a place], must pay for it."[46]

The dilapidated hall and the refusal of the guild women to accept the obligation to pay for its improvements are emblematic of problems in the state that brought the Old Regime to a close. The bickering guild members reflected the byplay of notables' councils called during the 1780s to find a solution to the state's fiscal crisis. As many nobles clung to their

---

44. Ibid., 211, recto, 3 November 1784. The syndics appealed the decision (211, verso), demonstrating an occasion when officers sued members of another trade within their guild.

45. Ibid., session of 8 January 1785.

46. ADSM C 146. The *lingères en vieux* did not hesitate to protest that Director General Necker had mistakenly linked them to the sellers of used furniture (*fripiers-tapissiers*) instead of the used clothes dealers (*fripiers d'habits*), and Tolozan agreed with them. Letter, Tolozan, 5 December 1779.

privilege refusing to accept deeper taxes, the *lingères* used their status and the regulations of the guild to defend their recalcitrant position. Appeals on the basis of fairness and utility were unpersuasive. The king's house, like the Cloth Hall, would soon fall from disrepair.

October 1790 brought a summons from the guild's board, to the linen-drapers. After reading that the guild gave a subvention to the linen-drapers by paying for the repairs and the rent of their hall, and that the women made a formal refusal to pay at the guild meeting of 12 August 1788, Pottier declared that they would press the matter until it was settled definitively because the needed monies "are allocated in their accounts."[47] The guild had also imposed an additional fee of 6 livres on each new *lingère* inducted, and the women resisted paying this fee as well. Finally the guild went to the departmental authority, which authorized fines to be imposed on the *"lingères en vieux* who refuse to pay various expenses." Even the revolutionary officer, the *procureur general sindic du Département de la Seine Inférieur*, was unable to extract the outstanding funds.[48]

While the tailors' syndics and assistant officers took steps to get the money the guild imposed on the linen-drapers of old clothes, the women appealed to higher authorities. They complained to the Bureau of Commerce that the 2 livres impost earmarked to pay back the guild for repairing the hail and paying the rent was an illegal fee. They also objected to paying an extra 6 livres fee for new linen-draper mistress. To their credit, the government supported both monetary claims. Accusing the tailors' syndics of extorting money, Intendant of Commerce Tolozan insisted that the tailors stop these unauthorized practices. Evidently the state considered this breach of regulations an important test case. Of each *lingère*'s 300 livres entrance fee, the guild kept 56 livres, which was enough to pay rent and repairs on the hall.[49] But the linen-drapers' grievances did not end with finances; they had a list of additional problems that needed attention and an equal roster of solutions to propose.

The problems with the hall where they sold their goods had to do with intrusion of the tailors' officers into the *lingères'* space. To avoid arguments

47. ADSM 5 E 675, "Délibérations de la communauté des marchands tailleurs, fripiers d'habits en neuf et en vieux, chasubliers, brodeurs, 1779 à 1787." The following account of the *lingères en vieux*'s refusal to pay repair and rent expenses comes from this register.

48. ADSM 5 E 675, "Délibérations." The government's reduction of the *capitation* and the *industrie* taxes from 1609 livres to 1405 livres supports the *lingères'* complaints of bad economic times. It also demonstrates the guild's success in negotiating with royal officials.

49. Ibid., session of 12 May 1787 with ten deputies in attendance.

among themselves, the linen-drapers drew lots for the stalls every fortnight, and they complained that the syndics tore up the numbered chits on each booth forcing the women to make their drawings at the guild office. Objecting to this irritation, they also complained that the officers had taken the administration of the hall into their own hands. They proposed reestablishing their old practice of renting the hall directly from the city and subletting part of it to others (which used to earn them 60 livres); they also wanted to draw lots for their places right in the hall.[50] Mixing money issues and issues of precedence, the women were nevertheless trying to gain more control over the conditions of their work. And Tolozan was shrewd enough to sense their underlying motive.

The guild women knew that only by pursing each detail of their independence could they hope to manage their business to their own benefit. Their status would produce economic advantages only if they insisted on taking into account every possible boon in their regulations. The thicket of legal rules and the process of court procedure were rich fields for them to pluck the fruits of protections. Contrary to the general denigration of law and lawyers as dangerous areas to entrap the unwary, the complications were resources of protection for the *lingères*. They had honed their skill in making use of restrictions and loopholes for centuries, and they still were using these means of reaching for economic success.

A subsequent memoir claimed that the tailors had no understanding of how the linen-drapers of old cloth cut and sewed used clothes. The linen-drapers had a shred of justification in this since they were obliged to sew seams in a particular backstitch (*à la tacquette*). The pretext, however, was a slender thread on which to base their request that they should therefore have the right to "make apprentices," to have them execute the necessary masterpiece, and to present them for the swearing in when skilled enough to become mistresses.[51] Their reasoning was even less convincing when they insisted that their craft had no similarity with that of the old clothes dealers in their guild who, in Tolozan's words, "were occupied every day in cutting and sewing old linen." He warned that if the government acceded to the linen-drapers' wishes, entrants to the guild would have to make a separate apprenticeship to sell used linen. Such an

---

50. ADSM 5 E 689, "Délibérations de la communauté des marchands tailleurs, fripiers en neuf et en vieux, casubliers, et brodeurs, 1787 à 1791." Session of 12 August 1788. The following discussion is based on this register.

51. Ibid., session of 28 October 1790.

exception to the general rule would encourage all the separate trades to impose their own disciplines and make an illusion of guild amalgamation. As Tolozan concluded, the *lingères en vieux* were "sharing the advantages attached to the profession of tailors and old clothes dealers." (The advantages included the right to hire workers to make and sell any of the guild's products.) But at the same time, "without daring to request their independence, even far from wishing it, these women have as their ambition the power to govern alone and not to be subordinated to the laws of the guild . . . they put all their effort into participating in the functions of syndics and associate officers, and to forming a small separate guild."[52]

The Paris administration accurately viewed all the other grievances of the linen-drapers in the same light, as pretexts to gain control of their affairs. In fact, with each complaint the women offered a solution that would let them function like guild officers, as if they were a separate guild within the larger group. Insisting that they were the only ones who understood their craft and that the tailors' syndics failed to conduct the obligatory four annual inspections, the linen-drapers suggested that they should choose two among them to conduct their own examinations. This would also help conditions at the hall where, instead of making the proper inspections at their workshops, the tailors' syndics stationed themselves on Fridays during market hours and imposed a fee of 20 sous on every batch of goods sold to merchants from out of town. In addition, getting back the right to keeping track of stolen goods in a register as they had done in the past would enable the linen-drapers to curtail illegal resale. It would promote the public good, the women insisted, since the tailors' syndics ignored the theft of cloth and tolerated the peddling of stolen goods from house to house.[53]

These were serious accusations, and the administrators in Paris asked Rouen's intendant to investigate the truth of the charges. The officials concluded that most of the complaints were "unfounded and that the *lingères en vieux*, or especially four of them, jealous and constrained by the tailors' and old clothes dealers' inspection, only multiplied their complaints to try, if it is possible, to shake the ties [to the guild] and become free, or at least to participate in the honors of administration invested

---

52. ADSM L 2409, letter to the committee of the tailors, 24 December 1790.
53. ADSM C 146, letter from Tolozan [to de Crosne], Paris, 16 April 1785.

in the syndics and assistant officials of the guild." Tolozan suggested that the women chaffed against the officers' close scrutiny, which alerted the police to any stolen goods they put on sale. As for the intrusion of the syndics in the hall, their inspection of the goods sold was precisely to guard against passing stolen cloth (but if there was an inspection, naturally it had to be paid for). The accusations around drawing lots seemed equally insubstantial: the officers collected the numbered tags to keep them from getting lost and to make the women choose their stalls in the privacy of the bureau; in fact, these officials "merited hymns of praise rather than reproaches on the part of the *lingères*."[54]

Finally tipping their hand, the *lingères en vieux* accused the guild officers of overcharging the linen-drapers when they were compiling the tax rolls "in order to make it lighter on themselves." They assessed the impost "without regard to the means of each woman, to the effect that it became arbitrary."[55] The women's proposed solution was to learn the total sum the guild expected them to pay and to decide on each individual *lingère*'s portion themselves. To solve the problem of vending stolen goods, the women suggested allowing them to select three linen-drapers, among themselves, to apprehend the peddlers. After all the rhetoric, Tolozan declared that in their tracts "the linen-drapers delivered themselves of a sort of declamation against the tailors [and] old clothes handlers . . . to obtain, if it is possible, an absolute independence from the rules of this guild." This was all the more ironic, he jibed, since this was the group "with which they had asked to be linked."[56]

Tolozan received the burden of the linen-drapers' complaints with the skepticism he thought they deserved. The linen-drapers were full of eloquence, but if they really had evidence that the tailors' officers paid so little attention to stolen goods, "they should do them the favor of denouncing them to the public ministry of police in the *bailliage* of Rouen, who have their eyes on [the officers] without cease." As for the *"bien public"* that the *lingères* adduced as their rationale, the Bureau of Commerce

---

54. ADSM C 146, letter from Tolozan [to de Crosne], Paris, 17 October 1784.
55. ADSM C 146, letter from Tolozan [to de Crosne], Paris, 24 October 1784.
56. ADSM C 146, letter from Tolozan [to de Crosne], 26 February 1785. "C'est ainsi, mon cher colleague, que les lingères en vieux, en partagant les avantages attachés à la profession des tailleurs fripiers. . . . Sans oser demander leur désunion, bien éloignée même de la désirer, ces femmes ambitionnent le pouvoir de se gouverner seule et de n'être pas subordoné aux . . . loix de la communauté, dont elles parties . . . elles font leurs efforts pour participer aux functions des syndics et adjoints, et former un petit corps séparé."

commissioners considered it much less worthy than the public good of "obeying the imperative disposition of the edict of 1779, which prohibits girls and women from attending assemblies and exercising public office in men's guilds."[57]

Thus the ostensible assistance to women workers of allowing them to enter men's guilds resulted in cutting off their access to directing the general guild. The few women whom we find in male guilds through the centuries had probably attended the assemblies without causing comment. Women had become officers in guilds of mixed sex like the spinners and ribbonmakers, and they certainly consulted with male and female masters to formulate policy. In the days before 1779, guild masters competed in legal battles without reference to sex; each master or mistress was a privileged person, and privilege diminished, though it did not erase, the importance of gender. Flattening the categories, however, vitiated the distinctions of privilege, allowing other differences to become prominent. Women might be equal as guild members, but in the public realm of governance they had no standing. All the autonomy they had practiced in determining policy, apprehending illegal workers, defending their guild at court, negotiating with officials over taxes—all that was stripped from them if they were in male guilds. Given the king's order to reduce the number of guilds, many mistresses found themselves becoming minorities in male guilds. As Tolozan put it, their contribution to the public good was not so much faithful craft work and honest accounts, but rather obeying the law to stay silent and away from the chief guild assemblies.

Gender and Reform

In the decade and a half between the restoration of guilds in 1776–79 and their final suppression in 1791, competing projects vied for reform. The burden of financing the midcentury's wars shrank the public resources that administrators would have used to promote new industrial initiatives. Economic difficulties paved the way for innovative assemblies to discuss taxation and eventually to convoke the Estates General in 1789. National productivity and commerce also became problematic, as French

---

57. Ibid.

manufacturers tried to market their own goods against cheaper British products. These troubles stimulated ideological competition as the government tried to find its way among various reform suggestions. Some believed that manufactures should be freed from industrial regulations, others blamed the last twenty years of lax enforcement by the inspectors of manufacture as the key cause of economic problems. Without a political mandate to make wholesale changes, administrators could only legalize partial flexibility while maintaining the rest of the regulatory industrial system. Even with a stronger hand, the chief financial officers might not have made sweeping changes since they were as tentative as the public about the right road to prosperity.[58]

Director General Jacques Necker's "intermediate system," begun in May 1779, typified the mixed nature of old and new institutions in this period. After an inconclusive survey of opinions among entrepreneurs, guilds, and inspectors of manufacture about the benefits of industrial regulations or freedom, Necker allowed manufacturers to choose whether to make their products according to the regulations or to use no authorized specification—and label them as free goods. In a sense this double posture was a logical outcome of the policy begun in the 1750s, which stopped penalizing cloth made in the countryside by nonguild workers. Decriminalizing the manufacture of cotton calicoes and finally allowing their import into France were other measures weighing in on the side of laissez-faire economics at the same time that rewriting the industrial code for textiles maintained the older policy of regulation that was begun by Colbert. Jean-Pierre Hirsch has characterized the merchants of this era as having simultaneously *"les deux rêves de commerce,"* the two dreams of regulation and freedom.[59]

The uncertainties of this transitional period provoked other apparently opposite solutions. A system of parallel paths continued in the laws restoring the guilds. The edicts reestablishing the guilds institutionalized economic differences in a society that still separated groups according to privileged orders. The widest gulf had always differentiated free crafts from guild production. In the countryside, peasant cottage craft and

---

58. See Levasseur, *Histoire*, and Minard, *La Fortune de colbertisme*, esp. chap. 8, "L'Inspection contestée ou la réglementation en question" on the ambiguity of inspectors of manfacture toward industrial regulation.

59. Jean-Pierre Hirsch, *Les Deux rêves du commerce: Entreprise et institution dans la region liloise, 1780–1860* (Paris: EEHESS, 1991).

clustered industry were free from guilds. Now in cities too, those who worked alone and sold goods from their dwelling or found jobs as day workers *(journaliers)* had no obligation to join guilds. In the guilds themselves, there had always been separation between apprentices, journey workers, and masters. For the first time, skilled workers themselves were put into different categories. Along with masters, whose higher entrance fees allowed them to participate in guild governance, were ranged the associates, separated from making policy and confined to abiding by the rules of the old guild for their products. Among the masters, the ideal of universal participation fell before the program of selecting a panel of twenty-five deputies to direct affairs along with the guild officers.

The separations and categories embedded in society seemed to legitimate a variety of roles for women workers. Thus in women's guilds, women remained officers. In men's guilds, their legal handicap overpowered the equalizing capacity of being *"marchande publique,"* which applied only to commercial activities. They could run businesses as masters or associates, but they had to go "inside the tent" when it came to the management of mixed-sex guilds. The multivalent nature of women's economic roles caused anomalies as lawmakers shifted from treating them like men to preserving exceptions for their special qualities as females. An inquiry on handling difficulties in the 1779 edict, which took up questions about rules for women, gives us a sense of the administration's dual approach.

The questionnaire asked if women may become masters in guilds where their own husbands were not masters. The answer is yes, women might become masters independently of their husbands, or take on trades with or without their husbands, and they could also do business in several guild trades after registering, just as men could. In order to enter into men's guilds, are girls and women required to undertake an apprenticeship? In this case, the answer was no, based on the particular nature of female workers. "To require girls and women to undertake an apprenticeship before they may be admitted into men's guilds would seem to impose on them a very harsh obligation. It would be enough to keep them from choosing to enter. It is doubtful if one could find anybody who would want to go through it." The occasion of this question was women's request to enter the woolens' guild in Sedan, which required apprenticeships of male workers. The questioner asks if "such an exception for girls and women would be contrary to equity? Would it cause the masters to complain?" The response ignores the standard of evenhandedness to rest on the basis of female difference, transforming work requirements into charity. "In subjecting girls and women [only] to a simple trial or to a simple examination, they would be treated in accord with the way that the weakness of their sex and decency requires."[60] (The same issue in Lyon was answered differently. There an apprenticeship was required for female workers.) Like the rationale in Turgot's 1776 legislation and tracts favoring the entrance of drawgirls to Lyon's silk guild, opening guilds to women was presented as a means of achieving benevolence and virtue, removed from economic considerations. Equity with male workers was not a consideration because the females were on a different plane.

But economic and political considerations underlay the administration's support of women's entrance into the guilds. Although never articulated, the lower salaries that women earned and their earlier exclusion from most male guilds made the females ideal candidates to undermine guild exclusiveness and power. Whether the inspiration for women's opportunity was "an integral part of the general project of reforming the country and regenerating its *moeurs*," as Judith Coffin has written, or a charitable enterprise, it remained an administrative means to subvert the guild system.[61] The subtext was to sap the power and monopoly of guilds and open up the workforce of France to more productivity. These steps, shown in Steven L. Kaplan's thorough analysis, were part of a conscious approach to modernizing French industry to compete in the European marketplace. Just as Colbert had constructed a system of regulations and guilds to bring French production up to international standards, a century later the government undertook to reorganize the guilds, the regulatory structure, and the workforce for the same ends. By changing the basis of female labor the government entered into the economic field hoping to cut men's salaries and spread industriousness; of course, reducing the number of poor women on charity and eliminating prostitution were also persistent goals.

The lieutenant of police in Rouen helped the *lingères* to break into the tailors' guild, and in Lyon the central administration proposed having girls enter the *grande fabrique* as silk weavers. The Chamber of Commerce brought pressure to bear on behalf of female ribbonmakers seeking to

---

60. AN F12 677B, "Questions et observations sur les nouveaux règlements."
61. Judith H. Coffin, *The Politics of Women's Work: The Paris Garment Trades, 1750–1915* (Princeton: Princeton University Press, 1996), 38.

enter the *passementiers'* guild. Ruling that women were not required to undergo apprenticeship just to demonstrate their competence, lowered the bar for their entrance. The male guilds' resistance showed not only their misogyny but also their determination to oppose the government's pressure and to maintain the guild in its traditional privilege. But what was sauce for the goose was sauce for the gander; if women could enter male guilds, then it followed that men could enter those formerly relegated to women. This, too, was part of the government's effort to impose symmetry and modernization on French economic structures.

In guilds of mixed sex, like the spinners and ribbonmakers, the widowers of female masters traditionally had the right to inherit the business, just as widows inherited the guild rights of their husbands who had been masters. With the rules spelled out, now the widowers' rights were universally applied in all guilds. In addition, as the economic situation worsened, male workers began entering traditional female trades. They were enticed by the lower entrance fees and shorter spans of apprenticeship. In Rouen, for example, some 200 males chose to become women's hairdressers through the new women's guild of knitters, hairdressers, and feather merchants rather than by purchasing their offices through the master wigmakers. The wigmakers' harassment prompted the male hairdressers to request an official judgment on their right to the trade. They received assurances that "as men may be received into women's guilds . . . nothing prevents the male hairdressers from acquiring this mastership."[62]

The officials reckoned without the new sensibilities relegating particular trades to specific genders. Judith Coffin cites the outrage of social critic Louis Sébastien Mercier at the entrance of men into traditionally female occupations. "It is grotesque to see male hairdressers, men pushing a needle, handling a shuttle, and usurping the sedentary life of women. . . . It is immoral . . . for strong and robust persons to invade areas which nature has particularly designed for persons of the opposite sex."[63] The gendering of work, always in the background, was gathering emphasis as the century wore to a close, and men were scorned if they used tools associated with women, like the needle and the shuttle, worked in trades

62. ADSM C137. The men wanted to pay their fees and receive letters of mastership from the new guild of knitters–hairdressers–feather workers (*bonnetières-coeffeuses-plumassières*).
63. Coffin, *Politics*, 41. Her translation of Sébastien Mercier, *Les Tableaux de Paris*, 9:178–79.

that catered to female frivolity like hairdressing, or adopted the passive behavior of sitting assigned to women. From a different source came other criticism as the female masters objected to the men as competitors. The guild women drew heavily on new standards of modesty and appropriate behavior. The men were not only interlopers in a traditional women's trade, they would insinuate themselves into the furthest recesses of the house and perform services too intimate for decency. Besides, female hairdressers had little hope of displacing the men because the customers preferred them.

When guild women themselves used essentialist arguments to defend their position, the rhetoric of guild argumentation came to its opposite point. Once enjoying the status simply of adults in guilds where scant reference was made to gender, they now turned to the new and limiting definition of female as weak and in need of special protection and particular etiquette. Current laws gave them increased economic opportunity but curtailed their chance for political action. Administration policy took note of women workers' skill and their ability to act capably, but at the same time, the government used the women's lower pay scale to help undermine the system of guilds. As the touchstone of privilege waned, sex difference came to stand in its place. While setting a standard for assertive self-direction, the lessons that guild women had learned over the centuries in managing their own destiny could not always triumph over the new economic and political obstacles.

The economic difficulties that fed into the Revolution brought new exigencies to bear on working women's lives. Not only did the aristocratic taste and style that had sustained the luxury trade of the Old Regime pass from popularity, the old networks of commerce found themselves disrupted by political uprisings and warfare.[64] Producers and traders who had learned to switch from domestic to foreign markets now had to find new avenues of commerce where the fluctuating French currency would be honored. Wholesale commerce of linen cloth and thread that the new linen-drapers struggled to keep in their own hands faced competition from larger, better-financed trading companies. The war made crossing national borders problematic so that raw materials the women

---

64. Pierre Cayez analyzes the elements of Lyon's economic disruption in *Métiers jacquard et hauts fourneaux: Aux orgins de l'industrie lyonnaise* (Lyon: Presses Universitaires de Lyon, [1978]), 78–96. For a discussion of the confusion in Paris and the provinces, see Kaplan, *La Fin*, 519–28, 546–65.

needed for their workshops became scarce and overpriced, and the merchants who expedited finished goods were less obliging in their terms of trade.

As male family members were drafted, women lost the resources of extra labor and homestead that might have enabled their business to succeed. Credit became a severe problem for the guild women who amassed goods from rural Normandy and transshipped them to Paris and elsewhere. Inevitably, the journeywomen and apprentices lower on the commercial rung suffered from irregular orders and payment. The fragile personal networks that sustained guildwomen through the eighteenth century were disrupted by bankruptcies that left scores of women with empty hands and cupboards. It profited them naught to be skilled in manipulating the local administrators and the thicket of time-honored laws: new tax collectors and new courts had even more pressing needs and more ideological reasons not to make decisions with a light hand. The pocket of privilege that had enabled guild women to subsist fell away. Wealth, from family sources or one's own earnings, skill, and above all, luck were to determine the fate of Rouen's former guild women as they struggled for survival in a new economic era.

Lyon Resists the King

The royal decree to reform Lyon's guilds came on 24 January 1777. Like the edicts reinstalling guilds in other cities, this document established a table of fees for entrance to masterships, who would have the right to direct guild affairs, and another for associates (*agrégés*), former masters who would not take part in guild governance. Artisans who had been masters in the old guilds paid only one-quarter of the new fees to become masters or associates in the new guilds. Other entrants had to pay one-half the new fee. Workers without earlier membership paid the entire fee. For the silk merchants and weavers the fees for mastership ranged from master merchants at 500 livres, to master weavers at 100 livres; other trades in Lyon cost between 400 and 600 livres for entrance.[65]

The government's pressure on artisans to join the new guilds was one of the most maladroit and resisted campaigns of the late reform effort.

---

65. AN F 12 768, "Édit du Roi, pour les communautés d'arts et métiers de la ville de Lyon, January 1777."

Lyon was proud of its free craft heritage and flexible approach to commerce. Whereas Rouen's guild masters complained about being linked to incompatible trades in the reform, many of those in Lyon protested against being made into a guild in the first place. They cited past practice as their rationale. For two centuries, the trades that prepared thread and finished the cloth were at the disposal of the silk industry, hiring on as many workers as needed, advancing the silk yarn from one workshop to the next, and accommodating the press of business rather than being preoccupied with the concerns of individual guilds. The *grande fabrique*, which included the silk weavers and merchants, was like a sun pulling into its orbit the auxiliary trades and bending their trajectories from independent guild functions into service work for silk weavers and merchants.

Guild rules existed, but business needs came first. Or, one might say, guilds in Lyon pursued their regulations to the letter when it suited them but closed their eyes to infractions when profit lay in that direction.[66] In any event, guilds were far fewer than free trades. In the silk industry, the various parts of silk processing in specialized workshops were engaged on the basis of contracts with individuals outside the guild. As artisans pointed out when the edict of 1777 began to be enforced, few of the auxiliary trades had belonged to guilds, and even fewer had a tradition of being formally merged with other trades. Although there were some guilds of mixed sex, and even some women's guilds in Lyon, a strong tradition of independent guilds, which enabled women to become mistresses and officers in Rouen, was not part of Lyon's silk culture. Indeed, when the possibility of giving women masterships in the silk guild came under discussion, one hostile tract asserted that if women became the heads of ateliers, they would have to hire male proxies (who were in bad

66. AN F 12 768, Guilds also occasionally tolerated nonguild work. Laurant Chabout, clincailer [sic], in Lyon, said that his father "avoit de tout tems fait des boutons de metal, étampes, et calotes sur moules de bois et sur ciment sans avoir jamais éprouvé aucun empechement ni opposition de la part des maîtres Boutoniers et Enjoliviers, qu'au moyen de cette longue tranquilité" (original spelling). He thought he would make buttons as well. In another such accommodation, the widow Cornet and her daughter are discussed in AN F 12 1430, "Mémoire," no. 3216, and letter, Lyon, 16 December 1767, M. de la Verpillière to the Prévôt de Marchands. Having refused another woman permission to join, the guild had authorized the arrangement with Widow Cornet in 1745, perhaps because her pay far exceeded the usual fee of 130 livres for apprenticeship, *compagnonage*, and mastership. See also Archives Municipales de Lyon (hereafter AML) HH 580, Grande Fabrique, Registre, 29 September 1773. Femme Boisson was allowed to work in silk making, "en qualité de maîtresse sous le nom de son mary," who had completed his apprenticeship but had fallen gravely ill before he could take it up.

repute) to carry on their business. Such a comment would have been unimaginable in Rouen!

When officials asked the trades to declare their structure and rules in order to group similar ones together, the unorthodox nature of Lyon's guilds became clear. The carders and spinners of wool had been a guild since 1641, but their officers left the simple artisans at liberty to function as they wanted, revoking all the previous regulations. The shoe makers and carvers of the wooden *sabot* had formed a guild, but both received freedom from guild membership in 1756.[67] Wheelwrights and makers of stocking machines were not in guilds; instead they made spinning and knitting devices on individual orders.[68] There was confusion over the status of blacksmiths. According to one document, they formed a guild with pin makers and shoesmiths, incorporating the retail hardware sellers only in 1775 and incorporated the nail makers two years later in the general reform.[69] But de Flesselles, intendant in Lyon from 1768 to 1784, told Paris that neither coppersmiths nor tinsmiths were in guilds. The tapestry makers, grocers, mercers, and carpenters had also been free trades. Officers of the newly created guild of hat makers, furriers, feather merchants, and fur shearers asserted that only the hat makers had earlier status as a guild and that the other trades had been separate. As for matching the trade to the sex of workers, in Lyon the metal founders' guild in existence before 1777 included men and women masters.[70] But the linen-drapers (*lingers*)—so important among the women's guilds in Rouen—were exclusively men in Lyon. And despite the fact that the females did virtually all the work, only males could be masters in the trades of spinning, silk throwing, making the warp, folding warp threads around the beam, carding, and combing silk yarn.[71]

---

67. AN F 12 768, *Cardeurs* and *fileurs de laine; cordonniers* and *savetiers* received an *arrêt du conseil*, 29 March 1756.

68. AN F 12 762. The tradition of women workers in these metal trades paved the way for them to become masters when the guild was established.

69. AN F 12 763 gives material on *marechaux* (shoesmiths), *forgeurs* (blacksmiths), *ferretiers* (hardware venders), *épinglières* (pin makers), and *cloutiers* (nail makers).

70. AN F 12 774, letter from de Flesselles, 16 July 1770.

71. AML HH 424, "Les maîtres moulineurs de soie," 31 January 1669, accusing Simonde du Lièzedes of occupying a mastership illegally, the guild officers asserted that sons of masters have the privilege of owning a workshop, but not daughters of masters. Nevertheless, as a special exception, the *gardes* awarded Simonde this favor, because of their great "respect" for her mother, who became a mistress in the guild! Thus they signaled two anomalies in guild practice.

Because of the mixture of free and guild trades in Lyon before the 1777 edict, the reinstallation of guilds had unexpected results. When the government joined several trades that it considered similar, often only one had previously enjoyed guild status. That trade ended up dominating the others in the new guild. For instance, the new guild of dressers of silk cloth—workers who gave a *moiré* or watered pattern—was joined to *apprêteurs* and cleaners in 1777. But only the *apprêteurs* had constituted a guild before, and they alone signed up as masters. The other trades—specialists in using machines for *moiré*, calendars, cylinders, and cleaning—enrolled in the lower ranks as associates.[72] This meant that the trade with the masters made all the guild decisions, turning informal cooperative relationships between the trades into more rigid practices and ensuring that the dominant trade squeezed the most profit from contracts for itself.

Other amalgamations brought different problems. The most straightforward charge was that officials had misunderstood the technical processes and had joined together trades as different as cheese and chalk. (Blacksmiths warned against linking "*dans la même main les functions les plus incompatibles, la lime et le rabot*").[73] More subtle political issues arose in other unions. Pastry chefs, restaurant keepers, chefs, and innkeepers complained that forcing them to join with the wine shop owners gave those sellers of drink unfair access to the more serious food preparation trades.[74] In chapter 3, we saw that the hat makers made a similar complaint about the shearers of pelts using their newfound guild entrance to become hatters. Eventually, the hatters managed to reduce the pelt shearers to the rank of associates, who needed to undergo an apprenticeship to become master hat makers. The specialized dyers of silk thread called *chineurs* resisted joining with the ordinary silk, cotton, and wool dyers, arguing that the *chineurs*' trade was really an art, unlike the routine activities of the dyers. Their underlying motive was probably that the ordinary dyers far outnumbered them, but this was the very reason

---

72. AN F 12 768 documents the status of finishers (*aprêteurs des étoffes*), who gave a moiré or watered pattern (*moireurs*), calenderers, cilindreurs, and cleaners (*dégrasseurs*).

73. AN F 762, The blacksmiths (*forgeurs*) claimed incompatibility with the wheelwrights (*charons*) in order to exclude them from the new guild. The two trades were as dissimilar, they asserted, as "*la lime*," a file, was to "*le rabot*," a plane. The first was used on metal; the second on wood.

74. AN F 12 762. The 1777 edict combined pastry chefs (*patissiers*), restaurant keepers (*traiteurs*), chefs (*cuisiniers*), and inn keepers (*taverniers*) with the wine shop owners (*cabaretiers*).

why officials insisted on their amalgamation—that they were too few to constitute a guild on their own.[75]

The *grande fabrique* was a guild that had split into its two factions of merchants and workers with some three hundred wealthy master merchants who kept their own workshops and gave out work to the eight hundred or so master weavers. Some one hundred "*petits marchands*" formed an intermediate group of merchants who gave out work and sold the products until an economic downturn forced them to return to the category of master weavers.[76] The government's pressure to open the *grande fabrique* to women, as part of its general guild reform, received stiff opposition. As the eighteenth-century struggle of the master weavers to maintain control over their independence and economic fortunes gave way to the merchants' dominance, the status of female workers became ever more central.[77] Master weavers, who themselves hired unrelated female weavers illegally, were fiercely opposed to allowing them legal entry into the guild since the women would then become competitors rather than hired labor.[78]

The commercial decline of brocades and other rich silk fabrics rippled through Lyon, with trades dependent on the silk industry the first casualties. Those who had not purchased their masterships in good times were in no position to buy them now. Those already masters were reluctant to pay again for a license they already enjoyed. To the dismay of royal officials, the master merchants and master weavers of the *grande fabrique* largely honored the edict reorganizing the guilds in the breach.

This pattern was not immediately obvious, however, because in the first year of the new edict, 2,104 artisans entered the new guilds, paying

---

75. AN F 12 762 [1780]. The specialized silk thread dyers called *chineurs*, made weft designs called *chine à la branche*. They were differentiated from the ordinary dyers, who were called *teinteurs*.

76. Ernest Pariset gives a clear description of the evolving classes of silk merchants and weavers in *Histoire de la fabrique lyonnaise: Étude sur le régime social et économique de l'industrie de la soie à Lyon depuis le XVI siècle* (Lyon: Rey, n.d.), 79–89.

77. See Daryl M. Hafter, "Women Who Wove in Eighteenth-Century Lyon," in *European Women and Preindustrial Craft*, ed. Daryl M. Hafter (Bloomington: Indiana University Press, 1995), 42–64.

78. See the restrictions that the provost of merchants and aldermen of Lyon made in 1723 against master weavers for hiring drawgirls to weave. The officers "reçoivent des fréquentes plaints que plusieurs maîtres s'ingerent d'employer en qualité des journalières les filles tireuses de cordes, contre les défences des ordonnances consulaires du 5 Aoust 1704 et 14 Février 1718, ce qui porte un préjudice considerable à ceux qui suivant les règlements," "A Messieurs, les Prévost et Échevins de la Ville de Lyon," February 1723, p. 179.

the grand sum of 128,635 livres. Warning themselves not to expect the same outcome in subsequent years, the next year officials inscribed 291 artisans who paid a total of 41,446 livres. The milliners (*marchandes de modes*), the only women's guild besides the midwives to respond, showed only 4 entrants in 1777, for a combined 150 livres, and none in 1778.[79] Royal officials did not have much cause to celebrate the obedience of Lyon's artisans in entering the new guilds. Although the numbers in one report may have been exaggerated, they illustrated a real trend. A local official wrote that as many as 800 mercers, hardware vendors, and silk retail merchants had plied their business in the era of free commerce before 1777, but only 15 signed up to enter the new combined guild.[80]

While the small guilds were not unimportant, it was the merchants and weavers of the *grande fabrique* that the economic administration was watching. In the class of master weavers, 107 men had found their way to the intendant's office in 1777, along with 14 master merchants and 1 master weaver who paid the requisite 500 livres to become a master merchant. But in 1778, only 15 men enrolled as master weavers, and 3 as master merchants. The master weavers with their designated guild officers pressed to have the entrance fees to the new guild reduced. They also wanted guarantees that their own children could keep the right to weave as wage earners in the ateliers of fellow master weavers and that their sons would accede to the mastership on easier terms than those for journeymen. In addition, the uncertain status of guild widows troubled them, and they held out for full guild privileges at no extra fee for their widows. The master merchants balked at the new entrance fees and complained of being subject to the onerous job of guild officer, which would put a crimp in their profits. Facing this opposition, the government's campaign to convince the silk industry to enroll in the new guild went on for the next fourteen years, and it showed the limits of royal persuasion in the economic realm.

Trying to explain the silk manufacturers' intransigence, officials singled out the workers' past independence. Lyon resisted setting up new guilds, one wrote, "because the republican spirit rules here more than in

---

79. AN F 12 768. The "État" for 1777 lists only 16 entering this guild.
80. AN F 12 768. Master weavers were called "fabricans d'étoffes de soye, d'or, et d'argent, maîtres ouvriers à façon ou travaillant pour le compte d'autrui." The terms designating master merchants were "maîtres marchands, fabricans d'étoffes de soye, d'or, et d'argent travaillant et faisant travailler."

other cities."[81] The "republican spirit" referred to workers' belief in their right to what they considered fair treatment. It had in the past goaded silk weavers and journeymen hatters to strike for better wages and work requirements. It was behind the municipal consulate's practice of setting a tariff, a general pay rate for weavers and hatters, to deal with militant workers. Whether as master weavers and their journeymen or as journeymen hatters, who banded together to defend their rights, Lyon's guilds had large groups of male and female workers conscious of their role in the economic structure and experienced in organizing protests. Their penchant for obstreperous behavior can be gauged by the regulations for masters, masters' widows, and associates to receive the guild officers "with civility and respect" when they came to inspect the products. Often assertive and rowdy, the masters were told: "It is expressly enjoined on the masters to comport themselves in the assemblies with decency and circumspection . . . It is forbidden to make and foment any intrigue of party or cabal, whether in order to have a policy adopted or to nominate officers, under pain of fine and canceling the nominations."[82] With this sort of behavior as its standard, the labor force of Lyon caused officials administering the law to tread softly.

Ignoring the royal edict, the majority of weavers simply continued their business, working in infringement of the law. Various estimates put the number of weavers without license at 600, 800, 1,200, or even 2,000. The last thing administrators wanted to do, however, was to cause labor disputes in the silk industry, especially when the sales decline had already disrupted production. Another apprehension was that too much pressure from the government would cause the masters to bring suit and that this would serve as a pretext for them to reinstate the guild bureau or to borrow funds to support their court case. To support a policy of reducing guild involvement in fiscalism, the 1777 edict had explicitly directed that all guild bureaus—the buildings where guild business was done—be sold and that the guilds should borrow no money without permission from the king.

---

81. AN F 12 765, "Observations sur la communauté de la fabrique d'étoffes," [1777]. Robert Darnton showed how a contemporary printer used the "republic" as an ideal of work democracy, in which guildmen shared just conditions with all in the trade. See *The Great Cat Massacre* (New York: Random House, 1985), 82.

82. AN F 12 763, Article 16 and Article 18.

A mild course of action could avoid labor unrest, they hoped. Here the administration demonstrated it was willing to be flexible to avoid confrontation. Describing the realities in Lyon, an official wrote to Paris weighing possible actions: "It is doubtless an abuse to tolerate workers without licenses, but it would be too dangerous at the moment to choose to correct this abuse by seizures and confiscations of looms. That would throw the 'fat into the fire' [*le feu dans la fabrique*]. It would then seem as if we want to reduce the most desperately unfortunate beings to misery by removing the only means they have to earn their bread. It would perhaps cause some uprisings while there are still gentle ways to bring about order and tranquility. But we must add that there is no time to lose."[83]

Thus began a tug of war between the Paris commissioners of the Bureau of Commerce, who wanted the provisions of the 1777 edict enforced, and the master merchants and master weavers of the *grande fabrique*, who sought to have the fees lowered and the benefits increased before they would join the new guild. The mediators were the local and royal administrators who were sympathetic to the real misery of the silk workers but were themselves under pressure to have Lyon conform to national standards. As letters and memoirs sped back and forth from Lyon to Paris, the will of government and workers was tested. The masters proposed lowering the entrance fees for both merchants and weavers, but the Bureau of Commerce refused. Although collecting funds for the crown was not the primary goal of this reorganization, funds were needed to pay off the debts guilds had incurred in the past.[84] Moreover, it went against the grain to give exemptions to individual cities and crafts. If equal treatment was the key to reforming the guilds, any deviation or "individual consideration" was a step backwards from the modern homogeneity the edict was designed to achieve.

Although the Bureau of Commerce and the Royal Council refused to lower entrance fees, other observers continued to document the artisans' poverty. In 1779, the officers of the *grande fabrique* protested that the master weavers could not pay the fee set for entrance, and they asked for smaller fees and a longer period in which to pay. Paris officials at first refused both requests but then were convinced to give weavers a three-month grace period with an entrance fee of 25 livres before it rose to

---

83. AN F 12 765, 1778.
84. AN F 12 765. Note the report that at least 600 silk weavers avoided the guild and worked without masterships, causing a loss of some 45,000 livres to the king.

50 livres. In 1780, the officers again wrote that master weavers could not pay even the reduced entrance fee for masters. They could manage the fee for associates, but without permission to have apprentices, they would certainly fail in business. In fact, the work balance of the entire silk industry depended on a regular supply of apprentices. But the 1777 edict provided that masters alone, not associates, could have apprentices and the director general of economic affairs in Paris explicitly forbade this change in the law. Yet another petition from Lyon's silk *fabrique* for smaller fees and associates' use of apprentices elicited a further extension of the reduced fee payment but no change in the rule that only masters could have apprentices. "Messieurs the Commissioners of the Bureau have always been disposed to come to the aid of the master workers," the Paris report said, but "still they have to pay their fees if another expedient cannot be found."[85]

Letters and memoirs continued to be exchanged between Paris and Lyon. In 1781, the provost of merchants, Antoine Fay de Sathonay, wrote of the "miserable state of most silk workers, still unable to satisfy the confirmation tax of the 1777 edict." In 1783 and 1784 there were so few masters enrolled in the guild that it was difficult to find candidates to become officers.

Complicating matters, another element had entered the debate: the independent, intransigent spirit of the Lyon workers. Their experience in pressing their "republican" rights made them unwilling to fall in with the government's plan to set up new guilds. De Cotte, the intendant of commerce, wrote to De Flesselles that he was searching for some means of exempting poor workers from paying the entrance fee, but he was disappointed that "master workers who could afford to pay have not shown more good will [by doing so] than those who are without means."[86] Defying Paris became the political aim of the guild. As De Cotte suggested, some masters financially able to enter the new guild refused. At one point masters would have joined, but many feared the retaliation of the holdouts. How could the government make a guild function when the majority of its potential members dug in their heels and would not cooperate? In the absence of volunteers to become guild officers, the Lyon consulate had appointed men, but parts of the *grande fabrique* had balked

---

85. AN F 12 762, letter from de Cotte to De Flesselles, 9 October 1780.
86. AN F 12 762, letter from de Cotte to Fay de Sathonney, n.d.

at accepting this decision. Fay de Sathonay then suggested allowing the guild to choose officers from among the old masters, even if they had not yet entered the new guild! With the last syndic already serving for five years (the usual term was one), the problem was growing urgent. A group of old officers tried to compel a master named Fontetrune to accept the post. But he adamantly refused despite promises to pay the cost of his new mastership and to change the day of the guild court's séances from Wednesday to Thursday to accommodate him. Making a great commotion, his fellow silk master weavers threatened him and would not let him agree either to join the new guild or to become an officer.[87]

The master merchants were as stubborn as the master workers in boycotting the new guild and delaying the writing of new regulations. Moreover, they used the negotiations in progress to try to curtail the master weavers' rights. They avoided calling guild assemblies or "forgot" to inform the master weavers of the meeting dates. When guild assemblies did meet, the merchants ignored the master weavers' suggestions and said simply that "the majority does not adopt your proposition."[88] Royal patience was wearing thin. The intendant threatened that the king would stop asking for input and simply impose regulations that would restrict the master merchants' prestige.

By the year 1786 the *grande fabrique* still refused to join its new guild, and its officers still tolerated business as usual. They did so on sufferance, while the king was deprived of his fees, "but it is to be hoped that the situation will end," the *receveur des maîtrise* in Lyon wrote to Henri Léonard Jean Baptiste de Bertin, then secretary of state for manufactures. At any rate, this official showed his ongoing conciliation. "I hold out my hand to them, as well, with regard to everything within my power" (*mais il y a lui d'esperer qu'elle cessera; j'y tiendrai au surplus la main en tout ce qui pourra dépendre de moi*). The persistent obstinacy of the *grande fabrique* was all the more egregious in view of the acquiescence of other guilds elsewhere.[89] Despite the government's crisp refusals to give the silk *fabrique* extra time to comply with the 1777 edict, the deadline was extended

87. AN F 12 765, letter to de Colonnia, intendant of commerce, #5427, n.d.
88. AN F 12 762. Master weavers complained that the merchants preferred keeping the regulations of 1744, which favored their class, and so they procrastinated about drawing up new ones. They kept the master weavers from using the guild assemblies as a forum for like tribunals where the judges voted but did not discuss the material.
89. AN F 12 762, extract of a letter to M. Bertin from the Receveur des Maîtrise in Lyon, 19 January 1786.

to 1780, 1781, and then to 1783. No more than 528 masters had subscribed to the new guilds by the end of the guild regime.[90]

Meanwhile other political and economic conflicts were being fought within the process of forming the new guilds. Earlier in the eighteenth century, guilds like the silk master merchants and master weavers did business with the auxiliary trades, each of which was a separate entity. Whether part of a guild, a group of craft workers, or simply individual workers scattered throughout the city's tenements, workers unwound the silk from cocoons, spun, warped, and finished the woven fabric on the basis of each separate contract. The silk guild set out regulations for its own manufacture and also for the governance of the "other cloth, mixed with silk wool, animal hair [poil], linen and cotton of the city and outskirts of Lyon and for the manufacture of these textiles."[91]

The silk industry's domination of the auxiliary trades was evident in this comprehensive set of bylaws over cloth trades that existed in whatever form history and politics had left them. The 1777 edict sought to discipline the crafts by linking similar trades, making them into guilds, and weeding out those with casual or unskilled work as free professions open to all. After scrutinizing the various trades, the commissioners of the Bureau of Commerce came up with a plan to establish five guilds, which would then make up the *grande fabrique*. Nothing so exemplifies the modernizing spirit of the late 1700s as comparing the varied form of the trades before 1777 and the effort to synchronize, balance, and homogenize them into guilds afterwards.[92]

Presented with the roster of which trades would be amalgamated into each guild, the old masters and their officers began lobbying for the arrangement they considered best, just as the trades in Rouen had done. Several issues became flash points for their agitation: the trades that would be amalgamated, the eventual structure of the guild, and whether the guild would become part of the *grande fabrique* or remain with other auxiliary trades in the *petite fabrique*. Each memoir had its own hyperbole

90. Pariset, *Histoire de la fabrique*, 233n4.
91. AN F 12 763, "Projet et déclaration du Roi. Communautés d'arts et métiers. Ville de Lyon," [12 December 1781]. This appendix to the January 1777 edict established five guilds in the *grande fabrique*: (1) des fabricants d'étoffes d'or, d'argent, et de soye; (2) des guimpiers, fabricants de gase, mouchoirs de soye et fabricants de blonde; (3) passementiers, tissutiers, rubaniers, frangeurs, boutonniers, et enjoliviers; (4) plieurs de soye, cardiers de soye, moulineurs de soye, et autre préparateurs de soye pour être montée et employee sur le métier; (5) aprêteurs de toutes sortes d'après aux étoffes de soye, moireurs et calandreurs, cilindreurs et dégrasseurs.
92. Ibid.

to argue its point of view. The most fractious guild created by the edict of 1777 was the one that included the makers of gold and silver thread; weavers of gauze, silk kerchiefs, and "blonde" lace; decorative braid makers; weavers of narrow silk bands; ribbonmakers; makers of fringe; button makers; and cloth finishers.[93] Arguing against the new arrangements, the gold and silver thread makers traced the history of these disparate trades to show how illogical it was to join them together. The regulations of 1668 gave the gauze weavers and the spinners of gold and silver thread a loose association. But the gauze makers were not in a formal guild until 1777 when they were linked to the decorative braid makers and ribbonmakers. Only the gold and silver thread makers and these few gauze merchants were in a position to pay the designated guild fee of 300 livres. This put the precious thread makers into the intolerable position of having to support the entire guild. Clearly, some argued, the guild should be dissolved and allowed to let its separate trades go their own way.[94]

Other guild members opted for a united guild with many trades but with a single guild fee. For two hundred years there has been equality among the guild members, they claimed, but now that some workers had fallen on bad times with little work, the merchants wanted to shrink competition at their level and increase the number of workers. This group likened the outcome of a varied entrance tariff to the class fracture seen among the silk merchants and weavers. In fact, they asserted, the fees should be lowered for all, "since a great number of workers who established themselves without license do not have bread to eat and much less the 300 livres for entrance to the mastership."[95] While royal officials were sensitive to the difficulties of impoverished masters, they opposed breaking the guild into groups paying different entrance fees. This split would duplicate the problems of intraguild hostility that plagued the silk weavers. As one of the memoirs alleged, it would cause the small masters to become the "slaves" of those wealthy enough to be merchants.

Another faction of precious thread makers wanted to keep the guild in one body but to divide it into three classes, roughly corresponding to the master merchants, the small master merchants, and master workers

---

93. AN F 12 765, "Guimpiers et fabricants de gaze, mouchoirs de soye et fabricants de blondes, passementiers, tissutiers, rubaniers, frangers, boutonniers, enjoliveurs," [1777].
94. AN F 766, "Observations pour la communauté des guimpiers," [n.d.].
95. AN F 12 766, "Observations pour les maîtres de la main d'oeuvre de la communauté des passementiers et autres professions réunités à Lyon par l'édit de janvier 1777."

of the silk weavers. Masters supporting the "three-class" strategy furnished the information that since the two or three hundred workers could not afford to pay the entrance fee, the *gardes* simply excused them from registering in the guild and left them "at liberty in their workshops." Reducing entrance fees would enable all the workers to be legalized so that none were scofflaws. It would be a form of charity to the poor workers, allowing them to survive. Instead of the edict's fee of 300 livres for masters, they suggested the following schedule:

Precious thread makers	80 livres for master, 30 livres for sons of masters
Passementiers	120 livres for master, 27 livres for sons of masters
Button makers	100 livres for master, 30 livres for sons of masters
Women and girls	"only 6 livres each"[96]

The tariff recommended for women and girls is significant because it confirms the fact that this guild permitted female workers to become masters, although they were permitted only one loom in each of their workshops in comparison with the male masters' six. One loom supported a woman at subsistence level, but at this point few of these women practiced the trade as independent masters. There were so many female employees doing piecework for other masters that Lyon's intendant, de Cotte, and other officials mistakenly asserted that "in the old regulations '*les personnes du sexe*' can work only if they are employed by masters and merchant *passementiers*."[97]

---

96. AN F 12 766, "Sur la requête présentée au Roy . . . par les guimpiers." Requiring women and girls to pay "only 6 livres" suggests that despite their legal access to mastership, it must have been usual for them to be employed as permanent journeywomen.

97. AN F 12 770, letter # 4965, to de Cotte, courtesy of M. Deflesselles, [n.d. but after 1777]. In response to the request of Catherine Guerin and Heleine Delhomme, *filles majeures*, to enter the *passementiers*' guild, officials declared, "que les femmes et filles ne pouvoient être admises dans la nouvelle communauté et qu'à la somme des anciens règlemens [sic] les personnes du sexe ne pouvoient travailler que pour le compte des maîtres et marchands passementiers, à titre de simples ouvrières." See also de Cotte's request to let a daughter of Sr. Lafabreque into the guild to weave gauze, letter of de Cotte to Rivereux, 10 June 1777. In both instances, the misunderstanding originated with Bertin's ignorance of the *guimpiers*' pre-1777 statutes. Letter #4965 shows that Bertin thought requests for women's entrance were based solely on the edict of 1777, and he objected, declaring that they could work only

The many different functions of the guild may also have led to confusion about the various ranks of artisans. For example, one branch of the guild (*guimpiers*) made metal thread, others employed cloth-covered wire to construct countrywomen's hats, still another wove silk cloth and constructed bodices and wimples with fluted decoration. In fact, this was the only trade in the silk industry that opened its doors to women masters. But the female masters among the *guimpiers* were so few that their status was not well known either among royal or municipal officials or in the silk industry at large. As we shall see, this fact would have surprising and important consequences.

The internal constitution of the guild was not the only issue of contention: technology also was a contested area. The *guimpiers* wanted to keep the rights to prepare gold and silver thread and to weave cloth of pure silk and silk mixed with other materials. These techniques put them into competition with the silk weavers of the *grande fabrique*, who also had legal rights to these processes. The silk weavers insisted that the *guimpiers* be kept from weaving pure silk since it was the silk weavers' specialty. They also wanted to differentiate between the *guimpiers*' gold and silver thread and their own, insisting that the *guimpiers*' ornaments should be backed by grill-like open weave, not the solid weave normal to the silk workers.[98] A fierce struggle over technology raged for permission to weave on the tall brocade loom (*à la grande tire*), with its capacity to make large designs, and the button loom, which was used for small designs.[99] Naturally, the *guimpiers* hinged their assertions on the fact that in 1726 the enlarged guild of *guimpiers*–gauze makers had won the right to use the *grande tire* brocade loom, in competition with the silk weavers of the *grande fabrique*.[100]

---

as simple *journalières*. In fact, this was true only of the decorators (*enjolivieurs*), who had been employed by *passementiers* before the two trades were united.

98. AN F 12 765, "Statuts des passementiers, Grande Fabrique." *Passementiers* also had to obey the limitation of raising the warp half by half [*levant la chaîne moitié par moitié*] to keep from producing cloth of more than a stipulated length. For a description of the grill-like background weave called *grille* and *à jour*, see Phyllis G. Tortora and Robert S. Merkel, *Fairchild's Dictionary of Textiles*, 7th ed. (New York: Fairchild Publications, 1996), 254, 297.

99. In the button loom (*métier à bouton*) the cords of the patterning device were "passed through a perforated board (button board) and fitted with buttons at the end." The drawgirl turned a rotary device through which the cords were wound to advance the pattern. See Annemarie Seiler-Baldinger, *Textiles: A Classification of Techniques* (Bathurst, Australia: Crawford House Press, 1994), 85–86.

100. AML HH 558, "Pièce relative au procès avec les guimpiers gaziers qui demandent exclusivement la fabrication des gazes et mouchoirs de soie."

When their products were in demand, guilds defended the technical monopoly that enabled them to dominate the market, vigorously rejecting the claims of rival guilds to the same tools and processes. In this vein, the silk weavers of the *grande fabrique* continued to emphasize whatever differences they could find between their techniques and those of the *guimpiers'* guild, chafing at competition with the gauze makers. But when the taste for brocades waned, they found it expedient to reverse their strategy. By 1776, the silk weavers were claiming that since the *guimpiers-passementiers'* techniques "emanated" from the *grande fabrique*, it should give up its independence and become part of the silk weavers' guild. Now they emphasized the similarities of the two groups, fortuitously coming upon regulations from 1557 that allowed both the *guimpiers* and the silk weavers to use tall drawlooms (*à la grande tire*), to weave silk and gauze, to spin, and to make gold and silver thread.[101]

This time it was the turn of the silk weavers to promote amalgamation on the basis of the shared technology that they had earlier resisted. They claimed that the 1777 statutes separated the guilds only as to the wording of regulations and that underlying logic argued for their integration. But the real motives of the *grande fabrique* had to do with profits and control. By amalgamating with the *guimpiers*, the *grande fabrique*'s idled silk weavers could conveniently use their traditional drawloom technology to make more popular cloth. They could elbow out the gauze makers' domination of new fabrics now exclusively on the gauze makers' looms: mixtures of raw silk with threads of linen, wool, goats' hair, and *galette*—a silk yarn spun from cocoon wastes. With these cheaper threads, silk weavers could produce far more economical textiles, which would still be embellished with large or small designs made on drawlooms. Thus the male weavers and the drawgirls and drawboys, no longer employed to produce brocades in gold and silver, could find work again. The similarities between the techniques of *gaziers* and silk weavers could be turned to the latter's benefit. It was none too soon to discover alternative jobs for the skilled drawloom operators. The census of 1777 found that looms producing brocades had declined to 4,924 while there were 6,432 looms with plain silk, already a surplus of 1,508 of the less lucrative looms employing fewer persons per machine. Silk entrepreneurs hoped the chance

---

101. AML, Grande Fabrique, Tome 2, 1763, lawsuit over the regulation of 30 July 1726 between *fabriquants de soie* and *passementiers*.

to make popular new fabrics like gauze would restore economic health to the *grande fabrique*.[102]

The same logic pressed the *grande fabrique* to try to incorporate the embroiderers, who had taken over decorating silk as brocades fell out of fashion. At first the embroiderers successfully warded off amalgamation, but the *grande fabrique* overwhelmed them, insisting that left on their own, the embroiderers could not be trusted to avoid using "false" gold and silver thread. The *fabrique*'s real motive surfaced when they had to justify this expansion to Paris officials. While entirely absent from earlier regulations, it seemed "only fair that the embroiders should pay the incorporation fee to the *grande fabrique* . . . since they will enjoy the benefits of the *fabrique*, and since they form today a branch of very extensive commerce, developed to the detriment and the ruin of brocaded cloth."[103]

The proposed 1787 regulations directed all merchant embroiders to sign up as a guild within the *grande fabrique*, each member paying the 300 livres entrance fee within the three-month grace period or a 500-livre fine. The new rules would provide that ordinary embroiderers, *"ouvrières de l'un et de l'autre sexe,"* could work at home without joining the guild as long as they did not have "a shop or atelier, train students, buy and sell work made by others, or send out work." The master merchant embroiderers and master silk manufacturers had the right to put out work to as many of these nonguild workers as they wished. Despite its specious claim that this linkage would greatly benefit the embroiderers, the dominance of the silk *fabrique* is evident since the silk weavers would gain the right to deal in embroidered objects, but the merchant embroiders were specifically forbidden to sell cloth.[104]

While the commissioners preferred to disband the embroiderers rather than implant embroidering within a guild in the *grande fabrique*, the *guimpiers*–gauze makers were finding it harder to fend off incorporation. Since 1781 when amalgamation with the *grande fabrique* was suggested officially, memoirs repeated old arguments painting the *guimpiers*–gauze makers as a distinct trade with technology too distinctive to encourage linkage. They cited the gauze makers' irregular history to reinforce its

---

102. Tortora, *Fairchild's Dictionary*, s.v. galette. See also AML HH 558 for the census of 1777 and documents on the dispute between the *grande fabrique* and the *guimpiers*' guild.
103. AN 12 766.
104. AN F 12 766, "Projet des règlements," 1787, Article 4. An added note reveals that the commission at first rejected this new amalgamation and had to be convinced of its justice.

special privileges and even alluded to lawsuits between the silk weavers and the *guimpiers*–gauze makers to demonstrate their incompatibility.

But the economic pressures on the *grande fabrique* to gain access to gauze weaving were irresistible. The *guimpiers*–gauze makers pulled out their last card, expecting that it would make an invincible argument. They could not join the master weavers, they reminded officials, because the structure of the *guimpiers*–gauze makers' guild permitted women not only to work as *compagnonnes* (journeywomen), *but to rise to the mastership!* This would introduce a situation of such unpopularity that the journeymen would riot as they did in 1744, when females without ties to guild families were allowed to accept work as daily weavers. These artisans believed they had found the ultimate safeguard against amalgamation with the silk weavers.

The atmosphere in the 1780s, however, was very different from that of the 1740s. To the *guimpiers*' shock, the argument against women coming to weave was no longer persuasive. The thirty-five years since midcentury had been filled with debate at every level over the policy of French industry. Keenly aware of the increasing competition with England, Holland, and Spain, of the situations posed by colonial markets, and of changes in the flexibility and scale of merchandising, the Bureau of Commerce in Paris and its inspectors of manufacture in the field had concerned themselves with improving French commerce.

Arguments in favor of freedom of manufacture and suppressing the silk guilds began to circulate in the 1750s when economic liberals initiated their far-ranging discussion over natural rights. Early suggestions for change had come from tracts by the intendant of commerce in Lyon, Vincent de Gournay, an official heavily influenced by the Physiocrats. His rationale for eliminating the silk guilds evoked a frisson of objection from the guilds' officers in 1752, but it fell on receptive ears in Paris. In 1759, responding to the *grande fabrique*'s complaints that female workers, especially drawgirls, were scarce, Henri Bertin, then controller general, asked whether more girls would be convinced to enroll as drawgirls if they could become weavers after a certain period of labor. At the same time, an anonymous memoir challenged the silk guild's ten-year term of apprenticeship, the utility of the journeyman's rank, and the limit of four looms and one sole apprentice in each silk weaver's atelier. It promoted "the admission of girls and women, even of drawgirls, to weaving." In marginal notes, an officer of the *grande fabrique,* no doubt one representing the master weavers, admitted that "the ideas are seductive and striking, and the author seems to know the silk industry well." He warned, nevertheless, that "the ideas are extremely prejudicial to the interests of the industry" and that they "had been adopted by the master merchants."[105]

The issue of female work came to the fore in 1759 because the Seven Years' War and the royal court's conversion to the plain black fabric of mourning threw brocade commerce into a temporary decline. Always sensitive to changes in style, the *grande fabrique* immediately found itself without work for drawgirls who were crucial to brocade weaving. These female employees managed the patterning device of brocade looms, pulling down weighted cords to advance the design. The physically ruinous job was in the hands of migrants to Lyon, so needy that they had no reserves to weather even a small term of unemployment.[106] Caught short by the commercial slump, the master weavers reneged on their yearlong contracts to the drawgirls, dismissing them without pay. A general exodus of unpaid drawgirls and spinners, who returned to their native Savoy and Bugey, suddenly brought many looms to a halt. Master weavers and merchants complained bitterly, appealing to Paris for help, and Controller General Bertin responded by suggesting that the arduous task of the drawgirl might be sweetened if it led to a legal place at the loom. For the next twenty years, the possibility of allowing female workers into the guild attracted support from merchants and free trade ideologues and apprehension from master weavers.[107] This struggle exemplifies Sheilagh Ogilvie's assertion that the "social capital" of community expectations kept women from entering some guilds.[108]

With the plan of 1781, the administration turned from suggesting a way for women to become masters in the silk guild, to the first concrete

---

105. AML, Registre Grande Fabrique, December 1760. Vincent de Gournay's first memoir of 1751 blamed the silk guild's monopoly for the success of foreign imports because it raised the price of French goods and enforced regulations that made silk work "disagreeable." Pariset, *La Fabrique lyonnaise*, 250, 363–64.

106. See Daryl M. Hafter, "The 'Programmed' Brocade Loom and the Decline of the Drawgirl," in *Dynamos and Virgins Revisited: Women and Technological Change in History*, ed. Martha Moore Trescott (Metuchen, N.J.: Scarecrow Press, 1979), 49–66.

107. According to Pariset, on 28 March 1778, Lyon's Chamber of Commerce "insisted energetically" that a regulation curtailing the length of training for apprentices and journeymen and permitting women to weave should be given to the silk fabrique. *La Fabrique lyonnaise*, 232.

108. Sheilagh Ogilvie, *A Bitter Living: Women, Markets, and Social Capital in Early Modern Germany* (Oxford: Oxford University Press, 2003), 267, 340–44.

steps requiring the guild to take them in. Perhaps the government thought this plan would be validated by the surge of women into the ranks of weavers since the 1740s. (By 1774 more than half of the 4,246 journey weavers were women, either related to male masters or hired illegally, but none with the eventual promise of becoming masters.)[109] The long negotiations with the *grande fabrique* to enroll its male masters in the new guild had no doubt taken their toll on ministerial patience. The government's irritation grew as it watched factions contend for their own advantages while resisting the king's edict. As silk weavers and merchants continued to protest that they could not afford to join the new guild, they must have aroused administrators' distrust, especially when they blamed their lack of resources on the scarcity of drawgirls and spinners. But the coup de grâce for Lyon appears to have been the precious thread and gauze makers' claim of exemption from the *grande fabrique*, on the basis of its guild mistresses. The trump card played by the *guimpiers*–gauze makers pulled down the house of cards of exclusive male mastership.

By 1781, royal administrators took actions specifically to impose on Lyon the freedom for women's work that had been the law throughout France since 1777. The regulations permitted women and girls to enter any of the five silk guilds as apprentices and journey workers, to work at the masters' ateliers, "and thus progress in succession to the mastership." But unlike the men, the women's entrance to the guild would rest on the pretext that it was a means of furnishing the industry with drawgirls and silk thread winders. (Perhaps this was a sop to mollify the silk weavers who were so adamantly arrayed against the proposal and whose businesses were suffering from the drawgirls' absence.) A commentary accompanying the proposed regulations required "all hired girls" to serve four years as drawgirls or silk thread winders before they could begin a two-year apprenticeship and a four-year *compagnonage*. It concluded, "Thus after ten years of work and experience, girls or women could become mistress weavers." To add teeth to the new system, the proposal added, the law should come from the king, be deliberated in the royal council, and registered by *parlement*, and it should be proclaimed without explanations. Nevertheless, to avoid the guilds' "murmuring on the occasion of a new

---

109. L. Bosseboeuf, *Historie de la fabrique de soieries de Tours, des origins au XIXe siècle* (Tours: P. Bousiez, 1900), 293.

regime," the commentary went on, "it would be expedient to accustom their disposition [to it] little by little."[110]

These regulations posed a radical change in practical and theoretical terms. They largely followed in the footsteps of "the capitalists of the late medieval cities," who, in Martha Howell's words, "sought to cheapen labor by subdividing the production process, a goal often achieved by circumventing the established labor force and . . . by employing women or workers from the countryside."[111] Bringing women into the weaving process legally had major implications. It overrode the guild's power to set work standards and entrance requirements, and it did so by ignoring privileged and natural distinctions. By a stroke of the pen, nonguild workers were as good as guild workers and women were as qualified as men.

In an unusual step, the Bureau of Commerce itself wrote the new rules. They appeared as an appendix to the silk guild's regulations, which were finally patched together and registered in 1783. The germ of Turgot's reform ideology was alive in the provisions. Weavers could now set up shop in the suburbs; apprentices needed only four years instead of five in rank; and women could now enter the guild.[112] Subsequent consular ordinances of 17 June 1785 and 3 September 1786 repeated the permission for women to weave, at the same time allowing master weavers to have an unlimited number of looms (while canceling weavers' right to move outside the city).[113] With the 1786 ruling, the municipality announced that it was reneging on an earlier pledge to set a new tariff for silk weaving; henceforth the price for each commission would be set by negotiations between the merchant and each weaver, and workers were forbidden to collaborate for a general wage.

110. AN F 12 736, "Projet de Déclaration du Roi," [12 December 1781], "Les corps de métiers à Lyon ne connoissant rien au dela de l'intérêt du moment, pourront murmurrer à l'occasion du nouveau régime; on a donc jugé qu'il convenoit d'y accoutumer peu à peu leur génie, en faisant précéder changemens par une loi du Prince, délibéré en son conseil, et registrée au Parlement."

111. Martha Howell, *Women, Production, and Patriarchy in Late Medieval Cities* (Chicago: Chicago University Press, 1986), 36.

112. Pariset, *La Fabrique*, 231–32. Freedom to move to the faubourgs where the artisans would be policed by seigneurial justice, along with continuance of municipal enforcement of the industrial regulations, were provisions of the declaration of 30 August 1782, made public by the intendant on 19 January 1783.

113. Louis Trénard, "La Crise sociale lyonnaise à la veille de la Révolution," *Revue d'histoire moderne et contemporain* 2 (1955): 14–15, cites the "Ordonnance consulaire portant règlement pour la police des garçons, femmes et filles, occupés à tirer les cordes à journée," 17 June 1785, Registre Grande Fabrique. The liberty to establish workshops in the faubourgs was rescinded by this law.

Neither the *guimpiers* nor the master weavers could continue to shelter behind guild regulations excluding women. Pushed by its reforming faction, the Bureau of Commerce stripped away the institutional restrictions against women's entrance. Past practice and respect for tradition could no longer justify social conventions discredited by natural law. The terms of dialogue had changed. On one side, social critics' challenge of what was artificial, purely customary, and contrary to nature gained the day (even in the midst of ministerial hesitation). On the other, the logic of Turgot's program of 1776, that the right to work was a basic element in natural rights, had become compelling. Abbé Jean Marie Terray a former controller general, echoed these ideas when, as intendant of Lyon, he supported the 1786 legislation. As nature was the touchstone of appropriate civil law, the rationale for institutions had to conform to the natural propensities of human beings. Thus the propaganda around women's guild entrance—both pro and con—rested on essentialist arguments.

An administrator in support of female weaving in 1781 asserted that "in every profession where strength is not used as a necessary agent and first mover, it is well known that women perform the craft with more address, assiduity, and perfection than men." In order to demonstrate that silk weaving was appropriate for women, he continued by using the successful example of master weavers' female relatives. "The girls and wives of workers making cloth, making gauze, tassels, ribbons, buttons, and decorations, etc. furnish the proof of this assertion. They are completely comfortable working. They rarely leave their looms and their houses. They are more sober than the *compagnons* and their cost of upkeep is less." The last comment highlighted the most striking feature of women's labor, the one that recommended them or damned them according to point of view. Women required less food than men and were satisfied if they did not receive money for the tavern and wine shop. Because they were cheaper to support than male employees, "their labor gives an advantage, more profit for masters and merchants."[114]

The overseers of the poorhouse declared that when females wove, "The cloth is more skillfully woven, more uniform and better made; the work may be slower, but it will be more constant."[115] The *guimpiers* and

---

114. AN F 12 764 B, "La premier établissement de la fabrique de Lyon," [1768?].

115. AN F 12 678, n.d. [after 1786], "Mémoire sur divers objets d'amélioration dans l'ouvre dont l'hôpital de Lyon est chargé tant pour le soulagement des vieux et vieilles infirmes que pour les enfans trouvés, délaissés, ou adoptifs." The administrators wanted to place thirty

makers of gauze and decorative braid justified the female masters in their guild "as being naturally more adroit than men in this kind of manufacture."[116] From the Academy of Lyon's prize-winning essay inquiring which trade and manufacture would be best for Lyon came the exhortation: "Why exclude [women] from a kind of manufacture which nature and their intelligence boldly calls them? Their delicacy is not an obstacle; it is an additional incentive in an art where one needs more taste than strength."[117]

Essentialist arguments also served against women's entrance to the loom. Master weavers asserted that, contrary to their opponents' ideas, strength was indeed a crucial element for weaving and that women were too weak. "Even if in each workshop the *maîtresse* worked like a man, if her privilege conferred that right upon her, it would certainly not have the power to give her more strength." The scheme of using drawgirls as eventual weavers was flawed by "their ineptitude, their weak constitution, their caprices, their illnesses, and their stubborn nature so different from that of an active and robust male weaver."[118] Moreover, women did not have the inventiveness to make new textile structures. They could not conjure up the cloth novelties, the tasteful decoration, the harmonious combination of pattern and background that had put the city of Lyon ahead of its rivals. As a final point of debate, the critics warned that sometimes the weaver had to climb up and rearrange the cordage at the very top of the loom. To think of women performing this task (in a time when many wore no underclothes) was to imagine a circumstance at the height of immodesty![119]

Whether using women's natural capacities to justify or discredit their weaving skills, both sides of this debate agreed that their salaries would be lower than men's. Since their upkeep cost less, master weavers could save the difference. Best of all, when work took a downturn, these females would be encouraged to return to their native villages in the Savoy, as the female embroiderers did, thus allowing the master craftsmen associated

---

members of "*le sexe*" in spinning jobs, with the promise that they might become masters in the *grande fabrique* after six years of work.

116. AN F 12 762, #4977, memoir to the Bureau of M. de Vergennes.

117. Abbé Pierre Bertholon, *Du Commerce et des manufactures destructives de la ville de Lyon* (Montpellier: Jean Martel, aîné, 1787), 193.

118. AML HH 235, Liasse 40, Côte E, Claude Rivey, "Report aux Prévôt des Marchands," 29 May 1781.

119. Cited by Godart, *L'Ouvrier*, 358.

with them to save the cost of their upkeep. From the opposing master weavers came the warning that work stoppage would be catastrophic for the female weavers since it would be more difficult for them to find employment or to join the army as unemployed journeymen did. Instead, they would fall into "dishonest" habits. The worst results, however, would come from their success, as their low salaries would undercut the employment of the journeymen. Where, then, would the former drawgirls find husbands? If the *grande fabrique* became feminized, the master weavers themselves would be unable to survive in Lyon and would emigrate to one of France's competitors.

In spite of the complaints of the master weavers, the government successfully opened the *grande fabrique* to female weavers. With this act, it succeeded in two goals of the 1777 legislation. The first was to increase the number of workers employed at productive tasks. Full employment of artisans—both male and female—was an aim of the official policy. But there was another purpose, less articulated to the public but still firm in the administrators' letters to each other: to break the guilds' hold over production and labor without suppressing the organizations. Turgot's failure to abolish the guilds cancelled the politics of radical reform, and many thought the corporations still contributed a necessary discipline to society to prevent a repetition of the Paris workers' chaos in spring 1776. Steven L. Kaplan emphasized the guilds' importance in regulating workers, policing manufacture, ensuring standards, fostering emulation, encouraging the exchange of information, and above all, maintaining the status of masters within the privileged orders. And the king still valued the guilds as a reliable source of funds, as critics skeptical of high-minded natural rights rhetoric pointed out.

With these elements in mind, the royal ministers sought to exert what influence they could to bring the guilds' idiosyncratic pretensions to heel. Each step of administrative reform, each regulation of the number of guilds in the cities, the number of guild officers, the creation of a twenty-five-man governing assembly, and so on, was designed not only to standardize guilds throughout the kingdom, but to gain control of them. Forbidding the new guilds to borrow money was yet another step toward putting an end to the guild masters' intransigent behavior. Opening the privileged crafts to women was perhaps the ultimate nail in the coffin of guild independence. Even though it appeared to expand the guilds' power by creating more masters and spreading technical standards over a wider field, the act undermined the guilds' power of self-government and wage control. With the general low standard for women's salaries, it would be harder for male masters to maintain their high fees. This dynamic was played out most overtly in the government's assault on the *grande fabrique*. As Maurice Garden reasoned, freedom to increase the number of looms and to hire girls as weavers was "in fact, a formal and definitive attack against the guild itself and its regulations."[120] Having split the silk industry into its component parts by creating separate guilds, royal officials expected the entrance of hired women to weaving to further dissipate the cohesion and power of the *grande fabrique*. The stage was being set for the next century's division of industry into industrialists and hired workers—both males and "persons of the other sex."[121]

Conclusion

The late eighteenth century was a time of transition for France when administrators and manufacturers both were challenging the traditional system of regulated industry. The liberalism of the 1760s and 1770s had encouraged some inspectors of manufacture to apply the industrial regulations "softly," and numerous manufacturers had become accustomed to ignoring specifications. Increasing competition and consumer demand for novelty, as shown in Daniel Roche's research, pressed merchants to order cloth of more varied patterns and content.[122] The guilds themselves were changing in response to these new market demands, and despite the economic problems of the last third of the century, they were still holding strong. When Turgot's reforms temporarily suppressed them in 1776, vested interests caused that minister's downfall and guilds were reestablished in a new format.

These royal programs were greeted with skepticism and antagonism throughout the kingdom. In 1776 the guilds had been abolished only in Paris. Nevertheless, in 1777 the king ordered that masters should act as if all guilds had been suppressed and that the various regional *parlements*

---

120. Garden, *Lyon*, 578.
121. See Garden's explanation of local pressures, *Lyon*, 580–82.
122. See Daniel Roche, *La Culture des apparences: Une histoire du vêtement* (Paris: Fayard, 1989) and *Histoire des choses banales: Naissance de la consommation XVIIe–XIXe siècle* (Paris: Fayard, 1997).

should accept the edicts creating new guilds. Although each area received an edict tailored to its special characteristics, there was general aversion to putting the decrees into effect. *Parlements* dickered over details of the order, intendants worried about its impracticality, and masters resisted paying new entrance fees. Rouen's guilds responded to the royal government's guild reform with vigorous hostility, and the local administrative officers helped them. The trades that were cast out of corporations and opened for any individual to join tried every stratagem to maintain guild membership. Although they argued for preserving the public well-being, they were actually trying to keep their own technical and market monopolies. If the authorities refused to restore their former corporate structure, they then lobbied to join another guild. Other trades officially amalgamated to form one of the forty new guilds raised a storm of protest claiming that the technologies the administration had forcibly linked were incompatible.

The new guilds dashed liberals' hope for establishing wholesale freedom of work but still retained some of the reforming goals—reducing and standardizing entrance fees, consolidating similar crafts to avoid lawsuits, and removing unskilled crafts from guild control so that anyone could work at them. These were steps toward enabling France to produce goods more competitively and to come closer to the ideal of full employment. But the government also wanted to pay off the debts that guilds had incurred borrowing money to satisfy the king's taxation, and that pressed administrators to collect the new fees for guild entrance. Ironically, the fiscal agenda that pulled against laissez-faire reform caused administrators to establish guilds where they had not existed, for instance, in Lyon, in order to extract the new entrance fees.

In Paris, officials were startled and angered to learn that not only were the guilds themselves resisting the new rules, they were being helped by royal administrators in Rouen and elsewhere who had been co-opted by local factions. Like many other edicts from the royal pen, this one became an issue through which the *parlements* could oppose the king. The contradictory goals of the reform legislation also provoked confusion.

While Parisian journeymen responded to the new legislation with labor unrest and strikes, believing that they had won freedom of action, Lyon's trades obstinately refused to cooperate with the new laws. In effect, they were protesting against the government's insistence on changing the flexible auxiliary crafts that had cooperated successfully without guild structures into guilds. We might say that while Rouen fought against trade liberty, Lyon protested against guild discipline. As for the silk weavers in the *grande fabrique* who balked at joining the new guilds, their preoccupation was to maintain their traditional system of workshop industry while opposing the entrance of the women weavers.

For women, the reformed guilds had benefits and opportunities. If they could succeed in entering formerly male guilds, they gained the protection and support of a prestigious economic community. Changing many handicrafts from guilds into free trades also helped female seamstresses, spinners, and the like to do small jobs without being harassed by patrolling *gardes*. Registering with the police entitled them to do business at home, earning a fragile living for themselves and their families. This measure had a long history of encouraging women's work as a form of charity or public morality, helping widows to earn their mite, keeping women from prostitution, and enabling mothers to care for their young.

But essentialist reasoning was called into question when administrators considered women in their aspect as workers. What was the place of these artisans in the wider perspective of the economy? This question underscored the ambiguities of women's role in society. In the old-fashioned guilds, they had been treated as legal equals and as the new corporations came into being, officials maintained the principle of this custom. Except, of course, that in political terms, women were not the equal of men, and the new law prevented them from participating in the public governance of mixed-sex guilds. Nor did women workers earn salaries commensurate with those of men. In dealing with problematic industries, like the *grande fabrique*, the authorities used women workers' differences as a means of breaking the cohesion and demands of the skilled workforce. But from the women's point of view, guild membership provided the most favorable shelter in which to seek their own economic survival.

PATHS TO THE REVOLUTION

In Rouen

The revolutionary period brought together many of the themes that had been emerging throughout the eighteenth century, even if their realization came in surprising forms. As privilege, which had favored many enclaves of French society, became discredited, all forms of separation from the state's reach lost their rationale.[1] Theoretically, the laws enacted during the Revolution aimed to level the status of citizens and eliminate the three estates and the various groups with hereditary privileges. Taxation was to be based on income rather than family status; noble prerogatives disappeared in favor of civil equality; and the guilds—as privileged entities—were suppressed. The traditional honeycomb of special groups instituted by royal grant disappeared leaving instead Rousseau's ideal of a state composed of separate and equal citizens. Civic responsibilities now weighed on individuals; the individual, not the privileged group, became the module unit of the commonwealth.

In many ways, this individualistic manner of envisioning society emerged from earlier bureaucratic efforts to modernize the state. The pressing economic goals of government officials in the period leading up to the Revolution were to increase revenue by levying taxes proportionate to income and to stimulate manufacture and commerce. Information from the entire kingdom was considered the first instrument of this policy. But in trying to measure resources with political arithmetic, the reforming administrators constantly tripped on the irregular and the privileged elements making up French society. To overcome the distortions, comparative charts of wages, output, and cost of food in the various regions were drawn up. When the opportunity to reform the guilds

---

1. See William H. Sewell Jr., *Work and Revolution in France: The Language of Labor from the Old Regime to 1848* (Cambridge: Cambridge University Press, 1980), chap. 4, "The Abolition of Privilege," esp. 77.

presented itself in 1777 and 1778, standardized entrance fees, the number of guilds permitted in each city, and technical regulations became the means of introducing rational performance. Intense reforming zeal led administrators to make membership in the guilds equal for males and females. But here their political arithmetic reached a major stumbling block: the Revolution was essentially hostile to awarding women all the same rights and roles as men. As Lynn Hunt and Joan Landes have written, the dynamics of revolutionary politics excluded women from formal political affairs.[2] While a few feminist voices demanded equality, claiming, for instance, that since women paid taxes they were entitled to vote,[3] many others—both men and women—believed that women should confine themselves to the private sphere of domestic nurture.

Ironically, the inspiration for this frame of mind came from the same source as the insistence on the importance of the individual in the state—from Jean-Jacques Rousseau, who applied the Enlightenment's emphasis on nature to the different roles of male and female. Following ideas current at the time, Diderot's *Encyclopédie* defined human beings as animals embedded in the natural world. Rousseau refined this conception by emphasizing the idea that each sex had unique talents and therefore different roles in life. The nurturing female should find her natural place within the home; the assertive male should deal with the public sphere. Since the revolutionary era still held the belief that the mother was responsible for her children's food, prejudice against working women did not reach the level that it would in the nineteenth century. Nevertheless, the attributes that the new way of thought defined as feminine trapped women in a work situation that was unskilled, low paid, and subservient. In this formulation, women were physically weak, detail-oriented, and unable to visualize complicated projects like transferring a complex pattern

---

2. Joan B. Landes, *Women and the Public Sphere in the Age of the French Revolution* (Ithaca: Cornell University Press, 1988), and Lynn Hunt, *The Family Romance of the French Revolution* (Berkeley and Los Angeles: University of California Press, 1992).

3. See, for instance, the "Cahier de doléances et réclamations des femmes, par Madame B***B***," 1789, Pays de Caux, in *Cahiers de doléances des femmes en 1789 et autres texts*, ed. Paule-Marie Duhet (Paris: Édition des Femmes, 1981), 50, "Ce n'est point aux honneurs du gouvernement ni aux avantages d'être initiées dans les secrets du ministère que nous aspirons; mais nous croyons qu'il est de toute équité de permettre aux femmes, veuves ou filles possédant des terres ou autres propriétés, de porter leurs doléances au pied du trône; qu'il est également juste de recueillir leurs suffrages, puisqu'elles sont obligées, comme les hommes, de payer les impositions royals et de remplir les engagemens du commerce."

to a loom. As the harsh economic conditions of the revolutionary period bore on them, some female workers turned these clichéd phrases around and used them to make a case for help and protection. Gone were the days when the female masters of guilds, as *marchandes publiques,* pitted their business skill against male guild masters without reference to sex. The privileged institution that had made these women into honorary men fell with the collapse of privilege. They were thrown back upon the expedient of using essentialist ideas as a protection.

Another element also emerged from the new social norms: as political theory came to promote the individual as the authentic source of power and responsibility, it discredited the system of proxies that had sustained the Old Regime. In theory, every individual represented himself alone. This contributed to an insistence that magnified personal characteristic as the telling identification for each member of society. The status of "legal persons" that had given corporate privileged bodies like the council of treasurers or the guilds exemption from general laws was rejected. It was now considered unethical for persons to gain their rights from membership in a special group or even to have representatives unlike themselves. The revolutionary women who seized on this idea insisted that females must be allowed to participate in the legislative assemblies, for only they could adequately represent *citoyennes*.[4] But unfortunately, bias against women and fear of their collective power caused the legislature to turn away from such logic, relegating women to the role of passive citizens with curtailed civic rights. Females had been minors under Old Regime law, but they were granted exemptions in a society that abounded in exemptions; the Revolution made them political minors in a new society based on the removal of exemptions.

The history of Rouen's guildwomen demonstrated these themes within the political economy of a transitional age. Beliefs that informed lawmakers in the halls of royal administration and later in the Revolution's

---

4. Ibid. As the anonymous author of the earlier cited pamphlet argued, it is incorrect to deny women participation in the Estates General on the pretext that they can be represented by a surrogate (*par procuration*). "On pourroit répondre qu'étant démontré, avec raison, qu'un noble ne peut représenter un roturier, ni celui-ci un noble; de même, un homme ne pourroit, avec plus d'équité, représenter une femme, puisque les représentans doivent avoir absolument les mêmes intérêts que les représentans: les femmes ne pourroient donc être représentées que par des femmes." (You could respond [to women's claim to vote], it has been reasonably shown that a noble cannot represent a non-noble, nor the latter a noble; just so, a man cannot, in all equity represent a woman because the representatives must have absolutely the same interest as their constituents: women may be represented only by women.)

legislatures changed the circumstances of these artisans' working lives. When the d'Allarde law of March 1791 suppressed the guilds, masters and mistresses were cast loose from their legal and economic advantages. No longer limited to even two crafts, individuals could set themselves up in whatever business they chose. From the legal aspect at least, it was a new era, full of possibility for advancement or bankruptcy. The Revolution disrupted old business networks and opened new ones for artisans and industrial workers. The shortages, the shifting political orthodoxies, the repression of the church and the anti-Christian movement all presented difficulties that female artisans had to negotiate if they were to survive. Wars curtailed trade but generated new contracts for equipment.

The chance to establish a commercial empire was there for anyone who was clever, well connected, and supplied with deep pockets. The possibility of failure and destitution, without the support of guild charity, also stood alongside the prospering businesses. Once again, women grappled with these new conditions, a few becoming proprietors of large networks, the majority subsisting as small-scale artisans, day laborers in the newly mechanizing workshops, or paupers. These possibilities were bound up with the bruising events of the last quarter of the century. The years preceding the Revolution presented France with overwhelming problems as well as the ferment of new political consciousness. Rouen's guildwomen were intent on using their special prerogatives to manage the difficult economic circumstances rather than devoting themselves to political debate.

The Revolution came gradually to the guildwomen of Rouen. Although their business with the wealthy did not protect them from the general downturn, they were able to pay their taxes and contribute to a fund for the poor. But the failed grain harvests of 1787 and 1788 spread misery throughout the Normandy region, and normal business became impossible as unemployed spinners and their families filled Rouen's streets. As these workers protested the high price of bread and demanded work, the extent of the economic deterioration throughout the region became apparent. The brisk production and trade that had occupied rural industry and urban guilds until 1787 declined severely. Market loss disrupted the countryside's woolen manufacture, cotton spinning, glassmaking, and tanning. The second poor harvest raised the price of bread again from 2.5 sous to 4 sous, while cotton spinners' wages fell from 15 sous a day to 3.[5] Spinners and agricultural laborers could afford no more than half their families' food needs. The ordinary family had to invest in the bare essentials rather than clothing and other manufactured goods. Food scarcity became the preoccupation of working people and the poor.

This was not the first time grain shortage had lowered wages and caused unemployment in Normandy. Similar problems in 1768 left merchants with a thread surplus and no need to purchase more from spinners. Rouen's intendant then called a committee of influential persons who decided to offer charity to more than 4,000 cotton spinners (in the hope of avoiding a run on public relief, rather than to stimulate the industry). The group lent funds to underwrite a public spinning atelier in each parish.[6] The rising price of raw cotton kept poor families from supplying their spinning wheels, and those who did manage to produce thread were doubly hurt by the low price of spun thread. An inquiry in 1775 showed that poverty remained widespread among cotton spinners and their families.[7]

The 1780s brought problems to several other industries, especially those in the countryside. In part, French goods came up against the obstacle of recent tariffs like that imposed by Spain. In addition, as France confronted the consequences of the Seven Years' War, economic losses compounded her diplomatic decline. The treaty of August 1763 deprived France of her Canadian holdings and opened French colonies to foreign ships. The ramifications of this treaty stretched into the hamlets of Haute-Normandie, dampening markets for French pin manufacturers, woolen makers, and the linen cloth industry. Traditional industries like faience, glass, tanning, metallurgy, and woolen manufacture gave way to numerous bankruptcies in the general economic upset. From makers of goods as trivial as horsehair rings to the important *siamoises* destined to clothe colonial slaves, French producers had to trim their operations and seek new strategies.

In the midst of this downturn, high grain prices caused by a midsummer hailstorm in 1784 increased workers' need not just for work

5. Marc Bouloiseau, *Cahiers de doléances du tiers état du bailliage de Rouen* (Paris: Presses Universitaires de France, 1957), liv–lv.
6. Camille Léon, "Notes sur les travaux publics et filatures de cotton établies à Rouen dans les paroisses de St-Maclou, St. Vivien et St. Nicolas en 1768 et 1769," *Bulletin de la Société Libre d'Emulation du Commerce et de l'Industrie de la Seine-Inférieur* (1932): 353–67.
7. Eugene Le Parquier, "Une enquête sur le paupérisme et de la crise industrielle dans la region rouennaise en 1788," *Bulletin de la Société Libre d'Emulation* (1935): 147.

but for a raise in their wages. The unusually cold winter of 1784 brought flood waters into Rouen's streets. Growing misery caused administrators again to organize public workshops and private charity for the beggars and vagrants increasingly drawn to urban centers. Rumors of marauders circulated through the Norman countryside and towns increasing economic problems. Five years later, the rumors became a self-fulfilling prophecy as bands of peasants grabbed their tools to use as weapons and marched in search of grain hoards and the "brigands" who supposedly harbored them. Once on the move, they entered the storage rooms of chateaux and burned land deeds they found there. In cities, the accusation that grain merchants and certain monasteries were hoarding supplies led to riots and pillaging of stores. The crowds in traditional fashion effected "popular taxation" by forcibly buying grain and flour at prices lower than those the merchants were charging. As Georges LeFebvre, Albert Soboul, George Rudé, and Olwen Hufton have taught us, women were usually in the forefront of these appropriations because they were less likely to receive punishment than male rioters.

The Cotton Crisis

The harvest failures of 1787 and 1788 that raised the price of bread coincided with the continuing crisis in the hand-spun cotton thread industry.[8] As William M. Reddy has pointed out, machine-spun Manchester thread could undersell French thread by 20 to 30 percent even including the 12 percent for import duty and a 15 percent profit.[9] This cotton was too poor in quality to be popular among French consumers, but it suited the needs of export trade for cheap cloth used to furnish garments for slaves. As French merchants turned to the low-priced English thread, they undercut the price domestic hand-spinners could afford to set. Cotton hand-spinning was a cottage industry that had made some Norman farm families prosperous during the preceding twenty years, but when

---

8. Florin Aftalion suggests that Necker's intervention in the grain market perversely helped to cause farmers to withhold their grain from sale, contributing to the shortage. *The French Revolution: An Economic Interpretation*, trans. Martin Thom (Cambridge and Paris: Cambridge University Press, 1990), 42. Originally published as *L'Economie de la Révolution française* (Paris: Hachette, 1987).

9. William M. Reddy, *The Rise of Market Culture: The Textile Trade and French Society, 1750–1900* (Cambridge: Cambridge University Press, 1994), 55.

the price of thread dropped, many could no longer afford to buy raw cotton or to invest their time in spinning. Without the sale of cotton thread, these families had scarcely enough to feed themselves and nothing left with which to acquire the stylish accessories and linens that urban artisans produced.[10] The fall in agricultural wages compounded their misery. Urban women working in proto-industrial settings as spinners and cloth finishers in their homes also suffered. An estimated third of the 6,000 women and girls in this trade lost their jobs to mechanization.[11]

Faced with street protests as unemployed urban and rural people gathered in towns, Rouen's administrators and merchants vociferously blamed the Anglo-French Eden-Rayneval Treaty of 1786 for lowering duties on cotton yarn and woven cloth. The Rouen Chamber of Commerce complained that cheap English machine-spun thread and woven goods were flooding into France, undercutting local spinning and displacing French production of exports. In 1788 the newly formed Bureau of Encouragement, which Reddy calls "a kind of committee to save the Normandy cotton trade," offered 300,000 livres to provide women with 600 spinning jennies to replace the outmoded handwheels, and to retrain women to process linen thread.[12] While functioning as a means to help the indigent earn their bread, a workshop set up by the bureau in the St. Maclou district also aimed at training women to use new English spinning jennies. The bureau, in addition, offered spinning jennies at less than cost to rural and urban workers. A few rural spinners acquired the machines as gifts from their noble landlords and another few found their way into ateliers in town, but widespread prejudice against them persisted. Ordinary handworkers focused their blame for the entire imbalance of wages and bread price on English machines, which could not produce thread of high quality. In the workers' judgment, spinning machines capable of producing only rough thread condemned their operators to unacceptably low wages. Not until the early 1800s did spinning jennies proliferate in France.[13]

10. Bouloiseau, *Cahiers*, xl–xli.
11. Claire Le Foll, "Les Femmes et le mouvement révolutionnaire à Rouen (1789–1795)," in *À Travers la Haute-Normandie en Révolution, 1789–1800*, ed. Claude Mazauric and Yannick Marec (Rouen: Comité régional d'histoire de la Révolution française, 1992), 33. Le Foll's information comes from Louis-Eszéchias Pouchet, *Traité sur la fabrication des étoffes* (Rouen: Deboucher, 1788), 103.
12. Reddy, *Market Culture*, 55.
13. Ibid. In a cahier from the village of Perriers-sur-Andelle it was noted, "There ought to be a certain balance between the price of bread and the profit to be had from the spinning of cotton." Reddy's translation, p. 58.

With the perverse variations that the preindustrial economy so often displayed, colonial trade and commerce with other European countries kept some guilds and rural industry afloat.[14] The women's guilds were affluent enough to contribute substantial charity to the poor (*lingères en neuf*, for instance, budgeted 300 livres in 1788 to be distributed at the city hall).[15] If cheap thread undercut cottage spinners' income, it helped the hand knitters to maintain their production of caps, stockings, gloves, mittens, and money pouches. Merchants who could shift these products to foreign markets managed to maintain themselves as domestic consumption dried up. But the collapse of domestic sales drove a stake into the heart of the French economy. The role that increasing domestic consumption played in the course of the eighteenth century now made its importance felt by its comparative absence.[16]

Repercussions of the 1778 Guild Reform

While all businesses were forced to deal with the general economic slowdown, the guilds also came under pressure from structural changes. The edict of February 1778 required masters of the old guilds to reregister for the new ones if they wished to maintain their status as full members. It is not surprising that former masters were outraged at having to pay again for a license. Even at the 50 or 75 percent reduction (for the Rouen's cord makers–spinners) that they were allowed, many former masters could not afford the expense. The new license costs were also an excessive sum for beginning masters.

Work in guild trades required some form of paid authorization, but the provision made for workers unable to pay for a master's license was

---

14. Alan Forrest commented that "colonial trade had been the most dynamic single sector of the French economy, increasing tenfold between 1716 and 1787." *The Revolution in Provincial France: Aquitaine, 1789–1799* (Oxford: Clarendon Press, 1996), 246.

15. Archives départementales de la Seine Maritime 5 E 508, Compte 1788 submitted by Mademoiselle Desmarets, *garde comptable*.

16. In *Revolution in Provincial France*, Forrest comments that the rise in bread prices not only brought immediate privation to the poor, it also prevented the moderately well-off from spending surplus capital on manufactured goods. For comments on a "clothing revolution," see Daniel Roche, *The Culture of Clothing: Dress and Fashion in the Ancien Régime* (Cambridge: Cambridge University Press, 1996), passim. Originally published as *La Culture des apparences* (Paris: Librairie Arthème Fayard, 1989). "Agricultural underproduction" also curtailed income that farm workers would have spent on manufactures. Aftalion, *French Revolution*, 39.

degrading. Steven L. Kaplan has explored the wound to their professional honor that the new requirements imposed, but underlying the personal insult was a serious economic blow. Defying the law, some unscrupulous guild officers imposed exorbitant costs on would-be entrants. In other cases, Parisian authorities made reductions for special circumstances. A lesser fee would enable one to work at the trade as an associate (agrégé) in the guild, but these individuals had neither a voice in the guild assembly nor the right to have apprentices. They could not carry on more than one trade, unlike the new masters who were given the right to work at two or three. Moreover, the associates were limited to abiding by the industrial regulations in place when they entered the new guild; they could not legally take advantage of new rules simplifying or modernizing technology. Nevertheless, a number of large-scale producers remained agrégés, according to Jeff Horn, while their less fortunate compatriots became hired day workers.[17]

As they lost their inner integrity, the guilds also lost political and economic influence.[18] Steven L. Kaplan and Maurice Garden have argued that weakening the corporate hold over industry was an important goal of the reforming members of the royal administration. But the administration imposing the new law had certainly not foreseen the complications and difficulties to which it would give rise. Aggrieved former masters took on apprentices and other workers illegally and hired themselves out as well. Some took up production of unregulated goods. Their skills and their lingering ties with others in the trade gave these "false workers" an inside track that frustrated the officers of the new guilds. In the confusion of determining who had signed up for the new guild and whose credentials had been verified (baptismal records and marriage contracts counted for women), the new guild was also competing with a sizeable body of equally skilled, recently unincorporated workers. As in Lyon, Rouen's male and female masters and widows of the ribbon-making and spinning guilds, and especially the former masters, were said to "daily hire a number of male and female workers without claims to being either guild members or apprentices, whom they show and teach their trade." In guild deliberations the officers warned, "This is and will become in the future

17. One example in Rouen was the amalgamated tailleurs-fripiers-lingères en vieux, which had a total membership of 414 masters and 52 agrégés. Kaplan has found that there were fewer permanent agrégés in Paris than in the provinces. See his discussion in Steven L. Kaplan, La Fin des corporations (Paris: Fayard, 2001), 230–32.
18. Ibid., 172–74, and personal communication from Jeff Horn.

very prejudicial to the new guild."[19] While laissez-faire sentiment in some towns discouraged the reestablishment of guilds, as Steven L. Kaplan has shown for Villefranche-en-Beaujolais, lack of funds, personal irritation, uneven municipal policing, and confusion were likely overall causes.[20]

Rouen's workshops contained a great variety of personnel in this unsettled time. When Fille Anne Monique Dormesnil, mistress in the former guild of spinners, was caught working as a day laborer at the home of Sieur Landormy, member of an old spinning family, the guild fined them both. Neither Landormy's influence ("he claimed that his name excused his infraction"), nor one official's offer of grace for the spinner ("perhaps she was unaware of the penalties and fines pronounced by the regulations") could turn away the guild's condemnation.[21]

While most of the cord maker–spinner masters worked at home with an apprentice and one or two workers, some had large workshops. In September 1783, Antoine Martin des Isles declared he lived at rue Écquerie with two unmarried spinners who worked for him, and that he also had an atelier in Saint Aignon, where another two unmarried women spun. But one of these women, Fille Lefevre, kept at her own house another workshop with five married women, six unmarried women, and six men at work.[22] Another woman responded to the guild survey of April 1784 that she had fifteen employees as outworkers, in addition to three in her home. Madeleine Harde declared that she had three workers, two women and one man, who lived and worked in her house and also another female employee living in the working class area, the faubourg Cauchois, on the western side of the city.[23] A sort of chaos spawned by institutional confusion was present even within legitimate guild workshops. Outsourcing, similar to the subcontracting that Michael Sonenscher discovered in Paris, seemed at this point in the century not only tolerated but even praised for its role in spreading employment.[24]

19. Archives Nationales (hereafter AN) 5 E 449, "Registre Cordiers et Filassiers," Rouen, January [?] 1784.
20. Kaplan, *La Fin des corporations*, 168–69.
21. AN 5 E 449, 9 June 1784. Three masters of the guild were members of the Landormy family at the time. Bouloiseau, *Cahiers*, 185. There was confusion in identifying the woman; others described her employer as Sieur Languement, *marchand mercier*, rue aux Juifs, and asserted that she was now a mistress *filassière*, whose father was also in that trade.
22. Ibid., 28 August 1783.
23. Ibid., 4 April 1784.
24. Michael Sonenscher, *Work and Wages: Natural Law, Politics and the Eighteenth-Century French Trades* (New York: Cambridge University Press, 1989), 210–43.

The flexibility that guilds adopted, however, did not stop them from maintaining many of their traditional objectives. Technical monopoly still permeated the guild outlook: officers diligently surveyed the streets and alleys to impose confiscations and fines on workers making or selling goods without guild membership. The technical regulations that had governed the guilds before 1778 remained in force, not necessarily bending to new consumer demand. Individual craft professionals sometimes fell afoul of all these complications. Consider the example of Elisabeth Martine, wife of Robert Thérard, mistress in the ribbon-making guild since 1759. An experienced worker, she knew that "ribbonmakers are permitted to make and sell all sorts of ribbons, lace, and fringe in thread of gold, silver, silk, wool, or simple linen. They can also sell raw material. They have the right to sell thread in competition with the spinners, although the spinners protest this and claim the sole right." But she acknowledged that ribbonmakers did not have the right to sell thread in balls (*en pelleton*). "This frivolous distinction is a constraint," she alleged, "because nowadays the public only wants to buy thread in balls."[25]

Martine had a further problem. Apparently she could not afford to pay for a new mastership in the ribbonmakers' guild. It was suggested that she prepare instead to become a master spinner. Even though that would have allowed her to continue her business selling balls of thread, Martine rejected the idea of undertaking another apprenticeship (with the spinners). Her legal representative explained her rationale. "At the age of forty-five, after twenty-five years of being a mistress in the ribbon trade, an apprenticeship of whatever sort would be a reduction to the absurd. She knows how to finish thread to facilitate sales just as well as the spinners do. They ought to appreciate the sacrifice she would have to make to become an apprentice again." The spinners were unmoved by her reasoning and refused to let "Dame Thérard" enter their guild.[26]

To be sure, the tumultuous conditions of 1790 weighed against taking up new masterships. Money was in short supply, businesses were disrupted, and many artisans had been able to afford only the rank of associate. As local officials lost control of the streets, many tradespeople felt little need to register. In the confusion, it was hard to distinguish which

25. AN 5 E 449, 5 April 1784.
26. Ibid., After twenty-five years in the ribbon trade, "un apprantissage quelconque c'est la reduire à l'impossible; elle connoit comme les fillassières la manière d'aprester le fil pour en faciliter lavante" (original spelling).

trades were declared to be free and which were still under guild control. The chef d'atelier might not be able to tell if job applicants were licensed industrial workers or home laborers claiming the right to produce the occasional fichu or bonnet. Given the pressure to lower costs, artisans could not afford to ignore the crowd of unauthorized day laborers willing to work at low wages.

Conditions were not so chaotic a decade earlier when the guilds had just been restored. Guilds could still manipulate their regulations to protect exclusive trade rights, even as these same institutions stretched to incorporate nonqualified labor in far-flung workshops. In the 1780s, workers' discipline modeled itself after the "intermediate" system of privileged and free work instituted by Jacques Necker. Just as manufacturers could choose whether to follow industrial regulations and have their products certified by inspectors or ignore traditional rules and have their goods labeled "Libre," masters could cling to guild membership or, at least in trades that had been officially declared free of guild restraint, set up shop as they liked. Economic luck and personal circumstance probably determined which path would be taken. Steven L. Kaplan has called this "a labor market split into two classes" that could benefit an emerging group of small capitalists, some of whom operated at a distance.[27] It is worth noting that the dual labor market existed not only between craft workers inside and outside guilds; it was present within the guilds themselves as the edict of 1778 made clear. Sometimes those fortunate enough to become new masters were able to hire workers who had formerly been masters or journeymen as associates. These employees were then paid as day laborers.

The late 1780s saw guild discipline straining at the seams. As increasing numbers of guild members could not pay their taxes, the sums weighed more heavily on remaining masters. Ribbonmakers and linen weavers resisted paying the fees for inspections. Day laborers demanded pay raises and behaved with so much menace that the masters warned the guild's tax collectors not to press too hard. The *livrets*, booklets listing the employers and contracts of workers in order to regularize the hiring of labor, became ineffective as workers ignored them or wrote in their employers' permission themselves. Female silk workers took their projects home where they might conveniently "lose" them. The mercers continued to resist the right of the female ribbonmakers to inspect their

27. Kaplan, *La fin des corporations*, 169.

ribbons at the hall where sales took place. This dispute had a long history between the two guilds, but earlier it had not been expressed in terms of gender conflict.[28]

But skilled women had another avenue of possibility that had been opened by the 1778 edict; they had the legal right to enter men's guilds if they could do the work. Since men's guilds received better pay than traditional women's guilds, this was an attractive option. It has been difficult, however, to learn the extent to which this new regulation actually opened new trades to women. Bureaucrats' records are filled with complaints from women who were kept out of male guilds by every conceivable dodge. Although the new rule, like so many others, was honored more in the breech than the observance, some women in other cities managed to enter male guilds

In spite of the irregularities at the end of their tenure, the guilds still managed to provide an avenue of professional training and protection for women that was not replaced in the era of free markets. Judith Coffin's view that the guilds fell of their own weight is rebutted by the documents. Statistics show that in 1787, one-fifth (20 percent) of the more than 7,000 guild members in Rouen were women. But they were arrayed differently in the various guilds. Of the 1,460 female guild masters, 850 widows were in groups that were considered "men's" guilds. Only 62 married women and 41 unmarried women also had masterships in the "men's" bailiwick; they represent the total number of women who benefited from the 1778 reform. Thus 4 percent of the privileged women workers were installed in trades that would have been closed to them in earlier times. By contrast, 50 percent of the women workers who received masterships in the men's guilds were widows following tradition and would probably have achieved the same status in the past. These were women whose entry to the guilds was justified through their late husbands' brevet. They were carrying out a family tradition, making their living for the minor children they had to feed, and maintaining a place in the trade for their children to inherit. (Were daughters then brought into the guilds of their fathers? The system didn't last long enough to tell.) We can presume, however, that while their widowed mothers headed the household, these guild families put their children to work in home ateliers. In this way, their daughters and sons may have been saved the cost of formal apprenticeship.

28. ADSM, 5 E 612. Papers of the ribbonmakers, linen weavers, and *passementiers*.

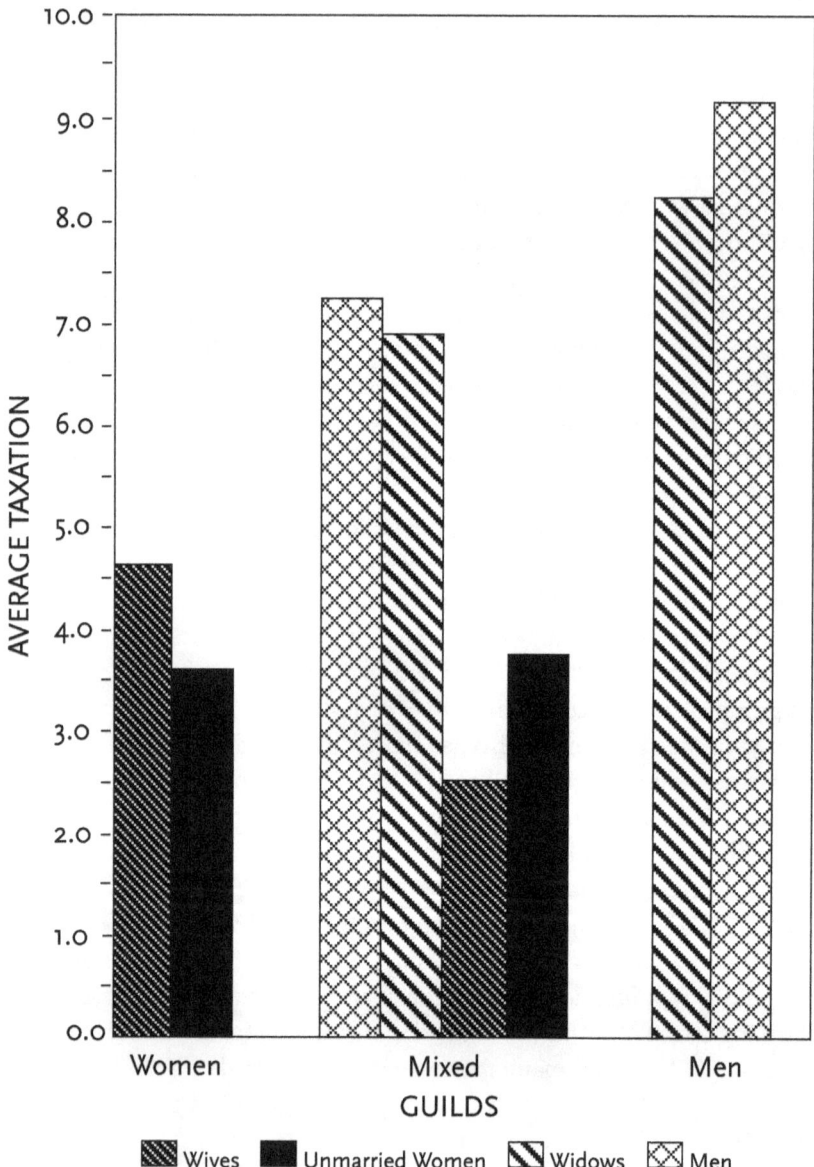

Figure 15. Rouen guild capitation, by status, 1787. The comparative tax rolls of masters in women's, mixed, and men's guilds show that widows fare better in their late husbands' guilds than as mistresses in their own name in mixed guilds. From Archives départementales de la Seine Maritime, C 389.

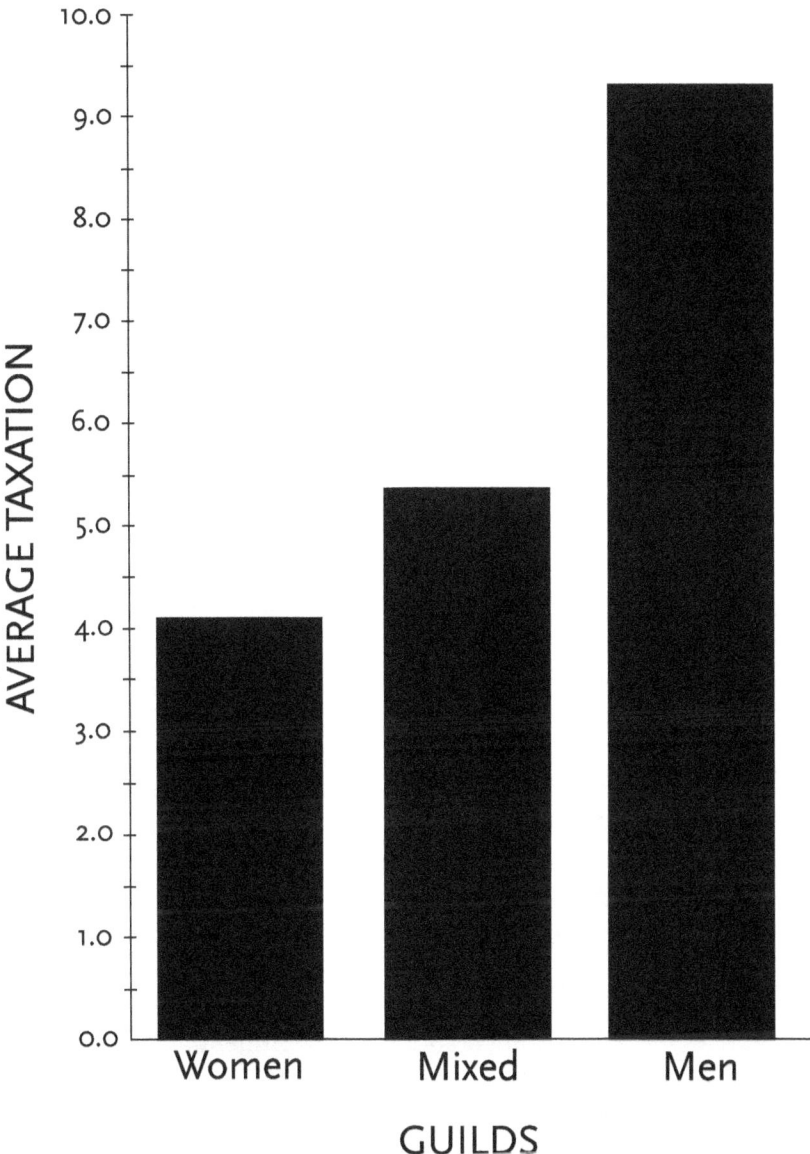

Figure 16. Rouen guild capitation, by average, 1787. The comparative tax rolls of women's, mixed, and men's guilds shows that the male guilds earned more than twice the income of female guilds, and the guild with both male and female masters had an income between the two. From Archives départementales de la Seine Maritime, C 389.

A different story was told by the two all-female guilds that lasted in Rouen after the 1778 reform, first, the linen-drapers of new cloth (*lingères en neuf*) and second, the knitters (*bonnetières*) amalgamated with fashion merchants, milliners (*marchandes de modes*), button makers, lacemakers, and fringe makers. The all female linen-drapers were now also called merchants of linen cloth, a function their statutes had traditionally given them. Not one widow joined this group; instead there were 139 wives and 84 unmarried women in 1787. The knitters and fashion merchants had a similar composition: no widows, 172 wives, and 116 unmarried women. How can we understand this difference?

While entrance fees for "female professions" had been lower than those for traditional male guilds, the fees were now standardized. At 200 livres for the mastership of the linen-drapers of new cloth and 300 for the female knitters and fashion merchants, the women's entrance fees were on the low side, and many other guilds imposed fees that were equal to these. But if a woman were not already associated with one of the male trades, it was harder for her to enter those guilds. Perhaps the possibility of being able to manage their own professional life, which was the legacy of the women's guilds, also attracted them. For most of these women, the prospect of large earnings could not have been the lure. A rough comparison of the *capitation* tax that fell on estimated income gives the average tax on male masters as 14 livres, 9 sous. The average tax on the all-female guilds of linen-drapers was 5 livres, 9 sous and on knitters, 2 livres, 17 sous. Economic gain was a more obvious reason that widows chose amalgamation with men's trades when they could; had they been in a women's guild, they might have earned three times less. The average tax on female masters in the two womens' guilds was 4 livres, 1 sou.[29]

Guildwomen and Self-Government

In the balance sheet for guildwomen on the eve of the Revolution, the gains and losses were far from apparent. On the positive side, men's guilds were legally open to women who could prove competence in the craft. Nor were they forced, according to one discussion of the law, to go through a formal apprenticeship in some instances. They could bequeath

29. Le Foll, "Les Femmes,"Annex 7.

their trade privileges to their widower husbands, on the same basis that male masters could pass on their license to their widows. From a strictly mechanical calculation, the presumption of female workers as privileged actors within the scope of guild action maintained its weight. Women could still become guild masters, with legal prerogatives—in terms of business practice—that were equal to those of male masters. In fact, the opening of men's guilds to women, and the reflexive policy of admitting men to women's guilds, bespoke a continuing emphasis on the work rather than the sex of the worker.

On the negative side, women often found it difficult to enter men's guilds. Frequently they had to enlist officials' help to overcome the obstacles men put in their way.[30] In the reorganization, trades with similar technologies were joined in order to curtail the endless court suits that these trades brought against each other. One effect of this change was that most women's guilds were deprived of their independence and power, either being amalgamated with male guilds or becoming free trades, which could no longer take shelter in guilds. Although Turgot's rhetoric had praised opening the needle trades as a means to let poor women earn their living, the suppression of the couturiers' guild status actually led to sweatshop conditions for seamstresses.[31] Reimposing mastership fees may have thrown many women into the ranks of the associates or even of day laborers. And shortening to one year the length of time widows controlled of their husbands' business probably forced many into impoverishment. Finally, the most egregious discrimination forbad female masters in guilds of mixed sex to take part in the general assembly or to become officers. This meant that in guilds with male masters, the mistresses would have no part in determining policies the guild would pursue, nor would they participate in public activities implicit in master's status. They would no longer negotiate the tax impost with the government, divide it among the masters, keep the accounts, make protests to the lieutenant of police, bring suit on the guild's behalf, or hire jurists to promote their causes with legal memoirs. It would not be wrong to see prohibition of women from guild assemblies and guild office as a predecessor of the final segregation of women from active political life in 1795.

30. See the correspondence listed in AN 135–36.
31. See Steven L. Kaplan's comments on Turgot's calculated use of rhetoric and purposeful ignoring of history. See also Clare Crowston and Judith Coffin for condition of seamstresses after the 1778 edict.

But even while practical considerations curtailed their opportunities, in reality guildwomen still exerted influence over their destiny. The prize for female independence was held by the group of linen-drapers of old clothes, who were linked to the tailors in 1778. In earlier chapters we have seen them voting to decide policy about drafting guild sons for the militia, withholding payments and information from civic authorities, and refusing to contribute to repairs for the market building. The national official in charge of Seine Inférieur was amazed by their obstinate refusal to help take care of their part of the Halle aux Toiles. Citing prescriptive legislation of the sixteenth century, they continued to ignore the tailors' demands for money until the end of the guilds in 1791.

In more conventional ways, too, guildwomen exercised their customary roles. Officers of the two female corporations continued to apprehend unauthorized craft workers and peddlers. In 1783, the male and female spinners with permission to dye thread paid for a mass on the first Sunday of the month and on the feast day of the Sacred Virgin, through the agency of their confraternity of Saint Anne.[32] The ribbonmakers, most of whom were women, continued to insist on their right to inspect their own goods in opposition to the *marchand merciers'* claim of jurisdiction in the city market. Arguing against the powerful merchants' assertion that the regulations now only applied to ribbon length, the ribbonmakers consulted lawyers and accompanied the bailiff Fabulet to the market on a tour of inspection. In 1786 the authorities decided to continue their earlier practice of supporting rival guilds, including those with female artisans, against the merchants mercers' claims; Goy, the principal inspector of cloth, ordered the merchants mercers to give the ribbonmakers a corner in their own office where the women could examine samples and swatches from different manufacturers.[33]

This policy was in place when the merchants mercers insisted on their right (specified in their new bylaws) to inspect stalls of the *lingères en neuf*. The *lingères* complained that the mercers' scrutiny amounted to harassment, and they reminded the authorities that the mercers did not have the right to retail goods made by the linen-drapers, nor to decorate them. In fact, the all-female guild asserted, "it would be [only] justice and equity to give the *marchandes lingères* that privilege, equal to that which

---

32. ADSM, 5 E 447.
33. ADSM, 5 E 612.

the mercers claim to exercise over them." It is evident that neither the tradeswomen nor their lawyers shrank from asserting their equality to their economic rivals or employing terms that reflected the current interest in natural rights. The case concluded by condemning the mercer Sieur Mattuieur le Fevre for taking *lingers'* products and peddling them on the rue de Gros Horloges. He gave the proceeds of the sales to the *lingères* and promised not to repeat his actions.[34]

We can almost visualize officers of the reconstituted guilds tiptoeing around the new regulations as they tried to make the new corporations function. Despite the rules keeping tradeswomen from policy-making positions, the very process of setting up the new guilds involved the women. Because industrial specifications carried over, the new guild syndics and *adjoints* needed documents kept by the suppressed guilds' officers. To bolster their claims against the powerful merchants, the new officers of the ribbonmakers went to the home of the two Perniers to see the old papers. "And the said dames replied to them that the statutes and titles in question were in the hands of M. Le Breton, notary, whose return they awaited."[35] Even though the law forbad women to appear in the guild's general assembly, assigning taxes and recording receipts also required the women to be present. The mixed-sex guild of spinners recorded an expense of 6 livres for printing up notice of *"une séance général de toutes les maîtres et maîtresses aux nombre de 160,"* to distribute notices of the first half of the *capitation d'industrie* and to register the fees which were deposited with guild officers.[36] When they prosecuted cases brought by the suppressed guilds' officers having to do with women's crafts, it was literally impossible for the new guilds to ignore their female workers. The difficulty of dealing with women's labor while ignoring their personhood came home to officials in all strata of the bureaucracy.

In refusing to pay for the market repairs, the linen-drapers of old clothes (*lingères en vieux*) showed more obstinate independence than most

---

34. ADSM, 5 E 508, The memoir read, "Il est de la justice, et l'équité, d'accorder aux marchandes lingères, sur les merciers, un droit, égal à celui qu'ils prétendent exercer sur elles." The tone of raillery in the *lingères'* argument should not obscure its serious thrust. Their lawyer had served the *Haro*, a binding accusation in Norman law, on merchant le Fevre to make sure that he was brought to trial. Valérie Toureille, "Cri de peur et cri de haine: haro sur le voleur," in *Haro! Noël! Oyé!: Practiques du cri au Moyen Âge*, ed. Didier Lett and Nicolas Offenstadt (Paris: Publications de la Sorbonne, 2003), 169–78.

35. ADSM, 5 E 612.

36. ADSM, 5 E 455.

artisans. Many guildwomen, however, did take advantage of the mechanism by which the reorganized guilds incorporated the various trades. It was customary for the incoming trade to keep itself as a separate unit under the umbrella of the newly enlarged association. The guild's name changed to include the new group, but it usually did not share the new technology among all the guild members.[37] Although each amalgamation brought its own particular quirks as the groups jockeyed to gain precedence, there was a long tradition of separation within the guild framework. Amalgamation of trades that represented the victory of some groups over their close competitors had been an active form of guild politics for centuries. The forced uniting of professions after 1778 had a different dynamic, since it represented the state's attempt to snuff out some of the guilds' pretensions and their habit of endless litigation. Complaints about the unsuitability of the trade partners were attempts by craft workers to regain their autonomy or, at second best, to show that the protesting artisans had such a lack of affinity with the other trades that the women needed to police themselves.[38] With this assertion, the women's groups managed to keep their technological monopoly to themselves and to govern their everyday affairs. Judith Coffin points out that the Paris seamstresses objected to meeting in a separate assembly from the tailors.[39] This maneuver precluded their becoming officials of the guild as a whole, but under the circumstances the tactic offered their best chance at maintaining authority over their own affairs.

Steven L. Kaplan shows that combining the thirty some male cutters (*découpeurs*) in Paris with the three thousand female seamstresses resulted in the women's advantage. Fearing that the amalgamated trade would be classified as a "women's guild," depriving the men of any public role, the cutters objected to the union. (Even if the guild had been classified as a men's guild, the cutters might still have been under the jurisdiction of female inspectors, since the *couturières* were so much more numerous.) Officials settled the dispute by transforming the cutters into a free trade and leaving the seamstresses in their own guild. While the discourse used by the cutters may have stressed their reluctance to

---

37. For instance, although the cord makers and spinners had been amalgamated, a cord maker was fined in 1788 for having hemp in his shop. ADSM, 5 E 455.
38. See AN F 12 203–204 for numerous requests to alter the 1778 guild composition.
39. Judith G. Coffin, *The Politics of Women's Work: The Paris Garment Trades, 1750–1915* (Princeton: Princeton University Press, 1996), 42.

be overseen by females, it freed the women to remain under their own guidance.[40]

It is easy to see the hand of political compromise in the contradictory structure of an ill-assorted work discipline created by the reform of 1777–78. Believers in laissez-faire and those preferring regulations found a balance by restoring some trades to guild status and liberating others. The charitable impulse to give women alternatives to prostitution and starvation became translated into opening male guilds to women. Faced with the problem of dealing with female artisans who were legal minors, the architects of the reform forbad them to meet in the assembly or to become guild officers. Privileged industry could continue to exist—bowing to the uproar condemning Turgot's suppression of guilds—but some egregious abuses were curtailed by amalgamating guilds, limiting their number, and lowering entrance fees. The most powerful motive behind the ill-matched assortment of rules was the pressing need for tax revenue. No matter how much enlightened bureaucrats believed in freeing opening industry to all, no matter how chagrined the guild supporters were about the admitted abuses of the system, the king could not do without the immediate guild revenue. Therefore, the restoration of guilds, with a nod to the reformers' opportunity to modernize the old institution, became a chance to extract new taxes for the state.[41] The royal treasury took three-fourths of the new entrance fees to liquidate guild debt and to support its own obligations.[42] As Emile Coornaert commented, French kings had always acted in response to their own fiscal needs rather than carrying out a rational, nationwide plan of guild reform.[43]

The Revolution Approaches

Deficits at the end of the eighteenth century posed serious financial problems to the royal administration. Besides the declining tax revenues

40. Kaplan, *La Fin des corporations*, 171.
41. David D. Bien suggests that revenue from privileged sources stood against the king's becoming a constitutional monarch. "Offices, Corps, and a System of State Credit: The Uses of Privilege Under the Ancien Régime," in *The Political Culture of the Old Regime*, ed. Keith M. Baker (Oxford: Oxford University Press, 1987), 89–114.
42. Émile Levasseur, *Histoire des classes ouvrières et de l'industrie en France avant 1789*, 2nd ed., rev. (Paris: Arthur Rousseau, 1901), 2:646.
43. Emile Coornaert, *Les Corporations en France avant 1789* (Paris: Les Éditions Ouvrières, 1968), 148–51.

generated by its current economic troubles, the budget crisis of the French state was compounded by its investment in the rebellion of the English colonies and its inefficient tax collecting system. Although the king managed to increase tax on aristocrats' earnings, nobles and clergy paid disproportionately less in revenues than the Third Estate.[44] Prevented by the pressure of lenders from defaulting on the debt, the king sought a legislative solution.[45] From 1778 on, ministers created a series of provincial assemblies to generate acceptance of new forms of taxation, but their solutions aroused general hostility. The long-standing enmity of Rouen's *parlement* toward the king guaranteed that it would reject any suggestions from bodies, such as the assemblies, that were seen as royal tools. The *parlement* viewed the assembly members as bourgeois upstarts, without the right to rule on serious issues like taxation. When the government failed to establish a process to find new revenue from the clergy and nobles, the king felt obliged to seek new taxes by convening the Estates General.

What caused the administrative search for taxes to begin a revolution was the coincidence of political dissatisfaction of the privileged and famine and hardship of the people. From the viewpoint of political players, the fiscal crisis provided an opportunity to "institutionalize a national assembly that would meet regularly."[46] But the political activities went on against a background of confusion and need. By the summer of 1789, the price of bread had again risen to unacceptable heights. Lack of food caused poor laborers to gather in search of bread or flour set aside in warehouses. Foiled by militia that the bourgeoisie had organized to protect their shops, a crowd in Rouen, composed mostly of women, attacked the workshop of George Garnett, an English artisan who made jennies and carding machines for the Bureau of Encouragement. In the week of July 14, when a crowd in Paris was attacking the Bastille, its counterpart in Rouen was wrecking a machine shop and burning machines.[47] Attacks on machinery in the charity workshop of the St. Maclou district and in

---

44. Michael Kwass, *Privilege and the Politics of Taxation in Eighteenth-Century France* (Cambridge: Cambridge University Press, 2000).

45. By the end of the eighteenth century, the government debt was funded by a much wider and more varied group of lenders than the Paris financiers. The new lenders turned public opinion against royal default, an expedient used as recently as 1740. See the extensive discussion of the political significance of monetary policy by Philip T. Hoffman, Gilles Postel-Vinay, and Jean-Laurent Rosenthal, *Priceless Markets: The Political Economy of Credit in Paris, 1660–1870* (Chicago: University of Chicago Press, 2000), 136–76, esp. 174–75.

46. Ibid., 194.

47. Ibid., 59–60.

other cities followed. As Jeffry Kaplow put it, "Coincident with the fall of the Bastille, Rouen was the scene of a veritable revolt on the part of the poor who also attacked and destroyed cotton spinning machines whenever they could lay their hands on them."[48]

The scale of continued unrest and hostility in the streets seemed to overwhelm the local authorities. As royal and municipal bureaucracy failed to respond to the rioting, the bourgeoisie, fearing for its property, established executive committees and militias to step into the breech. In Rouen, the administrative problem was complicated by hostility among the *parlement*, the town aldermen, the bishop, and the provincial council. As the most economically developed city in the region, Rouen also had the largest financial split between economic groups; 50 percent of the population composed of workers and small tradesmen and 16 percent of more affluent members, involved in wholesale business and selling to the personnel in local law courts. The remaining third of the inhabitants, who were guild masters, shopkeepers, or agents in the free trades, resented the bourgeoisie's takeover of town offices and their control of the National Guard that grew out of the local militia. Added to the food scarcity, high bread prices, and generalized fear circulating through the countryside, the craft workers' perception that they were being ill treated stiffened their antagonism to the more fortunate groups.[49]

Continued Quarrels About the 1778 Reform

All sides of the political spectrum had complaints to bring to the Estates General when it convened in May 1789. The king had requested constituent groups to draw up notebooks of grievances (*cahiers de doléances*) for the assembly and to elect delegates. Historians have shown how the process of electing deputies and drawing up the cahiers politicized many ordinary people throughout France. In Rouen, these steps were complicated by the antagonism between the wealthy—including wholesale merchants and professionals—and the guilds. The worsening economy furnished the guilds with hard-bitten complaints, and no doubt they would have liked to blame the wealthy for their troubles and to have sent

---

48. Jeffry Kaplow, *Ebeuf During the Revolutionary Period, 1770–1815: History and Social Structure* (Baltimore: Johns Hopkins University Press, 1964), 128.
49. Gabriel Désert, *La Révolution en Normandie* (Toulouse: Privat, 1989), 30–31.

numbers of articulate masters to Paris. But with fast footwork, Rouen's bourgeoisie, like others in northern cities, excluded a number of guild masters from their share of representation in municipal elections and elections to the Estates General. By increasing the electoral slots of the more prosperous guilds and exerting their cultural predominance, the urban notables triumphed over the network of ordinary guilds as well as poor city artisans and rural cottagers.[50]

In the elections of winter and spring 1788–89, all men over the age of twenty-five, with a fixed address were eligible to vote, but only half of the guild members did. In general terms, 68 percent of the rich but only 7 percent of the less affluent raised their hands in these elections. Nevertheless, some guild masters showed their political awareness by commenting on the heated debate over the Estates' voting procedure in a tract they sent to Paris. Their memoir laid out propositions, some of which became the standard platform of the Third Estate regarding the voting procedure in the Estates General. They requested doubling the number of deputies for the Third Estate, deliberation in common and vote by head, assigning deputies according to population and wealth, and ensuring an equitable representation between city and countryside.[51]

The king's call to choose representatives for the Estates General were directed to all his subjects: "It is the king's will that his subjects were all called to convene at the elections of deputies who must form this great and solemn assembly."[52] Women in convents and noble women in possession of a fief were explicitly offered representation by proxy. But guild women in trades of mixed sex may not have gathered in the meetings that drew up the cahiers or selected deputies to the Estates General. Marc Bouloiseau suggests that because the rules for voting were based on the text of the edict of 1778, which forbad women in guilds of mixed sex to attend guild assemblies or become officers, officials did not invite them to take part in elections of the Estates General.[53]

---

50. Désert, *La Révolution*, 31, and Judith A. Miller, *Mastering the Market: The State and the Grain Trade in Northern France 1700–1860* (Cambridge: Cambridge University Press, 1999), 121–22.

51. Désert, *La Révolution*, 26.

52. Tiroir 217, Archives Municipales de Rouen, Bibliothèque Municipale de Rouen, "Lettre du roi pour la convocation des États-Généraux et Règlement y annexé," "Le Roi a voulu que ses sujets fussent tous appelés à concourir aux élections des deputes qui doivent former cette grande et solennelle assemblée."

53. Bouloiseau, *Cahiers*, "Although this interpretation may be rather arbitrary," he commented, "the women do not seem to have protested" (76). (Bien que cette interprétation soit assez arbitraire, elles ne semblent pas avoir protesté.)

There is evidence, however, that Rouen's masters in traditionally female guilds considered the king's call to engage in the Estates General like any other royal directive they needed to obey. Of the two remaining women's guilds in Rouen, the linen-drapers of new cloth and the knitters, the latter has left a record of participation in the voting process and drafting a cahier. On 23 March 1789, the entire membership of the knitters-ribbonmakers' guild—masters and associates alike—convened to draw up their cahier and choose delegates. Ceding their chance to place women among the delegates to Versailles, they elected François Monnais, père, and Henry Adam as their representatives in the Third Estate.[54] Claire Le Foll insists on the openness that surrounded the question of women's participation, citing a memoir to the city government drawn up in 1788 by the "guilds, corporations, and citizens" of Rouen. Mesdames Demare, Viard, and Mattard, the three women who signed this discussion of the rules for convening the Estates General were officers of the linen-drapers.[55] They may have been the last women in Rouen to take their legal place in the public discourse of the Old Regime.

Unfortunately, the *bonnetières'* cahier has not survived among the sixty-two collected by Marc Bouloiseau. Nevertheless, two documents purporting to have been written by females, expressed the complaints of Norman women. The anonymous "Cahier des doléances et réclamations des femmes" by Madame B***B*** dated 1789, Pays de Caux, was a wide-ranging tract that struck a blow for female equality. The author(s) complained that men discriminated against women, giving them an inferior education and subjecting them to the provincial Norman customary law that gave the bulk of an inheritance to the eldest son and a slim portion to the daughters. Since women have an equal burden of work as men, only prejudice keeps them from having equal access to political activity, the pamphlet asserted. They pay taxes, so why not include them in councils of state? Instead, they are expected to work, obey, and be silent. While its range of topics suggests that this tract was written by a male politician, it remains a striking feminist declaration.[56] The second pamphlet,

---

54. ADSM, 5 E 612.
55. Claire Le Foll, "Les Femmes et le mouvement Révolutionnaire à Rouen, 1789–1795," master's thesis, Université de Haute-Normandie, 1985, 39–40. Le Foll also shows evidence that in one of Rouen's suburbs three widows participated in one of the preliminary assemblies as heads of families. A total of sixty noble women owning fiefs in the nearby baillages were represented by male family members (41).
56. "Cahier de doléances et réclamations des femmes, 1789," 47–59.

"Rémonstrances des mères et des filles Normandes de l'ordre du Tiers," also castigated the legal system for giving fathers the power to marry off their daughters for their own gain. Written by two Rouennaise women, this tract also urged the Estates General to give women rights and to let them have suitable education.[57] Cahiers and petitions from Paris and other cities made many of the same requests, emphasizing that women needed to be protected from vice by gaining decent employment and that women's work should earn them a living wage.[58]

Women's Status at a Turning Point

In the last quarter of the eighteenth century, women's status continued to be one of the compelling questions under discussion.[59] As they reevaluated the nature and purpose of society, enlightened thinkers inevitably began to examine the role of women in the past and future. The intensity of this discussion is reflected in the quantity of commentaries by modern historians.[60] In keeping with new ideals, many eighteenth-century writers advocated educating women and giving them more equitable property rights. Most of the discussion focused on middle-class women and their relation to the legal strictures of marriage; however, the role of working women had been an object of concern in administrators' discourse for some time.

We can distinguish at least three norms for working women. First was the generalized misogynistic picture constructed from classical myth and scriptural directives of the ignorant, incompetent female who ought to give way before masculine mental and physical superiority. Although belittled in folk wisdom as a shrew, a jezebel, a conniver, or even a witch,

---

57. "Remonstrances des mères et des filles Normandes de l'ordre du Tiers," Np875, p. 31, Bibliothèque Municipale de Rouen. See the comments of Claire Le Foll on these pamphlets, "Les Femmes," 45–49.

58. See the texts and discussions in Paule-Marie Duhet, ed., *Les Femmes et la Révolution* (Paris: Éditions Julliard, 1971); Darlene Gay Levy, Harriet Branson Applewhite, and Mary Durham Johnson, eds., *Women in Revolutionary Paris, 1789–1795* (Urbana: University of Illinois Press, 1979); and Duhet, ed., *Cahiers de doléances*.

59. Karen Offen views the "woman question" as one of the most persistent and central issues through French social and political history. *European Feminisms, 1700–1950* (Stanford: Stanford University Press, 2000), 27–49.

60. See, for instance, Samia I. Spencer, ed., *French Women and the Age of Enlightenment* (Bloomington: Indiana University Press, 1984) and Dena Goodman, *The Republic of Letters: A Cultural History of the French Enlightenment* (Ithaca: Cornell University Press, 1994).

the workingwoman was usually taken on her own merits in eighteenth-century business. Nevertheless, law codes labeled her a minor and required a male guardian for public transactions. General prejudice justified the fact that almost always she received less for her work than a man.

The second norm focused on the female worker's economic function. Society expected women to earn their own living if they were single and to contribute to the household if they were married. To be sure, women's legal and social disabilities hobbled them, but the law provided some measure of relief with such devices as the award of the status—*marchande publique*—that gave business women the legal rights of adults. Civil separation performed a similar function. Wives whose husbands were temporarily absent took on the role of proxies, carrying out the family business at hand. Thus the Old Régime assigned a double role to women, making them independent without taking away their dependence. This double view enabled women to participate as artisans and businesswomen without creating a revolution in the legal system. Although it had a practical basis, it gave rise to a new theoretical program for women's role in society: as simply a member of the state, producing, tax paying, and competent to participate in domestic and public spheres. We will return to this category again, because its potential for revolutionary change, seldom explored, bore on the guildwomen.

The third norm for workingwomen was posited by Rousseau and his followers. The seventeenth-century aristocratic reaction had already set the stage for hostility to women's participating in court politics. Fénelon articulated this notion as a compelling ideal, that the state preserved its balance only when women kept to family duties and men took charge of public affairs.[61] In the eighteenth century Rousseau drew on this view of a "domestic republic," arguing that women were by nature the mothers and keepers of the home, and he placed them firmly in the domestic sphere. While their intellectual inferiority and linkage to the senses could be accommodated by education tailored to their capacity, it went against common sense to think that they could ever take on the role of political citizen, even by proxy. As persons who do not contribute to productive labor,[62] women in Rousseau's tableau did not manage to gain a role in the market economy.

61. Landes, *Women and the Public Sphere*, 28.
62. Susan Moller Okin reasoned that (1) private property, which belonged to the husband, could be increased only by [his] manual labor and (2) "the work assigned to his wife is not

As a program for workingwomen, however, Rousseau's domestic ideal could not even begin to take hold. Employers had no intention of providing a family wage to husbands so they could keep their wives and children at home. The primitive state of mechanization required the largest number of hands possible; women and children were needed to provide labor in the workshop and to contribute salaries to the household. Such a tradition fostered an attitude toward the female worker that considered her, in the words of Albistur and Armogathe, as *"la femme-outil,"* the woman as implement or machine.[63] This was the being found in large and small manufactures throughout the land, a cheap and dependent laborer, a source of the next products in the industrial process. Her work was the important thing, not her feminine attributes; or rather, one could say only the womanly traits that shaped her work discipline counted. Both general misogyny and her role as mother fell away before the mundane consideration of her productive capacity.

Evaluating women solely as workers in certain circumstances was appropriate for the old system of proxies and privilege, but it also fit the royal administrators' vision of a modern state. As an individual separated from the practice of a family trade, the woman-machine could be admitted to any guild, on the same basis as a man. The 1778 guild reform used the principle of symmetry, referring to women as workers. In the revolutionary era, the notion of equality in work became a rallying cry that justified equitable pay as well as political participation. From the Pays de Caux in Normandy came the statement that women work as hard as men and at the same jobs. The author wrote, "I saw, with as much surprise as admiration, that in the popular class, whether by design [*par raison*] or by need, men permit women to share in their work, some to dig up the soil, to hold the plough-share, to distribute the mail; others to undertake long and arduous trips in the worst weather for the sake of commerce."[64] Women filled administrative posts creditably, becoming inspectors for public hospitals, serving as postmasters, and even judging cloth quality in the countryside. Feminist writers like the Dutch Belle van Zuylen

---

considered to be productive labor," but only domestic duties. See *Women in Western Political Thought* (Princeton: Princeton University Press, 1979), 112–13n21.

63. The authors use this term in discussing agriculture and industry from the post-Roman era through the Middle Ages. Maité Albistur and Daniel Armogather, *Histoire du féminisme française du moyen âge à nos jours* (Paris: Éditions des Femmes, 1977), 1:45.

64. "Cahier de doléances . . . . par Madame B*** B***," 48.

drew the conclusion that there is no natural inequality between men and women.[65]

Indeed, the proposition that women ought to be equal to men in terms of civil property rights had entered into the Enlightenment debate about women.[66] Demonstrating a thrust against the biases of traditional society, such ideas were debated early in the Revolution. The right to work, free basic education, and state-sponsored welfare were ideals to strive for. Marriage became a civil contract and divorce was legalized. Women acquired more equitable inheritance rights and both sexes gained the chance to marry at the age of twenty-one without parents' permission.[67]

If the sexes were equal in capacity for work and in some civil functions, then why should they not have equal political rights as feminists in the revolutionary era demanded?[68] As the Marquis de Condorcet wrote: "The rights of men result only from this, that men are beings with sensibility, capable of acquiring moral ideas, and of reasoning on these ideas. So women, having these same qualities, have necessarily equal rights."[69] Here the paradigm of the woman-machine broke down. No matter how often women workers were measured and found equal to men, their female essence cast them into a different rank. Even wealthy women who paid taxes and owned property did not qualify for the vote. Just when the trend toward modernizing and ideas about the equality of human beings might have coincided to lift women's civil disabilities, the new view of women as destined to be nurturers, kept in the private sphere, carried the day. In fact, this change was not accidental. As the horizontal divisions between

---

65. Joke Hermsen, "Proto-Feminism pendant la Révolution? Belle van Zuylen et Mme. de Stael: A Propos de Kant et Rousseau," in *Les Femmes et la Révolution Française: Actes du Colloque International, 12–14 Avril 1989* (Toulouse: Presses Universitaires du Mirail, 1989), 298–99.

66. See Offen, *European Feminisms*, 31–49, for a discussion situating feminism in the eighteenth-century context.

67. Mary Durham Johnson, "Old Wine in New Bottles: The Institutional Changes for Women of the People During the French Revolution," in *Women, War, and Revolution*, ed. Carol R. Berkin and Clara M. Lovett (New York: Holmes & Meier, 1980), 121–22.

68. The debate over the Revolution's response to women's political rights has an extensive literature. Representative works are Joan B. Landes, *Women and the Public Sphere in the Age of the French Revolution*; Landes, *Les Femmes et la Révolution Française: Actes du Colloque International, 12–14 Avril 1989* (Toulouse: Presses Universitaires du Mirail, 1989); and Dominique Godineau, *The Women of Paris and Their French Revolution*, trans. Latherine Streip (Berkeley and Los Angeles: University of California Press, 1998).

69. Translation by Karen Offen, *European Feminisms*, 57. See her discussion of feminism and the French Revoluton, 50–76.

estates and privilege fell away, the vertical division of sex separation emerged to take its place as the prime organizing principle of society. Harkening back to Greek ideas, women and men received definitions that cast them as binary opposites, women in the home caring for the family, men in the public world laboring, making political decisions.

Even though working-class women continued to labor for wages or piecework, the ideal of the thoroughly domestic female homebody persisted. Women's waged employment began to acquire the taint of inappropriate behavior that would become so stultifying in the nineteenth century. Joan Landes relates this to a general trend "that foreclosed women's earlier independence in the street [and] in the marketplace."[70] The expectation that women had the responsibility to provide food for their children paled before the growing ideal that family support was the task of husbands and fathers. Only two legitimate reasons for women to work outside the home remained: to support themselves if they had no other resources and to preserve themselves from prostitution. Thus the right to work described by Turgot in 1776 and elaborated in revolutionary tracts became hedged about by excuses and provisos.

The revolutionary era was not the first in which women protected work options by asserting the importance of gender and claiming that only they were capable or appropriate practitioners of a trade. The most important example is that of the Paris seamstresses and their struggle, in the seventeenth century, to keep as sizeable a part of clothes making as they could from the male tailors. Clare Crowston describes the founding of the Paris *couturières* in 1675: they gained the legal right to establish their own workshops without the interference of tailors, but the provisions of their guild limited them to sewing for women and children and to leaving the dress bodice, skirts, and stays to the tailors. To break into the manufacture of these lucrative articles, the seamstresses successfully emphasized their dainty needlework and the need for feminine modesty in fittings. Sequestering certain trades on the basis of innate female characteristics was not always done in the Old Regime. During the revolutionary era this rhetoric became a common means of keeping a place for women as male competition threatened to put them out of business.[71]

---

70. Landes, *Women and the Public Sphere*, 22. Landes identifies the eighteenth century as a "turning point" for women of the people and elite women whose influence also was curtailed.

71. Clare Haru Crowston, *Fabricating Women: The Seamstresses of Old Regime France, 1675–1791* (Durham: Duke University Press, 2001).

If work outside the home was theoretically becoming the province of males, females began to reassure society that they would not become any the less womanly by performing waged tasks. The "Petition of Women of the Third Estate to the King, 1 January 1789" asked to have education and work "not in order to usurp men's authority, but in order to be better esteemed by them, so that we might have the means of living out of the way of misfortune and so that poverty does not force the weakest among us . . . to join the crowd of unfortunate beings . . . whose debauched audacity is a disgrace to our sex."[72]

Yet even if they could do a job, the question remained of whether they should. The new ideal of the republican mother, focused on inculcating patriotism and morality in her children, was replacing the old belief in the mother as provider of food to her children. As Louise Keralio, coeditor of the *Mercure National,* told her colleagues in the Société Fraternelle des Jacobins, women inspectors could contribute greatly to running public hospitals. But "their domestic duties, sacred duties important to the public order, prohibit their taking on any administrative functions, and I do not claim to draw them from their sphere."[73]

Earlier employment trends, which brought difficulties for guild mistresses, continued to plague female workers in the revolutionary period. As the economic downturn in the late 1780s increased competition for jobs, there was more intense focus on whom the candidates for employment would be. Royal administrators had tried to structure work discipline to ignore sex, but a combination of job scarcity and ideological turmoil sharpened the sexual politics of the economy. Some men's guilds mobilized to keep women from becoming members, but other males entered guilds, like that of the hairdressers, that had been kept earlier for females. Women complained that men were now infiltrating the "feminine" trades, even though there had been male embroiderers and needle workers in guilds for hundreds of years. The difference, of course, was that professional embroidery and needlework had not been gendered "female" before the 1770s. Men used the advantages of having more capital and prestige to elbow women out of employment, as in the hairdressers' trade. Angela

---

72. Levy, Applewhite, Johnson, eds., "Petition of Women of the Third Estate, 1 January 1789," *Women in Revolutionary Paris,* 20.
73. Quoted by Jan Aubray, "Feminism in the French Revolution," in *The French Revolution in Social and Political Perspective,* ed. Peter Jones (London: Arnold, 1996), 249. Aubray is citing Marc de Villiers, *Histoire des clubs de femmes et des ligues d'amazons* (Paris, 1910), 59.

Groppi comments that widespread discrimination against women in the revolutionary years curtailed their work at skilled and unskilled tasks.[74]

Women fought back by using the new emphasis on gender-specific trades for their own benefit. They turned essentialist bias on its head by identifying jobs especially appropriate for the female hand, and then pressing the authorities to reserve them for women. After detailing the misfortunes facing impoverished women, a typical 1789 tract declared: "To prevent so many ills, Sire, we ask that men not be allowed, under any pretext, to exercise trades that are the prerogative of women—such as seamstress, embroiderer, *marchande de mode*, etc., etc.; if we are left at least with the needle and the spindle, we promise never to handle the compass or the square.... May you assign us positions, which we alone will be able to fill, which we will occupy only after having passed a strict examination, after trustworthy inquiries concerning the purity of our morals."[75] While men had access to work on the basis of skill, women's protected employment required moral purity as another justification. This extra criterion may have made women's work acceptable at the time, but in the long run it contributed to the notion that female labor need not be well paid since women were not *real* workers.

Of course, women's work was not restricted to textile and needlework, and the dispute over appropriate employment shifted similar arguments to different professions. The bureaucratic posts that some women filled also came under discussion. The altercation over administrative posts is revealing. In 1791, the mail deliverers of Paris denounced women who were directors of the post, claiming that working for a woman would put him under the "yoke of caprice ... when everyone knows that woman, in terms of physical strength, has no more than half his *vertus*."[76] Commenting on a bureaucratic job three years earlier, rhetoric on the opposite side had declared of female workers, "this class of women is very capable, sirs, of exercising an infinity of lucrative posts, occupied until now by men; wouldn't it be fair to abolish this practice, and to reserve for women, all kinds of distribution offices, and all other employments whatsoever which lie within their capacity?"[77]

74. Angela Groppi, "Le Travail des femmes pendant la Révolution," 37 (1979): 27–46.
75. "Petition des femmes du Tiers-État au Roi, 1er janvier 1789," in *Women in Revolutionary Paris*, ed. Levy, Applewhite, Johnson, 19–20.
76. Cited by Groppi, "Le Travail des femmes," 37.
77. Cited by Amédée Le Faure, *Le Socialism pendant la Révolution française* (Paris: E. Danter, 1863), 126, from "Cahier de doléances et réclamations des femmes, 1789."

Although these tracts made use of the ideological arguments at large, they reflected the grim situation of working women in the revolutionary era. Darlene Gay Levy and Harriet B. Applewhite suggest that with their request for trades dedicated to them, the "women of the Third Estate" were reflecting a new economic reality. By asking for "honorable places in a transitional economy and society, these subjects of modest means, with trade-specific interests, revealed their awareness of needing new strategies and special government protection in order to cope with dignity and with a fair chance of success in a highly competitive marketplace."[78]

In terms of the political economy of work, however, the impulse to foster women's employment by setting aside certain trades for them was much more congruent with the Old Regime's structure of orders than with the free market's assault on work dignity. The anomalies inherent in women's status did bring paradoxes, as Joan Wallach Scott has written, paradoxes that could be overcome only by sequestering women in a special category.[79] Separating workingwomen from a domestic norm allowed the emotionalized home to persist as the ideal for all classes. Writing in 1788, Mercier was able to promote a workplace free of women, except for the feminine trades that would be preserved as a refuge for needy single females. Thus the trope of guaranteeing women's work in a separate setting served both the practical cause of maintaining employment and the conservative ideal of keeping women in a domestic setting. Providing dedicated professions for women could be considered a form of affirmative action, sheltering female workers from the immediate effects of the market by offering them a form of the "just price."[80]

Guild Widows in Rouen

Contention over the rights of guild widows shows the lasting strength of the family economy. Whereas men (like the postmasters) who found themselves in direct competition with nonfamily women tried to exclude them from trades, guild masters took the opposite stance toward widows.

---

78. Darlene Gay Levy and Harriet B. Applewhite, "Women of the Popular Classes in Revolutionary Paris, 1789–1795," in *Women, War & Revolution*, 13. The document they refer to is "Pétition des femmes du Tiers-Etat au Roi, 1er janvier 1789."

79. See Joan Wallach Scott, *Only Paradoxes to Offer* (Cambridge, Mass.: Harvard University Press, 1996).

80. Louis-Sébastien Mercier, *LeTableau de Paris* (Hamburg: Virchaux, 1789) 12:35.

The relation of widows to privileged work was a persistent theme because of its significance for guild families. Half of Rouen's thirty-two guild cahiers argued in favor of restoring the right of widows to continue in their husband's trade without making an additional payment. In earlier days it had been common practice for each guild to establish its own bylaws concerning widows of masters. Many allowed widows to carry on under certain stipulations; widowers of some female masters might also continue their wife's business. With its concern for standardizing guild practice, the edict of February 1778 imposed one rule concerning widows on all guilds.

Because women were now allowed to enter guilds in their own right, the administration foresaw a way to raise revenue. It gave widows a year of grace before they were obliged to join the guild in their own name, paying a new mastership fee. Objections to this system were still powerful in the revolutionary era and they found their way into guild cahiers. The amalgamated tailors–old clothes dealers–chasuble makers–embroiderers painted a pathetic scene of widows of artisans who are usually "encumbered with children, poor, and forced into RUIN [sic]" to pay a second finance charge.[81] The glovers–perfumers–powder makers "had the sad experience that the widows of our profession at the death of their husbands were stripped of their status [état] because they could not pay the fee."[82] The joiners–carpenters–woodworkers–sculptors–lute makers declared that the "widow is despoiled by a disastrous law ... [at] the moment when she needs all her strength to support herself and her children, she is forced to close the shop or to pay for a mastership."[83] The lock makers lamented that "a number of poor widows have had the bad luck to lose their husbands. Encumbered with children, most are without the resources that would let them enter the new guild, so they are reduced to the most extreme misery."[84]

The rhetoric did not stop at portraying the widows as destitute, which was sometimes accurate; it also argued that the widows had been illegally stripped of property that "law and custom" considered theirs. The husband's mastership was "a right [droit] that she acquired when she married a master-husband."[85] It was also possible that the wife had helped

81. Bouloiseau, *Cahiers*, 195.
82. Ibid., 161–62.
83. Ibid., 172.
84. Ibid., 193.
85. Ibid., 195, "un droit qu'elle avait acquis en contractant avec un mari maître."

her husband to earn it and therefore had a claim to its continuance. Or, the license might have been "recently acquired with difficulty and the assistance of his friends," which argued for a sort of homespun justice of ownership.[86]

In any event, the mastership was "hereditary," the guilds agreed. Paying a new entrance fee amounted to unfairly imposing a double charge, the cahiers argued. The familial nature of the mastership also evoked support for the late masters' children. They were entitled to inherit their fathers' guild rights. These privileged children should be excused from undergoing an apprenticeship and creating a masterpiece; they should pay only a nominal sum for entrance. The cord makers–spinners (a guild with many women members) suggested that masters' children should pay one-quarter of the rate. Makers of faience–bottle makers–glass makers and other guilds rejected any payment at all.[87] One cahier even offered a means of making up the lost revenue for the guild: the blacksmiths–tinsmiths–edge-tool makers suggested that entrance fees be raised for all masters, perhaps because their widows could then be assured of compensation.

Although the emphasis on providing a role for wives in their late husbands' trades may appear to signal a step toward the modern companionate marriage, it actually demonstrates the opposite.[88] The insistence of guild masters on widows retaining the license to work shows their backward-leaning reliance on the rights of the guild family. A widow's right to work was hedged about with the traditional notion that the master's family partakes of innate training and learns the mystery of the craft, enabling the widow to carry on and the children to do without an apprenticeship. It was such reliance on family privilege that enlightened writers and the Revolution's lawmakers sought to eradicate. Neither primogeniture nor inherited rank for the aristocracy; neither family mastership (an excused apprenticeship) nor widows' privilege for the workers! The apparent egalitarianism in the masters' plea to endow the widows rested on the old acceptance of proxies. Instead, the 1778 edict allowing only

---

86. Ibid., 172, "une maîtrise que feu son mari vient d'acquitter, souvent avec peine et l'aide de ses amis."

87. Ibid., 182, 135, 126, 158, 205.

88. See Kaplan, *La Fin des corporations*, 199–200, for an argument that promoting guild widows' rights demonstrates a move toward a new aspect of equality between husband and wife.

a one-year grace period before the widow had to register in the guild in her own name put into action the modern formula that individuals must appear on their own merits.

The End of Guilds

The guilds' continual bickering over precedent, status, and technical detail was interrupted by the d'Allarde law that abolished the corporations in March 1791. The suppression was not unexpected, but legislators hesitated to do away with an institution whose important economic and social functions were so deeply rooted and complex. The issues of industrial productivity, labor discipline, indemnification of masterships, and guild debt complicated prospective action.

But as the National Assembly worked to create a modern state structure for France, the time-honored principle of privilege fell into discredit. On 4 August 1789, aristocrats gave up their rights to preferences founded on their nobility. As equality became a leitmotif, laws were oriented, theoretically, to apply equally to every citizen. New territorial departments supplanted the traditional provinces with their inheritance of individual relationships to the crown and special rights. Primogeniture was suppressed, all children, even those born out of wedlock, were to receive equal inheritance from their fathers, and the tax system measured income rather than privileged status.

Legislators revisited earlier arguments criticizing the guild system. They argued that even with reduced entrance fees, the guilds discriminated against poor workers. The corporations retarded French industry, the rhetoric declared. Their debts and fees were passed on to consumers, making French goods uncompetitive on the world market, and they kept domestic manufactures from responding to consumers' taste. Moreover, the industrial regulations to which the guilds clung did not make their products appreciably better than goods made by nonguild artisans. Beneath these "enlightened" rationales lay a deeper issue: the reformers' hostility to an organization that had supplied the king with funds, helping to relieve the monarch of the need to submit his tax requests to a legislature.

In suppressing the guilds, the legislators required liquidation of guild assets in order to apply them to the organizations' debts. As in the 1778 guild legislation, the sale of furniture, buildings, and effects in guild halls would be a further contribution. Funds were also needed to repay the guild members for their masterships.

The d'Allarde law, proposed by Pierre Gilbert Le Roi, baron d'Allarde, achieved what Turgot had not succeeded in doing, permanently suppressing the guilds. From this time on workers could set themselves up in any trade and, in addition, take on any number of additional businesses. A worker's sex would no longer be a legal obstacle to performing a job. But the law also followed earlier precedents. As in the 1778 legislation, guilds were required to liquidate their assets in order to apply them to the organizations' debts. The government hoped that the sale of furniture, buildings, and effects would contribute to the funds needed to repay the guild members for their masterships.

But the prospect of completely freewheeling artisans, beholden only to themselves, did not sit right with the legislators. The legislature agreed that registration with the police and payment for a license, or *patente*, was required for every independent businessperson selling to the public. The law exempted poor workers employed by others or self-employed, and passive citizens whose taxes were worth only three days' wages. These were the artisans whose small home production of cheap, everyday objects and repairs was already classified as free craft.

Whatever hesitations the lawmakers might have had over d'Allarde's proposal were turned aside by the link he made to revenue collection. In the confusion and breakdown of controls, the revolutionary government was suffering from a lack of taxes. The regressive *octroi* tax imposed on goods entering cities was now generally ignored, to the extent, officials complained, that cheaper wine and beer encouraged drunkenness. In any event, as the legislature continued to elaborate a system of universal taxation, eliminating the *octroi* in February 1791, it charged the Comité des Contributions to find another tax to replace it. A new license, the patent imposed on workers' place of business, would make up the lost revenue, they believed. It would also establish a record of businesses for the police. To encourage the patent's payment, the law offered those who reported delinquent artisans half the confiscated goods and fine imposed.[89]

Despite the threat of punishment for noncompliance and the incentive for whistle-blowers, the patent system was ineffective, and it petered out by the end of 1792.[90] This was one of the unforeseen consequences of the

89. Liana Vardi, "The Abolition of the Guilds During the French Revolution," *French Historical Studies* 15, no. 4 (fall 1988): 716.
90. Marcel Marion, *Histoire financière de la France* (Paris, 1914), 2:88–98 and 218–28.

revolutionary legislation. Another was the workers' reaction to the d'Allarde law, which they interpreted as doing away with all the constraints the guilds imposed. Journeymen in Paris and elsewhere demanded higher pay, and forced recalcitrant compatriots to join them in strikes and threats to their employers. The legislators' fears of rampant workers' chaos seemed to be coming true. When the Paris carpenter journeymen made a protest, the situation became incendiary. With this preoccupation in mind, Isaac René Le Chapelier drafted the law that prohibited any organizations or meetings for the purpose of regulating wages or any other economic issues. The spontaneous gatherings of any economic players were tarred as surreptitious ways to reconvene the guilds.

Passed in June 1791, the Le Chapelier law aroused considerable debate over the way to express fundamental revolutionary principles. The right of citizens to assemble to express political opinions was a bedrock of the Revolution, but there was an equal fear of reestablishing privileged groups that sought special exemptions from the established law. Like earlier labor legislation, the Le Chapelier law suppressed workers' trade associations or brotherhoods (*confrèries*), which had sustained social welfare, religious activities, and artisans' strikes in the Old Regime. It forbad workers to collaborate in demanding higher wages and employers to collude in setting wage norms. Each contract was to be negotiated job by job and worker by worker.

There were to be no intermediate interests claiming the loyalty of citizens between the individual and the state. Although Le Chapelier acquiesced to the right of citizens to gather for a political purpose, he added, "but it must not be permitted to citizens of certain professions to assemble for their supposed common interests. There are no longer corporations in the State; there is no longer anything but the particular interest of each individual, and the general interest (*il n'y a que des intérêts individuels et l'intérêt général de la chose publique*). It is permitted to no one to inspire an intermediary interest in citizens, to separate them from the public interest by a spirit of corporation." William Sewell and Steven Kaplan emphasized that the assembly did not construe the provisions of the law as giving an edge to employers, but rather as a necessary precaution against the return of groups claiming to be entitled to exemptions from the law.[91]

91. Translated by William H. Sewell, Jr., in *Work and Revolution in France: The Language of Labor from the Old Regime to 1848* (London: Cambridge University Press, 1980), 88. See also pp. 89–91, and Kaplan, *La Fin des corporations*, 540–59.

The irony of a law intended to free ordinary individuals from the negative weight of privilege, while it actually prevents them from bringing effective pressure to gain a living wage has been much discussed by historians. This unintended consequence hampered French workers until labor legislation in 1864 permitted the establishment of unions. In addition, the provision of indemnifying the former masters kept some guilds in effect. As repositories of documentation, the guilds provided government officials with information about the former masters' length of service and whether they had paid recent taxes in order to verify claims for repayment. In the general turmoil, with guild propagandists still agitating for their continuation, some guilds continued to collect fees and elect officers.

If the Revolution willed the abolition of intermediate bodies in order to promote a nation of individuals, the suppression of women's guilds also had unintended consequences. The patent tax itself frustrated one of the reformers' goals: to cause male and female artisans to be considered interchangeable workers from an administrative point of view.[92] The state laid down the norm that labor should function as a collection of individual workers, each of whom would negotiate separate contracts with employers. But the requirement to pay the patent in order to be recognized as a public merchant caused virtually all married women to disappear from the official register. Of the women who paid for patents in Rouen during 1791 and 1792, the overwhelming majority were widows. Unmarried women came next, but married women were conspicuously absent. Only widows or unmarried women who had no possibility of working under the guise of a family enterprise spent the funds for the patent. Instead of freeing individual women to create new businesses that multiplied national resources, increased employment, and fostered productivity, the patent system may well have bound many women to their husbands' trade. For working families, this lack of product diversification contributed to their fragile economic position so common in the early modern world. It also kept married women in the position of lifelong journey workers, under the direction of husbands who had received formal training. Nevertheless, wives, who could offer their products in their husbands' shops, may well have chosen to save the price of another license fee. If that meant abandoning their entrepreneurial independence, so be it! For

---

92. The 1792 patent clearly shows more widows than married or single women enrolled.

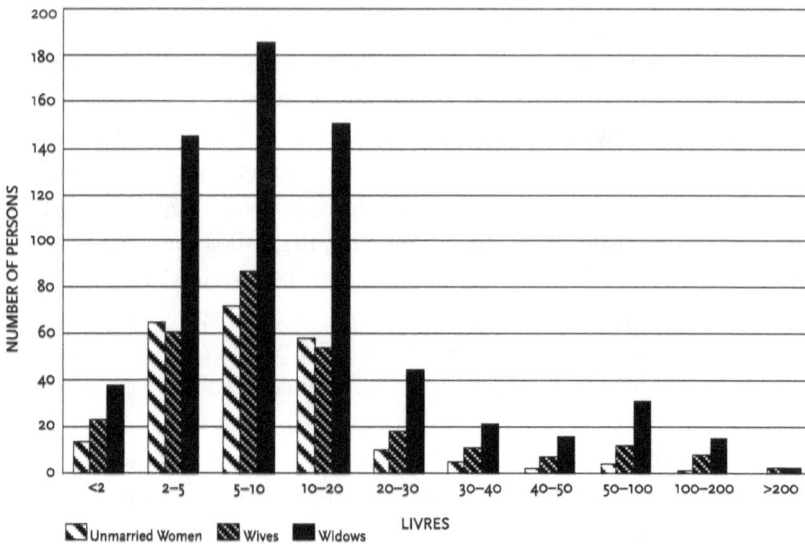

Figure 17. Patent tax on women artisans, Rouen, 1792. In every tax bracket, widows outnumber wives and unmarried women numerically and by value of their place of business. Apparently widows were more likely to establish their own businesses—and pay the tax—than wives or unmarried women. From Archives départementales de la Seine Maritime, L 2463.

small artisans in the 1790s, the difficult economic situation put a damper on personal preferences and turned people toward simple survival.

Even those wives who opted to maintain themselves in their own trade set up shop with their husbands or incorporated husbands into their trade while they remained the skilled but silent partner. Legally they no longer controlled their own businesses, finances, or strategies for manufacture or commerce. With this retreat, the new regime pushed women back into the closed, undifferentiated unit of the family that it was trying in other spheres to undo. The pressure of contradictory revolutionary ideals is nowhere so apparent as in the Revolution's praise of the new republican hearth and its condemnation of the old aristocratic family and the guild master's circle. The stage was set for Napoleonic legislation that perpetuated the husband's complete control over the wife's earnings. And by relinquishing the social basis of the proxy and suppressing the laws that enabled individuals to stand in for one another, the National Assembly stripped the family of its ability to shelter resources in the wife's independent business.⁹³ In effect, the family structure with husband as boss carrying ultimate power over his minors—women and children—replicated the pattern of the republican state with its pervasive control of citizens.

Nor did the guilds' suppression release institutional resources to the former masters. The guilds' balance sheets showed debts and obligations that outweighed the cash on hand. After having enjoyed balanced budgets for much of the 1780s, the guild of ribbonmakers–hand knitters–button makers–lacemakers–fringe makers registered its last entry on 9 November 1791 with a closing account of 5,756 livres in assets and 6,153 livres in debts.⁹⁴ Selling the guild halls, if they owned such property, and the chests, tables, mirrors, ornaments, and curtains, did not recover enough to pay their debts.

Artisans' Troubles During the Revolution

The guilds' increasing use of wage labor and their selective enforcement of craft regulations toward the end of the eighteenth century may not have prepared the way for the new regime of the patent. Indeed, Haim Burstin suggests that guilds had become more rigorous in support of their privileges at the end of the century in reaction to the growth of unregulated business.⁹⁵ Even suspicions that the guilds were about to be suppressed did not reduce the shock of their being shut down without the possibility of appeal.⁹⁶ With the suppression of the guilds, former masters suffered business upheaval and loss of status and political power. No longer could the expenses of lawsuits be defrayed by charging them to the association. Nor would a plea for tax reduction come from a group that might shift the levy to those better able to pay. Without the assurance of guild credit,

---

93. In fact, the new configuration of male and female roles changed the ideal shape and function of the family. When Abbé Fenélon called for restoring the family to its place of honor in the state, he understood women's role as household matron to include managing family estates. See Joan B. Landes's use of this perception in *Women and the Public Sphere*, 28.

94. ADSM, 5 E 612.

95. See Haim Burstin, "Conditionnement économique et conditionnement mental dans le monde du travail Parisien à la fin de l'Ancien Régime: Le privilège corporatif," *History of European Ideas* 3 (1982): 24. For a contrasting view, see Coffin, *Politics of Women's Work*, 42.

96. ADSM, 5 E 508, *Lingères en neuf*, 24 December 1790, The royal council would ordinarily direct Sieur and Dame Noyer to buy a mastership from the *lingères*, wrote maître Destrouché, "Mais dans les circonstances présentes, l'équité vient que l'on en use autrement. C'est l'opinion générale que les maîtrises et communautés d'arts et métiers vont bientôt être abolies."

capital could be harder to attract. Sons and husbands would be more vulnerable to military draft when collective fees could not buy substitute soldiers.

Along with the institutional changes wrought by the suppression of the guilds, artisans of both sexes experienced major problems caused by the Revolution, as shortages of raw materials and money disrupted manufacture and trade. Historiography has shown how the poor interjected their own interests into revolutionary ideals by protesting the high prices of bread and other necessities. As popular pressure in Paris and other cities caused political clubs to add the right to sustenance to their revolutionary goals, legislators in 1793 established price ceilings on bread and other food and covertly followed customary ways of supplying the cities with grain. Nevertheless, the civilian population was still deprived of food and such essentials as soap, bleach, and rags. Some historians have persuasively argued that by creating disturbances in the streets, barging into shops, and forcibly buying goods at the modest prices they set, working class women were converting traditional protests into political gestures.[97]

Those who owned shops also suffered during this time. By 1792 in Rouen, anyone who had a shop was in danger of losing their stock. Patrols formed to guarantee personal safety did not protect those whom the crowd suspected of hoarding goods or manipulating money; one merchant, a M. d'André, was forced to flee to Paris to avoid popular fury. Others prudently reclaimed all their merchandise, emptying their warehouses, and transferred the goods to ships at Le Havre for safe keeping until conditions improved. It is doubtful that the female craft workers had the means for this subterfuge. We are left to wonder if they put revolutionary symbols on their doors in the hope that the crowd would pass them by in favor of shops that sold sugar, coffee, and soap.[98]

Business entrepreneurs and the crowd alike blamed the assignats, issued by the government beginning in 1790, for much of the inflation plaguing the economy. People reported that the paper money, which was secured by the sale of church lands, chased out good coinage. It saddled

---

97. Barrie Thorne asserts that the push for these economic imperatives became political demands as market women and others in Paris wrote petitions and brought their demands to the legislative bodies. Personal letter.

98. See Olivier Chaline and Gerard Hurpin, eds., *Vivre en Normandie sous la Révolution* (Rouen: Société de l'histoire de Normandie, 1989), 1:233, 238, 239, 242, for descriptions of merchant behavior in January and February 1792. Distributing counterfeit assignats was a serious crime that carried the death penalty. Ibid., 2:485.

merchants with numerous logistic problems. Through the years, assignats lost more and more value, causing prices to rise. Counterfeit assignats circulating in quantity disrupted business confidence. Most irritating was the lack of small bills to make change. A local society of some two hundred wholesale merchants and traders in Normandy tried to solve the problem by issuing script in denominations of 20 sous up to 3 and 6 livres. These promissory bills were designed to pay workers, but they had to be redeemed for assignats at an official bureau before anyone could use them as currency. Unsurprisingly, workers shrank from accepting wages in this form because they had to turn in notes exactly equivalent to assignats to receive the exchange. Uneven lots became worthless, and they were a pure loss to the person left with them. Retail shops were even more reluctant to accept the script, especially when they had to make change; some merchants utterly refused the paper notes.[99] When the chaos of the Terror further disrupted the distribution and sale of goods throughout France, the value of assignats was shaken.[100]

Along with so much else, the issue of when to open or close shops was politicized. When the revolutionary calendar was installed in autumn 1793, officials required manufacturers' boutiques and ateliers to close on the tenth day of each ten-day week and to remain open on Sundays and Christian holidays. If they refused to follow this regime, they were regarded as suspect and punished. Observers recorded the waning of revolutionary fervor by noting that businesses began closing on Sundays again in 1795.[101]

Economic Shifts, Production, and the Cat in the Liberty Bonnet

As aristocratic garments fell out of favor and the wealthy left France, orders for the luxury goods that were the staple of women's guilds declined sharply. A further blow to the bespoke industry was the ruling in October 1789 that clerics should no longer wear ecclesiastic robes. Logistic problems also hampered the clothing industry. Raw materials were

---

99. Called *"billets de confiance,"* this substitute currency, signed by *députés du négoce*, was distributed from bureaux in several towns, which apparently issued bills in a variety of unstandardized denominations. Bills given out in Bolbec and Fécamp apparently could be redeemed only in the environs, not in Rouen. Ibid., 1:197, 200, 210–12.
100. Hoffman, et al., *Priceless Markets*, 201.
101. Chaline and Hurpin, eds., *Vivre en Normandie*, 2:510.

more expensive and hard to find, and trade networks had trouble distributing the products. Nevertheless, the Revolution itself provided work for the needle trades as new garments came into fashion. In 1789 the liberty cap and the cockade became spontaneous early symbols of the new regime; a royal decree of 19 May 1790 required men and women to wear the tricolor cockade of straight pieces of white, red, and blue ribbons in a hat or a buttonhole. Popular enthusiasm encouraged highly symbolic dress that supported the new ideals by the wearing of all three colors. Women sported red liberty bonnets and blue coats (the color of those worn by the National Guard) with red collars. Bourgeois men wore red waistcoats and white stockings with blue decoration while workers wore red caps and trousers with white and blue stripes. Royalists wore yellow and black in 1791 and later adopted a white cockade or other accessories coded as aristocratic.[102]

The potent symbolic value of badges of political orthodoxy can be seen in the police work that went into their enforcement. In Rouen, 1 May 1793 was distinguished by the arrest of someone wearing a hat cockade made of violet, white, and red silk ribbons. The punishment was an eight-day prison term and a fine of 50 livres. A regulation longer than the decree itself specified that only the three national colors should be worn, and that the ribbons must be of wool, goat hair, or dimity, and printed (*peinte*) on both sides. To emphasize the rule, a notice four months later declared, "All women [in Rouen] will wear the national cockade on their heads, in a visible manner. Every cockade of ribbons must conform to the regulation. Anyone breaking this law will be subject to eight days in prison for the first offence and for the second, will be declared a suspect and will be locked away until peace is declared."[103]

In spite of the advice of the Société Populaire et Républicaine des Arts that all citizens should wear similar clothing to underscore their equality, the revolutionary government found it expedient to dress officials in distinctive uniforms to indicate their rank and responsibility.[104] The

---

102. In *Dress in France in the Eighteenth Century*, Madeleine Delpierre writes that "in 1790 a few young aristocrats adopted the costume known as *demi-converti*." In mourning for the death of "THE HEIR APPARENT," they also expressed "their regret at losing their privileges and their resignation" to the loss. Trans. Caroline Beamish (New Haven: Yale University Press, 1997), 121–22. Originally published as *Se vêtir au XVIIIe siècle* (Paris: Socété Nouvelle Adam Biro, 1996).

103. Chaline and Hurpin, eds., *Vivre en Normandie*, 2:479, 500.

104. Ibid., 122–24. In 1794, the painter Jacques-Louis David was asked to design clothing

blue-coated National Guard, the soldiers of various regiments, the constitutional clergy, even members of the national legislature who clung to formal wear reminiscent of the old regime, all had to be supplied by the cadre of handicraft artisans. Technology that had been used to manufacture ribbons for aristocratic dresses, embroidery once setting off elegant vests, and passementerie that had emblazoned royal officers' coats now found new work in cockades, liberty hats, and banners.[105]

As keenly as under the Old Regime, textiles bore political and ideological messages. In the early years, the national tricolor emblem was linked with Christianity as the self-styled *"dames citoyennes de Rouen"* arranged a mass at the cathedral asking the Virgin Mary to safeguard the constitution and the well-being of France. Dressed in white with belts of three colored ribbons, the women donated a tricolor flag on which an image of the Virgin was painted. In other semi-religious, semi-secular ceremonies, the market women convinced the curé to lead them in a procession with the Virgin's picture, and along the way they embellished a street altar and a statue of Joan of Arc with tricolor ribbons. Later, when they were by themselves, they decorated many statuettes of the Virgin located near the market with little tricolor hats.[106]

The death of Count Honoré-Gabriel Mirabeau in 1791 called forth innumerable church services dignified with commemorative flags. Wildly popular because he served as a brilliant orator for the Third Estate, rather than the nobility, Mirabeau received homage from a wide range of male and female trades in Rouen. Five groups, among them the female woolen cloth bleachers, the market women, and the laundresses, each donated a flag in his honor.[107] Banners and flags for newly formed battalions of volunteers and later for national soldiers ensured that some silk workers had employment.

---

for all branches of French society. See Delpierre's discussion of the keen interest in new garment styles.

105. For an indispensable discussion of dress and its meaning, see Roche, *Culture of Clothing*, esp. chap. 9, "The Discipline of Appearances: The Prestige of Uniform."

106. Chaline and Hurpin, eds., *Vivre en Normandie*, 2:383, 385.

107. In April 1791, engravers and painters of calico, poor diggers, journeymen stocking makers, and journeymen linen weavers held masses for Mirabeau. In May, he was commemorated by women who bleached unfinished woolen cloth and men who finished it. In June it was the turn of the water carriers, manufacturers of faience and their journeymen, market women, journeymen turners, cabinetmakers, decorators who added painted designs and feathers to clothing, and laundresses. The female day laborers who wove woolen cloth, and the *"garçons et filles"* in the professions of cook, pastry chef, restauranteur, wine merchant, brewer, and billiard room attendant also paid their respects with church services in June.

To breath life into its new ceremonies, the administration specified that participants wear inspiring and dramatic garments. One *fête de la fédération* was scheduled for each month, and other parades and celebrations to generate civic devotion took place frequently. For each of these events, women dressed in white empire-style dresses with wreaths of artificial flowers or laurel leaves in their hair. Costume for men and for children was also designed especially for each event. Like the 400 boys and 60 girls of Rouen's free schools who marched on 21 July 1793, many wore small flags, either in tricolor or embroidered with Liberty trees. Municipal officials were also garbed in dress uniforms to set them apart from the crowd. Although revolutionary supporters in Paris agitated to require prostitutes to wear distinctive clothing, public women in Rouen were forbidden to have any identifying sign on their windows. The public and the lawmakers understood the power of symbols, sometimes displayed, sometimes omitted.[108]

During a 1792 bread riot in Rouen, the police alert was signaled by shop closings, the call of the tocsin, and hanging a martial flag outside the city hall. When all was quiet, officials substituted a white flag of peace. Spontaneous popular expression reached first for symbolic objects. Reacting to the news that the king and his family were imprisoned in August 1792, royalist sympathizers "tore off their national cockades, threw them into the fire, and grabbed them off passersby. Crying '*Vive le roi, au diable la République et les Jacobins!*' they put cockades made of white paper on their hats and their bonnets." During the terrible bread shortage of March 1795, officials in Rouen reported that "several women tore down a flag . . . , yelling '*des propos inciviques.*'"[109]

In an amusing inflation of the symbolic, an old woman whose cat had played some dirty tricks in her absence yelled at the animal that she was tying a red liberty bonnet on his head as punishment. Her neighbors in the same stairway were scandalized that she would treat the *bonnet rouge de la Liberté* so disrespectfully. They broke open her door, beat her up, and dragged her down to the municipality for punishment. Because it was late, she was locked up with the vagrants. Fortunately, after hearing

---

108. Chaline and Hurpin, eds., *Vivre en Normandie*, 2:461.
109. Ibid., 2:442, 2:460-61, and Miller, *Managing the Market*, 180. In the uprisings, hungry workers forced the officials to help them search for grain and they wreaked havoc on liberty trees and tricolor cockades, 181.

her explanation, the judge of the correctional court sent her home.[110] Because this event happened in Rouen in July 1792 rather than during the Terror, the old woman's words were dismissed.[111] Later, insults to the *bonnet rouge* would have incurred harsher punishment because the red cap was a potent national symbol. In every parade, procession, and celebration, the red cap festooned the displays. On the end of pikes, on carts bearing canons, worn by officials requisitioning supplies, the red cap accompanied by tricolor ribbons lent an air of national authority to the participants and symbolically transformed instruments of war into guardians of the idealized nation. Whether or not their work was recognized, the female artisans of the needle trades played a significant role in the community's political cohesion by producing these national symbols.

Requisitioning Workers for the Army

By autumn of 1793, a shortage of clothes and other furnishings for the army became apparent. Local officials in Rouen went door-to-door collecting stockings, shoes, shirts, leggings, and money for the ill-clothed soldiers. Citizens were asked to donate beds, pallets, mattresses, pillows, coverlets, and woolen blankets. Chairs were taken from churches. Upholsterers, used clothes dealers, and other textile makers had their merchandise requisitioned. One can imagine the reaction of needle workers, living on the edge of poverty, at having to donate their goods to the national effort. But even these efforts were not enough to furnish what was needed. With the guilds suppressed, the government stepped in to organize the trades, and former guild masters found themselves impressed into forced work with no chance to negotiate conditions or wages. Similar central workshops were organized in Paris where the women went on a successful campaign, complete with public assemblies, petitions, and lobbying the legislature, to restore the work to the sections.[112]

110. Chaline and Hurpin, eds., *Vivre en Normandie*, 2:383, 385,433. The old woman complained that she had lost two days of sale for her herbs, which were now wilted.
111. The old herb seller had more luck than several men who were lynched or stoned by a Paris mob for trampling on a tricolor flag in May 1790. See J. F. Bosher, *The French Revolution* (New York: W.W. Norton, 1988), 169.
112. Dominique Godineau, *The Women of Paris and their French Revolution*, trans. Katherine Streip (Berkeley and Los Angeles: University of California Press, 1998), 72–75. Originally published as *Citoyennes Tricoteuse* (Paris: Alinea, 1988).

The National Assembly blamed the administrators in Rouen's district for being lax in getting the clothes and equipment ready for the first draft of soldiers. In order to get the needed items quickly, the legislators established workshops and had the skilled needle workers rounded up and installed there. This hothouse production may have taken its inspiration from factories already established in Rouen. The authorities recognized that "the easy distribution of clothes within the communes of the district makes supervision [of the workers] almost impossible. The only way to accelerate and manage to have the clothes finished is to gather all the workers employed by the district into one single place, and to form ateliers which will be under the immediate and continuous surveillance of some good citizens." Therefore, orders came for all the tailors, whether experienced or not, to gather in the capital city of their district, and to work exclusively on the army assignment. Shoe makers were put under the same discipline. An atelier of women was also to be established for those who "wished to" make shirts, leggings, collars, and other accoutrements for the "new defenders of the fatherland."[113]

As the unsympathetic Rouennais Horchelle described it in his *Journal d'un bourgeois de Rouen ou la Révolution observée*, the government's response to this crisis was to "requisition" the entire population for the necessary tasks. Commenting wryly on the forced enthusiasm the republic demanded, he wrote, "All the male and female citizens and the children are put into 'requisition.' The young people and married men, to the army; the women work on tents and other implements appropriate for soldiers. They take care of the diseases in the hospitals; the children make rags; old people are carried to the public squares to preach to the people about the horror of royalty, the happiness of the republic (in which they are dying of hunger) and the angel of Reason."[114] The needle workers' small wages were probably less valuable than the tickets to the soup

---

113. ADSM, L 139 (1), "Arrêtes des Représentants du people française envoyés par la Convention national dans les departments de la Seine-Inférieure et circonvoisins," 19 Nivôse, Year II, Delacroix, Legendre, and L. Louchet. I am endebted to Jeff Horn for furnishing me with this reference.

114. Chaline and Hurpin, eds., *Vivre en Normandie*, 14 November 1793, 2:512. "Tous les citoyens, citoyennes et les enfants sont mis en requisition. Les jeunes gens et les hommes mariés pour l'armée; les femmes travailleront aux tentes et autres ustensiles propres aux soldats. Elles garderont les maladies dans les hopitaux; les enfants feront de la charpie; les veillards seront portés dans les places publiques pour y precher au people l'horreur de la royauté, le bonheur de la République (où on meurt de faim) et l'évangile de la Raison, etc." This commentary was from an acknowledged bourgeois perspective.

kitchen that they received, in the view of Jeff Horn. Without concerning itself overly much with the women's skill, authorities also rounded up former guild masters and *journalières* for a large workshop at the district of Saint-Ouen. There they turned out the blankets, knapsacks, and socks that Rouen furnished to the war effort. With the guild system abolished, the government frequently conscripted the former guildwomen into this work.[115]

What happened to the former guildwomen of Rouen? Changing economic conditions altered their options and their problems. The scarcity of male labor encouraged women to fill agricultural jobs. It is possible that among those who remained artisans in Rouen some had the opportunity experienced by some female artisans in Paris by taking the place of men who become soldiers and receiving the specialized training formerly reserved for males.[116] The collapse of the colonial trade in 1793, which brought stagnation to Nantes and Bordeaux, also reconfigured the production of artisans. Gradually, the external market stabilized as North America and Eastern Europe substituted for the lost English and Spanish consumers. With printed cottons from the new calico manufactures, founded in the last third of the eighteenth century and afterwards, artisans supplied bourgeois Europeans rather than Spanish and French slaves. As calicos and chintzes grew in popularity, cotton production flourished once again in Normandy, occupying many who had spun cotton or linen before the Revolution began. Cloth workers made destitute when the traditional industries of linen and hemp gave way to the cheaper linens of Silesia and Saxony may have found places at the new mechanized spinning jennies. Others who could not survive the collapse of the linen trade joined the ranks of the poor who drifted to Paris, hoping for jobs or charity. The flying shuttle proliferated both in urban and rural settings as France brought her technological practices up to English standards, if not to her rival's output.[117]

What the former guildwomen did depended on their skill, their connections, and luck. Without the institutional verification of quality that guilds had provided, personal experience of trustworthy dealings had to be the link between merchants. After guilds were suppressed, women

115. My thanks to Jeff Horn for sharing his archival research about this material.
116. Godineau, *Women of Paris*, 54.
117. Philippe Minard, "L'industrie," in *Atlas de la Révolution Française*, ed. Gérard Béaur, Philippe Minard, and Alexandra Laclau (Paris: EEHESS, 1989), 10:72–75.

in the trades found themselves scrambling to take advantage of the individual ties they had formed in their businesses. The census of 1790 shows that women's jobs in Rouen were mostly as salespersons in boutiques and as artisans in ateliers, especially as *modistes* and seamstresses. Only in the eastern sections of the city were women's jobs were more diversified.[118]

Propagandists of the time as well as contemporary historians have suggested that the closure of guilds opened unprecedented economic opportunity for women. It is true that former guild members already had the technical and managerial expertise to launch new businesses or to reconfigure traditional ones. Lobbying municipal and central administrations for favors and using the courts to gain economic advantages were strategies well known to them. They had a disciplined workforce capable of adapting to many new machines. As enticing as the possibilities appeared, however, we must not discount the economic and cultural obstacles that stood in their way.

The primary need for businesses after 1791, as always, was for capital and that was particularly hard for women to get. There were cultural hindrances to women's acquisition of financial support. As Jean-Yves Grenier reasoned in *L'Économie d'Ancien Régime,* the sort of information key to profitable commerce—knowledge of manufacturing techniques and worldwide market conditions—was the necessary precursor to credit worthiness. Only the merchant who already had a large network of correspondents and markets of high volume could be in a position to exert the kind of confidence to attract support. Access to "large, reasonably priced credit presupposes that the wholesale or retail merchant already has a strong reputation capable of sustaining confidence" by a history of commercial success with large investment and personal integrity. Only then were the business instruments of the letters of change, loans, and mutual credit accounts (*comptes mutuels*) between merchants accessible to the entrepreneur.[119] While some women in major commercial families satisfied these requirements, most guildwomen had not done business on this scale.

Instead, bankruptcy records suggest that craftwomen's business associates were likely to be women, and the sums of money they circulated

---

118. Le Foll, "Les Femmes et le mouvement révolutionnaire à Rouen," 32.
119. Jean-Yves Grenier, *L'Économie d'Ancien Régime: Un monde de l'échange et de l'incertitude* (Paris: Albin Michel, 1996), citation p. 418, see also 318–21, 417–20.

within their networks were small. Unless the woman's business was extraordinarily brisk when she married, her dowry probably went to underwrite the enterprise of her new husband. The women who did have considerable amounts at their disposal—wealthy widows—preferred conservative investments like life annuities and pensions. The guilds had attracted such subsidies but individual female artisans were unlikely to provide the long-term assurance of the former privileged corporations. That required a dedicated group, assets used as collateral, and sure expectation of long-term industrial and commercial continuity. Even though women's investments increased throughout the century, they were still characterized by their risk avoidance and relatively small scale.[120] The difficulties were exemplified by the woman who took advantage of the new liberty to open a bakery but found she could not sustain it when government regulations decreed that bakers had to keep a large amount of expensive grain on hand.[121]

The particular circumstances of the Revolution also weighed against women's enterprise. In *Priceless Markets*, Philip T. Hoffman and fellow authors argue that one long-term result of inflation during the Revolution was to deplete most sharply the savings of women, the elderly, and small investors. This population did not participate in the speculation over changes of currency and shifts in monetary worth; therefore, it was not able to offset the inflation accompanying revolutionary events with strategic injections of profit. When currency was stabilized in 1797, wealthy women found that their living conditions declined along with their assets, and unless they had family money behind them, they were dealt out of profitable enterprises in the new regime.[122]

As much a change of scale as of institutional revolution, certain corners of production after the guild regime tended to increase in size and scope, putting them outside the reach of female artisans and entrepreneurs. As before, the merchants who dominated international networks earned the big profits. Supplying the army was another source of large-scale profits. Virtually 60 percent of national resources went into war production in the mid-1790s.[123] Small craft workers found themselves pushed out of commerce and into the role of piece workers when one

---

120. Hoffman et al., *Priceless Market*, 166–68.
121. My thanks to Judith Miller for this information.
122. Hoffman et al., *Priceless Market*, 177–206.
123. See Miller, *Mastering the Market*, 202.

industry or another found an international market. During the guild era, industrial regulations had maintained the need for guilds, and manufacturing was so fragmented that they could survive with niche production. With the abolition of guilds, the female artisans were competing against rationalized production and big investment. When the era of machines became full-blown, they could not buy the machines or compete against them successfully with hand devices. In early days, the scale of business for the individual craft worker had been measured by the output of relatively small manufactories. Although we no longer believe that all guild industry was conducted in units of individual family ateliers, even those guilds whose outreach included extra urban workshops and rural networks of cottage industry did not produce the volume of goods that industrialization anticipated. Unless some special circumstance intervened, where handicraft was valued for its own sake, the artisans' atelier shifted production to supply only portions of the industrial products. Nor could the individual artisans gain the planning advantages of wholesale merchants who were constantly in touch with market conditions and changes in styles. But this scenario anticipates advances in industrialization that took place in the early years of the nineteenth century. During the Revolution, artisanal production prevailed and women continued to labor throughout the various industries as wage earners and sometimes as heads of workshops.

Scarce credit did not keep a number of women from organizing large businesses that they ran themselves as Dominique Godineau has shown. If their business situation started during the Revolution, these women may have been the true beneficiaries of guild suppression. With as many as two hundred workers, these contractors directed their own manufacturies of soap, beer, faience, and porcelain.[124] Women also functioned as supervisors in individual workshops and as intermediary entrepreneurs over large networks of female workers producing ornaments, polished metal letters, buttons, embroidery, artificial flowers, pearls, and other goods in Paris. Lace and other fashion items were made in the city and other areas, stretching into the surrounding regions. Female workers brought already acquired skills as metal polishers into copper and steel industries. Some in the metal industries attained the exceptional salaries

---

124. Of course, females heading royal manufactures of faience, porcelain, and glass during the eighteenth century provided precedents for businesses found during the Revolution.

of 2 or 3 livres per day, still only one-half the men's salaries for the same job. Others in needlework earned 1.5 livres, not enough to live on. With rare exceptions, these wages were not more than half that of men working in the same trades.[125]

Godineau points out that while the complaints of working women about insufficient wages and frequent unemployment did not automatically knit together a full-blown class consciousness, the protests of the Paris women told to work on goods provided by central offices did amount to the first organized women's job action. Their lobbying and speaking at the section was effective in having the auspices of their work switched from central offices to the sections. Clearly we need more extensive research to learn the how women, both the former guild elite and the traditional day laborers, fared after the end of the guilds. While some caught the tiger's tail of success in a more ruthless economy, most of the former guildwomen found themselves stripped of the protection that had sheltered them under the Old Regime. Without special status, they fell into the ranks of the urban proletariat, to eke out a living by continuing their handicraft production or applying their skill and discipline to the developing industrial world.

In Lyon

The Revolution came to Lyon when the silk industry was in a decline, many of its workers unemployed and suffering from the high cost of bread; Arthur Young estimated that 20,000 persons were receiving food on charity in the late 1780s. The poor harvest of Italian silk worms in 1788–89 had raised the cost of raw silk and the unusually cold winter caused ice to interrupt river transportation, further harming business. The Eden-Reyvenal Treaty of 1786, stimulating trade with England, was blamed for allowing the French silk market to be unpatriotically supplanted with cloth of English "whimsical" taste. English wallpaper began to replace silk wall coverings. Many unemployed silk weavers requested passports to seek work outside the country and were refused by officials

---

125. Godineau, *Women of Paris and Their French Revolution*, 52–67. See also Raymonde Monnier, "L'Évolution de l'industrie et le travail des femmes sous l'Empire," *Bulletin d'histoire économique et social de la Révolution française* (1979): 47–60, for the estimate that at least 45,000 women workers existed in Paris at the time.

afraid to let their expertise leave France. Others left without benefit of official sanction. As a result of so many problems, the consulate's survey of 1788 reported, 63 percent of the 14,777 looms in the city were idle.[126] The industry was so shaken that when new orders for fabric arrived in 1789–90 and 1791–92, merchants and weavers scrambled to hire skilled workers from other French cities and the Italian Piedmont.[127]

Historians have commented that the decline in the silk industry was not caused solely by prerevolutionary agitation or by the bread shortage, keen though they were, but that changes in clothing styles, increased duties, and competition from other European silk centers had brought Lyon's output down from its high point in the 1770s. Contention between merchants and master weavers, another of the major issues in the *grande fabrique*, continued to preoccupy the industry throughout the period. The small upsurge of orders at the start of the Revolution soon reversed as war and lack of capital disrupted Lyon's commerce. From 1792 to 1807 the silk industry foundered, and neither private nor institutional refuges for the poor and sick could sustain the unemployed.[128]

Wage Disputes and Workers' Derogation

Having lost their struggle to sell their products directly to consumers without paying the 800 livres fee required, most of the master weavers now dealt only with the merchants who provided patterns and warp for the new cloth. A price for each job resulted from bargaining over the difficulty of the design and the problems it would pose for execution in the master weavers' judgment. The rate of pay came from a tariff that the *grande fabrique* levied as a standard of payment for all who worked in the industry. Periodically the master weavers, often accompanied by their journeymen, demonstrated to raise the tariff. In 1759, 1774, and 1779 they

---

126. Arthur Young, *Travels in France During the Years 1787, 1788, 1789*, ed. Jeffry Kaplow (Garden City: Doubleday, 1969), 344. Louis Trénard, "La Crise sociale lyonnaise à la veille de la Révolution," *Revue d'histoire moderne et contemporain* 2 (1955): 8. Trénard cites "Résultats de la visite de 1777," claiming that "40,000 ouvriers au moins ont abandonné nos murs. Il faut dix ans pour réparer nos pertes." See Archives Municipales de Lyon (hereafter AML), Grande Fabrique. Carton 55.

127. Pierre Cayez, *Métiers Jacquard et hauts fourneaux: Aux origines de l'industrie lyonnaise* (Lyon: Presses Universitaires de Lyon, [1978]), 59–60.

128. E. Leroudier, "La décadence de la fabrique lyonnaise à la fin du XVIIIe siècle," *Revue d'histoire de Lyon* 10 (1911): 429–31. Trénard, *Crise*, 6–7.

made formal requests for increases, asserting that the merchants ought to share their profits in good times. The fees for women's work in auxiliary trades also conformed to set standards, but there is no evidence that they protested their rate of pay, only taking abrupt leave when they were not paid at all.

With the decade of the 1780s the silk industry began a serious decline and the silk weavers demanded higher pay simply to survive. Markets continued to shrink because of rising tariffs in Germany, England, and Spain; distribution problems caused by war; and switches in fashion to lighter fabrics. What production there was suffered from the scarcity of servants to pull cords on brocade looms and of journeymen, 500 of whom had left to do military service. Even the journeymen, the drawgirls and drawboys, and those women processing silk thread within masters' ateliers presented a problem for the master weavers, since legally they had to be paid whether or not there were orders for them to fill. And the brocades themselves, being a bit passé, now fetched lower prices.[129]

As merchants tried to make up for the loss of business by shortchanging the weavers, silk workers' lives became increasingly miserable. A graphic view of this situation can be seen in the declining number of masters in the silk *fabrique,* from 45.3 percent in midcentury to 17 percent in 1786. Meanwhile the number of silk weavers who were permanent journeymen or masters forced to work as journeymen in another master's shop increased from 18.9 percent in midcentury to 66.5 percent between 1786 and 1788.[130] With only their labor to sustain them, the silk weavers were separated more than ever from the wealthy merchants who now employed them. Besides accepting charity, their last recourse was to find refuge in the Hôpital de la Charité, which accepted poor people who were sick and abandoned children over the age of seven, or the Hôtel-Dieu, which opened its doors to the old and infirm, abandoned children, and the "honest" poor. These were the institutions where drawgirls, injured from years of pulling down the loom weights, often ended their days and where destitute unwed spinners gave birth.[131]

129. AN F 12 762 [1780], "Mémoire ... au Roy et nosseigneurs de son conseil ... les syndics et jurés de la fabrique des étoffes de soie, or, et argent."

130. Maurice Garden, *Lyon et les lyonnaises* (Paris: Société d'Édition "Les Belles-Lettres," 1970), 282.

131. AN F 12 678, "Mémoire sur divers objets d'amélioration" discusses plans to improve the inmates' work, especially allowing thirty members of "le sexe" to graduate from spinning to a mastership in the *grande fabrique* after six years [after 1786].

The economic conditions that caused the *grande fabrique*'s malaise, however, encouraged the government to stimulate industry by freeing up some aspects of the economy, including granting permission for women workers to enter guilds. The continuing emphasis of Colbert's seventeenth-century effort to draw women into the workforce can be seen with this step. In terms of women's work, the fourteen-year period between opening all guilds to female employment in 1777 and 1791, when the guilds were abolished, stands out as a time of great opportunity. If women were able to become mistresses throughout the crafts, they would be party to the financial and legal advantages of privileged trades beyond the traditional needlecraft and textile areas. Even with the truncated roles the new law imposed—exclusion from the general assembly and from becoming guild officers and spokespersons—women could come closer economically to their male counterparts. The chance to acquire new skills within the protection of the guild could be considered the best of both worlds—the prospects of freedom and the protection of privilege. Steven L. Kaplan suggests that the law opened a new epoch for women's work and "a radical change in corporate practices and in more general social mores."[132]

The reality, of course, did not always attain this ideal. All over France, privileged crafts were coming to terms, more or less, with female workmates. Guilds forcibly united by the law suffered much controversy from the men and women who continually protested their union. Some male guilds were more open than others to the new members. In Lyon, the small-scale master weavers were still vigorously combating this change while they tried to survive the latest slump by hiring hundreds of women as clandestine weavers. Diatribes insisting on women's lack of ability multiplied. As Olwen Hufton has observed, "The contest between the sexes was bitterest when the demand for work far outstripped the supply."[133]

With unparalleled ill timing, Paris officials chose 1786, at this economic low point, to enforce the guild regulations of 1777 on the silk industry. For this reason, the year 1786 has special significance in Lyon as the time when the government seriously brought its authority to bear on the obstreperous silk masters. The *grande fabrique* was formally divided into a separate guild for each of its five major products: gold and silver cloth, *passementerie*, knitwear, gauze fabric, and products made of tulle. As elsewhere in

---

132. Kaplan, *La Fin des corporations*, 232.
133. Olwen Hufton, *The Prospect Before Her: A History of Women in Western Europe* (New York: Alfred A. Knopf, 1996), 493.

France, masters in the old *fabrique* had to purchase new licenses in order to enter the restructured guilds. Those directives comprised the conservative aspects of the guild law. The laissez-faire elements can be seen in permission to have an unlimited number of looms, to set up shop outside the city limits, and to allow women to become masters in all the silk trades. The main benefactors at the time were the merchant manufacturers, well able to hire dozens of female weavers to staff their large workshops.

If merchants could legally hire untrained women to weave, they would be able to do without the chef d'atelier and the hard negotiation each contract entailed. We can imagine the emotions of a master weaver, crestfallen at having to weave as a simple journeyman in another master's atelier, finding himself sharing tools with a former drawgirl. Documents do not tell whether the women thought their situation would improve if they were hired as *compagnonnes* rather than day laborers.

In the midst of confusion caused by changes in guild law and the decline in trade, an unfortunate rise in wine prices provoked strikes by a number of trades. The silk weavers immediately marshaled themselves to demand that the city government enforce the wage tariff and increase it by 2 sous and accompanied their request by trooping through the streets and starting brawls. In this uprising, journeymen made common cause with their masters, leading some observers to believe, mistakenly, that the masters were reconciled to remaining wageworkers, dependent on the merchants for contracts. According to David L. Longfellow, after midcentury, requesting cost of living increases in piecework rates became the major strategy that silk weavers adopted to express their grievances.[134] The consulate of Lyon acquiesced to the raise but then called in royal forces. When the workers were subdued, the king outlawed the practice of setting tariffs for the entire industry and declared that future contracts were to be arranged between merchant and weaver on an individual basis.

Guild Suppression and New Possibilities

By abolishing the wage tariff, the economic administration took another step toward making French industry competitive in international markets. The action flowed from the same body of thought that denigrated privilege

134. David L. Longfellow, "Silk Workers and the Social Struggle in Lyon," *French Historical Studies* 12, no. 1(spring 1981): 114.

and fostered the emergence of natural rights. Liberal economic theory shunned the possibility that groups within the state would have special privileges. The National Assembly put this belief into practice with the d'Allarde law in March 1791, dissolving the guilds, and the Le Chapelier law in June, forbidding workers' associations. The suppression of guilds shocked the silk enterprise, and one might think it left the master weavers without a rhetorical platform. But their continuing efforts to restore industrial rules gave them a forum to lobby for reinstalling the detailed production standards and the prohibition of women weavers. The two laws put male master weavers into an even more precarious position. Now they competed directly with low-salaried female workers without the strength of an organization to make some sort of balance against the wealthy merchants.

With established relationships set aside and the flow of capital temporarily halted, confusion overcame the industry. Weavers and merchants alike were unsure of what the new norms should be. The law suppressed the examination at the end of apprenticeship but kept the training period itself. The detailed industrial regulations were suspended and standards of quality were uncertain. But in the midst of this disruption, the industry maintained its traditional structure of urban family craft, although the former masters were now called chefs d'ateliers. Although the merchants had clearly won the struggle to dominate silk making, the master weavers resisted pressures to turn the industry into a factory model and clung to the relative autonomy their family workshops gave them. Customarily doing business with several merchant manufacturers each season, the chefs d'ateliers were able to negotiate with each of them and to function as patron of their own journeymen, journeywomen, and apprentices. Contributing to the family economy, their wives, along with their children, continued to work at silk production at home or as hired labor for other master weavers.[135]

Women's Work and Poverty

How did the female silk workers fare throughout these vicissitudes? The silk industry's decline was particularly hard on the auxiliary workers,

---

135. Ernest Pariset, *Histoire de la fabrique lyonnaise: Étude sur le régime sociale et économique de l'industrie de la soie à Lyon depuis le XVIe siècle* (Lyon, 1901), 267, 275.

whose livelihood was entirely bound up with the chefs d'ateliers' business, and the guild officials were aware of their suffering. A survey at the beginning of the Revolution emphasized that the 15,000 persons then in the *fabrique* of silk cloth had so little work that in order to buy food for their families, they were two and even three terms behind in their rent. Their only recourse was to pawn their tools or borrow from the Monte de Piété, but it was hard to retrieve the instruments for a new contract. M. Terret, syndic of the master merchants, wrote: "Among the most wretched workers attached to the *fabrique*, the *devideuses* must be singled out. Their labor is paid at the rate of two francs the pound of silk and scarcely can they process one-third [in a day]. The result is even less if the silk is of bad quality, in all [it produces] a notable lack [of funds]. This class consists of about 3,500 individuals."[136]

The *fabrique* of stockings and tulles had about 1,900 female workers, who were also poorly paid. A day's work at the knitting machine for stockings or for tulle earned 1 franc 25 centimes, and often there was no work to be had. Frequently their machines, too, were pawned. While the knitters were badly off, the female workers who prepared the silk for these processes were especially destitute. "The silk destined to be worked up as tulle and other stockings undergoes a preparation called the *oval*. The class of workers who are in charge of the process is very miserable because of the slowdown experienced by this branch of work."[137]

The *ovalistes*, as such workers were called, undertook a particularly delicate task, preparing thread for stockings and tulle, "a fine, machine-made net with a hexagonal mesh . . . used for millinery and dress trimming or embroidered to form lace."[138] Since the silk used to create these goods could not be hidden under other threads, it had to be especially pure in color. Such silk was identified in the Condition, the building given to unwinding cocoons, and to specialists for milling the filaments and turning them into skeins and then bobbin thread. Only material brought from the Piedmont came up to this standard, and it had to be meticulously worked by the *ovaliste*. Any obstruction in the silk trade raised its cost

---

136. AML F 2, "Tableau de la situation des quatre principales manufactures de la ville de Lyon," [1787]. Leroudier, *Décadence*, 421–23.

137. AML F 2, "Tableau" "La soie destinée au travail du tulle et du bas subi une préparation applée *oval*. La classe douvrière qui s'en occupe est très malheureuse en raison de l'état de langueur qu'éprouve cette fabrique."

138. Phyllis G. Tortora and Robert S. Merkel, *Fairchild's Dictionary of Textiles*, 7th ed. (New York: Fairchild Publications, 1996), s.v. "tulle."

prohibitively, pricing stockings out of reach of a wide market. Sudden fluctuations in style also caused tulle sales to decline. Either event immediately threw *ovalistes* out of work because they prepared thread exclusively for these products. The mills used by these workers had as many as twelve bobbins on which silk thread was wound at one time. The process required sustained attention to catch and repair any broken threads. Although the nineteenth century saw males entering the trade, this was traditionally female work and it remained mostly in women's hands.[139]

The *fabrique* of ribbons and *passementerie* had declined to 300 individuals, equally unable to earn enough to support themselves. The cost of necessities out priced their daily pay rate of 1 franc. The *fabrique* making hats was still as numerous as 1,500, but the male and mostly female *coupeurs de poil* who cut the pelt, female wool carders, and women who pulled out the animal hair (*éjareuses*), some 340 in all, were "*extremement malheureuses.*"

The fluctuating market stimulated employment in some sectors, while it curtailed work in others. Many women's craft specialties in 1789, still in women's hands in 1800–1801, saw the numbers rise slightly: *lingères* went from 150 to 200; milliners (*marchandes de modes*) from 30 to 36, preparers of silk thread from 18 to 48. Tailors of women's clothing, now were counted among tailors of men's clothing, increased from 443 to 611. But these numbers do not tell us whether the women workers were subsumed into men's workshops or whether they set up their own businesses, catering to male and female customers. While the production of silk cloth and clothing had an economic surge in the early years of the Revolution, the artificial flower trade fell badly, from 43 masters in 1789 to 20 in 1801, and the number of journeymen and women declined from something like 3,000 to 307.

To ameliorate the situation, current and former guild officials held an extraordinary meeting at the city hall to set up a charitable fund with contributions from wealthy Lyonnais, 5,000 livres from the silk guild's treasury, and additional money from the king. The silk cloth master weavers also put in a plea, without success, to permit the guild to keep one-half the price of mastership instead of the one-quarter allowed by the 1777 legislation.

---

139. See Dennis Diderot, *Encyclopedia: The Complete Illustrations, 1762–1777* (New York: Abrams, 1978) 4:2737. Cayez, *Métiers*, 69.

Revolution Co-opted by Workers

The Revolution provided opportunities for Lyon's workers to continue their struggle for equitable wages against the merchants. In a city where workers were being discouraged from gathering to elect representatives to the Estates General, the first day of deliberation saw more than 2,650 silk workers in attendance, and second day, 3,400. These men were the boldest and most contentious of the masters, the more moderate ones having been frightened into staying home. They completely shut out the merchants from participating, much less from dominating the meeting, and they elected thirty-four representatives from among the most "*turbulents*" leaders who had been involved in the actions of 1786. The merchants demanded the chance to meet by themselves or with other trades in order to put forth their own representatives, but finance minister Jacques Necker refused their request, declaring that the silk workers' meeting was legitimate. As Maurice Garden wrote, the silk masters' action was more important as a successful confrontation with the merchants, a vindication of their loosing demands for a just wage, than as a selection of delegates to Paris.[140]

The weavers' *cahier de doléance* is striking among the expressions of the Third Estate in its trenchant complaints about workers' misery and the merchants' role in causing it. They wrote, "This manufacture, formerly a fertile source of wealth, which enabled 20,000 workers to earn an honest living, is for them today nothing more than painful and forced work, whose wage [they know] will cover only two-thirds of their necessities." A recent law—they must surely be referring to the suppression of the tariff—"put them completely at the mercy of the big manufacturer." The weavers also detailed the effect on their families of the merchants' repressive, calculated underpayment: "For that reason since this law, many big merchants have been seen constraining the citizen to labor at half-price and to force the fathers of families to work, they, their wives and their children, seventeen to eighteen hours a day. And for this they receive so little that they must take charity in order to survive."[141] Not only was

---

140. Garden, *Lyon*, 590–92; Trénard, *Crise*, 39–43.
141. Émile Levasseur, *Histoire des classes ouvrières et de l'industrie en France*, 2nd ed. (Paris: Arthur Rousseau, 1901), 2:854–55, cites the text: "Cette fabrique, source autrefois si féconde en richesses, qui procurait à 20,000 ouvriers une honnête subsistance, n'est plus aujourd'hui pour eux que l'objet d'un travail pénible et forcé dont le salaire ne saurait suffire aux

this cahier outspoken about workers' complaints, it was also unusual in pointing to the contribution of the masters' wives and children for family survival.

After experiencing the successful meeting of workers, Lyon's officials were adamantly opposed to a second such gathering. As in Rouen, adroit political maneuvers, this one by Louis Tolozan de Montfort, provost of Lyon's merchants, managed to exclude most of the artisans from the next electoral assemblies.[142] (The crowds, however, responded to Tolozan's antiworker attitude by damaging his house and hanging him in effigy!) Inspired by news of the Paris uprising against the taxes imposed on wine and foodstuffs as they entered the city, Lyon's male and female artisans attacked their own customs offices in late June 1789, burning them and celebrating an end to the *octroi* by dancing in the street. They demanded that the authorities permit men earning as little as 30 sous a day to vote and allow those paying a mere 5 livres to run for office.[143] They also showed their resentment that only bourgeois were admitted to the National Guard.[144] By excluding workers from the quickly mobilized National Guard, the municipality laid up a store of resentment that erupted in conflict. Finally the bourgeoisie suppressed the uprising by surrounding and disarming the district of Pierre-Scieze, the most important of the weavers' quarters, but not before they had managed to install a red flag on the city hall. While this gesture was not the first step in a socialist program, it did confirm a gulf between the artisans who produced goods and the merchants who sold them.

Suppressing the indigent artisans did nothing to solve the problem of unemployment and misery. The workers again asked for a tariff to establish at least a subsistence wage, this time successfully petitioning the government in Paris. They reasoned that a contract negotiated between weaver and merchant could never be as between equals. In the interest

---

deux tiers des besoins de la vie." The weavers wrote that they were "totalement à la merci du fabricant." "C'est ainsi que depuis cette loi, on a vu plusieurs négociants contraindre l'ouvrier à travailler à moitié prix et forcer des pères de famille en travaillant, eux, leurs femmes et leurs enfants, dix-sept à dix-huit heures par jour, à ne pouvoir subsister sans recevoir les bienfaits de citoyens par les souscriptions ouvertes en leur faveur."

142. Longfellow, *Silk Weavers*, 114.

143. Maurice Wahl, estimated that 4,450 men were eligible to become officers of the municipality. *Les Premières années de la Révolution à Lyon 1788–1792* (Paris: Armand Colin, 1894), 136.

144. Edmond Soreau, *Ouvriers et Paysans de 1789 à 1792* (Paris: Société d'Édition "Les Belles Lettres," 1936), 110–111n51, cites AN F 12 1430.

of fairness, their petition declared, "A contract made privately and with a negotiated price must and should be made between equals, and the craftsman working by the piece (as a jobber) for somebody else, cannot be free to make a private contract; consequently, the tariff becomes an absolute necessity."[145] The *arrêt* of 29 November 1789 gave permission for the *grande fabrique* to have a provisional tariff, and it was finally put on the books in 1790. But even this concession was vitiated since the scarcity of jobs enabled merchants to ignore the tariff and offer workers cut-rate wages, adding insult to injury by calling it a charitable gesture. In their distress, the weavers objected to these "make believe" alms and even to the money donated by merchants; the workers declared that the charity funds were nothing more than the wages they should have received for their labor.

The conflict over wage rates and the right to vote continued through 1790. The master weavers mobilized their ranks and protested against the merchants in early May 1790. They demonstrated again in July against the privilege the bourgeoisie enjoyed to retail silk fabric. The *octrois* also came under their attack again; since Lyon depended for much of its financial support on this food tax, municipal officers had restored it in August.[146]

The Revolution actually put Lyon's silk masters into an ambiguous position. No doubt the heightened political atmosphere encouraged them to bring their grievances against the master merchants into the public sphere again and to demonstrate vigorously for their rights. The meeting of groups to elect representatives for cahiers and deputies for the Estates gave them organizational means for further protest. But they were essentially conservative, skilled craftsmen who did not support the most radical agenda of the Revolution. They believed the merchants were being unfair when they suppressed or skimped on wages, but they did not go along with the Jacobins' schemes of stripping the entrepreneurs of wealth and forbidding individuals to amass more than 500 livres in belongings. As one observer noted in the *Journal de Lyon* wrote, "The large merchants know

---

145. Workers' petition of 16 January, cited in C. Riffaterre, *Le Mouvement antijacobin et antiparisien à Lyon et dans le Rhône-et-Loire en 1793 (29 mai-15 août)* (Lyon: A. Rey, 1928; Paris: A. Picard, 1928), 1:341n2. "Le traité de gré à gré et de prix débattu ne peut et ne doit avoir lieu qu'entre égaux, et l'ouvrier travaillant à façon pour le compte d'autrui, étant sous la coulpe et dépendance du marchand qui le fait fabriquer pour son compte, ne peut être libre à traiter de gré à gré; en consequence, le tarif devient d'une nécessité absolue."

146. Soreau, *Ouvriers et Paysans*, 139–40.

too well, by their daily experience, that workers and merchants can have but one and the same interest, that of making manufactures flourish."[147]

Although the master weavers railed against the starkness of their lives, they petitioned those they regarded as theorists not to condemn or discourage the wearing of luxurious ornament. They could not help regretting the flight of the wealthy and aristocrats who were their customers. As a silk worker named Grégoire commented about the scarcity of royalists: "I don't know any [still here]. Those who gave [us] work have been made to leave Lyon."[148] Joining in the discussion of schemes to promote an egalitarian outfit for France, the weavers spoke out in favor of a national costume but proposed that it be made of silk. They were just as unhappy as the merchants and captains of their industry at the prospect of continuing political chaos, fearing that it would undermine the credit on which the business community depended. As for the petition from more than 2,000 Lyonnais that the National Assembly received in February 1791 favoring the suppression of guilds, it surely did not come from master silk weavers, who were devoted to guild monopoly and industrial regulations.[149] As Maurice Garden explained, the former masters used the means of modern labor disputes—walkouts, demonstrations, collaboration with other trades, careful preparation of strike funds, and even violent uprisings—in the service of the old-fashioned ideals of perpetuating their guild and being paid a living wage.[150]

Revolutionary Expedients for Hardship

Women who worked so closely with the male masters and journeymen also took part in their public protests and demonstrations, and they were preconditioned to participate in revolutionary actions. Certainly, the troubles curtailing the silk industry bore directly on their employment as well.

147. Ibid., 270. *Journal de Lyon*, 11 August 1792, cited by Soreau.
148. Herriot, *Lyon n'est plus*, 1:198. His words were: "Je n'en connais point. On a fait partir de Lyon ceux qui donnaient du travail."
149. Soreau, *Ouvriers et Paysans*, 153.
150. Garden, *Lyon*, 580, asserts that the master weavers reconciled themselves to remaining workers (giving up the ambition to once again join the merchants' ranks). As a self-confirmed working class, they bent their efforts to extracting higher pay and a tariff from the merchants. But they clung to archaic work discipline. "Sa position est devenue très ambiguë: il mène un combat avec des formes et des revendications nouvelles, mais avec des survivances marquées de l'idéal du passé."

With 30,000 workers out of work by winter of 1792, once again female unemployment was widespread.[151] A contemporary estimate concluded that 16,359 women workers were idle, not counting masters' daughters, drawgirls, embroiderers, women workers employed in the process of watering silk fabric (*moirage*), makers of gold thread, and female workers in numerous other auxiliary crafts. Women's joblessness was reported throughout the city, as the empty looms of half the *fabrique* told their story. Naturally, the crafts allied with the weaving were also idle. Advice for getting rid of unemployment generally suggested that idle men should enlist in the army, that destitute married women should be given needlework, and that single women and widows should be pressed into domestic service.[152]

The assembly of the section *Egalité* called for charity for the ill and the old, and especially for women and children whose husbands or fathers were away in uniform, because the lack of available work made them needy.[153] Like officials in the Old Regime, the revolutionary government knew that unemployed women workers took up prostitution and were a burden on charity funds. As in Paris, Rouen, and other cities, Lyon also established public workhouses. Officials in Lyon conceded that this charity work did not solve the problem, but the blame lay partly with the artisans themselves. A local commission complained that unemployed silk spinners refused to accept work spinning linen, cotton, or wool, "even though this kind of work very much resembles theirs."[154] What the commission considered misplaced pride or obstinacy may well have been the spinners' understanding that making thread from materials other than silk required different skills from those they had.

The poor conditions convinced a sizeable group of silk workers to move away from Lyon, reminding us that silk was a regional industry, with production centers in Italy, Germany, and Switzerland. These were the destinations of men, families, and unmarried women, while the exodus

---

151. W. D. Edmonds, *Jacobinism and the Revolt of Lyon, 1789–1793* (New York: Oxford University Press, 1990), 121.

152. C. Riffaterre, *Le Mouvement antijacobin*, 522, quotes Déglise, "Manuscrit contenant les produits rares et variés de la manufacture de soie classés dans les divers gendres de leur fabrication . . . depuis 1789 jusqu'à l'an X," 1:177n1.

153. C. Riffaterre, *Le Mouvement*, 2:555.

154. Herriot, *Lyon n'est plus*, 1:124. "Ils ne voudraient même pas faire des toiles de fil ou de cotton ou des étoffes de laine, quoique ce genre de travail se rapproche beaucoup du leur."

of unmarried female workers spread especially throughout the regions of Dauphiné, Savoy, and the Lyonnais from which they had been recruited. So large was this emigration that silk merchants and chefs d'ateliers complained about the shortage of labor when new orders came in for small figured upholstery silks, brocaded gauze for dress material, and gold braid decoration for military uniforms.

Women as Revolutionaries

Just as labor disputes took the form of revolutionary uprisings, women protested against bad conditions through the newly founded *Association des Citoyennes Dévoués à la Patrie*. Women also acted as supervisors of bureaux that the *Société Philanthropic* set up in each quarter of the city to distribute money to the indigent.[155] By summer 1792, Lyon had to deal with severe grain shortage, suspicion of hoarders, and depreciation of assignats as well as the continuing decline in the silk market. People condemned roving merchants (*revendeurs*) who raised the price of grain by hurling "fecal material or any other objects that came to hand" at them through the window.[156]

In the disorder, the clubwomen had ample opportunity to promote the politics of need. They demonstrated vigorously against the rising price of grain, cheese, wine, soap, oil, mocha coffee, candles, and wood, and they gave the municipal government a tract suggesting lower prices for these goods. Crowds of women barged into stores of small traders, confiscating any of these goods it found and leaving on the counter a sum of money they judged appropriate for payment. They stationed some women outside the store to take away goods passed out by those inside.[157] This "popular taxation" spread throughout the city, the luxuries on the list of overpriced goods showing that the middle class as well as the poor thought prices too high.[158] The clubwomen set themselves up as custodians of

155. Wahl, *La Révolution à Lyon*, 15, 18, 155. These "dames [qui] faisaient l'office de commissaries" enrolled more than 1,600 donors and helped 25,000 poor.
156. Herriot, *Lyon n'est plus*, 1:118. The Corps Municipaux, on 25 December, forbade people to throw "matières fécales ou autres objets quelques" out the window.
157. Ibid., 125. Edmonds cites a letter from the municipality to Roland declaring, "C'est le people, le people presque tout entire qui force les magasins, pour faire délivrer tous les comestibles, toutes les femmes à peu de chose près, se sont mises en avant pour se les faire délivrer."
158. Edmonds, *Jacobinism*, 125–26. Edmonds's comment suggests that workers in Lyon were not accustomed to buying coffee.

economic justice, patrolling the markets to see that the price controls were kept and carrying pikes to enforce the point that they would not allow indiscriminate looting. As Susan Desan has written, "Faced by empty markets, continual rioting, the desertion of the National Guard, and the bewildering emergence of self-appointed 'female police commissioners' [*commissaries de police femelles*], the municipal and departmental authorities finally agreed to set low price controls and to seek out counterrevolutionary agitators."[159]

Women also participated in the clubs and the thirty-four sectional assemblies of Lyon during the campaign in October 1792 to raise the tariff for silk weavers. Not only had the tariff remained the same since 1790, weavers complained that merchants took advantage of the scarcity of work to depress their salaries and to force them to stand the cost of tools, like the teeth of the loom, which were traditionally paid by merchants.[160] Confusion about money interjected another difficulty. While printing more assignats temporarily revived commerce in 1790–91, many workers received their pay in promissory notes that were hard to use.[161] In addition, the rapid depreciation of assignats effectively cut silk workers' salaries. Several patriotic clubs suggested giving the silk workers an indemnification like that given the bakers. The proposed 33 percent supplement had the support, according to officials, of almost 3,000 persons, "especially many women."[162] To expedite this change, silk workers put forth a petition with "eight large pages of signatures." With no response, the club members went further, submitting a plan to all the clubs to increase silk workers' wages.[163] Finally, in January 1793, a request with 4,000 workers' signatures caused the municipality to preside over a meeting of silk master workers and master merchants to increase the tariff. In March and April, the *bonnetiers* also convinced the council general of

---

159. Susan Desan, "'Constitutional Amazons': Jacobin Women's Clubs in the French Revolution," in *Re-creating Authority in Revolutionary France*, ed. Bryant T. Ragan, Jr., and Elizabeth A. Williams (New Brunswick, N.J.: Rutgers University Press, 1992), 15, 18, citation p. 23.

160. Herriot, *Lyon n'est plus*, 96. This silk workers' memoir, dated 26 October 1792, complained about paying for "*des peignes.*" AN F 12 501b.

161. Soreau, *Ouvriers et Paysans*, 190–91.

162. Riffatere, *Le Mouvement*, 1:338–39.

163. Herriot, *Lyon n'est plus*, 1:122–23. They asked for a new revolutionary catechism to teach their children.

the Commune to help them formulate a new tariff for the manufacture of black luster taffetas.[164]

As the local clubs and the sections took further action to secure drastic new measures, they became alienated from the local government and its liberal ideals. The master weavers and their journeymen must have had conflicting thoughts about the Jacobins' plans to level distinctions in the *grande fabrique*. Depriving the merchants of their privileges might have had an initial appeal, but weavers worried about the loss of their business function. Many on both sides of the loom asserted that diatribes against rich clothing and furnishings were not helpful to the silk industry. Indeed, through 1792 silk weavers and merchants were united in the hope that that the silk trade would pick up; despite their differences, both groups opposed the Jacobins' rhetoric against luxury, and they could only regret the loss of orders for elaborate church vestments.[165]

The spring of 1793 saw increasing pressures on the city. The death of the king and the political rift between those who voted for or against it, the protests over drafts for the army, royalist uprisings, increasing repression of priests who had not agreed to the Civil Constitution of the Clergy, and activities of émigrés all combined to provoke civil unrest in Lyon and in the surrounding areas. The ferment aroused rumors and hostility, as the establishment of a national universal male suffrage drew workers into expressing their fears through their political associations.[166] Bystanders witnessed a demonstration when women, "lead by five chefs d'ateliers and a silk carder," were joined by male workers.[167]

In May 1793, Lyon joined several other cities protesting that the Revolution was on the wrong path, marshalling an armed force to march on Paris.[168] Paris retaliated by sending national troops to suppress the uprising in Lyon and a siege ensued. During the first week of the siege that followed, thousands of male and female silk workers and club members fled the city.[169] Finally, after months of siege and bombardment, the

---

164. Ibid., 1:340–41. Besides knitting caps, stockings, and other goods, *bonnetiers* also wove certain fabrics.
165. Garden, *Histoire*, 295; Edmonds, *Jacobinism*, 155.
166. Edmonds, *Jacobinism*, 155.
167. Riffaterre, *Le Mouvement*, 1:349–50.
168. Garde, *Histoire*, 296–97.
169. Riffaterre, *Le Mouvement*, 2:553. They also expelled people who were declared suspect—including 200 club members of which 80 were women.

rebellion came to an end on 8 October. Lyon was a conquered city, and she had to pay the price of her disloyalty.[170]

Terrible repression followed the end of the siege, in which almost 2,000 suspects were tried and executed. Buildings in Lyon were destroyed in an attempt to make the city an example. Even its name was to be expunged; it was to be called Ville-Affranchie. Governmental policy exacerbated the difficulties and hardships of the workers, beset with the random violence, disorganization of industry, and population shrinkage.[171] The excesses of punishment, the committees of surveillance set up even in villages, and the reach of courts, which condemned silk workers and domestics in one-third of the cases, spread antirevolutionary sentiment among all levels of Lyon's population.[172]

After these devastations, Lyon found herself in an economic crisis that was more serious than the one of 1787–89. Silk workers appealed unsuccessfully to Paris to indemnify them for the looms that had been destroyed in the city's bombardment. Bouts of inflation, the scarcity of investment capital, and the poor condition of roads contributed to the malaise. Uncertain international conditions kept luxury goods from reaching the West Indies or European markets. The deep decline in Atlantic trade threw French seaports into distress, and that in turn caused unemployment in inland cities since few in France could buy the goods formerly exported. It was not until 1807 that the Lyon reconstituted its productive capacity and found accessible markets.[173]

A Labor Shortage: Who Benefits?

Emigration from Lyon during the Revolution shrank the population by half, from 150,000 to 88,000. The depopulation was compounded by the evacuation of the 20,000 mostly silk workers, women, and children during the siege in the summer and autumn of 1793. Those who left early and reached silk centers in Italy, Switzerland, and Germany were the

170. Garden, *Histoire*, 298–301.
171. Ibid., 294–303.
172. See Richard Cobb's evocative description of Lyonnaises who spied on national soldiers "as they walked down from la Croix-Rousse or crossed over from la Guillotière, by female scouts, standing in doorways or apparently going about their normal business, by prostitutes, on their usual beats, by girls looking out of upper windows." *The French and Their Revolution* (London: John Murray, 1998), 444.
173. Garden, *Histoire*, 304–5.

fortunate ones. The thousands who remained behind to exit later lost their tools and goods to fire. If they did not take refuge in another city where they found jobs producing silk, not even their "arms" were enough to gain their living, as a contemporary wrote, "because the male and female silk workers have very little aptitude for any other kind of work."[174]

But the wealthy merchants retreated only as far away from Lyon as their suburban estates during the worst days of the Terror of 1793, claiming that they were "absent on business trips." When Napoleon began to restore the French silk industry, they quickly returned to extend their commerce into Italy, now dominated by France. The political economy in these years underscored the international reach of the silk industry. The makers of lace and tulle were dependent on Italian silk thread. By manipulating tariffs in favor of Italy's raw and spun silk and against her silk cloth, France managed to "drain" Italy's silk thread and subdue her silk industry. Italy was forced to import French silk cloth instead of Swiss fabric.[175] Lyon once again became a key entrepôt and financial center, transshipping products from the Illyrian coast, the Piedmont, Switzerland, and the eastern Mediterranean.[176] The strong revival of silk in Lyon between 1807 and 1810 also benefited from Napoleon's support for the manufacture and his blockade of English goods. While the military draft and the disrupted economy had created a severe shortage of male labor in the ateliers, hundreds of journeymen from Turin and other cities managed to find their way to Lyon's silk neighborhoods. They may not have numbered 800 as Jean-Claude Déglize claimed, but "*étrangers*" were certainly seen in many workshops. That critic proposed that the government should exempt silk workers from the draft and offer inducements to lure French silk workers home from foreign countries.[177]

174. Riffaterre, *Le Mouvement*, 2:555n1, quoting a letter from "representatives of the people to La Pape, Minister of the Interior, 23 September, 1793," "L'inhumanité des rebelles de Lyon a fait sortir de cette ville vingt mille individus qui ont tout abandonné; la plus grande partie a perdu son mobilier dans les flammes; il lui restait des bras que nous ne pouvons employer, parce que les ouvriers et ouvrières en soie ont très peu d'aptitude pour tout autre genre d'occupation."
175. Cayez, *Métiers*, 126–30; see also Louis Bergeron, *France Under Napoleon*, trans. Robert R. Palmer (Princeton: Princeton University Press, 1981), 173. Originally published as *L'Épisode napoléonien: Aspects intérieurs, 1799–1815* (Paris: Éditions du Seuil, 1972).
176. F. Rivet, "Avant le chemin-de-fer: problème du transit rhodanien," *Cahiers d'histoire* (1956): 365–92, estimates that one-sixth of Lyon's population, some 15,000, was then occupied in the transit trade.
177. AML I-2, 46 bis, Jean-Claude Déglize, "État des ouvrages faits pour la restauration des arts et du commerce de la ville de Lyon," "Tableau de la Visite Générale," 1788, An X, p. 65v. Also classed as MS 2401 in the Bibliothèque Municipale de Lyon.

The labor shortage contributed to women's opportunities in weaving. We can see their success in the complaints of Déglize, who thought the increase of women weavers demonstrated the worst result of the new liberal regime. An unbending conservative, he predicted that the supposed 4,159 female weavers who far outnumbered the 286 male weavers would lead to the industry's demise. Their competition had lowered the profits to such an extent that male French workers no longer contemplated a future in silk weaving, he complained, pointing out that salaries dropped below the levels of 1789 while necessities rose by one-third. Instead, the industry had to rely on the influx of male weavers from Turin and suffer from ruinous commerce in stolen materials and illegal trade. In addition, Déglize blamed the female weavers' ineptitude for causing the decline in brocade fabrics.

In fact, of course, the popularity of brocade had receded through no fault of the women weavers, and they were able to gain employment in their specialty of plain, undecorated fabric. These less costly fabrics continued to find mass markets, signaling a "democratization" of silk products. In 1810, of the 11,699 working looms, plain silk (*étoffes unies*) accounted for 9,079 while brocades (*étoffe façonnée*) were made by only 1,354. The same trend applied to velvet with 538 looms making plain velvet (*velours unis*) and only 161 making patterned velvet (*velours façonné*).[178]

In the past these female weavers would have been hired as servants, sitting at the loom when inspectors were absent; now they were journeywomen and potential heads of workshops. Even taking the numbers as only an approximation, Déglize's unofficial survey of the silk cloth manufacture in early nineteenth century gives an idea of the comparison between male and female workers.

By the Year X (1801–2), some 1,500 journeywomen (*compagnonnes*) were listed next to 1,090 journeymen (*compagnons*).

Chefs d'ateliers	4,449
Wives and children	13,043
Apprentices	90
Journeymen	1,090
Journeywomen	1,562
Girls receiving wages	1,112

178. AML F 2, "État de la fabrique de Lyon en 1809 pour servir de comparaison à celui ci derrière de 1810."

By this count, there were 11,195 female workers and 10,150 male workers, a much more balanced sex ratio than during the previous century. But this survey leaves out the auxiliary workers, the *ourdisseuses, dévideuses, faiseuses de remittes, metteuses en main, faiseuses de lacs, appreteuses de cordages*, who could total another 5,600 to 10,000 female workers. It is also impossible to tell whether any of the 90 apprentices were female.[179]

By 1809 the picture in the silk industry had changed to reflect the new status of female workers not only as *compagnonnes* but as heads of workshops. Although the 1786 regulation had brought in a surge of female weavers who were permitted to become chefs d'ateliers, apparently none did so. It is unclear whether the obstacles were lack of skill, difficulty in getting funds together, or a hostile business climate. Despite the legislation allowing women to enter any guild whose work they could perform, legislation that encouraged urban women throughout France to try new professions, Lyon seems to have obscured the situation with continuing controversy. But the 1791 suppression of guilds definitively opened *all* the silk trades to women and many became heads of their own businesses. Approximately one-third of the silk-weaving ateliers were headed by women according to the census of 1809 prepared for Fay de Sathonnay, now count of the Empire and mayor of the city.

Chefs d'ateliers (male) occupying looms	3,596
Chefs d'ateliers (female) occupying looms	1,155
Wives of chefs d'ateliers who were weaving	974
Wives occupied with unwinding cocoons	1,171
Sons of chefs d'ateliers who wove	595
Daughters of chefs d'ateliers who wove	1,034
Compagnons and apprentices (male)	1,707
Compagnonnes and apprentices (female)	2,266
"Demoiselles" spinning	289 employed by chefs d'ateliers
Wage-earning girls spinning	1,023
Drawboys	288
Drawgirls	292
Merchants	365

179. Ibid., "Tableau de la Visite Générale," 1788, An X. Using Déglize's statistics, I have counted the 90 apprentices as male since none were designated as female. Given 4,449 chefs d'ateliers, I am assuming that at least 4,000 of them had wives. Subtracting this number from the total of wives and children, I then divided the number of children into half girls, half boys. See Pierre Cayez's comments on the problem of the statistical information, *Métiers*, 42–51, 72.

By this estimate, 8,204 women worked in silk-cloth production in contrast to 6,6262 men. (Of course this survey, like the earlier one, did not include the thousands of female auxiliary workers.) The significant statistic for this study is that 1,155 women opened their own ateliers, ready to take the risks and the profits of their own businesses. Unfortunately the survey does not indicate what sort of fabric the women produced or how many of the 875 looms making gauze and crêpe or other cloth were in their ateliers.[180]

The manufacture of stockings and tulle (*fabrique de bas et tulle*) saw a smaller improvement of women workers' condition. Taking 1809 as a year for comparisons, we see 825 male chefs d'ateliers compared with 20 females. Virtually the same number of male and female children worked for their parents, 108 sons, 92 daughters. As for journeymen and apprentices, 763 males and 63 females worked in these capacities. Brokering of goods in this area of production continued to be open to both women and men.

The stocking and knitwear trade maintained steady production in the first decade of the Revolution. The total number of its workers was approximately the same in 1789—6,630—and in the Year IX (1800–1801)—6,024. The tasks seem to have remained sex specific, except for the category of sons and daughters of masters working at the looms, male and female workers occupied at the *ovale* and at other preparations of silk, and as brokers or stock-jobbers. This knitwear had maintained steady production from 1789 to 1801, with some 6,000 employed, but by 1809 it had fallen by half. Although it still produced stockings in single colors, stockings decorated with flowers, cotton goods, and mittens in smaller quantities, its chief product by then was the production of tulle.[181]

The section of *passementerie*, including ribbons; lace of gold, silver, and silk; and buttons, declined drastically from its high point in the 1770s. The shift in fashion from showy garments to sober egalitarian styles shut down many looms, and gold and silver disappeared as an industrial material. Pierre Cayez estimated that *passementerie* declined by 80 percent,

---

180. AML F 2, "État comparatif de la fabrique d'étoffes de soie de la ville de Lyon, des années 1807, 1808, et 1809." The group consisted of 214 merchants who manufactured (*marchands fabricans*), 52 wholesale silk merchants, 24 retail ones, and another 75 manufacturers working with direct access to the market.

181. AML F 2, "Fabrique de Bas et Tulle, Résultat comparatif entre les années 1807 et 1808"; "Fabrique de Bas et Tulle, Résultat comparatif entre les années 1807, 1808, 1809, 1810, 1811."

embroidery by 50 percent, and gold thread making by 90 percent between 1789 and 1801.[182]

The manufacture of hats, Lyon's second largest industry, also suffered a 50 percent loss of workers between a high of 4,733 in 1789 and a low of 1,984 in 1809. But the decline in employed women was only 38 percent, going from 1,474 in 1789 to 559 in 1809. The 70 percent decline in male workers managed to exclude skilled workers receiving 3 and 4 francs a day—manufacturers, journeymen, dyers, finishers, and workers stripping off the fur from pelts. In their place, women workers paid 1.5 francs a day took over virtually all the "unskilled" work as cutters stripping off the fur (*coupeuses de poils*), workers plucking out the hair from pelts (*éjareuses*), wool carders (*cardeuses*), and finishers (*garnisseuses*). In this era, hat making serves as an example of a feminized industry offering steady but low-paying work to women. Much the same process had occurred in the silk manufacture, with the loss of brocade work for males and the increase of plain fabric for women.[183] Cotton works in the outskirts of Lyon that were already flourishing in 1780 also experienced an increase of female workers. One popular type of cloth may serve as an example. Workers—the majority of them women—making *mousselines de France* increased from a low of 650 in 1802 to 1,200 in 1805.[184]

The city's formal industrial inquests show that more than 1,000 women took advantage of the new climate of economic liberty to found their own silk cloth weaving enterprises in the period from 1786 to 1811. The new freedom also applied to the other trades related to the silk industry. Déglize's composite listing for Year IX and Year X (1800–1802) shows that a few women now appeared in a complex aspect of the dyeing industry, coloring the warp threads in skeins so precisely that they formed an intentionally blurred geometric pattern when woven (*chiné à la branche* or *ikat*). They were listed as 14 *chineurs et chineuses de soie*, and 20 *ouvriers et ouvrières chineux de soie*, without designating the number of each sex. This gain can be contrasted to the fact that males were now entering other parts of silk production once reserved by tradition in Lyon for women. While the embroidery trade in many parts of France had always employed

---

182. Cayez, *Métiers*, 87–89.
183. AML F 2, "Chapelerie et professions y relatives." Males also worked in the unskilled auxiliary trades, but in small numbers: *coupeurs de poils* 14, *coupeuses de poils* 203; *cardeurs de laines* 32, *cardeuses* 153.
184. AML F 2, "Tableau générale de la chapelerie de Lyon, 1807," and "État des filatures de cotton."

men and women, Lyon's embroiderers had been overwhelmingly women. The 2,000 wage-working embroiderers in gold, silver, and silk thread, as well as the 410 apprentices, were now both male and female (*brodeurs* and *brodeuses, apprentices* and *apprentisses*). During the last two decades of the eighteenth century, boys (*tireurs*) entered the ranks of the drawgirls pulling down cordage for the brocade looms, a task formerly exclusive to female workers (*tireuses*).

Within the scanty documentation of this period, I have found only one trade that lets us glimpse the structure of ateliers. The 1810 survey of *ovalistes* and *mouliniers* listed 41 operators, 27 men and 14 women, who were heads of their own business. Like the earlier guildwomen in Rouen, most of the females in this trade, 10 out of 14, were married, 1 was unmarried, and 3 were widows. Equally similar to Rouen's experience, the male chefs had more workers than their female counterparts, and one Pierre Buffonier had an establishment with 42 workers. Excluding this prosperous entrepreneur, the other 26 men averaged 7 workers apiece, while the women averaged 3.[185] This equation is reminiscent of Rouen's guild mistresses who were generally less affluent than the members of male guilds. It seems that for the most part, despite the privilege enjoyed by the former guild mistresses and the nineteenth-century entrance of women into trades as heads of businesses, they were still behind their male counterparts in size of enterprises.

The mass of women working in the silk industry continued to perform the necessary and mostly ill-paid auxiliary tasks. The official census of the silk cloth industry in 1808 gives a total of 5,911 women processing thread, pulling cords, and twisting warps, in short doing all the preparatory work needed before weaving could begin. The 3,770 *dévideuses* who unwound silk cocoons and spun thread lived with the chef d'atelier's family or by themselves. The far less numerous and better-paid readers (*liseuses de dessin*) circulated through the ateliers as in the past century.

New Technology, Old Attitudes

Although much about the silk industry remained tied to its past development, some inventions foreshadowed the path silk making would take into the nineteenth century. The most important was the invention of the

---

185. AML F 2, "État nominatif des ovalistes d'après le recensement de 1810," and "État nominatif des mouliniers d'après le recensement de 1810."

Jacquard device, a so-called lantern set on top of the high loom, which controlled the weaving of brocades without the assistance of a drawgirl or drawboy to advance the design. Conceived in 1801 by an inventive Lyonnais named Jacquard during his sojourn at the Conservatoire des Arts et Métiers in Paris, the device named after him combined elements of earlier inventions. By advancing precut cards that caused certain threads to be depressed or to be lifted, the Jacquard put brocading skill into the hands of those trained only to weave plain cloth. With much easier loom dressing, the Jacquard loom speeded up production of figured material by one to three months. Without all the specialists needed for the traditional draw loom—the maker of various cordage, finishers, drawgirls, and drawboys—the Jacquard device saved money and time. The invention considerably lowered the price of silk fabric and restored brocades, the most profitable part of the silk production. It did not go without notice that the labor saved was that of women workers.[186]

Another of the late eighteenth-century inventions, mechanical spinning slowly made its way into the ateliers early in the century where it competed with the hand spinning still in common use. In addition, a new cleaning agent for silk fabric, invented in 1780, continued to be developed. Most important at the time was F. Gensoul's new system for unwinding the silk cocoon. In the earlier system cocoons were unwound in water of a basin heated by a wood fire "with all the disadvantages that that implies: irregular heating, wasting of wood, particularly uncomfortable working conditions for the spinner." (The *dévideuse* had to dip the cocoon in her hand into the boiling water to start the unwinding process and sit in an uncomfortably hot space.) In 1803, Gensoul, a silk merchant, suggested that instead of heating each basin separately, a battery of basins should be heated by steam from a boiler. He also developed a system of crossing filaments, first suggested by Vaucanson, which improved the quality of thread. Gensoul's system of basins won fast approval because it was a cheap way to control temperature. One admirer noted callously, "The spinner is not bothered by the heat of the oven, she must do more work, she is less tired, she will be paid less." (La fileuse n'est pas incommodée

---

186. Cayez, *Métiers*, 105–7, observes that the permission for females to weave had encouraged the drawgirls (and drawboys) to leave their painful occupations and begin weaving. Thus Lyon's brocade weavers had more interest in a device that replaced them. As someone commented in An X, "Les moyens de faire des étoffes avec moins de bras existent par les mécaniques qui épargent le travail des femmes." Cited on p. 106.

par la chaleur du four, elle doit faire plus d'ouvrage, elle est moins fatiguée, elle sera moins payée.) Gensoul himself reckoned that with this system, the spinners, obliged to process at least fifty kilograms of raw silk, would be kept to a standardized rate calculated in relation to a specific number of cocoons.[187]

The invention of this process led to the creation of four buildings that functioned as Conditions where raw silk thread could be weighed, assessed for quality, and priced. During the eighteenth century Lyon had only one Condition, and the addition of another three increased the amount of unprocessed silk available to the industry. Although inexpensive to operate, the Gensoul process was very costly to install, and it was within the reach of only wealthy merchant manufacturers. Thus the devices were naturally set up in large establishments, on Lyon's outskirts. This trend pointed to one of the new aspects of silk making—huge factory-like establishments staffed by women workers.

In fact, the postrevolutionary era saw four different directions for manufacture of the costly fabric and each of them was facilitated by female employees. The first was the effort by wealthy *marchands fabricants* to establish large manufacturing firms with vertically integrated industry outside the city. There each part of the process—from unraveling the thread from the cocoons in one of the large Conditions to making the finished cloth—could be managed at a central location. Already by 1810, nine *marchand fabricants* had firms with more than 200 looms, twenty-three had firms with 100–200 looms, and forty-six had between 50 and 100 looms in their establishments. These manufactures were also the first to exploit the facility of the Jacquard loom for mass production. The weavers were women, participating in a new technology within a modern built environment.

The second step toward a modern silk industry came as the Jacquard technique enabled another group of women to enter the silk industry. Women in the countryside surrounding Lyon gave up their agricultural and small craft work and took up weaving instead. As the Jacquard device spread to the countryside around Lyon by 1815, women in countless farms and hamlets began to weave table linen, coverlets, and silk cloth. They became part of a rural putting-out system, closely tied to the wholesale merchants and their link with the world market. Receiving silk

---

187. Ibid., 108.

and newly programmed Jacquard devices from itinerant agents, the output of these women became an important source of competition for the handloom weavers still in the center of Lyon. This was a case of protoindustrialization stimulated by invention and organized by large-scale merchants.

Weaving women were also instrumental in the third aspect of Lyon's nineteenth-century manufacturing history, the persistence of the urban family handloom ateliers when the draft and wartime disruptions caused a severe shortage of male labor. These unrelated women integrated themselves into the family workshops headed by chefs d'ateliers and were crucial to the survival of traditional silk works. The predominantly male chefs d'ateliers' chance to maintain their handlooms where they could produce technically intricate silk brocades rested, one might say, on the arms of the journeywomen who accepted low salaries and room and board with the silk-making families. A nineteenth-century historian attributed the *compagnonnes'* acquiescence to the unstable, low wages to the fact that "they have fewer needs."[188] Their low wages and steady output of nonbrocaded silk fabric, combined with the work of wives and children, enabled urban workshops to withstand the competition from the large enterprises and the Jacquard country loom.

The fourth business pattern was found in the establishments that more than a thousand women headed, both for silk weaving and stockings, tulle, and *passementerie*. Like the family ateliers whose flexibility contributed to the industry's success, the small workshops with female leaders also specialized in a variety of products, though they probably turned out more plain fabric than brocades.

Thus alongside the beginnings of big industry and the new widespread system of cottage industry, the conservative structure of the industry *within* Lyon acted to support and maintain its success. In the city, even without the guild system's rules, family workshops and small female-headed workshops prevailed. While women in the family and hired "girls" turned out plain silks or worked at auxiliary tasks, the skilled male weaver busied himself with complex figured cloth. George Sheridan credits the work of female wage earners unrelated to the family for providing enough support to enable the male head of the workshop to continue weaving the superb luxury brocades by hand. Women's role as daily wageworkers,

---

188. Pariset, *Histoire*, 275.

which began with the fifteenth-century origins of Lyon's silk works, continued to be a vital source of labor in the modern era.[189]

Moreover, the continuing structure of the silk industry in Lyon, depending on family ateliers and other small workshops, enabled the French silk industry to compete successfully against competitors who sought economies of size. When Alain Cottereau compared the Spitalfields silk works in London with the still artisanal production in Lyon, the French industry came out ahead. In terms of refining patterns and solving production difficulties, the French weavers had the skill to overcome problems and ensure quality control. They could easily adapt to new styles and the fluctuations in business cycles. These qualities enabled them to survive in the face of the competition of foreign mass produced silks and domestic cottage industry. With these advantages, silk manufacture restored many of the features that had made it successful during the early centuries and supported its revival in the nineteenth century.[190] While competition from the rural Jacquard weavers caused many city looms to become quiet, in Lyon their sisters spun and wove to keep a critical mass of small urban workshops afloat.[191] The new category of female heads of ateliers surely conformed to this small workshop pattern. In an ironic counteraction, the act that helped to break the guild—allowing women to weave—actually enabled the old guild format of the family atelier to survive.[192]

Conclusion

As a luxury industry, Lyon's silk workers suffered disproportionately from the disruption that war and revolution brought. Not only did the international commerce that silk depended on become unattainable, but the

---

189. George J. Sheridan, Jr., "Household and Craft in an Industrializing Economy: The Case of the Silk Weavers of Lyons," in *Consciousness and Class Experience in Nineteenth-Century Europe*, ed. John M. Merriman (New York: Holmes & Meier, 1979).

190. Garden, *Lyon*, 308-11.

191. Alain Cottereau, "The Fate of Collective Manufactures in the Industrial World: The Silk Industries of Lyons and London, 1800-1850," in *World of Possibilities: Flexibility and Mass Production in Western Industrialization*, ed. Charles F. Sabel and Jonathan Zeitlin (Cambridge: Cambridge University Press, 1997): 75-152.

192. Tessie P. Liu, *The Weaver's Knot: The Contradictions of Class Struggle and Family Solidarity in Western France, 1750-1914* (Ithaca: Cornell University Press, 1994), 40-43 and chap. 9. In cloth industries elsewhere in France, the male handloom weaver's place was maintained by daughters who worked outside the home. The daughter's honor was tied to facilitating her father's role as a skilled artisan

Revolution, by promoting egalitarian dress, undercut domestic consumption of the elaborate fabric in which the *grande fabrique* excelled. The cycles of prosperity and poverty that had always beset Lyon fell harder on the city, made even less resilient by its experience of siege and retaliation.

We can imagine the chaos as avenues of credit dried up, skilled weavers were drafted, and raw materials became scarce. The networks of workers and ateliers that had formed through the years were suddenly broken. Personal and professional ties, described so well by Richard Cobb, could not survive the emigration of half the city's population. The rich fled to country homes, nobility left on their own or were hustled out of town by officials. The *canuts,* as silk weavers were now called, traveled to the Piedmont, to Switzerland, or to Germany in search of jobs in other silk centers. Auxiliary workers took shelter in Savoie, the Lyonnais, Beaujolais, and Dauphiné, regions from which they had emigrated in search of work. The streets had once hummed with the calls of female workers bringing raw silk to the Condition and shuttling warps to weavers' ateliers, and with men trundling materials to repair looms. Now they rang with the sound of crowds celebrating the destruction of the tax booths, artisans marching to protest their low pay, and the hollow echo of impoverished silk workers offering to light the passerby's way for a few coins.

Even though the master weavers had dragged their heels when royal officials tried to have them sign up for Necker's reconstituted guilds, the suppression of the guilds on 17 March 1791 shocked the *grande fabrique.* Angry as they were with the merchants for causing them to become hired hands, loading them with new obligations, and shortchanging them, the master weavers were accustomed to arguing their complaints within the context of their guilds. The merchants, too, were loath to see the corporations disappear because they had won all the issues of contention—number of looms, industrial regulations, permitting women to weave, and domination of the market—and found the guilds to be convenient facilitators.[193]

Nevertheless, the d'Allarde law of March 1791 abolishing the guilds and the Le Chapelier law of June 1791 forbidding workers to form coalitions suppressed the traditional organizations. Without corporate structure, the silk industry became even more disorganized. With confusion over the industrial regulations, cloth was hard to evaluate and merchants

---

193. Longfellow, "Silk Workers," 114.

claimed that its quality had declined. The chefs d'ateliers requested that city officials restore at least some of the early manufacturing rules, and they continued to demand that a tariff, one guaranteeing higher wages, be reinstated. Laws governing the silk industry were debated throughout the first three decades of the century, as the *ci-devant* master weavers campaigned for a return to the old status.

By 1807 Lyon's silk industry was returning to vigor, aided by French domination of Italian silk centers and economic protectionism. Napoleon's orders for brocades to restore French palaces and to outfit his new nobility boosted silk production. Swiss capital that had disappeared during the Revolution once again funded Lyonnaise businesses. In the next few years, silk production in the outskirts of Lyon expanded with large industrial plants and a new cottage industry based on the Jacquard loom. Despite the competition posed by these two sources of less expensive silk cloth, family-based workshops in the heart of the city continued to turn out the complex, luxurious fabric for which Lyon was famous. Lyon weavers' ingenuity, developed from their continual need to pass from one cloth type to another, kept their production flexible and of high quality. The skilled chefs d'ateliers working in a time honored way with their wives, day workers, and apprentices were the resource that enabled Lyon to succeed against England's mass production of silk in Spitalfield.

As in the eighteenth century, female labor was the key to all four types of business after the Revolution. The large spinning and weaving factories were staffed by girls and women who used to do the auxiliary work needed in the heart of Lyon. They may have gained a small, steady salary, but they lost the variety and freedom of street that workshop labor permitted. The countrywomen who took up weaving with Jacquard looms provided a huge proto-industrial reservoir for merchant entrepreneurs dealing in mass-produced inexpensive brocades. The work of *compagnonnes*, female weavers without any possibility of becoming heads of their own workshops, enabled their chefs d'ateliers in central Lyon to maintain their family craft and to concentrate on brocades. At the same time, other female entrepreneurs managed to establish their own businesses turning out woven silk and other products.

By the time of the Empire, the silk industry had undergone some surprising changes. A number of women had taken advantage of the new economic freedom to become heads of ateliers in the period from 1807 to 1811. They excelled in some of the same branches of industry that women had dominated earlier, *passementerie*, knitting, weaving gauze, and fashioning tulle stockings. In addition, the one thousand or so Lyonnaises who managed to set themselves up as chefs d'ateliers of weaving, dyers, *ovalistes*, and other thread processors were the winners of the government's desire to suppress the traditional corporate system of work. Where family ateliers were the norm, the workshops headed by female chefs d'ateliers had their own advantages. Capitalists could easily invest in the small businesses of female masters where they might assess the skill of the *patronne* and her workers. The limited scale of these ateliers and their flexibility provided a safeguard against the possibility of large financial losses.

Rouen's history was different, as the end of the guild system cast the once-favored guild mistresses into an undifferentiated struggle with other women for employment. Gone were the protections of the guild to moderate an inopportune tax assessment, to pay legal fees, or to enjoy special commercial rights. The monopolies that protected their manufactures, giving members of corporations a ready-made consuming public, were a thing of the past. Just as damaging was their loss of special treatment by the government in terms of protection through lawsuits and the freedom to make citizen arrests of unregistered competitors. In all, their ability to govern their own lives, from voting in guild assemblies to collecting dues and investments, was suppressed in one blow.

Rouen remained a center of industry, commerce, and administration where skillful and well-financed women could still conduct shops as *lingères, marchandes de mode,* milliners, knitters, spinners, ribbon and lace makers, and flour merchants. But the emergence of large-scale manufactures, the growth of cotton mills and cotton calico factories, the change of style for men's and women's clothing dwarfed their small enterprises and made them vulnerable to new modes of business. In a development contrary to Lyon's, where cotton production was becoming dominant, the women's comparative lack of capital was a more severe handicap. The requirement of paying the patent tax to establish firms under their own name caused many women to restructure their enterprises as family businesses under the name of their husbands. And since the opening of guilds had been more favorable to women in Rouen than in Lyon, no doubt they had this to regret as well. In contrast, the many taverns, billiard clubs, and assorted crafts established in women's names were witness to the continuing vitality of businesswomen in northern France.

Despite the problems it created, the end of guilds opened a world of possibilities to men and women. Manufacture and commerce were now accessible to all who had the funding to establish enterprises. No longer would the incessant lawsuits of former days siphon off time and money from business initiatives. Innovators were free to push technology in any direction without intruding on guild monopolies. The thousands of women excluded from guilds by lack of funds could now hope for employment. Women workers could legally apply for work in every trade, their ambitions limited only by their own skill and the customs of the community. Lyon's end of guilds resulted in the rise of hundreds of women as heads of weaving and *passementerie* manufactures. In Rouen, female entrepreneurs set up their own businesses if they were widows or unmarried while others continued to work in their husband's boutiques. The freedom to succeed or fail was open to all in the expanding, competitive economy of the coming century.

CONCLUSION

Women's work in Old Regime France had a variety of meanings. It was crucial to the kingdom's economy and to the family, but because society had defined a woman as a legal minor, her role as a productive worker was problematic. Tradition associated her with unpaid work in the family and the Church emphasized her connection with charity so that women's work was often hidden and unpaid. In addition, there was a general presumption that women were less intelligent, more credulous, and less reliable than men. These prejudices justified their being considered unskilled workers and paid accordingly at half the rate of male workers. Thus women's contribution to the patriarchal society was a sort of bonus, by which her work came at a cut rate.

Informally, of course, women stepped into the shoes of their male relatives or of other male workers to undertake skilled work. But since the skill was considered to be in the worker, not in the job, female pay was almost always less than that of men. Seldom given formal training, the rare women acknowledged to have skill were wives and daughters of guild masters. Yet, Old Regime economics made it crucial for every person to work to earn one's keep. It was incumbent upon women to contribute to the family's sustenance, and there was a special charge on women to provide food for their children. Whether that meant working inside or outside the household, tending the cows, spinning at the doorstep, or fulling cloth at a nearby processing yard, women were everywhere seen as workers. And since preindustrial work included tools and machines, there was no prejudice against women's using them. Or hardly any prejudice, since everywhere gender ruled the tasks that men and women performed.

It is part of the slippery history of women's work, however, that there are virtually no absolutes to count on in the early modern world. Tasks were divided by gender, but in time of pressure, the gender division was forgotten. Moreover, in a condition that defies ordinary logic, tasks were both gendered and also ungendered at the same time. Certainly women were associated with professions linked to the home—bearing children, preparing food, making clothes, and other household tasks—but what are we to make of the fact that cooks, sellers of smoked pork (*charcutiers*), pastry makers, and bakers in Rouen were exclusively male? Perhaps we can liken this to our modern chefs, whose professionalization lifts it out of the realm of women's home cooking.

Does that same rationale apply to the fact that there were males as well as females in the embroidery guilds, as professional hairdressers, and as spinners in both Rouen and Lyon? The linen-drapers in Lyon were all men, and in Caen, both sexes held the craft in one guild. At the same time, while working with metal and metal tools has been gendered male, women could become masters in Lyon's foundry guild and in Rouen's pin making guild. In the bustle of workshops, female servants gained informal training and stepped into supposedly masculine professions, whether temporarily or for a lifetime of work. Was male honor in France less tainted by performance of supposedly female work than, for instance, in Germany. What did people think when the same work earned higher wages for men than women? The puzzle of this ambiguity has links to segmenting of tasks and salaries in our contemporary world.

In the preindustrial times, the issue of women's "otherness" was sometimes a problem that had to be mitigated by legal means. The fact that women could manage to produce goods and to engage in commerce presented a problem in a society where they were not considered to be adults in the law. Without abandoning women's flexibility and lower wage, the question was how could a woman carry on buying and selling, planning and going to court, taking part in the public sphere if she was not a legal adult?

European societies wrestled with this conundrum and found a solution based on a precedent handed down from classical antiquity: to give a woman trader special dispensation for her business without removing her basic definition in the law. French society was open to this device because the structure of the kingdom depended on privileged orders created by the king. Thus the society honeycombed with privilege—that is, private law—for nobles, for administrators who had purchased their offices, for sovereign courts, and for guilds—had no trouble conferring another privilege on women traders. It was a legal device called the *marchande publique*, analogous to the British *feme sole*. This legal loophole gave women adult status to conduct their businesses. It was automatically acquired by women who acquired training and became guild mistresses.

Guild activity was an important economic power in the preindustrial era. While its early life must have seen articles made from start to finish in the guild family workshop, as merchant capitalism grew, guilds adapted techniques to keep up with the more competitive market. Breaking their regulations, these professional organizations began to hire workers outside the guild, use clandestine workshops, subcontract processes, and make use of stolen materials. At the same time, they employed their status as privileged bodies to defend their monopolies and acquire the technologies of other guilds at courts of law. The women in guilds participated in the same practices, gaining permission to sell the raw materials as well as the finished products of their trade, expanding into retail and wholesale commerce.

They were able to take up arms as equals in the struggle of guild conflict because of their privileged status. Artificial as it was, or should we say constructed as it was, the municipal, provincial, and royal officials treated them as adults. Their male guild counterparts disputed with them on the basis of traditional guild rhetoric, using precedent and knowledge of techniques in their frequent court altercations. In Rouen, there was a notable absence of reference among the guild masters and mistresses to the sex of members. In the numerous mixed guilds, women frequently became the guild officers setting policy for the male and female members. Because of their privilege, these women leaped over the legal disabilities of being minors in the law and participated fully and profitably in guild governance and affairs.

By contrast, in Lyon's famous silk *grande fabrique,* the twenty thousand or so female auxiliary workers who prepared the silk thread were not admitted as mistresses into the silk guild. Although highly skilled, they received the wages of unskilled laborers. The silk *fabrique,* however, could not function without them, and so gradually they received some benefits of annual pay, sleeping quarters, or holidays, showing that female wage workers were not completely at the mercy of their patrons. They also used their ingenuity to participate in the underground economy helping to keep Lyon's silk industry afloat.

Mastering the luxury textile trade in Rouen, the guild mistresses found that they frequently won court cases over the ambitious and wealthy merchant mercers' guild and other competitors. From our perspective, it appears that the government was interested in using the women's guilds as a foil to maintain competition among the Normandy guilds and to keep something of an evenhanded distribution of goods throughout the city. Allowing women into all guilds in 1778 certainly encouraged female employment, while at the same time fostering another aim of the government, to mitigate the male guilds' aggressive sense of entitlement. But when the guilds were suppressed in 1791, the former guild mistresses lost the privilege that had made them equal to their male competitors. As the market expanded, their monopolies and wholesale business fell away, and they became simply workers in an exigent economy.

In Lyon, the royal government's reform of guilds led to breaking the male monopoly of the *grande fabrique*. No longer relegated to the auxiliary tasks, the *lyonnaises cannutes*, as they were called at century's end, flooded into the weavers' ateliers. Their employment was instrumental in undermining the cohesion of the silk guild, but in the early nineteenth century they helped to keep the skilled male weavers in business. Taking the opportunities that they found, women workers mastered the technology of the era and made their lives as substantial as they could. While the state may have used them to achieve its own ends, the women made themselves expert and indispensable actors in the economy of the time.

BIBLIOGRAPHY

ARCHIVES

Archives Nationales (AN)

Series F 12 Economic affairs and administrative correspondence
    37 Correspondence of economic administrators
    135 Correspondence, guilds
    203–204 Correspondence regarding 1777 guild reform and protests
    678 Lyon
    677B "Questions et observations sur les nouveaux règlements"
    700 Finances, liquidation of guilds
    751 Statutes, *lingères*, Rouen
    762 Complaints over new guild amalgamations in Lyon: *forgeurs, aprêteurs des étoffes, calendrers, cylindreurs, dégrasseurs, patissiers, traiteurs, cuisiniers, chineurs*; memoirs
    763 *Grande fabrique*, Lyon, papers, January 1777 edict
    765 *Grande fabrique*, Lyon, papers. 1777–78, *guimpiers, fabricants de gaze, passementiers*, royal edicts
    766 *Guimpiers, grande fabrique,* Lyon, *passementiers*
    768 "Édit du Roi, pour les communautés d'arts et métiers de la ville de Lyon"; other papers of guilds in Lyon
    722 *Grande fabrique,* Lyon, *tapissiers*
    762 *Grande fabrique,* Lyon, statutes
    763 Lyon, *chapeliers, plumassières, coupeurs*
    764 *Grande fabrique,* Lyon, memoirs
    765 *Grande fabrique,* Lyon
    766 *Grande fabrique,* Lyon
    768 *Grande fabrique,* Lyon, *boutonniers, chapeliers*
    770 *Grande fabrique,* Lyon, *passementiers*
    773 *Grande fabrique,* Lyon, *tourneurs*
    1430 Rouen guilds: *rubanières;* guilds, Lyon

Archives départementales de la Seine Maritime (ADSM)

C Series: *Capitation d'industrie* of guilds, financial issues
    137 Official correspondence, *bonnetières*
    142 *Couturières*
    146–149 *Capitation*, guild affairs *lingères en vieux*
    148 *Toiliers*
    149 1775
    146 *Lingères en vieux*
    154 Correspondence of economic administrators, legal documents 16c
    344 *Capitation* of guilds in Rouen
    350 *Capitation* of guilds in Rouen
    360 *Capitation* of guilds in Rouen
F 82 Master's degree dissertations
4 BP L B Registers of guild entrance
5 E Series: Guild papers, Rouen if not otherwise noted
    89 *Marchands merciers*, Le Havre
    200 *Brodeurs-chasubliers*
    447 *Filassières*
    449 "Registre Cordiers et Filassiers," 1784
    455 *Filassières*
    457 *Filassières*
    449 *Filassières*
    463 *Filassières*
    497 *Filassières*
    498 *Lingères en vieux*
    500 *Lingères en neuf, filassières*
    501 *Lingères en neuf, filassières*
    502 *Lingères en neuf, filassières*
    504 *Lingères en neuf, filassières*
    506 *Lingères en vieux*
    508 *Lingères en vieux*
    511 *Lingères en vieux*
    527 *Filassières, marchands merciers*
    592 *Bonnetières*
    598 *Bonnetières*
    599 *Lingères en neuf*
    603 *Rubanières, marchands merciers*
    607 *Marchands merciers*
    611 *Bonnetières*
    612 *Rubanières-lingères-passementiers*
    675 *Lingères en vieux, marchands tailleurs, couturières*
    689 *Marchands tailleurs, fripiers en neuf et en vieux, casubliers et brodeurs*, 1789–1791
    714 *Lingères en neuf*

L 139 Guild papers, Rouen and environs, revolutionary era
L 2409 *Tailleurs*, 1790

Archives Municipales de Rouen, Bibliothèque Municipale de Rouen
Historic books and papers held in the bibliothèque are classed as holdings of the Archives Municipales. See for material on the Revolution in Rouen.

F 1/22 *Recensement de 1790*
F 2 Revolutionary taxes
G 1 *Patentes* 1791, 1792

Archives Municipales de Lyon (AML)

HH *Registre Grande Fabrique*, Tome I, II, Registers with records of lawsuits and regulations
HH 85*Mouliniers, ourdisseurs*
HH 167 *Passementiers, tapissiers*
HH 235, Liasse 40, Côte E, "Claude Rivey, Report aux Prévôt des Marchands" 1781
HH 424 *Grande fabrique, maîtres moulineurs*
HH 558 *Grande fabrique, guimpiers, gaziers*
HH 586 *Grande fabrique*, papers, register of permission to weave for masters' daughters
I2, 46 bis, Jean-Claude Déglize, "*État des ouvrages*," "*Tableau de la Visite Générale*," 1788, An X. Also classed as MS 2401, Bibliothèque Municipale de Lyon.

Archives Départementales du Rhône

1 C 35.40 Guild records, correspondence

Published Primary Sources

Almanach Royal, 1775.
Anon. "Remonstrances des mères et des filles Normandes de l'ordre du Tiers." Bibliothèque Municipale de Rouen. Np875.
Bertholon, Abbé Pierre. *Du Commerce et des manufactures destructives de la ville de Lyon*. Montpellier: Jean Martel, ainé, 1787.
Ferrière, Claude-Joseph. *Dictionnaire de droit et de pratique contenant l'explication des termes de droit, d'ordonnances, de coûtumes, et de pratique*. 2nd ed. Paris, 1740.
Houard, David. *Dictionnaire analytique, historique, étymologique, critique et interprétative de la coûtume de Normandie*. 4 vols. Rouen: Le Boucher, L. Oursel, 1780–82.
Mercier, Louis-Sébastien. *Le Tableau de Paris*. 12 vols. Hamburg: Virchaux & Company, 1781–88.

Pouchet, Louis-Eszéchias. *Traité sur la fabrication des étoffes*. Rouen: Deboucher, 1788.
Rogue. *Jurisprudence consulaire et instruction des négotiants*. 2 vols. Angers: J. Jahyer, 1773.
Savary, Jacques. *Le Parfait négotiant, ou instruction générale pour tout ce qui Regarde le commerce et toute sorte de merchandises, tant de la France que des pays étrangers*. Paris: Louis Billaine, 1675.
Young, Arthur. *Travels in France During the Years 1787, 1788, 1789*, ed. Jeffry Kaplow. Garden City, N.Y.: Doubleday, 1969.

Selected Secondary Sources

Aftalion, Florin. *The French Revolution: An Economic Interpretation*, trans. Martin Thom. Cambridge: Cambridge University Press, 1990. Originally published as *L'Économie de la Révolution française*. Paris: Hachette, 1987.
Albistur, Maïté, and Daniel Armogather. *Histoire du féminisme française du moyen âge à nos jours*. 2 vols. Paris: Éditions des Femmes, 1977.
Aubray, Jane. "Feminism in the French Revolution." In *The French Revolution in Social and Political Perspective*, ed. Peter Jones. London: Arnold, 1996.
Bardet, Jean-Pierre. *Rouen au XVIIe et XVIIIe siècles*. Paris: SEDES, 1983.
Beik, William. *Absolutism and Society in Seventeenth-Century France: State Power and Provincial Aristocracy in Languedoc*. Cambridge: Cambridge University Press, 1985.
Bell, Susan Groag, and Karen M. Offen. *Women, the Family, and Freedom: The Debate in Documents*. Stanford: Stanford University Press, 1983.
Benamou, Reed. "Women and the Verdigris Industry in Montpellier." In *European Women and Preindustrial Craft*, ed. Daryl M. Hafter. Bloomington: Indiana University Press, 1995.
Bennett, Judith. *Ale, Beer, and Brewsters in England: Women's Work in a Changing World, 1300–1600*. Oxford: Oxford University Press, 1996.
———. "'History That Stands Still': Women's Work in the European Past." *Feminist Studies* 14, no. 2 (summer 1988): 269–71.
———. *Women in the Medieval English Countryside: Gender and Household in Brigstock Before the Plague*. Oxford: Oxford University Press, 1987.
Berg, Maxine. "What Difference Did Women's Work Make to the Industrial Revolution?" *History Workshop Journal* 35 (spring 1993).
———. "Women's Work, Mechanisation, and the Early Phases of Industrialisation in England." In *The Historical Meanings of Work*, ed. Patrick Joyce. Cambridge: Cambridge University Press, 1987.
———. *The Age of Manufactures: Industry, Innovation and Work in Britain 1700–1820*. London: Fontana, 1985.
Berg, Maxine, Pat Hudson, and Michael Sonenscher, ed. *Manufacture in Town and Country Before the Factory*. Cambridge: Cambridge University Press, 1983.
Bergeron, Louis. "The Revolution: Catastrophe or New Dawn for the French Economy?" In *Rewriting the French Revolution*, ed. Colin Jones. Oxford: Oxford University Press, 1991.

Bezucha, Robert J. *The Lyon Uprising of 1834: Social and Political Conflict in the Early July Monarchy.* Cambridge, Mass.: Harvard University Press, 1974.

Bien, David. "Offices, Corps, and a System of State Credit: The Uses of Privilege Under the Ancien Régime." In *The Political Culture of the Old Régime,* ed. Keith M. Baker. Oxford: Oxford University Press, 1987.

———. "The Secretaries du Roi: Absolutism, Corps, and Privilege Under the Ancien Régime." In *Vom Ancien Régime zur Franzoischen Revolution,* ed. Ernst Hinrichs, Eberhard Schmitt, and Rudolf Vierhaus. Göttingen, 1978.

Blackstone, William. *Commentaries on the Laws of England,* 11th ed. London, 1791.

Blondel, Geneviève. "Les Communautés rouennises d'arts et métiers à la veille de la Révolution et leur liquidation." Mémoire de D.E.S., Diplôme d'Études Supérieures d'Histoire. Caen, 1962.

Bosher, John F. *The French Revolution.* New York: W. W. Norton, 1988.

Bosseboeuf, L. *Histoire de la fabrique de soieries de Tours, des origins au XIXe siècle.* Tours: P. Bousiez, 1900.

Bossenga, Gail. *The Politics of Privilege: Old Regime and Revolution in Lille.* Cambridge, Cambridge University Press, 1991.

———. "La Révolution française et les corporations: Trois exemples lillois." *Annales: E.S.C.* 43 (1988): 405–26.

Bouloiseau, Marc. *Cahiers de doléances du tiers état du bailliage de Rouen.* Paris: PUF [Presses Universitaires de France], 1957.

Bray, Francesca. *Technology and Gender: Fabrics of Power in Late Imperial China.* Berkeley and Los Angeles: University of California Press, 1997.

Burstin, Haim. "Conditionnement économique et conditionnement mental dans le monde du travail Parisien à la fin de l'Ancien Régime: Le privilege corporatif," *History of European Ideas* 3 (1982).

Butel, Paul. *L'Économie française au XVIIIe siècle.* Paris: SEDES, 1993.

Cayez, Pierre. *L'Industrialisation lyonnaise au XIXe siècle: Du grand commerce à la grande industrie.* Lille: Service de Reproduction des Thèses Université de Lille, 1979.

———. *Métiers jacquard et hauts fourneaux: Aux origines de l'industrie Lyonnaise.* Lyon: Presses Universitaires de Lyon, [1978].

Cerutti, Simona. "Group Strategies and Trade Strategies: The Turin Tailors' Guild in the Late Seventeenth and Early Eighteenth Centuries." In *Domestic Strategies: Work and Family in France and Italy, 1600–1800,* ed. Stuart Woolf. Cambridge: Cambridge University Press, 1991.

———. *La Ville et les métiers: Naissance d'un langage corporatif (Turin, 17e–18e siècle).* Paris: EEHESS [Éditions de l'École des Hautes Études en Sciences Sociales], 1990.

Chaline, Olivier, and Gerard Hurpin, ed. *Vivre en Normandie sous la Révolution.* Rouen: Société de l'histoire de Normandie, 1989.

Chassagne, Serge. *Le Coton et ses patrons: France, 1760–1840.* Paris: EEHESS [Éditions de l'École des Hautes Études en Sciences Sociales], 1991.

———. *Une Femme d'affaires au XVIIIe siècle.* Toulouse, 1981.

Clark, Alice. *Working Life of Women in the Seventeenth Century.* London, 1919; rpt. London: Frank Case, 1988.

Cobb, Richard. "Counter-Revolution and Environment: The Example of Lyon." In

The French and Their Revolution, ed. David Gilmour. London: Croom & Meiers, 1998.
Cockburn, Cynthia. *In the Way of Women: Men's Resistance to Sex Equality in Organizations*. Ithaca, N.Y.: ILR Press, 1991.
Coffin, Judith G. *The Politics of Women's Work: The Paris Garment Trades, 1750–1915*. Princeton: Princeton University Press, 1996.
Collins, James B. "The Economic Role of Women in Seventeenth-Century France." *French Historical Studies* 16 (fall 1989): 436–70.
Coornaert, Émile. *Les Corporations en France avant 1789*. Paris: Les Éditions ouvrières, 1968.
Cottereau, Alain. "The Fate of Collective Manufactures in the Industrial World: The Silk Industries of Lyons and London, 1800–1850." In *World of Possibilities: Flexibility and Mass Production in Western Industrialization*, ed. Charles F. Sabel and Jonathan Zeitlin, Cambridge: Cambridge University Press, 1997.
Cowper, B. Harris. *The Apocryphal Gospels*. London: Williams and Norgate, 1867.
Crowston, Clare Haru. *Fabricating Women: The Seamstresses of Old Regime France, 1675–1791*. Durham: Duke University Press, 2001.
———. "Engendering the Guilds: Seamstresses, Tailors, and the Clash of Corporate Identities in Old Regime France. *French Historical Studies* 23 (spring 2000): 339–71.
Darnton, Robert. *The Great Cat Massacre*. New York: Random House, 1985.
Davis, Natalie Zemon. "Women in the Crafts in Sixteenth-Century Lyon." In *Women and Work in Preindustrial Europe*, ed. Barbara A. Hanawalt. Bloomington: University of Indiana Press, 1986.
———. "Women on Top." In *Society and Culture in Early Modern France*. Stanford: Stanford University Press, 1975.
Delpierre, Madeleine. *Dress in France in the Eighteenth Century*, trans. Caroline Beamish. New Haven: Yale University Press, 1997. Originally published as *Se vêtir au XVIIIe siècle*. Paris: Société Nouvelle Adam Biro, 1996.
Désert, Gabriel. *La Révolution en Normandie*. Toulouse: Privat, 1989.
Dessan, Suzanne. *The Family on Trial in Revolutionary France*. Berkeley and Los Angeles: University of California Press, 2004.
———. "Constitutional Amazons: Jacobin Women's Clubs in the French Revolution." In *Re-creating Authority in Revolutionary France*, ed. Bryant T. Ragan Jr., and Elizabeth A. Williams. New Brunswick, N.J.: Rutgers University Press, 1992.
De Vries, Jan. "The Industrial Revolution and the Industrious Revolution," *Journal of Economic History* 54, no. 2 (June 1994): 249–70.
DiCaprio, Lisa. *The Origins of the Welfare State: Women, Work and the French Revolution*. Urbana: Illinois University Press, 2006.
———. "Women Workers, State-Sponsored Work, and the Right to Subsistence During the French Revolution," *Journal of Modern History* 71, no. 3 (September 1999): 519–51.
———. "The Enterprise of Welfare: State-Sponsored Work for Women in Revolutionary Paris." Ph. D. diss., Rutgers University, 1996.
Diefendorf, Barbara. *Paris City Councillors in the Sixteenth Century: The Politics of Patrimony*. Princeton: Princeton University Press, 1983.

Dixon, E. "Craftswomen in the 'Livre des métiers.'" *Economic Journal* 5 (1895): 209–28.

Dolléans, Edouard, and Gérard Dehove. *Histoire du travail en France, mouvement ouvrier et législation sociale des origins à 1919*. Paris: A. Colin, 1936; rpt. Paris: Domat-Montchrestien, 1953.

Dubois-Butard, Louis. *Les Femmes dans la maîtrise a'Amiens au XVIIIe siècle*. Amiens: Imprimerie des Archives départementals de la Somme, "Éklitra," 1975.

Duhet, Paule-Marie, ed. "Cahier de doléances et reclamations des femmes, par Madame B***B***." In *Cahiers de doléances des femmes en 1789 et autres texts*. Paris: Édition des Femmes, 1981.

———. *Les Femmes et la Révolution*. Paris: Julliard, 1971.

Edmonds, W. D. *Jacobinism and the Revolt of Lyon, 1789–1793*. New York: Oxford University Press, 1990.

Emmanuelli, François-Xavier. *État et pouvoirs dans la France des XVIe–XVIIIe siècles*. Paris, 1992.

Epstein, Steven A. *Wage Labor and Guilds in Medieval Europe*. Chapel Hill: North Carolina University Press, 1991.

Faigniez, Gustave. *La Femme et la société française dans la première moitié du XVIIe siècle*. Paris: J. Gamber, 1929.

———. *Études sur l'histoire de la classe industrielle à Paris au XIIIe et au XIVe siècles*. Paris: F. Vieweg, 1877.

Fairchilds, Cissie. "The Production and Marketing of Populuxe Goods in Eighteenth-Century Paris." In *Consumption and the World of Goods*, ed. John Brewer and Roy Porter. London: Routledge, 1993.

———. "Women and Family." In *French Women and the Age of the Enlightenment*, ed. Samia Spencer. Bloomington: University of Indiana Press, 1984.

Farr, James. *Authority and Sexuality in Early Modern Burgundy, 1550–1730*. New York: Oxford University Press, 1995.

———. *Hands of Honor: Artisans and Their World in Dijon, 1550–1650*. Ithaca: Cornell University Press, 1988.

Forrest, Alan. *The Revolution in Provincial France: Aquitaine, 1789–1799*. Oxford: Oxford University Press, 1996.

Garden, Maurice. *Lyon et les lyonnaises au XVIIIe siècle*. Paris: Société d'éditions "Les Belles Lettres," [1986].

———. "Lyon et les lyonnaises au XVIIIe siècle: L'exemple lyonnaise et les problèmes de classification." *Revue d'histoire économique et social* 48 (1970).

Garrioch, David. *The Formation of the Parisian Bourgeoisie, 1690–1830*. Cambridge, Mass.: Harvard University Press, 1996.

———. *Neighbourhood and Community in Paris, 1740–1790*. Cambridge: Cambridge University Press, 1986.

Genestal, René. "La Femme mariée dans l'ancien droit normand." *Revue historique de droit français et étranger* 29 (1930).

Geremek, Bronislaw. *Le Salariat dans l'artisanat Parisien aux XIIIe–XVe siècles*. Paris: Mouton, 1968.

Gilonne, Georges. *Soiries de Lyon*. 2 vols. Lyon: Éditions du Fleuve, 1948.

Godart, Justin. *L'Ouvrier en soie*. Lyon: Bernoux et Cumin, 1899.

Godineau, Dominique. *The Women of Paris and Their French Revolution*, trans.

Katherine Streip. Berkeley and Los Angeles: University of California Press, 1998. Originally published as *Citoyennes tricoteuses: Les femmes du peuple à Paris pendant la Révolution française*. Paris: Éditions Alinea, 1988.

Goodman, Dena. *The Republic of Letters: A Cultural History of the French Enlightenment*. Ithaca: Cornell University Press, 1994.

Green, Rosalie, and Iso Rogusa, eds. *Meditations on the Life of Christ: An Illustrated Manuscript of the Fourteenth Century*. Princeton: Princeton University Press, 1961.

Grenier, Jean-Yves. *L'Économie d'Ancien Régime: Un monde de l'échange et de l'incertitude*. Paris: Albin Michel, 1996.

Groppi, Angela. "Le Travail des femmes à Paris à l'époque de la Révolution française." *Bulletin d'histoire économique et sociale de la Révolution française* 34 (1979): 27–46.

Gullickson, Gay. *Spinners and Weavers of Auffay: Rural Industry and the Sexual Division of Labor in a French Village, 1750–1850*. Cambridge: Cambridge University Press, 1986.

———. "The Sexual Division of Labor in Cottage Industry and Agriculture in the Pays de Caux: Auffay, 1750–1850." *French Historical Studies* 12, no. 2 (fall 1981): 177–99.

Hafter, Daryl M. "Women in the Underground Business of Eighteenth-Century Lyon." *Enterprise and Society* 2 (March 2001): 11–40.

———. "Female Masters in the Ribbonmaking Guild of Eighteenth-Century Rouen." *French Historical Studies* 20, no. 1 (winter 1997): 1–14.

———. "Women Who Wove in the Eighteenth-Century Silk Industry of Lyon." In *European Women and Preindustrial Craft*, ed. Daryl M. Hafter. Bloomington: Indiana University Press, 1995.

———. "Gender Formation from a Working Class Viewpoint: Guildwomen in Eighteenth-Century Rouen." *Proceedings Western Society for French History* 16 (1989): 415–22.

———. "Female Masters in the Ribbonmaking Guild of Eighteenth-Century Rouen." *French Historical Studies* 20, no. 1 (winter 1997): 1–14.

———. The 'Programmed' Drawloom and the Decline of the Drawgirl." In *Dynamos and Virgins Revisited: Women and Technological Change in History*, ed. Martha Moore Trescott. Metuchen, N.J.: Scarecrow Press, 1979.

Hanley, Sarah. "Social Sites of Political Practice in France: Lawsuits, Civil Rights and the Separation of Powers in Domestic and State Government, 1500–1800." *American Historical Review* 102 (February 1997): 27–52.

———. "The Monarchic State in Early Modern France: Marital Regime Government and Male Right." In *Politics, Ideology, and the Law in Early Modern Europe: Essays in Honor of J. H. M. Salmon*. ed. Adrianna Bakos. Rochester, N.Y.: University of Rochester Press, 1994.

———. "Engendering the State: Family Formation and State Building in Early Modern France." *French Historical Studies* 16, no. 1 (spring 1989): 4–27.

———. "Family and State in Early Modern France: The Marriage Pact." In *Connecting Spheres: Women in the Western World, 1500 to the Present*, ed. Marilyn J. Boxer and Jean H. Quataert. Oxford: Oxford University Press, 1987.

Hardwick, Julie. *The Practice of Patriarchy: Gender and the Politics of Household Authority in Early Modern France.* University Park: The Pennsylvania State University Press, 1998.
———. "Seeking Separations: Gender, Marriages, and Household Economics in Seventeenth-Century France." *French Historical Studies* 21 (winter 1998): 157–80.
Hausen, Karin. "The Family and Role Division: The Polarization of Sexual Stereotypes in the Nineteenth Century." In *The German Family: Essays on the Social History of the Family in Nineteenth- and Twentieth-Century Germany.* London: Croom Helm, 1981.
Hauser, Henri. *Ouvriers du temps passé (XVe-XVIe siècles).* Paris: Félix Alcan, 1909.
Herlihy, David. *Medieval Households.* Cambridge, Mass.: Harvard University Press, 1985.
Hermsen, Joke. "Proto-Feminisme pendant la Révolution? Belle van Zuylen et Mme. De Stael: A Propos de Kant et Rousseau." In *Les Femmes et la Révolution française: Actes du Colloque International 12–14 Avril, 1989.* Toulouse: Presses Universitaires du Mirail, 1989.
Herriot, Edouard. *Lyon n'est plus.* 5 vols. Paris: n.p., 1938–40. Vol. 1, *Jacobins et modérés.*
Hill, Brigit. *Women, Work, and Sexual Politics in Eighteenth-Century England.* Montreal: McGill-Queens University Press, 1994.
Hillaire-Pérez, Liliane. *L'Invention technique au siècle des lumières.* Paris: Albin Michel, 2000.
Hirsch, Jean-Pierre. *Les Deux rêves de commerce: Entreprise et institution dans la région lilloise, 1780–1860.* Paris: EEHESS [Éditions de l'École des Hautes Études en Sciences Sociales], 1991.
Hoffman, Philip T., Gilles Postel-Vinay, and Jean-Laurent Rosenthal. *Priceless Markets: The Political Economy of Credit in Paris, 1660–1870.* Chicago: University of Chicago Press, 2000.
Howell, Martha. *Women, Production, and Patriarchy in Late Medieval Cities.* Chicago: University of Chicago Press, 1986.
Hufton, Olwen H. *The Prospect Before Her: A History of Women in Western Europe, 1500–1800.* New York: Alfred A. Knopf, 1996.
———. *Women and the Limits of Citizenship in the French Revolution.* Toronto: University of Toronto Press, 1992.
———. "Women, Work, and Marriage in Eighteenth-Century France." In *Marriage and Society,* ed. R.B. London: Europa, 1983.
———. "Women and the Family Economy in Eighteenth-Century France." *French Historical Studies* 9, no. 1 (spring 1975): 1–22.
———. *The Poor of Eighteenth-Century France, 1750–1789.* Oxford: Oxford University Press, 1974.
———. "Women in Revolution 1789–1796." *Past and Present* 53 (November 1971).
Hunt, Edwin S., and James M. Murray. *A History of Business in Medieval Europe, 1200–1555.* Cambridge: Cambridge University Press, 1999.
Hunt, Lynn. *The Family Romance of the French Revolution.* Berkeley and Los Angeles: University of California Press, 1992.

Isambert, F.-A., Jourdan, A.-J.-L., and Decrusy, eds. *Recueil générale des anciennes lois françaises depuis l'an 420 jusqu'a la Révolution de 1789*. 29 vols. Paris, 1833.

Jacobsen, Grethe. "Economic Progress and the Sexual Division of Labor: The Role of Guilds in the Late-Medieval Danish City." In *Altag und Fortschritt im Mittelalter*. Vienna, 1986.

———. "Women's Work and Women's Role: Ideology and Reality in Danish Urban Society, 1300–1550." *Scandinavian Economic History Review* 30, no. 1 (1983): 3–20.

Johnson, Christopher. *The Life and Death of Industrial Languedoc, 1700–1920*. New York: Oxford University Press, 1995.

Johnson, Mary Durham. "Old Wine in New Bottles: The Institutional Changes for Women of the People During the French Revolution." In *Women, War and Revolution*, ed. Carol R. Berkin and Clara M. Lovett. New York: Holmes & Meier, 1980.

Juratic, Sabine, and Nicole Pellegrin. "Femmes, villes et travail en France dans la Deuxième moitié du XVIIIème siècle: Quelques questions." Institut d'histoire moderne et contemporaine–C.N.R.S. Occasional paper.

Kaplan, Steven L. *La Fin des corporations*. Paris: Fayard, 2001.

———. "Les Corporations, les 'faux-ouvriers' et le fauberg Saint-Antoine au XVIIIe siècle." *Annales: E.S.C.* 40 (March–April 1988): 253–88.

———. "The Luxury Guilds in Paris in the Eighteenth Century." *Francia* 9 (1981): 257–98.

———. "Réflexions sur la police du monde du travail, 1700–1815." *Revue historique* 261, no. 1 (1979): 17–77.

Kaplan, Steven Laurence, and Cynthia J. Koepp. *Work in France: Representations, Meaning, Organization, and Practice*. Ithaca: Cornell University Press, 1986.

Kaplow, Jeffry. *The Names of Kings: The Parisian Laboring Poor in the Eighteenth Century*. New York: Basic Books, 1972.

———. *Elbeuf During the Revolutionary Period, 1770–1815: History and Social Structure*. Baltimore: Johns Hopkins University Press, 1964.

Kelly, Joan. "Did Women Have a Renaissance?" In *Women, History and Theory: The Essays of Joan Kelly*. Chicago: University of Chicago Press, 1984.

———. "The Doubled Vision of Feminist Theory." In *Women, History, and Theory: The Essays of Joan Kelly*. Chicago: University of Chicago Press, 1984.

Kowaleski, Maryanne, and Judith M. Bennett. "Crafts, Guilds, and Women in the Middle Ages: Fifty Years After Marian K. Dale." *Signs* 14, no. 2 (1989): 474–88.

Kwass, Michael. *Privilege and the Politics of Taxation in Eighteenth-Century France*. Cambridge: Cambridge University Press, 2000.

Lacey, Kay E. *Women and Work in Preindustrial England*. London: Croom Helm, 1985.

Landes, Joan B. *Women and the Public Sphere in the Age of the French Revolution*. Ithaca: Cornell University Press, 1988.

Lanza, Janine Marie. *From Wife to Widow in Early Modern Paris: Gender, Economy, and the Law*. Aldershot, U.K.: Ashgate, 2007.

Le Faure, Amédée. *Le Socialism pendant la Révolution française*. Paris: E. Danter, 1863.

Lefebvre, Charles. *L'Ancien droit matrimonial en Normandie.* Rouen: Imprimerie L. Gy, 1912.
Le Foll, Claire. "Les Femmes et le mouvement révolutionnaire à Rouen." In *À Travers la Haute-Normandie en Révolution,* ed. Claude Mazauric and Yannick Marec. Rouen: Comité régional d'histoire de la Révolution française, 1992.
———. "Les Femmes et le mouvement Révolutionnaire à Rouen, 1789–1795." Mémoire de DES, Université de Haute-Normandie, 1985.
Lehmann, Andrée. *Le Rôle de la femme dans l'histoire de France au moyen âge.* Paris: Berger-Levrault, 1952.
Léon, Camille. "Notes sur les travaux publics et filatures de cotton établies à Rouen dans les paroisses de St.-Maclou, St.Vivien et St. Nicolas en 1768 et 1769." *Bulletin de la Société Libre d'Emulation* (1932).
Le Parquier, Eugene. "Une Enquête sur le paupérisme et de la crise industrielle dans la Region Rouennaise." *Bulletin de la Société Libre d'Emulation* (1935).
Leroudier, Emile. "La Décadence de la fabrique lyonnaise à la fin du XVIIIe siècle." *Revue d'histoire de Lyon* 10 (1911): 415–44.
Levasseur, Émile. *Histoire des classes ouvrières et de l'industrie en France avant 1789,* 2nd ed. 2 vols. Paris: Arthur Rousseau, 1901.
Levy, Darlene Gay, and Harriet B. Applewhite. "Women of the Popular Classes in Revolutionary Paris, 1789–1795." In *Women, War, and Revolution,* ed. Carol R. Berkin and Clara M. Lovett. New York: Holmes & Meier, 1980.
Levy, Darlene Gay, Harriet Branson Applewhite, and Mary Durham Johnson, eds. *Women in Revolutionary Paris, 1789–1795.* Urbana: University of Illinois Press, 1979.
Liu, Tessie. "The Commercialization of Trousseaux Work: Female Homeworkers in the French Lingerie Trade." In *European Women and Preindustrial Craft,* ed. Daryl M. Hafter. Bloomington: Indiana University Press, 1995.
———. *The Weaver's Knot: The Contradictions of Class Struggle and Family Solidarity in Western France, 1750–1914.* Ithaca: Cornell University Press, 1994.
Longfellow, David L. "Silk Workers and the Social Struggle in Lyon." *French Historical Studies* 12, no. 1 (spring 1981):1–40.
Marion, Marcel. *Histoire financière de France.* Paris: A. Rousseau, 1914.
Martin, Germain. *Les Associations ouvrières au XVIIIe siècle (1700–1792).* Paris: A. Rousseau, 1900.
Martin Saint-Léon, Étienne. *Histoire des corporations de métiers depuis leurs origins jusqu'à leur suppression en 1791.* Paris: F. Alcan, 1922; rpt. New York: Arno Press, 1975.
May, Gita. "Rousseau's 'Antifeminism' Reconsidered." In *French Women and the Age of Enlightenment,* ed. Samia I. Spencer. Bloomington: Indiana University Press, 1984.
Mazauric, Claude. *À Travers la Haute Normandie en Révolution.* Rouen, 1992.
Miller, Judith. *Mastering the Market: The State and the Grain Trade in Northern France, 1700–1860.* Cambridge: Cambridge University Press, 1999.
Miller, Lesley Ellis. "Paris-Lyon-Paris: Dialogue in the Design and Distribution of Patterned Silks in the Eighteenth Century." In Robert Fox and Anthony Turner, eds. *Luxury Trades and Consumerism in Ancien Règime Paris.* Aldershot, U.K.: Ashgate, 1998.

Minard, Philippe. *La Fortune du Colbertisme: État et industrie dans la France des Luminières*. Paris: Fayard, 1998.

———. "L'industrie." In *Atlas de la Révolution française*, ed. Gérard Béaur, Philippe Minard, and Alexandra Laclau. Paris: EEHESS [Éditions de l'École des Hautes Études en Sciences Sociales], 1989.

Monnier, Raymonde. "L'Évolution de l'industrie et le travail des femmes sous l'Empire." *Bulletin d'histoire économique et social de la Révolution française* (1979): 47–60.

Mousnier, Roland. *The Institutions of France Under the Absolute Monarchy, 1598–1789: Society and State*, trans. Brian Pearce. Chicago: Chicago University Press, 1979.

Offen, Karen. *European Feminisms, 1700–1950*. Stanford: Stanford University Press, 2000.

Ogilvie, Sheilagh. *A Bitter Living: Women, Markets, and Social Capital in Early Modern Germany*. Oxford: Oxford University Press, 2003.

Okin, Susan Moller. *Women in Western Political Thought*. Princeton: Princeton University Press, 1979.

Oldenziel, Ruth. *Making Technology Masculine: Men, Women, and Modern Machines in America, 1870–1945*. Amsterdam: Amsterdam University Press, 1999.

Olivier-Martin, François. *L'Organisation corporative de la France d'ancien régime*. Paris: Sirey, 1938.

Ouen-Lacroix, Charles. *Histoire des anciennes corporations d'arts et métiers et des confréries religieuses de la capital de la Normandie*. Rouen: Lecointe frères, 1850.

Pariset, Ernest. *Histoire de la fabrique lyonnaise: Étude sur le régime social et économique de l'industrie de la soie à Lyon depuis le XVIe siècle*. Lyon: A. Rey, n.d.

Parr, Joy. *The Gender of Breadwinners*. Toronto: University of Toronto Press, 1990.

Perrot, Jean-Claude. *Genèse d'une ville moderne: Caen au XVIIIe siècle*. 2 vols. Paris, La Haye: Mouton, 1975.

Pinchbeck, Ivy. *Women Workers and the Industrial Revolution, 1750–1850*. 1930; rpt. New York: Routledge, 1969.

Poni, Carlo. "Fashion as Flexible Production: The Strategies of the Lyons Silk Merchants in the Eighteenth Century." In *World of Possibilities: Flexibility and Mass Production in Western Industrialization*, ed. Charles F. Sabel and Jonathan Zeitlin. Cambridge: Cambridge University Press, 1997.

Portemer, Jean. "Le Statut de la femme en France depuis la réformation des coûtumes jusqu'à la rédaction du code civil." *Recueils de la Société Jean Bodin* 12, pt. 2 (1962): 447–97.

———. "La Femme dans la legislation royale des deux derniers siècles de L'Ancien Régime." *Études d'historie du droit privé offerts à Pierre Pétot*. Paris: Montchrestien, Dalloz, Sirey, 1959.

Povey, Mary. *Uneven Developments: The Ideological Work of Gender in Mid-Victorian England*. Chicago: University of Chicago Press, 1988.

Proctor, Candice E. *Women, Equality, and the French Revolution*. New York: Greenwood Press, 1990.

Quataert, Jean. "The Shaping of Women's Work in Manufacturing: Guilds, Households, and the State in Central Europe, 1648–1870." *American Historical Association* 90 (December 1985): 1122–48.

Reddy, William M. *The Rise of Market Culture: The Textile Trade and French Society, 1750–1900*. Cambridge: Cambridge University Press, 1994.

Riffaterre, C. *Le Mouvement antijacobin et antiparisien à Lyon et dans le Rhône-et-Loire en 1793 (29 mai–15 aout)*. Vol. 2. Lyon: A. Rey, 1928.

Roche, Daniel. *A History of Everyday Things: The Birth of Consumption in France, 1600–1800*, trans. Brian Pearce. Cambridge: Cambridge University Press, 2000. Originally published as *Histoire des choses banales: Naissance de la consommation XVIIe–XIXe siècle*. Paris: Fayard, 1997.

———. *The Culture of Clothing: Dress and Fashion in the Ancien Régime*, trans. Jean Birrell. Cambridge: Cambridge University Press, 1996. Originally published as *La Culture des apparences: Une histoire du vêtement*. Paris: Fayard, 1989.

Roper, Lyndal. *The Holy Household: Women and Morals in Reformation Augsburg*. Oxford: Oxford University Press, 1989.

Rosa, Annette. *Citoyennes: Les femmes et la Révolution française*. Paris: Messidor, 1989.

Rosenband, Leonard N. *Papermaking in Eighteenth-Century France: Management, Labor, and Revolution at the Montgolfier Mill, 1761–1805*. Baltimore: Johns Hopkins University Press, 2000.

Rothschild, Joan, ed. *Machina ex Dea: Feminist Perspectives on Technology*. New York: Pergamon Press, 1983.

Rule, John. "The Property of Skill in the Period of Manufacture." In *The Historical Meanings of Work*, ed. Patrick Joyce. Cambridge: Cambridge University Press, 1987.

Sargentson, Carolyn. *Merchants and Luxury Markets: The Marchands Merciers of Eighteenth-Century Paris*. London: Victoria and Albert Museum, 1996.

Scott, Joan Wallach. *Only Paradoxes to Offer*. Cambridge, Mass.: Harvard University Press, 1996.

———. "Gender: A Useful Category of Historical Analysis." In *Gender and the Politics of History*. New York: Columbia University Press, 1988.

Seiler-Baldinger, Annemarie. *Textiles: A Classification of Techniques*. Bathurst, Australia: Crawford House Press, 1994.

Sewell, William, Jr. "Social and Cultural Perspectives on Women's Work: Comment on Loats, Hafter, and DeGroat." *French Historical Studies* 20, no. 1 (winter 1997): 49–54.

———. *Work and Revolution in France: The Language of Labor from the Old Regime to 1848*. Cambridge: Cambridge University Press, 1980.

Sheridan, George J., Jr. "Household and Craft in an Industrializing Economy: The Case of the Silk Weavers of Lyons." In *Consciousness and Class Experience in Nineteenth-Century Europe*, ed. John M. Merriman. New York: Holmes & Meier, 1979.

Sledziewski, Elizabeth G. "The French Revolution as the Starting Point." In *A History of Women*, ed. George Duby and Michelle Perrot. Cambridge, Mass.: Harvard University Press, 1995.

Sonenscher, Michael. *Work and Wages: Natural Law, Politics, and the Eighteenth-Century FrenchTrades*. Cambridge: Cambridge University Press, 1989.

———. *The Hatters of Eighteenth-Century France*. Berkeley and Los Angeles: University of California Press, 1987.

———. "Mythical Work: Workshop Production and the *Compagnonnages* of Eighteenth-Century France." In *The Historical Meanings of Work*, ed. Patrick Joyce. Cambridge: Cambridge University Press, 1987.
Soreau, Edmond. *Ouvriers et paysans de 1789 à 1792*. Paris: Société d'édition "Les Belles Lettres," 1936.
Spencer, Samia I., ed. *French Women and the Age of Enlightenment*. Bloomington: Indiana University Press, 1984.
Strumingher, Laura S. *Women and the Making of the Working Class: Lyon, 1830–1970*. St. Albans, Vt.: Eden Press Women's Publications, 1979.
Sydenham, M. J. "The Republican Revolt of 1793: A Plea for Less Localized Local Studies." *French Historical Studies* 12, no. 1 (spring 1981): 120–38.
Tilly, Louise A., and Joan W. Scott. *Women, Work, and Family*. New York: Holt, Rinehart and Winston, 1978.
Tortora, Phyllis G., and Robert S. Merkel, eds. *Fairchild's Dictionary of Textiles*. 7th ed. New York: Fairchild Publications, 1996.
Trénard, Louis. "La Crise sociale lyonnaise à la veille de la Révolution." *Revue d'histoire moderne et contemporaine* 2 (1955): 5–45.
Truant, Cynthia. "La maîtrise d'une identité? Corporations féminines à Paris aux XVIIe et XVIIIe siècles." *Clio, Histoire, Femmes et Sociétés* 3 (1996).
———. "Parisian Guildswomen and the (Sexual) Politics of Privilege: Defending Their Patrimonies in Print." In *Going Public: Women and Publishing in Early Modern France*, ed. Dena Goodman and Elizabeth C. Goldsmith. Ithaca: Cornell University Press, 1995.
———. "The Guildswomen of Paris: Gender, Power, and Sociability in the Old Regime." *Proceedings Western Society for French History* 15 (1988): 130–38.
Utz, Erika. *The Legend of Good Women: The Liberation of Women in Medieval Cities*, trans. Sheila Marnie. Wakefield, R.I.: Moyer Bell, 1988.
Vaesen, J. *La Juridiction commerciale à Lyon sous l'ancien régime*. Lyon: A. Brun, 1879.
Vardi, Liana. "The Abolition of the Guilds During the French Revolution. *French Historical Studies* 15, no. 4 (fall 1988): 704–17.
Wahl, Maurice. *Les Premières années de la Révolution à Lyon, 1788–1792*. Paris: Armand Colin, 1894.
Wajcman, Judy. *Feminism Confronts Technology*. University Park: The Pennsylvania State University Press, 1991.
White, Lynn, Jr. "Dynamo and Virgin Reconsidered." *American Scholar* 27, no. 2 (spring 1958).
Wiesner, Merry. "'Wandervogels' and Women: Journeymen's Concepts of Masculinity in Early Renaissance Germany." *Journal of Social History* 24 (1991): 767–82.
———. "Guilds, Male Bonding, and Women's Work in Early Modern Germany." *Gender and History* 1, no. 2 (summer 1989): 125–37.
———. *Working Women in Renaissance Germany*. New Brunswick, N.J.: Rutgers University Press, 1986.
Wingrove, Elizabeth Rose. *Rousseau's Republican Romance*. Princeton: Princeton University Press, 2000.

INDEX

Abeille, Louis-Paul, 151–52
abuse, 79
Adam, Henry, 231
Aftalion, Florin, 212n8
Albistur, Maité, 234
Allarde, Pierre Gilbert Le Roi, baron d', 242, 243, 244, 264, 286
André, M. d', 248
Applewhite, Harriet B., 239
apprenticeship. *See* training
Armogather, Daniel, 234
army, 253–55
artisans, 247–49, 255–59, 255–59. *See also* guild masters; laborers
assignats, 248–49, 273
associates, 148–49, 176, 180, 214–15

Beik, William, 62
Bence, Antoine, 100
Bennett, Judith M., 37, 38
Bertin, Henri Léonard Jean Baptiste de, 189, 192n97, 196, 197
Bigault, 100
Binard, 167
black market. *See* underground economy
Blackstone, William, 10, 69
Boileau, Étienne, 42
Boisson, Femme, 181n66
Boittout, Jacques, 158
Bonnemaison, M., 168
Bonnet, Jean Louis, 158
bonnetières, 112–15, 155–57, 222, 231
Bouloiseau, Marc, 230
Bourdon, M., 159–60
bread marches, 57
Brunel, M., 122

Buffonier, Pierre, 281
Bunel, Femme, 107, 108
Burstin, Haim, 247

cahiers, 229–32, 240–41, 267–68
calendar, 249
capacity, legal, 10, 69–73. *See also* natures
capital, 256–57
capitalism, 3, 100–3. *See also* economy
Cayez, Pierre, 279–80, 282n186
Chabout, Laurant, 181n66
charity, 67–68
Chefderue, Pierre, 100
chefs d'ateliers, 264, 277–79, 284, 287–88. *See also* master workers
civil separation from bed and hearth. See *séparation de corps et d'habitation*
civil separation of property. See *séparation de biens*
Claire, David de, 19, 22
Clark, Alice, 39
class, 56–57. *See also* privileges
clothing, 249–55
Cobb, Richard, 275n172, 286
Coffin, Judith G., 147n3, 177, 178, 219, 226
Colbert, Jean-Baptiste, 32, 33, 175, 177
competition
 economy and, 174–75, 177, 179–80, 196–97
 in guild system, generally, 28–31, 33–35, 91, 100–3, 105–6, 164–66
 from merchant mercers, 13–14, 51–53, 63–64, 119–23
 for Rouen, 47–48
Conseil d'État, 45

contracts, 73–76, 87
Coornaert, Émile, 26, 34, 227
cord makers, 161–62
Cornet, 181n66
costs. *See* fees, entrance
Cotte, 188, 192
Cottereau, Alain, 185
cotton crisis, 212–14
Coulon, Femme, 93
courtly love, 59
Coûtumier de Normandie, 11
Couture, Jacques (wife of), 81–82
couturières, 116, 165–66, 167, 226–27, 236
Crestien, Gabriel, 100
Crosne, Louis Thiroux De, 157
Crowston, Clare, 43, 236
culture, 58–60. *See also* social order
customary law, 69–73. *See also* legal instruments; legal system
cutters, 226–27

Darnton, Robert, 186n81
David, Jacques-Louis, 251n104
Davis, Natalie Zemon, 60, 132
day laborers. *See* laborers
debts, 78–79, 82–85, 227–29, 242–43, 247
Delabos, Sieur, 90
Delanos, 90
Delhomme, Heleine, 192n97
Delpierre, Madeleine, 250n102
Demare, 231
Desan, Susan, 273
Destrouché, 247n96
Diderot, Denis, 208
discipline, 26, 202, 217–19. *See also* governance
Dormesnil, Fille Anne Monique, 216
douaire, 74
dowry, 73–76, 87
Dubos, Jean Raphael, 73–74
Duval, Jacques, 78

economy. *See also* capitalism
  competition and, 174–75, 177, 179–80, 196–97
  of family, 59, 291
  gender and, 64–69, 196–97, 233
  of guild system, generally, 28–31, 33–35, 100–3, 165
  legal instruments in, 11–12
  of Lyon, 44, 123–25, 272–75
  natures and, 3–6, 233
  of Normandy, 47–48, 87–88
  of Old Regime France, 9–10, 145–49, 174–75
  productivity in, 9–10
  reform and, 145–49, 174–75, 177, 179–89, 196–97, 203
  regulation of, 174–75
  of Revolutionary France, 207–8, 248–53, 255, 257–58, 263–64, 272–75
  of Rouen, 46–48, 91–92, 149–50, 209–12
  underground, 9, 135–42, 172, 173, 215–16
education, 54
embroiderers, 195
Encyclopèdie, 208
Estates General, 33, 228, 229–32, 267

Fagniez, Gustave, 43
family
  class and, 56
  economy of, 59, 291
  gender and, 56, 57–58, 59, 65–66, 233–34, 236, 237
  guild masters and, 24, 25, 239–42
  in guild system, generally, 24–25, 38, 66–67, 219
  industrialization and, 10
  lingères and, 94–95, 99–100
  natures and, 5–6
  in Revolutionary France, 245–47, 284–85
  ribbonmakers and, 117
  silk industry and, 131, 133, 185, 200, 264, 284–85
  training by, 24
Fay de Sathonay, Antoine, 188–89, 278
fees, entrance
  for *bonnetières*, 222
  for guild masters, generally, 148–49
  for *lingères*, 94–95, 157, 168–74, 222
  in Lyon, generally, 180
  in Rouen, generally, 150–51, 214, 217–18, 240–41
  in silk industry, 184–85, 187–90, 191–192, 195
Fenélon, Abbé, 233, 247n93
Ferrière, Claude-Joseph, 75, 77, 78n59
Fevret, Sieur (wife of), 82
filles majeures, 10n22

Flaust, Maître, 84
Flesselles, 182, 188
Fontetrune, 189
Forrest, Alan, 214n14, 214n16
France. *See* Napoleonic Era; Old Regime France; Revolutionary France

Garden, Maurice, 124–25, 203, 215, 267, 270
Garnett, George, 228
gender. *See also* natures
　of artisans, 255–59
　of *bonnetières*, 112–15
　class and, 56–57
　culture and, 58–60
　economy and, 64–69, 196–97, 233
　education and, 54
　family and, 56, 57–58, 59, 65–66, 233–34, 236, 237
　in Germany, 57–58, 59
　of guild masters, generally, 36–44, 56, 87–88, 91–93, 115–16, 132–33, 142–43, 219–22
　in guild system, generally, 56, 60–61, 63–64, 66–67, 68, 87–88, 237–38
　of hat makers, 135–37
　history of, 55–60
　of laborers, generally, 36, 43–44, 54–55, 142–43
　of *lingères*, 93–12
　of master workers, 196–203, 262–63
　in Old Regime France, 54–55, 58–59, 60–64, 291–92
　political rights and, 208, 209, 231–32, 233, 235–36
　power and, 54, 55–56
　privilege and, 60–64
　reform and, 157–60, 163–67, 176–80, 184, 192–93, 196–203, 205, 219–27
　religion and, 57–58, 64–66, 86
　in Revolutionary France, 208–9, 219–22, 245–47, 255–59, 270–74, 277–81, 287–89
　of ribbonmakers, 116–17
　sexuality and, 54
　in silk industry, 131–35, 137–42, 184, 192–93, 196–203, 262–63, 264–66, 270–74, 277–81
　in social order, 14–15, 54–64, 85–86, 86–88, 232–39, 291
　of spinners, 117–19
　taxation and, 109–12, 245–47
　technology and, 3–5, 6, 53, 64, 112–13
　training and, 37–38, 39–40, 198–99
　work and, 54–55, 86, 145–49, 152, 153–54, 164, 178–79, 200–1, 205, 222–23, 232–39, 291
Génestal, Renée, 69, 72n42
Geneva, 39
Gensoul, F., 282–83
Germany, 40–41, 57–58, 59, 80n64
Godineau, Dominique, 258, 259
Gournay, Vincent de, 196, 197n105
governance. *See also* discipline; regulation
　of *bonnetières*, 231
　exclusion from, 164, 165–74, 222–27
　in guild system, generally, 26–27, 28, 149, 164, 165–74, 202–3, 222–27, 230–31
　of *lingères*, 95–97, 231
　reform and, 164, 165–74, 222–27, 230–31
　of ribbonmakers, 117
　of spinners, 117–18
　taxation and, 225
government
　of Lyon, 44–45, 124, 187–90
　of Normandy, 46
　in Paris, 45, 169–74, 180–82, 184–90, 197–200, 203–4, 228–32, 242, 263–64
　of Rouen, 46, 110–12, 151–52, 172–73, 229
Goy, 224
Grégoire, 270
Grenier, Jean-Yves, 28, 256
Groppi, Angela, 237–38
Guerin, Catherine, 192n97
guild masters. *See also* master merchants; master workers; *specific trades*
　associate category created for, 148–49, 176, 180, 214–15
　family and, 24, 25, 239–42
　fees, entrance, generally, 148–49
　laborers compared, 89, 142–43
　lawsuits by, generally, 19–20, 21–23, 89–91, 105–6, 121–23
　in Lyon, generally, 8, 15, 130, 132–33, 142–43
　marchande publique and, 81
　oaths of, 25, 27–28
　overview of, 25–26
　in Rouen, generally, 7, 16, 18, 115–16, 132–33, 142–43

guild masters (*continued*)
   training by, 25–26
   women as, generally, 36–44, 56, 87–88, 91–93, 115–16, 132–33, 142–43, 219–22
guild system. *See also* guild masters; Lyon; Rouen; *specific trades*
   capitalism and, 3, 100–3
   competition and, 28–31, 33–35, 99, 100–3, 105–6, 164–68
   debts in, 242–43, 247
   discipline in, 26, 202, 217–19
   economy of, 28–31, 33–35, 100–3, 165
   end of, 242–49, 255–59, 263–64, 286–89, 294
   exclusion from, 5–6, 16, 40–42, 43, 58, 131–33, 157–60, 164, 167, 219
   family in, 24–25, 38, 66–67, 219
   gender in, 56, 60–61, 63–64, 66–67, 68, 87–88, 237–38
   in Geneva, 39
   in Germany, 40–41, 58
   governance in, 26–27, 28, 149, 164, 165–74, 202–3, 222–27, 230–31
   history of, 23–24, 28, 36–44, 100–1
   legal instruments and, 12
   membership in, 148–49, 219–22
   monopoly in, 91, 217
   overviews of, 12–13, 21–31, 48–50, 293–94
   in Paris, 39–40, 42–43, 45, 236
   privileges in, 1–3, 49–50, 60–61, 63–64, 162–63, 174, 175–80, 207–8
   reform of, generally, 16, 145, 146–49, 163–67, 175–84, 203–5, 207–8
   regulation in, 16, 31–35, 91, 92, 202–3
   religion in, 27–28
   in Revolutionary France, 5, 17–18
   subcontracting in, 29–31
   taxation of, 32–35, 169–70, 202, 204, 218, 220–21, 225, 227, 242
   training in, 21, 24, 25–26
   wages and, 67, 164
   widows' rights in, 68–69
guimpiers, 193–95, 195–96, 198

Harde, Madeleine, 216
harvest failures, 210–11, 211–12
hat makers, 135–37, 141, 280
Hauser, Henri, 29
Hebert, Margeurite, 93
Herlihy, David, 39

Heuye, Femme, 166
Hirsch, Jean-Pierre, 175
Hoffman, Philip T., 257
Horchelle, Rouennais, 254
Horn, Jeff, 215, 255
Houard, David, 12n26, 70, 71, 76, 80
Howell, Martha, 199
Hufton, Olwen, 36, 54–55, 57, 58n12, 262
Hunt, Lynn, 208

industrialization, 10, 203, 213, 258, 281–85
Inspectors of Manufacture, 3n5

Jacquard device, 281–82, 283–84
Joan of Arc, 251
Jourdain, Marie Catherine, 93n4

Kaplan, Steven L.
   on cutters, 226
   on guild system, 214–15, 216, 262
   on labor market, 218
   on Le Chapelier law, 244
   on reform, 147, 177, 202
   on work discipline, 114–15
Kaplow, Jeffry, 229
Kelly, Joan, 2, 59, 62n23
Keralio, Louise, 237
knitters. *See bonnetières*
Kowaleski, Maryanne, 37, 38

laborers
   guild masters compared, 89, 142–43
   in Lyon, 8–9, 18
   political rights of, 244–45, 268
   regulation of, 19–20, 21–23, 29–31, 134–35, 139, 141–42
   restrictions on, 9, 134–35, 139
   in Revolutionary France, 244–45, 259, 264–72, 275–81, 287–89
   in Rouen, 7, 218, 288–89
   in silk industry, 131–35, 137–42, 264–72, 275–81, 287–88
   women as, generally, 36, 43–44, 54–55, 142–43
Lafabreque, Sr., 192n97
Lamark, Sieur de, 19–20
La Motte, Marie Catherine, 83
Landes, Joan, 208, 236
Landormy, Sieur, 216
Languement, Sieur, 216n21
Laplanche, Dame de, 110–11

la Vaunudière, Madame de, 77–78
la Vaunudière, Sieur de, 77–78
lawsuits
  by *bonnetières*, 112–13
  by *couturières*, 167
  by guild masters, generally, 19–20, 21–23, 89–91, 105–6, 121–23
  by *lingères*, 51–53, 63–64, 100, 104, 107–9
Le Breton, M., 225
Le Cas, Dame, 169
Le Chapelier, Isaac René, 244, 264, 286
Lefevre, Fille, 216
le Fevre, Mattuieur, 225
Le Foll, Claire, 231
legal instruments. *See also* legal system; privileges
  marchande publique, 80–85, 87, 87–88, 292–93
  marriage contract, 73–76, 87–88
  marriage portion, 74
  overview of, 11–12, 15
  séparation de biens, 76–79
  séparation de corps et d'habitation, 76, 79
legal system, 1, 10–12, 15, 69–73. *See also* legal instruments
Le Gendre, Marie Barb, 19–20, 21–22
Le Guet, Dame, 159–60
Le Havre, 13–14, 51–53, 63–64
Le Jeune, Thérèse, 159
le Sauvage, Sieur, 84–85
Levy, Darlene Gay, 239
Lièzedes, Simonde du, 182n71
linen-drapers. *See lingères*
lingères
  family and, 94–95, 99–100
  fees, entrance, 94–95, 157, 168–74, 222
  governance of, 95–97, 231
  lawsuits by, 51–53, 63–64, 100, 104, 107–9
  of Le Havre, 13–14, 51–53, 63–64
  marriage and, 99–100, 111–12
  materials for, 104–5
  membership of, 93, 106, 157, 222
  merchant mercers and, 224–25
  monopoly by, 97–98, 103
  in Old Regime France, 7, 93–112
  old vs. new, 106–12
  privileges of, 97–100, 103–4
  reform of, 153, 155, 156, 157–60, 161, 167, 168–74, 224–25
  regulation of, 97–112

religion and, 106
  in Revolutionary France, 222, 224–25, 231
  ribbonmakers and, 161
  rural industry and, 104–5
  subcontracting by, 104–5
  tailors and, 157–60, 167, 168–74, 224
  taxation of, 93, 106, 109–12, 169–70, 222
  training of, 93–95
  underground economy and, 172, 173
  women as, generally, 93–112
Liu, Tessie, 67
Longfellow, David L., 263
Longuet, Abbé, 77–78
Lopez, Robert, 9
Lyon. *See also* silk industry
  assignats in, 273
  cahiers in, 267–68
  economy of, 44, 123–25, 272–75
  embroiderers in, 195
  fees, entrance, generally, 180
  government of, 44–45, 124, 187–90
  guild masters in, generally, 8, 15, 130, 132–33, 142–43
  guild system in, generally, 6–7, 7–9, 44–45, 66–67, 124–25, 130–33, 142–43, 150, 152, 180–84, 262–64, 286–87, 293, 294
  guimpiers in, 193–95, 195–96, 198
  hat makers of, 135–37, 141, 280
  laborers in, 8–9, 18
  labor shortage in, 275–81
  legal system in, 11
  passementiers of, 193n98
  poverty in, 261
  reform in, 150, 152, 180–203, 204–5, 262–63
  in Revolutionary France, generally, 259–60, 267–75, 285–88
  siege of, 274–75
  underground economy in, 9, 135–42

Machault, 104n24
maître marchands. *See* master merchants
maître ouvriers. *See* master workers
Malmaison, Marie, 73–74
marchande publique, 11–12, 80–85, 87, 292–93
marchands merciers. *See* merchant mercers
Marquis de Condorcet, 235

marriage. *See also* family; widows' rights
  contracts, 73–76, 87
  courtly love and, 59
  coverture, 10, 131
  in customary law, 69–73
  dowry in, 73–76, 87
  lingères and, 99–100, 111–12
  marriage portion, 74
  portion, 74
  privilege in, 72–73
  real estate in, 73, 74, 75, 87
  ribbonmakers and, 117
  separation in, 76–79, 87
  silk industry and, 131, 133
  wages and, 54–55
Martin des Isles, Antoine, 216
Martine, Elisabeth, 217
master merchants
  in Old Regime France, 130, 133–34, 141
  in reform era, 184–93, 197
  in Revolutionary France, 260–61, 264, 267, 269–70
master weavers. *See* master workers
master workers. *See also* chefs d'ateliers
  embroiderers and, 195
  gender and, 196–203, 262–63
  guimpiers and, 193–95, 195–96
  monopoly by, 194
  in Old Regime France, 130, 133–34, 138–39, 140–41
  in reform era, 184–203
  in Revolutionary France, 260–61, 262–63, 264
  wages and, 260–61
materials, 104–5, 118, 137–40
Mattard, 231
membership
  of *bonnetières*, 112, 155, 222
  of *couturières*, 116
  in guild system, generally, 148–49, 219–22
  of *lingères*, 93, 106, 157, 222
  of ribbonmakers, 116, 117, 160
  in silk industry, 125, 130, 184, 261, 265–66, 277–81
  of spinners, 116, 118
merchant in the public domain. *See marchande publique*
merchant mercers
  of Le Havre, 13–14, 51–53, 63–64
  lingères and, 224–25

ribbonmakers and, 160n32, 161, 224
  of Rouen, 119–23, 160n32, 161, 224–25
Mercier, Louis-Sébastien, 57, 178, 239
Minard, Philippe, 146, 151n12
Mirabeau, Honoré-Gabriel, 251–52
money, 248–49, 273
Monnais, François, 231
monopoly
  of *bonnetières*, 113–14
  in guild system, generally, 91, 217
  of *lingères*, 97–98, 103
  of master workers, 194
Montmiery, Dame, 108
Mouchet, Dame, 78–79
Mulat, Dame, 167

Napoleonic Era, 276, 277–81, 287–88
natures. *See also* gender
  economy and, 3–6, 233
  family and, 5–6
  past practice and, 53
  privilege and, 5–6
  in Revolutionary France, 208–9
  technology and, 3–5, 6, 53, 64
  work and, 178–79, 200–1, 232–39
Naval, Nicholas Laurent, 111
Necker, Jacques
  on gender, 153
  harvest failures and, 212n8
  lingères and, 157, 169n46
  regulation by, 175
  ribbonmakers and, 160–61
  silk industry and, 267
  on standardization, 152
Nicolle, Femme, 107–8
Normandy, 11, 46, 47–48, 84–85, 87–88
Noyer, 247n96
Noyon, Anne de, 100

oaths, 25, 27–28
Offen, Karen, 232n59
officers. *See* governance
Ogilvie, Sheilagh, 197
Old Regime France
  economy of, 9–10, 145–49, 174–75
  gender in, 54–55, 58–59, 60–64, 291–92
  legal system in, 1, 10–12
  privileges in, 1–2, 41–42, 60–64, 72–73, 292–93
  productivity in, 9–10
  reform in, 16, 145–49, 174–76

Ouin-Lacroix, Charles, 96
outsourcing. *See* subcontracting
ouvrières. *See* laborers
ovalistes, 265–66

Paris
  couturières of, 236
  government in, 45, 169–74, 180–82, 184–90, 197–200, 203–4, 228–32, 242, 263–64
  guild system in, 39–40, 42–43, 45, 236
  legal system in, 11
  reform in, 147–48
  tailors of, 236
Parr, Joy, 55–56
passementiers, 161, 163n37, 193n98
past practice, 52–53, 63–64
peddlers, 13, 162
Petit, Dame, 159–60
Pinchbeck, Ivy, 9
political rights
  of laborers, 244–45, 268
  of women, 208, 209, 231–32, 233, 235–36
Pontchartrain, 33
Portemer, Jean, 71
Pottier, Jacques, 159, 170
poverty, 210–12, 248, 261
Povey, Mary, 60–61
power, 54, 55–56
privileges. *See also* legal instruments
  of *bonnetières*, 113–15
  gender and, 60–64
  in guild system, generally, 1–3, 49–50, 60–61, 63–64, 162–63, 174, 175–80, 207–8
  of *lingères*, 97–100, 103–4
  in marriage, 72–73
  natures and, 5–6
  in Old Regime France, 1–2, 41–42, 60–64, 72–73, 292–93
  reform and, 162–63, 174, 175–80
  in Revolutionary France, 5–6, 16–18, 207–10, 242, 247–48, 263–64
  of ribbonmakers, 116–17
  in Rouen, 18
  of spinners, 118–19
productivity, 9–10

real estate, 73, 74, 75, 87
Reddy, William M., 212, 213
reform

auxiliary trades and, 190–3
of *bonnetières*, 155–57
of *couturières*, 165–66, 167, 226–27
economy and, 145–49, 174–75, 177, 179–80, 196–97, 203
gender and, 157–60, 163–67, 176–80, 184, 192–93, 196–203, 205, 219–27
goals of, 145–49, 164, 202–3, 215, 227
governance and, 164, 165–74, 222–27, 230–31
of guild system, generally, 16, 145, 146–49, 163–67, 175–84, 203–5, 207–8
of *lingères*, 153, 155, 156, 157–60, 167, 168–74, 224–25
in Lyon, 150, 152, 180–203, 204–5, 262–63
in Old Regime France, 16, 145–49, 174–76
in Paris, 147–48
privileges and, 162–63, 174, 175–80
of ribbonmakers, 160–61, 163n37, 224
in Rouen, 150–74, 176–78, 204, 209–10, 214–27, 229–32
in silk industry, 150, 152, 184–203, 204–5, 262–63
of spinners, 161–62, 211
subcontracting and, 215–16
taxation and, 152, 174–75, 227–29
technology and, 193–96
underground economy and, 215–16
wages and, 164, 201–2, 218–19
work and, 145–49, 152, 153–54, 164, 178–79, 200–1, 205, 222–23
Regnard, Pierre, 117
regulation. *See also* governance; taxation
of economy, 174–75
of guild system, generally, 16, 31–35, 91, 92, 202–3
of laborers, 19–20, 21–23, 29–31, 134–35, 139, 141–42
of *lingères*, 97–112
of rural industry, 47–48, 98–99
of silk industry, 134–35
religion
  bonnetières and, 112
  gender and, 57–58, 64–66, 86
  in guild system, generally, 27–28
  lingères and, 106
  in Revolutionary France, 251
  in Rouen, 251
  spinners and, 118

Revel, 137
revendresses. See peddlers
Revolutionary France
  army in, 253–55
  artisans during, 247–49, 255–59
  assignats in, 248–49
  calendar in, 249
  clothing during, 249–55
  economy in, 207–8, 248–53, 255, 257–58, 263–64, 272–75
  family in, 245–47, 284–85
  gender in, 208–9, 219–22, 245–47, 255–59, 270–74, 277–81, 287–89
  guild system in, generally, 5, 17–18
  laborers in, 244–45, 259, 264–72, 275–81, 287–89
  in Lyon, generally, 259–60, 267–75, 285–88
  master merchants in, 267
  poverty in, 248
  privileges in, 5–6, 16–18, 207–10, 242, 247–48, 263–64
  religion in, 251
  in Rouen, generally, 209–12, 228–32, 248, 250–59, 288–89
  silk industry in, 285–88
  social order in, 232–39
  spinners in, 212–14
  taxation in, 207–8, 227–29, 242–44, 245–47, 260–61, 268–69, 273–74
  wages in, 258–59, 265, 266, 267–70
ribbonmakers, 116–17, 121, 160–62, 163n37, 224
Rigot, Femme, 137
Roche, Daniel, 203
Roper, Lyndal, 41
Rouen
  artisans in, 247–49, 255–59
  bonnetières of, 112–15, 155–57, 222, 231
  cahiers in, 229–32, 240–41
  competition for, 47–48
  cord makers in, 161–62
  cotton crisis in, 212–14
  couturières of, 116, 165–66, 167, 226–27
  cutters of, 226–27
  economy of, 46–48, 91–92, 149–50, 209–12
  fees, entrance, generally, 150–51, 214, 217–18, 240–41
  government of, 46, 110–12, 151–52, 172–73, 229
  guild masters in, generally, 7, 16, 18, 115–16, 132–33, 142–43
  guild system in, generally, 6–7, 12, 45–48, 91–93, 94, 132–33, 142–43, 150–74, 209–10, 214–27, 242–49, 288–89, 293–94
  harvest failures in, 210–11, 211–12
  laborers in, 7, 218, 288–89
  legal system in, 11, 15
  lingères of, 7, 93–112, 153, 155, 156, 157–60, 161, 167, 168–74, 222, 224–25, 231
  merchant mercers of, 119–23, 160n32, 161, 224–25
  passementiers of, 161
  poverty in, 210–12
  privilege in, 18
  reform in, 150–74, 176–78, 204, 209–10, 214–27, 229–32
  religion in, 251
  in Revolutionary France, 209–12, 228–32, 248, 250–59, 288–89
  ribbonmakers of, 116–17, 121, 160–62, 224
  spinners of, 116, 117–19, 161–62, 211, 212–14
  subcontracting in, 215–16
  tailors of, 157–60, 161, 165–66, 167–74
  underground economy in, 215–16
  widows' rights in, 239–42
Rousseau, Jean-Jacques, 5–6, 208, 233
rural industry, 47–48, 98–99, 104–5

Sainte Croix, Bigot de, 151
Saint-Léon, Étienne Martin, 23n4
Savary, Jacques, 84
Scott, Joan Walloch, 10, 54, 55, 59, 64, 239
seamstresses. *See couturières*
separateness, 52–53, 63–64, 86–87
separation, legal, 76–79, 87
séparation de biens, 11–12, 76–79
séparation de corps et d'habitation, 76, 79
separation of sexes, 53
Sewell, William, 12, 244
sexuality, 54
Sheridan, George, 284
siege, 274–75
silk industry
  auxiliary trades in, 190–193
  chefs d'ateliers in, 264, 277–79, 284, 287–88

embroiderers in, 195
family and, 131, 133, 185, 200, 264, 284–85
fees, entrance, 184–85, 187–90, 191–92, 195
gender and, 184, 192–93, 196–203, 262–63, 264–66, 270–74, 277–81
guild system in, generally, 124–25, 184–196, 262–64, 293, 294
guimpiers in, 193–95, 195–96, 198
laborers in, 131–35, 137–42, 264–72, 275–81, 287–88
marriage and, 131, 133
master merchants in, 130, 133–34, 141, 184–93, 197, 260–61
master workers in, 130, 133–34, 138–39, 138–39, 140–41, 184–203, 260–61
materials for, 137–40
membership in, 125, 130, 184, 261, 265–66, 277–81
in Old Regime France, 7–8, 45, 121, 123–25, 142–43
ovalistes in, 265–66
reform in, 150, 152, 181–82, 184–203, 204–5, 262–63
regulation of, 134–35
in Revolutionary France, 17, 259–60, 285–88
spinners in, 126, 137–38, 282–83
subcontracting in, 140–41, 195
taxation of, 260–61, 263, 268–69, 273–74
technology in, 125–30, 134, 193–96, 265–66, 281–85
throwing in, 126–28
training in, 198–99, 277–79
underground economy in, 135–42
wages in, 130, 133–34, 201–2, 260–61, 265, 266, 267–70
warping in, 128–29, 138
weaving in, 129, 193–96, 281–82, 283–84
similarity, 52, 53
Six Great Corps, 33, 119
skill, 54. See also technology
slaves, 149n6
social order, 14–15, 54–64, 85–86, 86–88, 232–39, 291
society of orders, 61–63
Sonenscher, Michael, 109, 114–15, 216
spinners

cord makers and, 161–62
governance of, 117–18
materials for, 118
membership of, 116, 118
privileges of, 118–19
reform of, 161–62, 211
religion and, 118
in Revolutionary France, 212–14
ribbonmakers and, 161–62
in silk industry, 126, 137–38, 282–83
taxation of, 116
training of, 117, 118
women as, 117–19
St. Pierre, Françoise, 159
subcontracting, 29–31, 104–5, 114–15, 140–41, 195, 215–16. *See also* underground economy

tailors
couturières and, 114, 165–66, 167, 236
lingères and, 157–60, 167, 168–74, 224
of Paris, 236
ribbonmakers and, 161
of Rouen, 161, 165–66, 167–74
taxation. *See also* regulation
of *bonnetières*, 112, 155, 222
of *couturières*, 116
governance and, 225
in guild system, generally, 32–35, 169–70, 202, 204, 218, 220–21, 225, 227, 242
of *lingères*, 93, 106, 109–12, 169–70, 222
reform and, 152, 174–75, 227–29
in Revolutionary France, 207–8, 242–44, 245–47, 260–61, 268–69, 273–74
of ribbonmakers, 116, 160
of silk industry, 260–61, 263, 268–69, 273–74
of spinners, 116
women and, 245–47
technology
bonnetières and, 112–13, 114
gender and, 3–5, 6, 53, 64, 112–13
reform and, 193–96
in silk industry, 125–30, 134, 193–96, 265–66, 281–85
Terray, Abbé Jean Marie, 200
Terret, M., 265
throwing, 126–28
Tilly, Louise, 10, 59
toiliers, 100, 104, 104n24

Tolozan
  lingères and, 157n23, 169n46, 170, 171, 172, 173
  on reform, 174
Tolozan de Montfort, Louis, 268
training
  of bonnetières, 115
  family role in, 24
  in guild system, generally, 21, 24, 25–26
  of lingères, 93–95
  in silk industry, 198–99, 277–79
  of spinners, 117, 118
  of women, 37–38, 39–40, 198–99
Turgot, Jacques, 16, 68, 146–48, 202
underground economy, 9, 135–42, 172, 173, 215–16. *See also* subcontracting

van Zuylen, Belle, 233–34
Vasse, M., 151–52, 157, 158n25
Vaucanson, 282
Vauveurs, Dame, 167
Viard, 231
Virgin Mary, 64–66, 86, 251
Vorillon, Dame, 84–85

wages
  debasement of, generally, 14–15, 37, 54–55, 291
  in guild system, generally, 67, 164
  marriage and, 54–55
  reform and, 164, 201–2, 218–19
  in Revolutionary France, 258–59, 265, 266, 267–70
  in silk industry, 130, 133–34, 201–2, 260–61, 265, 266, 267–70
warping, 128–29, 138
weaving, 129, 193–96, 281–82, 283–84. *See also* master workers
widowers' rights, 75–76, 178
widows' rights, 68–69, 74, 178, 239–42
Wiesner, Merry E., 83n73
women. *See* gender
work
  gender and, 54–55, 86, 145–49, 152, 153–54, 164, 178–79, 200–1, 205, 222–23, 232–39, 291
  natures and, 178–79, 200–1, 232–39
  reform and, 145–49, 152, 153–54, 164, 178–79, 200–1, 205, 222–23
  skill and, 54
  wages and, 54–55

Young, Arthur, 259

www.ingramcontent.com/pod-product-compliance
Lightning Source LLC
Chambersburg PA
CBHW021354290426
44108CB00010B/235